"An impressive feat of journalism, monumental in scope and urgent in its implications...gritty and heartbreaking." —*BOSTON GLOBE*

DOPESICK

DEALERS, DOCTORS, *and*
THE DRUG COMPANY THAT ADDICTED AMERICA

BETH MACY

Author of *Truevine* and *Factory Man*

A ferocious piece of journalism distinguished by unyielding compassion."

—*ATLANTA JOURNAL-CONSTITUTION*

WINNER OF THE LOS ANGELES TIMES BOOK PRIZE FOR SCIENCE & TECHNOLOGY

"Comprehensive, compassionate, and forceful. No matter what you already know about the opioid crisis, *Dopesick*'s toughness and intimacy make it a must."

—*NEW YORK TIMES*

SHORT-LISTED FOR THE ANDREW CARNEGIE MEDAL FOR EXCELLENCE IN NONFICTION

"A terrifying, essential read."

—*PEOPLE*

FINALIST FOR THE KIRKUS PRIZE FOR NONFICTION

"Shifting effortlessly between the sociopolitical and the personal, Macy weaves a complex tale that unfolds with all the pace of a thriller."

—*THE GUARDIAN*

WINNER OF THE AMERICAN SOCIETY OF ADDICTION MEDICINE'S MEDIA AWARD

"You've probably heard pieces of this story before, but in *Dopesick* we get something original: a page-turning explanation."

—*USA TODAY*

PRAISE FOR BETH MACY'S
DOPESICK

SELECTED AS ONE OF THE
BEST BOOKS OF THE YEAR

New York Times Book Review...*Chicago Tribune*...
Washington Post...*Elle*...Amazon...NPR's *On Point*...
Literary Hub... American Library Association...
Atlanta Journal-Constitution...*Newsweek*

Short-listed for the 2019 Andrew Carnegie Medal for Excellence in Nonfiction; Finalist for the 2019 Library of Virginia People's Choice Award for Nonfiction, the 2019 Hele Bernstein Book Award for Excellence in Journalism, and the 2018 Kirkus Prize; and Winner of the 2019 Los Angeles Times Book Prize for Science and Technology and the American Society of Addiction Medicine's Annual Media Award

"A harrowing, deeply compassionate dispatch from the heart of a national emergency...A masterwork of narrative journalism, interlacing stories of communities in crisis with dark histories of corporate greed and regulatory indifference."
—Jessica Bruder, *New York Times Book Review*

"Comprehensive, compassionate, and forceful. No matter what you already know about the opioid crisis, *Dopesick*'s toughness and intimacy make it a must."
—Janet Maslin, *New York Times*

"Until I read *Dopesick* by journalist Beth Macy, I didn't grasp all of the factors that have combined to produce the present crisis...Although Macy's stories are set in Virginia, they could happen anywhere in the United States."
—Susan Okie, *Washington Post*

"Macy's strengths as a reporter are on full display when she talks to people, gaining the trust of chastened users, grieving families, exhausted medical workers, and even a convicted heroin dealer whose scheduled two-hour interview with the author ended up stretching to more than six hours." —Jennifer Szalai, *New York Times*

"Macy focuses on southern and western Virginia, though the lessons of her narrative apply broadly...Macy embedded herself in the lives of four heartsick families whose children's lives were ravaged—and sometimes lost—because of opioid addiction...For those new to the topic, there is much to learn." —Sally Satel, MD, *Wall Street Journal*

"Macy reports on the human carnage with respect and quiet compassion." —Gabriel Thompson, *San Francisco Chronicle*

"You've probably heard pieces of this story before, but in *Dopesick* we get something original: a page-turning explanation." —Matt McCarthy, *USA Today*

"Macy's book reveals a more complex truth of an epidemic that has been manufactured by the players of her subtitle." —John Warner, *Chicago Tribune*

"A masterful work." —Misty Hawkins, *Charleston Express*

"A ferocious piece of journalism distinguished by unyielding compassion." —Jeff Calder, *Atlanta Journal-Constitution*

"Beth Macy turns her prodigious reporting and writing skills to the opioid crisis...show[ing] how the pharmaceutical company pushed this powerful drug, giving million-dollar bonuses to sales reps and rewarding doctors with gifts and trips...A harrowing, infuriating, eye-opening book." —Laurie Hertzel, *Star Tribune*

"Macy is a terrific reporter, scrupulous in detailing the significance of her findings...*Dopesick*'s second section—filled with gut-wrenchingly candid interviews with addicts and their families—is the most essential, placing broken faces on horrifying data sets."
—David Canfield, *Entertainment Weekly*

"Heartbreaking, exhaustively researched...a fierce indictment of racism, corporate greed, and wily dealers...A terrifying, essential read."
—*People* (Book of the Week)

"Shifting effortlessly between the sociopolitical and the personal, Macy weaves a complex tale that unfolds with all the pace of a thriller. Her deep journalism—interviews with dealers, police officers, activists, and local politicians, as well as users and their families—is matched by a sense of barely suppressed anger at what is happening to communities like Roanoke, Virginia, where she has lived since 1989."
—Sean O'Hagan, *The Guardian*

"A dogged and empathetic reporter on the ills of Appalachia (see her earlier *Factory Man*), Macy sets her roving eye on the victims and villains of the opioid crisis...Macy's approach is fresh in its humanity and its outlook, which is at once comprehensive and hyperlocal."
—Boris Kachka, *Vulture*

"In *Dopesick*, Macy brings clarity to what she describes as the 'perfect storm' that created one of the most pressing health emergencies the United States has ever faced...Woven throughout Macy's story is a riveting and heartbreaking human narrative."
—Travis Lupick, *Los Angeles Review of Books*

"Beth Macy gives the opioid epidemic a human face, but not at the expense of historical and scientific context."
—*Plough Quarterly* (Editor's Pick)

"*Dopesick* pulls together [Macy's] decades of research and interviews to highlight why and how doctors, dealers, and drug companies conspired (in some cases knowingly) to get large swaths of the American population addicted to painkillers." —Jessica Roy, *Elle*

"Beth Macy charts the epidemic in small communities in Central Appalachia, wealthy suburbs, and everywhere in between and details the insidious, indiscriminate effects of addiction." —Cristina Arreola, *Bustle*

"It is difficult to imagine a deeper and more heartbreaking examination of America's opioid crisis than this new book by investigative reporter Beth Macy of Roanoke." —Jeff Debell, *Roanoke Times*

"[Macy] brings a clear eye for journalistic detail and a searching humanity to her account of the people who turn to crime to avoid dopesickness... *Dopesick* will enrage you and bring you to tears, often on the same page." —Steve Mitchell, *Lit South*

"With both compassion and no-bull reporting, Roanoke, Virginia–based journalist Beth Macy delivers the first book to completely chart America's current opioid crisis." —CJ Lotz, *Garden and Gun*

"*Dopesick* is nonfiction, but it unfolds like a tragedy, in a place that receives little national attention outside of election years... [and] accomplishes something American drug policy hasn't: It presents addicted persons as morally complex, fully formed human beings whose problems have medical and political solutions." —Sarah Jones, *Democracy Journal*

"A warning to everyone in America who thinks the opiate epidemic won't arrive at their doorstep." —Paula Rinehart, *The Federalist*

"Just as she did with her last book, *Truevine*, Macy is able to develop an intimacy with key individuals that allows her to understand and explain the heartfelt feelings of her characters... The end result is an on-the-ground survey of the crisis that explores it from both the head and the heart." —Paul Markowitz, *National Book Review*

"Macy's in-depth, personal portraits of those who have been lost and the family members left behind are both a gut punch and—beyond the righteous anger at those responsible—the heartbreaking beauty of the book." —800-CEO-READ

"Beth Macy is not satisfied with myths or sidebars. She seeks the very hearts of the people who are running the long marathons of struggle and survival—of Life. *Dopesick* is another deep—and deeply needed—look into the troubled soul of America." —Tom Hanks

"Beth Macy writes about our opioid epidemic, but *Dopesick* is not about the drugs. It's a book about kids and moms and neighbors and the people who try to save them. It's about shame and stigma and desperation. It's about bad policy, greed, and corruption. It's a Greek tragedy with a chorus of teenage ghosts who know how to text but can't express how they feel." —Senator Tim Kaine

"Everyone should read Beth Macy's story of the American opioid epidemic, of suffering, of heroism and stupidity, and of the corporate greed and regulatory failure that lie behind it. With compassion and humanity, Macy takes us into the lives of the victims, their families, law enforcement, and even some of the criminals. A great book!" —Anne C. Case, professor emeritus of economics and public affairs at Princeton University, and Sir Angus Deaton, FBA HonFRSE and winner of the Nobel Prize in Economics

"I'm still in withdrawal from *Dopesick,* a harrowing journey through the history and contemporary hellscape of drug addiction. Beth Macy brings a big heart, a sharp eye, and a powerful sense of place to the story of ordinary Americans in the grip of an extraordinary crisis."
—Tony Horwitz, Pulitzer Prize–winning author of the national bestseller *Confederates in the Attic*

"All prior books on this topic, including my own, were written as if describing the trunk, the ear, or the tail, without quite capturing the whole elephant. Journalist Beth Macy has packed the entire elephant and then some into one book. Her writing jumps from the page with a fast-paced narrative, colorful and inspiring characters, vivid historical detail, and a profound sense of place."   —Anna Lembke, MD, author of *Drug Dealer, MD,* psychiatrist and professor of addiction medicine at Stanford University School of Medicine

DOPESICK

ALSO BY BETH MACY

Truevine

Factory Man

DOPESICK

DEALERS, DOCTORS, AND THE DRUG

COMPANY THAT ADDICTED AMERICA

Beth Macy

BACK BAY BOOKS
Little, Brown and Company
New York Boston London

Back Bay Book / Little, Brown and Company
Hachette Book Group
1290 Avenue of the Americas, New York, NY 10104
littlebrown.com

Originally published in hardcover by Little, Brown and Company, August 2018
First Back Bay paperback edition, August 2019

Back Bay Books is an imprint of Little, Brown and Company, a division of Hachette Book Group, Inc. The Back Bay Books name and logo are trademarks of Hachette Book Group, Inc.

The publisher is not responsible for websites (or their content) that are not owned by the publisher.

The Hachette Speakers Bureau provides a wide range of authors for speaking events. To find out more, go to hachettespeakersbureau.com or call (866) 376-6591.

ISBN 978-0-316-55124-3 (hc) / 978-0-316-52317-2 (large print) / 978-0-316-55130-4 (pb)
LCCN 2017961068

Printing 3, 2020

LSC-C

Printed in the United States of America

Contents

PART THREE:
"A Broken System"

This evil is confined to no class or occupation. It numbers among its victims some of the best women and men of all classes. Prompt action is then demanded, lest our land should become...stupefied by the direful effects of narcotics and thus diseased physically, mentally, and morally, the love of liberty swallowed up by the love of opium, whilst the masses of our people would become fit subjects for a despot.

—Dr. W. G. Rogers, writing in *The Daily Dispatch* (Richmond, VA), January 25, 1884

A mother's love for her child is like nothing else in the world. It knows no law, no pity, it dares all things and crushes down remorselessly all that stands in its path.

—Agatha Christie, "The Last Séance" (from *The Hound of Death and Other Stories*)

In memory of Scott Roth (1988–2010), Jesse Bolstridge (1994–2013), Colton Scott Banks (1993–2012), Brandon Robert Perullo (1983–2014), John Robert "Bobby" Baylis (1986–2015), Jordan "Joey" Gilbert (1989–2017), Randy Nuss (1984–2003), Arnold Fayne McCauley (1934–2009), Patrick Michael Stewart (1980–2004), Eddie Bisch (1982–2001), Jessee Creed Baker (1982–2017), and Theresa Helen Henry (1989–2017)

Author's Note

In 2012, I began reporting on the heroin epidemic as it landed in the suburbs of Roanoke, Virginia, where I had covered marginalized families for the *Roanoke Times* for two decades, predominantly those based in the inner city. When I first wrote about heroin in the suburbs, most families I interviewed were too ashamed to go on the record.

Five years later as I finished writing this book, nearly everyone agreed for their names to be used, with the exception of a few, as noted in the text, who feared going public would jeopardize their jobs or their safety.

I'm indebted to the families I first met in 2012 who allowed me to continue following their stories as their loved ones grappled with rehab and prison, with recovery and relapse. I'm also grateful for insights gleaned from several rural Virginia families, advocates, and first responders, many of whom were quietly battling the scourge almost two decades before I appeared on the scene. Several law enforcement officials spoke with me on background and on the record, including a few who had arrested their own relatives for peddling dope. So did scores of doctors and other caregivers who, after working fourteen-plus-hour days, did not feel their work was complete without getting the story of this epidemic out there.

A few interviewees died before I had time to transcribe my notes, including one by his own hand after relapsing and fearing that his wife—whom he loved more than anything in the world—would divorce him. "If she ever figures out she don't need me," he confided, "I'm screwed."

Their survivors continued talking to me during their most fragile moments, generously texting and calling and emailing photographs long after their loved ones' battles were over. One requested my MP3 recording of her departed loved one's interview, so desperate was she to hear his voice again. Another shared her deceased daughter's journals.

I'm particularly indebted to four Virginia moms: Kristi Fernandez, Ginger Mumpower, Jamie Waldrop, and Patricia Mehrmann. More than anyone, they helped me understand the crushing and sometimes contradictory facets of an inadequate criminal justice system often working at cross-purposes against medical science, and a health care bureaucracy that continues pumping out hard-core pain pills in large doses while seeking to quell cravings and turn around lives with yet more medication.

In sharing their experiences, these mothers hoped readers would be moved to advocate for life-saving addiction treatment and research, health care and criminal justice reform, and for political leadership capable of steering America out of the worst drug epidemic in modern history. Until then, they hoped their children's stories would illuminate the need for patients not only to become more discerning consumers of health care but also to employ a healthy skepticism the next time a pharmaceutical company announces its latest wonder drug.

Riverview Cemetery, Strasburg, Virginia

Prologue

Two years into a twenty-three-year prison sentence, on a day pushing 100 degrees, Ronnie Jones had his first visitor. I'd spent almost a year listening to police and prosecutors describe Jones, imprisoned for armed heroin distribution, as a predator. After three months of requests, I walked along the manicured entranceway of Hazelton Federal Correctional Institution on the outskirts of Bruceton Mills, West Virginia. The air was so thick that the flags framing the concrete-block structure hung there drooping, as still as the razor wire that scalloped the roofs.

In the state's northeastern crook, bordering Pennsylvania to the north and Maryland to the east, Preston County had once been dominated by strip-mining. But by the mid-2000s, most of the mines had shut down, and the prison had taken over as the county's largest employer, with eight hundred guards and staff.

My August 2016 interview had taken several weeks to arrange with the Bureau of Prisons pecking order in Washington, D.C., but first I had to navigate weeks of curt back-and-forth with Jones, over the prison's monitored email, to get his OK. "Exactly who have you spoken to as of today that was involved with my case?" he wanted to know. What personal information about him did I intend to use?

Jones agreed to let me visit, finally, because he wanted his daughters, in kindergarten and first grade when their dad was arrested in June 2013, to understand "there's a different side of me," as he put it. The last they'd seen him, a week before his arrest, he had delivered birthday cupcakes to their school.

I thought of the "tsunami of misery" Jones had first unleashed in Woodstock, Virginia, as his prosecutor put it, before it fanned out in waves over the northwestern region of the state and into some of Washington's western bedroom communities in 2012 and 2013. In just a few months' time, Jones was presiding over the largest heroin ring in the region, transforming a handful of users into hundreds.

As I made my way to the prison, I calculated the human toll, the hundreds of addicted people who ended up dopesick when their heroin supply was suddenly cut by Jones's arrest: throwing up and sweating and shitting their pants. When Jones was jailed in 2013, many of the newly addicted Woodstock users began carpooling to the nearest big cities—Baltimore, Washington, and even Martinsburg, West Virginia, aka Little Baltimore—to score drugs, converging on known heroin hot spots and playing drug-dealer Russian roulette.

I didn't yet know that a single batch of heroin was about to land in Huntington, West Virginia, four hours west of Jones's cell, that would halt the breathing of twenty-six people in a single day, before the week was out. Those overdoses were fueled by the latest synthetic opioid, carfentanil, imported from China with a stroke on a computer keyboard. Carfentanil is an elephant sedative one hundred times stronger than fentanyl, which is twenty-five to fifty times stronger than heroin. For the fifth year in a row, the state of West Virginia's indigent burial-assistance program was about to exhaust its funds from interring opioid-overdose victims.

Similar surges were happening across the country, from Florida to Sacramento to Barre, Vermont. Every person I interviewed that summer, from treatment providers to parents of the addicted to the judges who were sending the addicted to prison or jail, was growing more burdened by the day. The enormity of America's drug problem was finally dawning on them and on the rest of us—two decades after the opioid epidemic first took root. (Although the word "opiate" historically refers to drugs derived from the opium poppy and "opioid" to chemical versions, the now more widely accepted term "opioid" is used in this book for both forms of painkillers.)

Drug overdose had already taken the lives of 300,000 Americans over the past fifteen years, and experts now predicted that 300,000 more would die in only the next five. It is now the leading cause of death for Americans under the age of fifty, killing more people than guns or car accidents, at a rate higher than the HIV epidemic at its peak.

The rate of casualties is so unprecedented that it's almost impossible to look at the total number dead—and at the doctors and mothers and teachers and foster parents who survive them—and not wonder why the nation's response has been so slow in coming and so impotently executed when it finally did.

Ronnie Jones had run one of the largest drug rings in the mid-Atlantic United States, a region with some of the highest overdose rates in the nation. But I wasn't driving to West Virginia for epidemiological insights or even a narrative of redemption from Jones.

I'd been dispatched to prison by a specific grieving mother, clutching a portrait of her nineteen-year-old son. I wanted to understand the death of Jesse Bolstridge, a robust high school football player barely old enough to grow a patchy beard on his chin.

What exactly, his mother wanted to know, had led to the death of her only son?

I'd been trying to address that same question for more than five years, in one form or another, for several mothers I knew. But now I had someone I could ask.

*   *   *

Three months before visiting Jones, in the spring of 2016, Kristi Fernandez and I stood next to Jesse's grave on a rolling hillside in Strasburg, Virginia, in the shadow of Signal Knob. She'd asked me to meet her at one of her regular cemetery stops, on her way home from work, so I could see how she'd positioned his marker, just so, at the edge of the graveyard.

It was possible to stand at Jesse's headstone—emblazoned with the foot-high number 55, in the same font as the lettering on his Strasburg Rams varsity jersey—and look down on the stadium where he had once summoned the crowd to its feet simply by running onto the field and pumping his arms.

In a small town where football is as central to identity as the nearby Civil War battlefields dotting the foothills of the Blue Ridge, Jesse loved nothing more than making the hometown crowd roar.

He had always craved movement, the choke on his internal engine revving long after his peers had mastered their own. As a toddler, he staunchly refused to nap, succumbing to sleep on the floor midplay, an action figure in one hand and a toy car in the other. This restlessness was part of the epidemic's story, too, I would later learn. So were the drugs Jesse's high school buddies pilfered from their parents' and grandparents' medicine cabinets—the kind of leftovers that pile up after knee-replacement surgery or a blown back.

Jesse had been a ladies' man, the boy next door, a jokester who began most of his sentences with the word "Dude." When he left his house on foot, the neighbors did a double take, marveling at the trail of cats shadowing him as he walked.

Kristi pointed out the cat's paw she had engraved at the base of Jesse's headstone, right next to the phrase MISS YOU MORE, a family shorthand they had the habit of using whenever they talked by phone.

"I miss you," she'd say.

"Miss you more," he'd tell her.

"Miss *you* more," she'd answer. And on and on.

Kristi takes pride in the way the family maintains Jesse's grave, switching out the holiday decorations, adding kitschy trinkets, wiping away the rain-splashed mud. "It's the brightest one here," his younger twin sisters like to say as they sweep away the errant grass clippings.

When I pulled into the cemetery for our first meeting, Kristi had taken it as an omen that my license plate included Jesse's number, 55. She's always looking for signs from Jesse—a glint of sun shining through the clouds, a Mother's Day brunch receipt for $64.55. To her, my license plate number meant our meeting was Jesse-sanctioned and Jesse-approved.

Kristi used to think that maintaining Jesse's grave was "the last thing we can do for him," she told me, choking back tears. But right now she's obsessed with the story of her son's swift descent into addiction—the missing details that might explain how Jesse went from being a high school football hunk and burly construction worker to a heroin-overdose statistic, slumped on someone else's bathroom floor. If she understood the progression of his addiction better, she reasons, maybe she could help other parents protect their kids from stumbling down that same path.

"I just want to be able to say, 'This is what happened to Jesse,' so I can be educated, so I can help others," Kristi says. "But in my mind, the story doesn't add up, and it drives me crazy."

Maybe a mother's questions about a child's death can never be totally answered, and yet Kristi's pain sits there between us, no less urgent today than it felt on the day he died. To comprehend how she was left with these questions—and how our country came to this moment—I needed to widen the scope of my investigation both in geography and in time. I would fold in questions from other mothers, too, who wanted to understand why their addicted sons were imprisoned now instead of in treatment; why their addicted daughters were still out on the streets, God only knew where.

When a new drug sweeps the country, it historically starts in the big cities and gradually spreads to the hinterlands, as in the cases of cocaine and crack. But the opioid epidemic began in exactly the opposite manner, grabbing a toehold in isolated Appalachia, Midwestern rust belt counties, and rural Maine. Working-class families who were traditionally dependent on jobs in high-risk industries to pay their bills—coal mining in southwest Virginia, steel milling in western Pennsylvania, logging in Maine—weren't just the first to experience the epidemic of drug overdose; they also happened to live in politically unimportant places, hollows and towns and fishing villages where the treatment options were likely to be hours from home.

Jesse Bolstridge was born in the mid-1990s, when opioid addiction first took root. His short life represents the arc of the epidemic's toll, the apex of which is nowhere close to being reached.

If I could retrace the epidemic as it shape-shifted across the spine of the Appalachians, roughly paralleling Interstate 81 as it fanned out from the coalfields and crept north up the Shenandoah Valley, I could understand how prescription pill and heroin abuse was allowed to fester, moving quietly and stealthily across this country, cloaked in stigma and shame.

Set in three culturally distinct communities that represent the evolution of the epidemic as I reported it, *Dopesick* begins in the coalfields, in the hamlet of St. Charles, Virginia, in the remote westernmost corner of the state, largely with the introduction of the painkiller Oxy-Contin in 1996.

From there, the scourge not only advanced into new territories but also arrived via a different delivery system, as the morphine molecule shifted from OxyContin and other painkillers like Vicodin and Percocet to heroin, the pills' illicit twin, and, later, even stronger synthetic analogs.

As the epidemic gained strength, it sent out new geographic shoots, moving from predominantly rural areas to urban and suburban settings, though the pattern was never stable or fixed. Heroin landed in the suburbs and cookie-cutter subdivisions near my home in Roanoke in the mid-2000s. But it wasn't widely acknowledged until a prominent jeweler and civic leader, Ginger Mumpower, drove her addicted son to the federal prison where he would spend the next five years, for his role in a former classmate's overdose death.

I covered Spencer Mumpower's transition from private-school student to federal inmate at the same time I witnessed the rise in overdose deaths spread north along I-81 from Roanoke. It infected pristine farm pastures and small northern Shenandoah Valley towns, as more users, and increasingly vigilant medical and criminal justice systems, propelled the addicted onto the urban corridor from Baltimore to New York. If you live in a city, maybe you've seen the public restroom with a sharps container, or witnessed a librarian administer Narcan.

While more and more Americans die of drug overdose, it is impossible to not look back at the early days of what we now recognize as an epidemic and wonder what might have been done to slow or stop it. Kristi Fernandez's questions are not hers alone. Until we understand how we reached this place, America will remain a country where getting addicted is far easier than securing treatment.

The worst drug epidemic in American history didn't land in the bucolic northern Shenandoah Valley until 2012, when Ronnie Jones, a twice-convicted drug dealer from the Washington suburbs, arrived in the back of a Virginia Department of Corrections van and set about turning a handful of football players, tree trimmers, and farmers' kids who used pills recreationally into hundreds of heroin addicts, as police officers told the story.

The transition here, in the quiet town of Woodstock, was driven by the same twisted math I'd witnessed elsewhere, as many users began with prescriptions, then resorted to buying heroin from dealers and selling portions of their supply to fuel their next purchase. Because the most important thing for the morphine-hijacked brain is, always, not to experience the crushing physical and psychological pain of withdrawal: to avoid dopesickness at any cost.

To feed their addictions, many users recruit new customers. Who eventually recruit new customers. And the exponential growth continues until the cycle too often ends in jail or prison or worse—in a premature grave like Jesse's adorned with teddy bears, R2-D2 action figures, and the parting words of mothers like Kristi engraved in granite: UNTIL I TAKE MY FINAL BREATH, YOU WILL LIVE IN MY HEART.

To reach Ronnie Jones, I head north on the nearest "heroin highway," I-81. I travel roughly the same path in my car, only in reverse, that Jones's drugs did by bus, his heroin camouflaged inside Pringle's cans and plastic Walmart bags on the floor beside him or his hired drug runners.

On the suburban outskirts of Roanoke, I drive near the upper-middle-class subdivision of Hidden Valley, where a young woman I've been following for a year named Tess Henry was once a straight-A student and basketball star. At the moment, she's AWOL—her mother and I have no idea where she is—although sometimes we catch glimpses of her on our cellphones: a Facebook exchange between Tess and one of her heroin dealers, or a prostitution ad through which Tess will fund her next fix.

I pass Ginger's Jewelry, the high-end store where parents of the addicted still drive from two hours away simply because they can think of nowhere else to turn. They've read about Ginger's imprisoned son in the newspaper, and they want to ask her how to handle the pitfalls of raising an addicted child.

Up the Shenandoah Valley on the interstate, I pass New Market and think not of the men who fought in the famous 1864 Civil War battle but of the women who grew poppies for the benefit of wounded soldiers, harvesting morphine from the dried juice inside the seed pods. Three decades later, the German elixir peddlers at Bayer Laboratories would stock America's drugstores with a brand-new version of that same molecule, a pill marketed as both a cough remedy and a cure for the nation's soaring morphine epidemic, known as "morphinism," or soldier's disease. Its label looked like an amusement advertisement you might have seen on a circus poster, a word derived from the German for "heroic" and bracketed by a swirling ribbon frame: heroin. It was sold widely from drugstore counters, no prescription necessary, not only for veterans but also for women with menstrual cramps and babies with hiccups.

Outside Woodstock, I pass George's Chicken, the poultry-processing plant where Ronnie Jones first arrived to work in a Department of Corrections work-release program, clad in prison-issue khakis. I pass the house nearby where a cop I know spent days, nights, and weekends crouched under a bedroom window, surveilling Jones and his co-workers from behind binoculars—a fraction of the man-hours the government invested in putting members of Jones's heroin ring behind bars.

I head northwest toward West Virginia, the crumbling landscape like so many of the distressed towns I've already traversed in Virginia some four hundred miles south, down to the same HILLARY FOR PRISON signs and the same Confederate flags waving presciently from their posts.

At the prison, I park my car and walk through the heavy front door. A handler named Rachel ushers me through security, making cheerful small talk as we head deeper inside the concrete maze and through three different sets of locked doors, her massive cluster of keys reverberating like chimes at each checkpoint.

We pass through a recreation area, where several men—all but one of the prisoners black and brown, I can't help noticing—push mops and brooms around the cavernous room, looking up and nodding as we pass. The manufactured air inside is cold, and it smells of Clorox.

Ronnie Jones is already waiting for me on the other side of the last locked door, seated at a table. He looks thinner and older than he did in his mug shot, his prison khakis baggy, his trim Afro and beard flecked with gray. He looks tired, and the whites of his eyes are tinged with red.

He rises from the chair to shake my hand, then sits back down, his hands folded into a steeple, his elbows resting on the table between us. His mood is unreadable.

The glassed-in room is beige, the floors are beige, and so is Rachel, in her beige-and-blue uniform and no-nonsense shoes, the kind you could run in if you had to. She tells us to knock on the window if we need her, then leaves for her perch in the rec room, on the other side of the window, the door lock clicking decisively behind her.

I open my notebook, situate the questions I've prepared off to the side, next to my spare pens. I'm thinking of Kristi and Ginger and of Tess's mom, and what Jones might say that will explain the fate of these mothers' kids.

Jones leans forward, expectant and unsmiling, and rubs his hands together, as if we're business associates sitting down to hammer out a deal.

Then he takes a deep breath and, relaxing back into his chair, he waits for me to start.

PART ONE

The People v. Purdue

Pennington Gap, Lee County, Virginia

Former coal-mining facility, Lee County, Virginia

Chapter One
The United States of Amnesia

Though the opioid epidemic would go on to spare no segment of America, nowhere has it settled in and extracted as steep a toll as in the depressed former mill and mining communities of central Appalachia, where the desperate and jobless rip copper wire out of abandoned factories to resell on the black market and jimmy large-screen TVs through a Walmart garden-center fence crack to keep from "fiending for dope."

In a region where few businesses dare to set up shop because it's hard to find workers who can pass a drug test, young parents can die of heroin overdose one day, leaving their untended baby to succumb to dehydration and starvation three days later.

Appalachia was among the first places where the malaise of opioid pills hit the nation in the mid-1990s, ensnaring coal miners, loggers, furniture makers, and their kids. Two decades after the epidemic erupted, Princeton researchers Anne Case and Angus Deaton were the first economists to sound the alarm. Their bombshell analysis in December 2015 showed that mortality rates among white Americans had quietly risen a half-percent annually between the years 1999 and 2013 while midlife mortality continued to fall in other affluent countries. "Half a million people are dead who should not be dead," Deaton told the *Washington Post*, blaming the surge on suicides, alcohol-related liver disease, and drug poisonings—predominantly opioids—which the economists later referred to as "diseases of despair." While the data from which Case and Deaton draw is not restricted to deaths by drug overdose, their central finding of "a marked increase in the all-cause mortality of middle-aged white non-Hispanic men and women" demonstrates that the opioid epidemic rests inside a host of other diseases of despair statistically significant enough to reverse "decades of progress in mortality."

At roughly the same time the Case and Deaton study was published, a Kaiser Family Foundation poll showed that 56 percent of Americans now knew someone who abused, was addicted to, or died from an overdose of opioids. Nationwide, the difference in life expectancy between the poorest fifth of Americans by income and the richest fifth widened from 1980 to 2010 by thirteen years. For a long time, it was assumed that the core driver of this differential was access to health care and other protective benefits of relative wealth. But in Appalachia, those disparities are even starker, with overdose mortality rates 65 percent higher than in the rest of the nation. Clearly, the problem wasn't just of some people dying sooner; it was of white Americans dying in their prime.

The story of how the opioid epidemic came to change this country begins in the mid to late 1990s, in Virginia's westernmost point, in the pie-shaped county sandwiched between Tennessee and Kentucky, a place closer to eight other state capitals than its own, in Richmond.

Head north as the crow flies from the county seat of Jonesville and you'll end up west of Detroit.

Geopolitically, Lee County was the ultimate flyover region, hard to access by car, full of curvy, two-lane roads, and dotted with rusted-out coal tipples. It was the precise point in America where politicians were least likely to hold campaign rallies or pretend to give a shit—until the unchecked epidemic finally landed on their couches, too.

Four hundred miles away, at the northern end of the Shenandoah Valley, a stressed-out preschool teacher would tell Kristi Fernandez around this time that her four-year-old son, Jesse, was too rambunctious for his own good. He was causing mayhem in the classroom, so Kristi took him to his pediatrician, who urged her to put him on Ritalin. She acquiesced two years later, the drug seemed to quell his jitters and anxiety, and the teacher complaints stopped.

But he was still her high-energy Jesse. You could tell he was hyper even by the way he signed his name, blocking the letters out joyfully and haphazardly, adding a stick-figure drawing of the sun with a smiley face below the first *E.* The sun's rays stuck out helter-skelter, like a country boy's cowlick, as if it were running and winking at you all at once.

Lieutenant Richard Stallard was making his usual rounds, patrolling through Bullitt Park in Big Stone Gap in Wise County near the Lee County line. This was the same iconic small town romanticized in Adriana Trigiani's novel and film *Big Stone Gap,* the one based on her idyllic upbringing in the 1970s, when a self-described town spinster with the good looks of Ashley Judd could spend her days wandering western Virginia's hills and hollows, delivering prescriptions for her family-run pharmacy without a thought of danger.

The year was 1997, a pivotal moment in the history of opioid addiction, and Stallard was about to sound the first muffled alarm. Across central Appalachia's coal country, people hadn't yet begun locking their toolsheds and barn doors as a guard against those addicted to Oxy-Contin, looking for anything to steal to fund their next fix.

The region was still referred to as the coalfields, even though coal-mining jobs had long been in steep decline. It had been three decades since President Lyndon Johnson squatted on the porch of a ramshackle house just a few counties west, having a chat with an unemployed sawmiller that led him to launch his War on Poverty, which resulted in bedrock social programs like food stamps, Medicaid, Medicare, and Head Start. But poverty remained very much with the coalfields the day Stallard had his first brush with a new and powerful painkiller. Whereas half the region lived in poverty in 1964 and hunger abounded, it now held national records for obesity, disability rates, and drug diversion, the practice of using and/or selling prescriptions for nonmedical purposes.

If fat was the new skinny, pills were becoming the new coal.

Stallard was sitting in his patrol car in the middle of the day when a familiar face appeared. An informant he'd been working with for years had some fresh intel. At the time, the area's most commonly diverted opioids were Lortab and Percocet, both of which sold on the streets for $10 a pill. Up until now, the most expensive painkiller of the bunch had been Dilaudid, the brand name for hydromorphone, a morphine derivative that sold on the black market for $40.

The informant leaned into Stallard's cruiser. "This feller up here's got this new stuff he's selling. It's called Oxy, and he says it's great," he said.

"What is it again?" Stallard asked.

"It's Oxy-*compton*...something like that."

Pill users were already misusing it to intensify their high, the informant explained, as well as selling it on the black market. Oxy came in much higher dosages than standard painkillers, and an 80-milligram tablet sold for $80, making its potential for black-market sales much higher than that of Dilaudid and Lortab. The increased potency made the drug a cash cow for the company that manufactured it, too.

The informant had more specifics: Users had already figured out an end run around the pill's time-release mechanism, a coating stamped with OC and the milligram dosage. They simply popped a tablet in their mouths for a minute or two, until the rubberized coating melted away, then rubbed it off on their shirts. Forty-milligram Oxys left an orange sheen on their shirtsleeves, the 80-milligrams a tinge of green. The remaining tiny pearl of pure oxycodone could be crushed, then snorted or mixed with water and injected.

The euphoria was immediate and intense, with a purity similar to that of heroin. Stallard wondered what was coming next. In the early nineties, Colombian cartels had increased the potency of the heroin they were selling in urban markets to increase their market share—the goal being to attract needle-phobic users who preferred snorting over injecting. But as tolerance to the stronger heroin increased, the snorters overcame their aversion to needles and soon became IV heroin users.

As soon as Stallard got back to the station, he picked up the phone.

The town pharmacist on the other line was incredulous: "Man, we only just got it a month or two ago. And you're telling me it's *already* on the street?"

The pharmacist had read the FDA-approved package insert for Oxy-Contin. Most pain pills lasted only four hours, but OxyContin was supposed to provide steady relief three times as long, giving people in serious pain the miracle of uninterrupted sleep. In an early concession to the potential for its abuse, the makers of OxyContin claimed the slow-release delivery mechanism would frustrate drug abusers chasing a euphoric rush.

Based on Stallard's news, the pharmacist already doubted the company's claims: "Delayed absorption, as provided by OxyContin tablets, is believed to reduce the abuse liability of a drug." If the town's most experienced drug detective was calling him about it just a couple of months after the drug's release, and if his neighbors were already walking around with their shirts stained orange and green, it was definitely being abused.

*   *   *

Approved by the Food and Drug Administration in late 1995, Oxy-Contin was the brainchild of a little-known, family-owned pharmaceutical company called Purdue Frederick, based in Stamford, Connecticut. The company was virtually unheard of when a trio of research psychiatrists and brothers—Mortimer, Raymond, and Arthur Sackler—bought it from its original Manhattan-based owners in 1952, with only a few employees and annual sales of just $20,000. The new owners made their initial fortunes specializing in such over-the-counter products as laxatives, earwax remover, and the antiseptic Betadine, used to wash down the Apollo 11 spacecraft after its historic mission to the moon. Expanding internationally in the 1970s, the Sacklers acquired Scottish and British drug companies and paved the way for their entry into the pain-relief business with the development of an end-of-life painkiller derived from morphine, MS Contin, in 1984. (*Contin* was an abbreviation of "continuous.") With annual sales of $170 million, MS Contin had run its profit-making course by the mid-1990s.

As its patent was set to expire, the company launched OxyContin to fill the void, with the intention of marketing the new drug, a reformulation of the painkiller oxycodone, beyond hospice and end-of-life care. It was a tweak of a compound first developed in 1917, a form of oxycodone synthesized from thebaine, an ingredient in the Persian poppy.

Famously private, the brothers were better known for their philanthropy than for their drug-developing prowess, counting among their friends British royalty, Nobel Prize winners, and executives of the many Sackler-named art wings from the Smithsonian to the Metropolitan Museum of Art.

Promotion and sales were managed by the company's marketing arm, Purdue Pharma, launched in the nation's best-known corporate tax haven—Delaware.

Purdue Pharma touted the safety of its new opioid-delivery system everywhere its merchants went. "If you take the medicine like it is prescribed, the risk of addiction when taking an opioid is one-half of 1 percent," said Dr. J. David Haddox, a pain specialist who became the company's point man for the drug. Iatrogenic (or doctor-caused) addiction, in the words of a 1996 company training session for doctors, was not just unusual; it was "exquisitely rare."

In the United States of Amnesia, as Gore Vidal once called it, there were people in history who might have expressed some skepticism about Haddox's claim, had anyone bothered reading up on them. Ever since Neolithic humans figured out that the juice nestled inside the head of a poppy could be dried, dehydrated, and smoked for the purposes of getting high or getting well, depending on your point of view, opium had inspired all manner of commerce and conflict. The British and Chinese fought two nineteenth-century wars over it. And opium was a chief ingredient in laudanum, the alcohol-laced tincture used to treat everything from yellow fever and cholera to headaches and general pain. In 1804, at the end of Alexander Hamilton's ill-fated duel, doctors gave him laudanum to numb the agony caused by the bullet that pierced his liver, then lodged in his vertebrae.

In the 1820s, one of Boston's leading merchants masterminded an opium-smuggling operation off the Cantonese coast, spawning millions for Boston Brahmins with the names of Cabot, Delano (as in FDR), and Forbes. This money would go on to build many of the nation's first railroads, mines, and factories.

Around that time, a twenty-one-year-old German apothecary urged caution when he published the first major opium breakthrough. Friedrich Sertürner had isolated the active ingredient inside the poppy, an alkaloid he named morphium after the Greek god of dreams, Morpheus. Sertürner quickly understood that morphine was exponentially more powerful than processed opium, noting that its side effects often progressed from euphoria to depression and nausea. He had not at all liked what the compound did to his dogs: It made them pass out drooling, only to awaken in an edgy and aggressive state, with fevers and diarrhea—the same state of withdrawal the opium-addicted in

China had long referred to as "yen." (What modern-day addicted users call dopesick or fiending, William S. Burroughs referred to as junk sick, gaping, or yenning.) "I consider it my duty to attract attention to the terrible effects of this new substance in order that calamity may be averted," Sertürner wrote, prophetically, in 1810.

But his medical descendants were not so conscientious. Dr. Alexander Wood, the Scottish inventor of the hypodermic needle, hailed his 1853 creation by swearing that, whereas smoking or swallowing morphine caused addiction, shooting it up would not. No one mentioned Sertürner's warning decades before. It was easier to be swayed by Wood's shiny new thing.

So when doctors departed from the homes of the injured Civil War veterans they were treating, it became standard practice to leave behind both morphine and hypodermic needles, with instructions to use as needed. An estimated hundred thousand veterans became addicted, many identifiable not by shirt smudges of orange and green but by the leather bags they carried, containing needles and morphine tablets, dangling from cords around their neck. The addiction was particularly severe among white Southerners in small cities and towns, where heartbroken wives, fathers, and mothers turned to drugs to cope with devastating war fatalities and the economic uncertainty brought on by slavery's end.

"Since the close of the war, men once wealthy, but impoverished by the rebellion, have taken to eating and drinking opium to drown their sorrows," lamented an opium dealer in New York.

By the 1870s, injecting morphine was so popular among the upper classes in Europe and the United States that doctors used it for a variety of ailments, from menstrual pain to inflammation of the eyes. The almost total lack of regulatory oversight created a kind of Wild West for patent medicines, with morphine and opium pills available at the nearest drugstore counter, no prescription necessary. As long as a doctor initially OK'd the practice, even injected morphine was utterly accepted. Daily users were not socially stigmatized, because reliance on the drug was iatrogenic.

Morphine did generate public debate, if tepid, from a few alarm-sounding doctors. In 1884, the Virginia General Assembly considered placing regulations on over-the-counter versions of opium and morphine, a move the local newspaper denounced as "class legislation." In response, Richmond doctor W. G. Rogers wrote an empathetic, impassioned letter urging the newspaper to reconsider its stance:

> *I know persons who have been opium-eaters for some years who now daily consume enough of this poison in the form of morphine to kill a half dozen robust men not used to the poison. I have heard them, with tears in their eyes, say that they wished it had never been prescribed for them, and... many of them [have] inserted into the flesh frequently during each day, in spite of the painful abscesses it often causes, until in some instances the whole surface of the body seems to be tattooed. I have heard one exclaim with sorrow that there was no longer a place to put it. Whilst they know it is killing them, more or less rapidly, the fascination and power of the drug [are] irresistible, and it is a rare exception if they ever cease to take it as long as it can be obtained until they have poisoned themselves to death.*
>
> *Should not this, then, be prevented, though the profits of [the drug-sellers] be diminished?*

The legislature declined to approve the bill, considering it government overreach, which allowed the tentacles of morphinism to dig in deeper. Fourteen years later, Bayer chemist Heinrich Dreser stumbled on a treasure in the pharmaceutical archives: the work of a British chemist who in 1874 had made a little-remarked-on discovery while researching nonaddictive alternatives for morphine.

Diacetylmorphine—aka heroin—was more than twice as powerful as morphine, which was already ten times stronger than opium. At a time when pneumonia and tuberculosis were the leading causes of death and antibiotics didn't yet exist, Dreser believed he had unearthed the recipe for an elixir that would suppress coughing as effectively as codeine, an opium derivative, but without codeine's well-known addictive qualities.

He ordered one of his lab assistants to synthesize the drug. From its first clinical testing in 1897—initially on rabbits and frogs, then on himself and employees of the Bayer dye factory—Dreser understood that the new drug's commercial potential was huge.

If they could pitch heroin as a new and nonaddictive substitute for morphine, Dreser and Bayer would both strike it rich. Presenting the drug to the German medical academy the following year, Dreser praised heroin's sedative and respiration-depressing effects in treating asthma, bronchitis, and tuberculosis. It was a safe family drug, he explained, suitable for baby colic, colds, influenza, joint pain, and other ailments. It not only helped clear a cough, it also seemed to strengthen respiration—and it was a sure cure, Bayer claimed, for alcoholism and morphine abuse.

Bayer's company doctor chimed in, assuring his fellow physicians: "I have treated many patients for weeks with heroin, without one observation that it may lead to dependency." Free samples were mailed to American and European physicians by the thousands, along with testimonials that "addiction can scarce be possible."

By 1899, Bayer was cranking out a ton of heroin a year and selling it in twenty-three countries. In the United States, cough drops and even baby-soothing syrups were laced with heroin, ballyhooed at a time when typical opioid consumers were by now not only war veterans but also middle-aged barbers and teachers, shopkeepers and housewives. Many were mostly functioning, doctor-approved users, able to hide their habits—as long as their supply remained steady, and as long as they didn't overdo.

At the dawn of the twentieth century, the pendulum began to swing the other way as a few prominent doctors started to call out their overprescribing peers. Addressing the New York Academy of Medicine in 1895, a Brooklyn doctor warned colleagues that leaving morphine and syringes behind with patients, with instructions to use whenever they felt pain, was "almost criminal," given that some were becoming hooked after only three or four doses. "Many cases of the morphine habit could have been avoided had the family physician not given the drug in the first place," he said. By 1900, more than 250,000 Americans were addicted to opium-derived painkillers.

And yet heroin's earliest years were mostly full of praise, as medical journals heralded Bayer's new cough suppressant, considering it distinctly superior to and apart from morphine, some promoting it as a morphine-replacement drug. Though a few researchers warned about possible addiction—"the toxic properties of the drug are not thoroughly known," one noted in 1900—for eight years you could buy heroin at any American drugstore or by mail order.

In 1906, the American Medical Association finally sounded a sterner alarm: "The habit is readily formed and leads to the most deplorable results." Heroin-related admissions to hospitals in New York and Philadelphia were rising by the 1910s and 1920s, and it was dawning on officials that addiction was skyrocketing among both the injured and recreational users (then called "vicious," meaning their use rose from the world of vice). Soldier's disease, in the words of New York City's commissioner of health, had now become "the American Disease."

The Harrison Narcotics Act of 1914 severely restricted the sale and possession of heroin and other narcotic drugs, and by 1924 the manufacture of heroin was outlawed, twenty-six years after Bayer's pill came to market. By the thirties, typical heroin users were working-class, and many of them were children of immigrants, along with a growing number of jazz musicians and other creative types, all now reliant on criminal drug networks to feed their vicious habit—and keep their dopesickness at bay. The addicted were now termed "junkies," inner-city users who supported their habit by collecting and selling scrap metal. The "respectable" upper- and middle-class opium and morphine addicts having died out, the remaining addicted were reclassified as criminals, not patients.

Gone and buried were the doctor-addicted opioid users once common, especially in small towns—think of Harper Lee's morphine-addicted eccentric, Mrs. Dubose, from *To Kill a Mockingbird,* or the morphine-addicted mother who inspired Eugene O'Neill's *Long Day's Journey into Night.* Think of the "Des Moines woman [who] gave her husband morphine to cure him of chewing tobacco," as one newspaper chortled. "It cured him, but she is doing her own spring planting."

Think of the time in 1914, decades before the term "neonatal abstinence syndrome" was coined (to describe the withdrawal of a baby born drug-dependent), when a Washington official wrote that it was "almost unbelievable that anyone for the sake of a few dollars would concoct for infant use a pernicious mixture containing…morphine, codeine, opium, cannabis indica, and heroin, which are widely advertised and which are accompanied by the assertion that they 'contain nothing injurious to the youngest babe.'"

Below the story, on the same newspaper page, appeared an ad for an opium "sanitorium," a sprawling Victorian home in Richmond in which Dr. H. L. Devine promised that he could cure opium addiction in ten days to three weeks.

But the yellowed newspaper warnings would become moot, like so many historical footnotes—destined to repeat themselves as soon as they receded from living memory.

Despite all the technical, medical, and political sophistication developed over the past century, despite the regulatory initiatives and the so-called War on Drugs, few people batted an eye in the late 1990s as a new wave of opioid addiction crept onto the prescription pads of America's doctors, then morphed into an all-out epidemic of Oxy-Contin's chemical cousin: Heinrich Dreser's drug.

No one saw the train wreck coming—not the epidemiologists, not the criminologists, not even the scholars who for decades had dissected the historical arc of *Papaver somniferum,* the opium poppy.

Like Alexander Wood promoting his syringes, and Dreser with his sleepy frogs, Purdue Pharma's David Haddox touted OxyContin for all kinds of chronic pain, not just cancer, and claimed it was safe and reliable, with addiction rates of less than 1 percent. Haddox heralded that statistic to the new army of pharmaceutical sales reps Purdue Pharma hired. They fanned out to evangelize to doctors and dentists in all fifty states with this message: Prescribing OxyContin for pain was the moral, responsible, and compassionate thing to do—and not just for dying people with stage-four cancer but also for folks with moderate back injuries, wisdom-tooth surgery, bronchitis, and temporomandibular joint disorder, or TMJ.

The 1996 introduction of OxyContin coincided with the moment in medical history when doctors, hospitals, and accreditation boards were adopting the notion of pain as "the fifth vital sign," developing new standards for pain assessment and treatment that gave pain equal status with blood pressure, heart rate, respiratory rate, and temperature. The seismic shift toward thinking of patients as health care consumers was already under way, as patients now rated their health care experiences in formal surveys, Press Ganey the largest among them, and doctors and hospitals alike competed to see who could engender the highest scores, incentivizing nurses and doctors to treat pain liberally or risk losing reimbursements. In 1999, the Joint Commission on Accreditation of Healthcare Organizations (JCAHO), the nonprofit health care and hospital accreditation body, took the idea a step further, approving new mandatory standards for the assessment and treatment of pain.

The next year, Purdue's bean counters gushed about the prospects: "This presents Purdue with the opportunity to provide true value-added services as the 'pain experts' in this key area," read the company's budget plan. "We have an opportunity to be seen as a leader in helping hospitals meet the JCAHO requirements in this area through the development of pain assessment and pain management materials geared to the hospital setting."

To underscore such opportunities, the company planned to pass out $300,000 worth of OxyContin-branded scroll pens, $225,000 worth of OxyContin resource binders, and $290,000 worth of "Pain: The Fifth Vital Sign" wall charts and clipboards. With any luck, every nurse and doctor would soon be wandering the hospital halls, their name badges dangling from a Purdue-branded lanyard.

A 2000 *New York Times* article reflected the new and widespread view among the vast majority of health care experts that pain had been grossly undertreated for too long. It featured the story of an older woman in a nursing home who'd been left to writhe in pain, given only Tylenol for the relief of her severe osteoporosis and pulmonary disease. The story demonstrated the growing concern that pain was woefully mismanaged due to outdated notions about addiction: "Many health care workers still erroneously believe that adequate pain relief can leave patients addicted to the drugs."

But what exactly was adequate pain relief? That point was unaddressed. Nor could anyone define it. No one questioned whether the notion of pain, invisible to the human eye, could actually be measured simply by asking the patient for his or her subjective opinion. Quantifying pain made it easy to standardize procedures, but experts would later concede that it was objective only in appearance—transition labor and a stubbed toe could both measure as a ten, depending on a person's tolerance. And not only did reliance on pain scales not correlate with improved patient outcomes, it also had the effect of increasing opioid prescribing and opioid abuse.

"Every single physician I knew at the time was told to be much more serious about making pain a priority," said Dr. John Burton, the head of emergency medicine for Carilion Clinic, the largest medical provider in western Virginia. "All it did was drive up our opioid prescribing without really understanding the consequences of what we were doing.

"I can remember telling my residents, 'A patient can't get hooked on fourteen days' worth of [opioid] pills.' And I was absolutely wrong."

The Press Ganey survey upped the pressure, recalled an emergency-room doctor who practiced in St. Louis. "We quickly found that drug-seeking patients or others sending off vibes we didn't like would give us bad reviews," remembered Dr. David Davis. "When you're really busy and interrupted all the time with seriously sick patients, it's so easy to give them an IV dose of Dilaudid or morphine, and kinda kick the can down the road.

"I did it myself, though I knew it was not the right thing to do. It was pushed on us big time, the idea that they can't become addicted if you're using opioids to treat legitimate pain. The advent of the pain score, we now think, got patients used to the idea that zero pain was the goal, whereas now doctors focus more on function if the pain score is three or four."

Compared with the New Zealand hospitals where Davis worked earlier in his career—often prescribing physical therapy, anti-inflammatories, biofeedback, or acupuncture as a first-line measure—American insurance companies in the age of managed care were more likely to cover opioid pills, which were not only cheaper but also considered a much quicker fix.

Little did Davis or the other ER docs understand that the routine practice of sending patients home with a two-week supply of oxycodone or hydrocodone would culminate by the year 2017 in a financial toll of $1 trillion as measured in lost productivity and increased health care, social services, education, and law enforcement costs.

Throughout OxyContin's earliest years, only a few voices of dissent rose to remind doctors that, historically, there had been risks associated with prescribing narcotics, and even those warnings were timid. Dartmouth medical school substance abuse researcher Dr. Seddon R. Savage argued that addiction risks for pain patients on narcotics tended to increase the longer the patients used the drugs. "It is tempting to dismiss all concerns regarding therapeutic opioid use as irrelevant," she wrote in a physician journal in 1996. "That would clearly be a mistake." A colleague argued in the same paper that there simply wasn't enough good data available to make a case for or against liberal opiate prescribing.

The first real dissent would come soon, though, in the unlikely form of a country doctor and one thoroughly pissed-off Catholic-nun-turned-drug counselor. Though Dr. Art Van Zee and his colleague Sister Beth Davies would sound the epidemic's first sentinel alarm from Appalachia, they were greeted with the same indifference as the Richmond doctor who demanded prompt action to curb the rampant use of opioids in 1884, and the inventor of morphine, who strongly urged caution in 1810. Their outsider status disguised both the depth and the relevance of their knowledge.

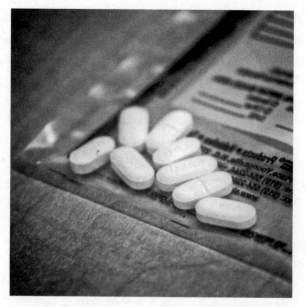

Evidence room, Lee County Sheriff's Office

Chapter Two
Swag 'n' Dash

Around the time the Big Stone Gap informant was leaning into the police officer's cruiser, the FDA loosened rules on pharmaceutical ads, allowing drugmakers to air detailed television ads touting specific medical claims for nonnarcotic drugs. Drug advertising ballooned from $360 million in 1995 to $1.3 billion in 1998, and nearly all pharmaceutical companies spent more plying doctors with freebies. At a time when there were scant industry or federal guidelines regulating the promotion of prescription drugs, the new sales strategies pushed the narrative of curing every ill with a pill and emboldened many patients to seek medicines unnecessarily.

From a sales perspective, OxyContin had its greatest early success in rural, small-town America—already full of shuttered factories and

Dollar General stores, along with burgeoning disability claims. Purdue handpicked the physicians who were most susceptible to their marketing, using information it bought from a data-mining network, IMS Health, to determine which doctors in which towns prescribed the most competing painkillers. If a doctor was already prescribing lots of Percocet and Vicodin, a rep was sent out to deliver a pitch about OxyContin's potency and longer-lasting action. The higher the decile—a term reps use as a predictor of a doctor's potential for prescribing whatever drug they're hawking—the more visits that doctor received from a rep, who often brought along "reminders" such as OxyContin-branded clocks for the exam-room walls.

The reminders were as steady as an alarm clock permanently set to snooze. Purdue's growing legion of OxyContin apostles was now expected to make more than a million calls annually on doctors in hospitals and offices, targeting the top prescriber deciles and family doctors, and aggressively promoting the notion that OxyContin was safe for noncancer patients with low back pain, osteoarthritis, and injury and trauma pain.

The practice became standard in rural Virginia towns like Big Stone Gap, Lebanon, and St. Charles—places that already claimed higher numbers, per capita, of dislocated workers and work-related disability claims. Now Purdue reps were navigating the winding roads and hilly towns in company-rented Ford Explorers, some pulling down annual bonuses of $70,000—the higher the milligrams a doctor prescribed, the larger the bonus. And they were remarkably adept. Five years earlier, cancer doctors had been by far the biggest prescribers of long-acting opioids, but by 2000 the company's positioning goals had been nailed, with family doctors now the largest single group of OxyContin prescribers.

Industrywide, pharmaceutical companies spent $4.04 *billion* in direct marketing to doctors in 2000, up 64 percent from 1996. To get in the doctor's door, to get past the receptionist and head nurse, the reps came bearing gifts, from Valentine's Day flowers to coupons for mani-pedis.

The average sales rep's most basic tool was Dine 'n' Dash, a play on the juvenile-delinquent prank of leaving a restaurant without paying the bill. For a chance to pitch their wonder drug, reps had long offered free dinners at fancy restaurants. But soon, to-go options abounded, too, for a busy doctor's convenience. Reps began coming by before holidays to drop off a turkey or beef tenderloin that a doctor could take home to the family—even a Christmas tree. Driving home from the office, doctors were also invited to stop by the nearest gas station to get their tanks topped off—while listening to a drug rep's pitch at the pump, a variation the reps nicknamed Gas 'n' Go. In the spring, the takeout menu featured flowers and shrubs, in a version some dubbed—you guessed it—Shrubbery 'n' Dash.

There seemed to be no end to the perks, or to the cloying wordplay: At a bookstore event titled Look for a Book, an invitation issued by SmithKline Beecham asked doctors to "come pick out the latest book about your favorite hobby or travel destination!" Purdue reps were heavily incentivized, buoyed by $20,000 cash prizes and luxury vacations for top performers and a corporate culture that employed terminology from the Middle Ages to pump up its foot soldiers. Internal documents referred to reps as royal crusaders and knights, and supervisors went by such nicknames as the Wizard of OxyContin, the Supreme Sovereign of Pain Management, and the Empress of Analgesia. Purdue's head of pain care sales signed his memos simply "King."

Physicians willing to submit to reps' pitches were routinely given not just branded pens and Post-it notes but also swing-music recordings labeled "Swing in the Right Direction" and freebie pedometers with the message that OxyContin was "A Step in the Right Direction."

A chain-smoking doctor in Bland, Virginia, was so blatantly in favor of graft that she posted a signup sheet in her office, soliciting reps to sponsor her daughter's upcoming birthday party at Carowinds, an amusement park—and one (not a Purdue rep) did. She even accepted cartons of cigarettes emblazoned with a sticker for Celexa, the antidepressant manufactured by Forest Laboratories: another gift from another clever rep.

Steve Huff was in medical residency training in the mid-1990s when he sampled his first taste of pharmaceutical swag—and not just by way of stickers, golf balls, and pens adorned with drug company names. "We were impressionable young doctors, fresh meat with a lifetime of prescribing ahead, and they flocked to us," he told me. "They took us golfing. It was standard to have a free lunch most days of the week because the drug companies were always buying, then you'd have a short educational seminar going on [about their drugs] while you ate."

By the time he progressed to a family practice, Huff decided the free meals were wrong and said so repeatedly, making a show of retrieving his cold leftovers from home from the office fridge, he told me. When he set about trying to coax the other doctors in his practice to ban the lunches, they demurred, saying the staff would be so disappointed if we "took away their free meals," Huff said.

The reps tended to be outgoing, on the youngish side of middle-aged, and very good-looking. "They were bubbly, they'd flirt a little bit, and it really would make you feel special. And yet intertwined in all those feelings is the name of a drug, which the rep is repeating over and over while you're eating this delicious, savory meal. And even if you say you're not swayed by such things, there is no doubt in my mind that you're more than likely to prescribe it," Huff added.

Huff didn't fall for the reps' pitches; in fact, he stopped accepting pharmaceutical gifts altogether, even Post-it notes and pens. At his first family medicine practice, in Stuart, Virginia, Huff prescribed OxyContin a time or two. But most of the patients returned, as miserable as ever and still complaining about pain, he said, along with new side effects that included sleepiness, confusion, constipation, and unsteadiness on their feet. "A few of them would stay on a stable dose once it was titrated properly, but more often than not it was causing problems" both for the patients and for Huff. He noted an uptick in depression and memory loss, too, among the long-term opioid users at the practice—as well as alarming news stories about drug seekers in the community breaking into those patients' homes or cars to steal their drugs.

When he moved his practice to the Carroll County hamlet of Laurel Fork to fill a spot left by two departing doctors in 2003, Huff was "deluged" with young-adult and middle-aged patients who'd been prescribed large amounts of OxyContin by his predecessors, concurrently with benzodiazepines such as Xanax, Klonopin, and Valium—"nerve pills," as most in Appalachia call them. There was nothing in their charts to justify why they were getting so many prescriptions, Huff said, and he knew the added benzos put the patients at enormous risk of overdose. As one recovering addict in Lee County schooled me: "Around here, pairing an Oxy with a nerve pill—we call that the Cadillac high. If you're gonna write this book, honey, you better learn the lingo."

Many of Huff's patients lived in nearby Galax, a factory town that had just witnessed the closing of two of its largest employers, Hanesbrands clothing and Webb Furniture, and continued downsizings in the town's remaining plants. In the wake of the 1994 North American Free Trade Agreement and China's entry into the World Trade Organization in 2001, many of the sewing factories and furniture plants were gravitating to cheaper-wage countries south of the border and in Asia.

OxyContin wasn't just numbing pain and the depression that came along with it; the drug was now its own resource to be plundered. "You could get a big bottle of eighty-milligram tablets and sell them for a dollar a milligram, and you could pretty much live on that for a month," Huff said.

Until Huff slammed the brakes on the Laurel Fork narcotics train.

"People freaked out on me," he recalled. They were sick and in withdrawal, some of them not yet understanding they were addicted.

"Just about every day I was having to go in and face another ten people, and tell most of them, 'I'm discontinuing your narcotics.' It was really strenuous. It drained me," he remembered.

One period was so awful that he got in his car and drove to Mississippi to see his sister for a long weekend. Two patients had threatened his life that week.

To one of the region's longtime health-department directors, Dr. Sue Cantrell, a former pharmacist, the premiere of OxyContin could not have been timed worse. With the exception of mining, production jobs in the coalfields had never paid much. Cantrell remembered setting up a mobile clinic in the parking lot of the Buster Brown apparel factory in the early 1990s because the women who worked there did piecework—they were paid by the number of sewn pieces they produced—and they had zero sick leave. "They couldn't leave work to have a pap smear or a breast exam, so we took the clinic to them," Cantrell recalled.

"Even though the pay wasn't great, those [production] jobs gave two things to our communities: One, families on the margin didn't always have to be on the brink of not having food on the table or money for utilities. And the second, more important thing was the behavior it modeled for families, where people got up in the morning and went to work. A lot of people never finished high school, just like the people who went into the mines, but they used to have a source of income before it dried up to nothing—and there have been no jobs to replace those," she said. Jobs in coal mining, once the number-one industry in central Appalachia, were cut in half between 1983 and 2012, owing to pollution regulations and competition from natural gas and cheaper low-sulfur coal out west. Automation in mining and the closings of factories that burned coal for power also contributed to the region's decline.

The closings were just sinking in when Cantrell took her first call about OxyContin from a doctor in tiny St. Charles, the next-to-poorest town (population 159 and waning) in the poorest county in the state.

Tall and skinny, Dr. Art Van Zee stood out. He was a Vanderbilteducated minister's son from Nevada who spoke softly, with no discernible accent. He'd come to the region in 1976 at the age of twenty-nine because he wanted to work in a medically underserved community. The town's new federally qualified community center, with its sliding-fee scale, was as close to the socialized medicine model he admired as he could find.

That's where he met his wife, Sue Ella Kobak, a firecracker lawyer and activist, a coal miner's daughter raised in a Kentucky coal camp just over the mountain in Poor Bottom Hollow. Introduced by mutual friends, the two had their first real date at an NAACP rally in Bristol, Virginia, called as a response to a planned KKK rally and ending with everyone holding hands and singing "We Shall Overcome." After they married a few years later—the flower girl was a three-legged goat—most locals began referring to the pair as "Doc and that woman," as Sue Ella tells it, because she refused to change her name.

Van Zee seemed to have all the time in the world for his patients, never mind that he worked sixteen-hour days, rising at four in the morning to type up his patient notes from the previous day's visits. A doctor who'd trained in Philadelphia recalled working with Van Zee during medical school and residency: "We'd rotate in and out of these big medical centers, and when we'd get back to school, it would occur to us, 'The best doctor in America is actually out in Lee County, Virginia,'" he told me.

Locals often compared Van Zee, with his salt-and-pepper beard and gangly frame, to Abraham Lincoln. If Lincoln had worn a paper clip for a tie clip to work. If Lincoln had been spotted routinely jogging on the winding mountain roads.

I had read about Van Zee in Barry Meier's deeply startling (but little-known) 2003 book, *Pain Killer,* which chronicled the country doctor's early David-versus-Goliath battle to get OxyContin off the market until it could be reformulated to be abuse-resistant. I had not yet met Van Zee in early 2016 when I ran into one of his patients coming out of a town-hall meeting on opioids sponsored by the Obama

White House. She was a nurse, a recent retiree with a thirty-year-old opioid-addicted son whose life, she swears, was saved by Art Van Zee. "When his patients are admitted to the ER, he comes there and sees them no matter what time of day. When my daddy died, he came to our house at two in the morning to pronounce his death."

Tales of Van Zee's dedication are as common in Virginia's coalfields as the rusted-out coal tipples that blanket the bluffs. There was the time he bent his lanky frame into the back of an ambulance to accompany a patient in cardiac arrest for the hour-long ride to the nearest hospital. The time he was so tired from all the house calls and beeper interruptions that some neighbors found him at a train crossing inside his idling car, asleep. The time when he cracked three ribs in the middle of a birding class on his property in the shadow of Wallens Ridge—he'd heard the spectacular clang of a two-car wreck in the distance and ran toward the road, only to find one of his own patients dead and the other driver flipped over, bottles of liquor and pills scattered around his car.

Van Zee sounded the alarm about OxyContin just as its makers were on the threshold of grossing its first billion on the blockbuster drug.

And though he didn't yet know it, he would spend the remainder of his career dealing with its aftermath—lobbying policy makers, treating the addicted, and attending funerals of the overdosed dead.

But back in the early days of OxyContin, Van Zee was as puzzled as he was concerned. He told Sue Cantrell about a new condition he'd spotted among some of his older opioid addicts—skin abscesses caused by injecting the crushed-up drug. He was beginning to think that OxyContin, especially in its 40- and 80-milligram forms, was another animal entirely from the 10-milligram Percocet pills some teenagers used recreationally on the weekends. His region had long been home to prescription drug abuse, though to a much smaller degree; before OxyContin, Van Zee treated only one to three narcotic-dependent patients a year.

But he was starting to get regular phone calls from worried parents about their young-adult kids. Jobs, homes, spouses, and children were being lost to OxyContin addiction. A banker he knew had already spent $80,000 of his savings after his son used his credit cards to buy items he could trade for Oxys.

Down the hall from his office, a physician colleague treated a septuagenarian farmer who had owned land worth $500,000. Within six months, the man had sold everything he had to keep his addiction fed. "It's over," he told his doctor. "The kids are gone. The wife's gone. The farm's gone."

The doctors were witnessing the same thing that Lieutenant Stallard had seen a year earlier, in 1997, on the streets. "We had always had people using Lortabs and Percocets, but they were five- or ten-milligram pills you could take every day and still function. They didn't have to have more," Stallard said.

"The difference with OxyContin was, it turned them into nonfunctioning people."

Convinced about the looming crisis, Cantrell, the region's top public health official, called the public health commissioner in Richmond in the late 1990s. "I said, look, we've had substance abuse problems for years," she said. "But this was a new kind of chemical, much more potent than anything we'd seen from the small subset of addicts we'd had since the seventies or eighties."

She was told it was a problem for the Department of Behavioral Health and Substance Abuse Health Services. Even though the infections put people at risk of tuberculosis, and the shared needles (and snorting straws) could hasten the spread of hepatitis C and HIV, the buck was passed. Officially, this was not a public health matter.

"Nobody would listen to her," said Dr. Molly O'Dell, then a fellow health-department director several counties to the east. "But she was right there in the epicenter of where the pills started. She's the first person I ever heard to name it. She called me and said, 'Molly, I think we've got an epidemic down here.'"

In 1997, the Roanoke-based medical examiner counted one Oxy-Contin death in southwest Virginia, the next year three, and the year after that sixteen.

But those numbers were inexplicably unexposed until 2001, five years after Purdue launched its drug. A Drug Enforcement Administration official told a Richmond reporter that illicit opioids were unlikely to spread beyond the mountains to the state capital, declaring southwest Virginia "a little bit unique," although he conceded there were other Oxy-abuse hot spots in rural Maine, Cincinnati, Baltimore, and Charleston, West Virginia.

Contacted by the same Richmond reporter, a spokesman for Purdue Pharma declined to discuss the illicit use of the company's drug.

So it happened that in the early 2000s Debbie Honaker, a happily married twenty-seven-year-old mother from the town of Lebanon, two counties to the east of Van Zee, recovered from a fairly routine gall-bladder surgery with a thirty-day prescription of "Oxy tens," followed by another script at her postsurgery checkup for another month's supply, this time for Oxy forties. When she called to complain that her incision was still hurting, the surgeon gave her a third prescription, for 7.5-milligram Percocet, designed to quell her "breakthrough pain," with instructions to take it not "as needed for pain" but as frequently as every two hours—concurrent with the twelve-hour Oxys. To remind her to take the Percocet, she was supposed to set an alarm for the middle of the night.

"The doctor didn't force me to take them," Honaker said. "But they're like a high-standard person, someone you're supposed to trust and believe in. My husband and I both understood that I was supposed to take the pills every two hours."

They have discussed that defining moment a lot in the intervening years. They've wondered aloud what might have happened had her gallbladder not given out at the same time the factories and mines were laying off and shutting down.

She might not have visited a neighbor, a well-known pill abuser, for advice on what to do when the pain wouldn't subside. "If you snort 'em up your nose, they hit you better," her neighbor told her.

She might not have found herself doubled over and dopesick the day her prescriptions ran out. "You're throwing up. You have diarrhea. You ache so bad and you're so irritable that you can't stand to be touched. Your legs shake so bad you can't sleep. You're as ill as one hornet could ever be," she recalled.

"And believe me, you'll do anything to make that pain go away."

She might not have later turned, in the throes of withdrawal, to her sixty-year-old neighbor, Margie, one of the growing legions of laid-off workers in town. Or suggested that, given Margie's bad hip from decades of standing on hard factory floors, she should go visit the town's so-called pain doctor and ask him to "write you"—parlance for coaxing a prescription out of a doctor by making the pain seem more debilitating than it really is. She might not have driven Margie to the appointment, then coached her on what to say.

"She didn't want to do it," Honaker recalled. "Margie would say, 'God knows I wouldn't be doing this if I didn't have to choose between paying a bill or going to the doctor to get the medicines I really need,'" for diabetes and high blood pressure.

Within the span of three months, Honaker had mastered the classic drug-seeking emergency-room trick, beginning with an impassioned complaint about kidney stone pain. "I'd say, 'My back's killing me,' and [in the ER bathroom] I'd pierce my finger, then put a drop of blood into my urine sample," she recalled.

She'd leave with a prescription for Percocet. She was a full-blown opioid addict when she resorted to stealing the money her husband set aside for paying the electric bill and spending it at the office of a well-known Lebanon doctor who began most of her visits to him with the question "What do you want?"

The Board of Medicine suspended Dr. Dwight Bailey's license to practice medicine in 2014 for excessive prescribing and poor record keeping, noting that five patients had died from drug overdoses while under his care—but that was more than a decade after Honaker first came through his doors.

Honaker went on to steal painkillers from her husband's elderly grandmother. She bought pills from people who paid one dollar for their OxyContin prescriptions using their Medicaid cards. "They've got to choose to eat or pay their electric bill. But if they're on Medicaid, they can sell their drugs to supplement their income," she said.

In an Appalachian culture that prides itself on self-reliance and a feisty dose of fatalism, peddling pills was now the modern-day moonshining. Some passed the trade secrets down to their kids because, after all, how else could they afford to eat and pay their bills?

"It's our culture now, taking pills," said Crystal Street, whose father, an octogenarian, got hooked on morphine and Dilaudid in the wake of a coal-mining injury. By 2016, he was on house arrest for selling prescription pills from his nursing-home bed. "I come from a long line of distributors," Street told me.

We spoke at an addiction clinic in Lebanon, where she and Honaker were being treated with the medication-assisted treatment (MAT) drug Suboxone. Like its methadone predecessor, Suboxone staves off dopesickness, reduces cravings, and, if prescribed appropriately and used correctly, doesn't get you high.

Both middle-aged, Street and Honaker had each been jailed. They took turns telling twin near-death stories, one beginning where the other left off. They'd both lost their teeth. "You get sick and throw up. Or you leave pills in your mouth and it takes the enamel off," Honaker said. Neither had ever had steady work. "You couldn't keep a job because you'd steal if you worked at a restaurant," Street added. "Or you just couldn't get up and go—you were too sick."

Honaker put in: "At the end of your journey, you're not going after drugs to get high; you're going to keep from being sick."

*   *   *

Art Van Zee saw it unfolding, and he was terrified. Within two years of the drug's release, 24 percent of Lee High School juniors reported trying OxyContin, and so had 9 percent of the county's seventh-graders. And Van Zee not only met with worried parents; he'd been called out to the hospital late at night about the overdose of a teenage girl he'd immunized as a baby. He remembered the exact position at the St. Charles clinic where he'd first held her. He was standing by the counter, made of materials recycled from a long-gone coal company's commissary where coal miners once gathered to collect their pay in scrip.

The miners had portions of their pay deducted from their salary to build the clinic in 1973. They'd also organized bake sales and talent shows, and spent years soliciting donations, many of the efforts shepherded by a trio of plucky nuns who'd migrated to the region a decade earlier, heeding LBJ's and Robert Kennedy's call to help Appalachia fight the War on Poverty. Nicknamed the Nickel and Dime Clinic, it was literally built by coal miners and community activists, people who chipped in every penny of their spare change.

These weren't simply Van Zee's patients who were showing up in the ER; they were also dear friends, many of them descendants of the coal miners whose pictures lined his exam-room walls. They hailed from nearby coal camps with names like Monarch, Virginia Lee, and Bonnie Blue. When patients recognized a relative in the old black-and-white photos, Van Zee took the time to write their names down on the back of the pictures.

In the spring of 2000, small-town newspaper stories weren't yet available online, and rural news typically didn't travel far. Van Zee had no idea that the force he was now wrestling with already had a hold elsewhere until a young doctor working in the clinic went home to visit relatives in the Northeast and hand carried a *Boston Globe* story back to the clinic in St. Charles. The story was headlined A PRESCRIPTION FOR CRIME.

Machias, Maine, was a remote town known for its juxtapositions—of coastal beauty and blueberries, of poverty and population decline. Its parallels to Lee County were stunning: In a region of just thirty-six thousand residents, the Washington County jail population had doubled in two years. It was overcrowded with young adults and middle-aged women and men, drug users and diverters who were facing charges of break-ins and robberies. A level of violent crime that was wholly unprecedented in the region had begun, including the fire-bombing of a police cruiser. The plainspoken sheriff blamed the new criminal landscape on OxyContin, and the DEA agreed, noting that Purdue's drug was being prescribed more than twice as often as in other parts of the state.

And though OxyContin's initial converts in Maine were fishermen and loggers, not coal miners, the results were the same:

People were "walking" prescriptions, or stealing prescriptions pads the moment a doctor turned his or her back. They were "shopping," too—quietly soliciting concurrent prescriptions from multiple doctors. Selling prescribed pills, available for a pittance with an insurance or Medicaid card, was now seen as a viable way of paying your bills in a county where the unemployment rate hovered around 22 percent.

In a place where people had once left keys in cars and didn't bother locking their homes, a forty-one-year-old resident told the *Globe* reporter, he now kept a loaded gun inside the house. A quarter of his former high school classmates had developed addictions to Oxy.

Van Zee's co-worker distributed copies of the *Boston Globe* story to others in the clinic, marveling: "That's us!"

Near the other end of the Appalachians, some eighteen hundred miles from Maine, it dawned on Van Zee and his wife that they were not alone. And they needed to get organized.

Within weeks, Van Zee had put on several public meetings under the auspices of the Lee Coalition for Health, a grassroots group of ministers, social workers, and other community-minded people. Edited and coached by his lawyer wife, a plucky former VISTA volunteer, he wrote letters of complaint to Purdue, noting injecting patterns, frequent overdoses, abscesses, and a higher incidence of hepatitis C.

"The extent and prevalence of the problem [are] hard to overemphasize," he wrote on August 20, 2000, in his first letter to Dr. David Haddox, then the company's medical director, beseeching him to investigate Purdue's prescribing patterns in the region. In another, he wrote, "My fear is that these are sentinel areas, just as San Francisco and New York were in the early years of HIV." The company replied by sending Van Zee and his medical partner some paperwork called Adverse Event Report Forms. At a forum for area doctors and families, Van Zee brought in Yale University substance abuse experts to describe the sudden physical and psychological stress caused by dopesickness, outlining a hard truth that many Americans still fail to grasp: Opioid addiction is a lifelong and typically relapse-filled disease. Forty to 60 percent of addicted opioid users can achieve remission with medication-assisted treatment, according to 2017 statistics, but sustained remission can take as long as ten or more years. Meanwhile, about 4 percent of the opioid-addicted die annually of overdose.

When the researchers recommended that area doctors prescribe other, less abuse-prone drugs to patients with severe pain, a Purdue Pharma rep who'd been sitting incognito in the crowd rose to sharply challenge him. The problem was inadequate pain treatment, he insisted, not OxyContin's abuse.

Sue Ella, Van Zee's wife, worried that the patient load was getting her husband down. But, instead, she witnessed a burst of energy and something she'd never seen in her mild-mannered husband: righteous anger. By November, his letters took on a sharper tone as he described patients who drove the five-hour round-trip to Knoxville, Tennessee, for maintenance methadone—including a twenty-three-year-old woman who woke at 4 a.m. and made the drive to the clinic with her four-year-old daughter in the car.

Van Zee attended a nearby meeting of the Appalachian Pain Foundation, a Purdue-funded professional association whose job was to capitalize on the growing pain-management movement of the 1990s and to amplify its organizing principle—that pain remained vastly undertreated. The invitation to the meeting featured a quote from a seventeenth-century English apothecary: "Among the remedies which it has pleased Almighty God to give man to relieve his suffering, none is so universal or efficacious as opium."

Van Zee presented the company with two major requests: stop the aggressive marketing of OxyContin for the treatment of noncancer pain, and reformulate the drug to make it less prone to abuse. As an example, he touted the makers of the painkiller Talwin, who in a 1982 reformulation had added a narcotic blocker, or antagonist, called naloxone, to the mix—and immediately reduced the drug's diversion and misuse.

In the fall of 2000, a newspaper story had run in nearby Tazewell County, Virginia, about an uptick in crime—between August 1999 and August 2000, 150 people had been charged with OxyContin-related felonies. In a county of just 44,000 people, there had been ten armed robberies of drugstores in the past eighteen months. Unemployed Tazewell miners like Doug Clark, who'd once made thirty-five dollars an hour, were now in legal trouble for ripping copper from an abandoned mining-equipment shop—to resell on the black market and fund his next OxyContin buy. Clark had gotten hooked after surgery to repair an injured neck and broken jaw; a rock had fallen on him inside a nearby Russell County mine, since closed.

Purdue's medical director, Haddox, called the reporter, Theresa M. Clemons, to complain about her crime coverage, and he seemed intimidating.

Now, at the meeting that followed Clemons's reporting, Haddox met with Van Zee, the county prosecutor, and other county officials, who told him about Oxy-related property crimes and check forgeries, and addicts who were doctor-shopping multiple physicians to feed their habit and to make a buck. Hypodermic needles were turning up at routine traffic stops.

While Purdue was concerned about the problem in the coalfields, Haddox said, he believed the worries were overblown. At the meeting, when Haddox and his colleagues steered the conversation toward the *under*prescribing of narcotics, prosecutor Dennis Lee was gobsmacked.

"We have never seen anything like this before," Lee interrupted. "There's just no comparison. Not just pill counting, but the human [tragedies]."

On the way out of the meeting, Van Zee pulled Haddox aside to reiterate his concerns about the promotional gimmicks the company was lavishing on doctors. The physician freebies needed to stop, Van Zee said.

"How is that any different from what every other drug company does?" Haddox fired back.

"People aren't stealing from their families or breaking into their neighbors' homes over blood-pressure pills," Van Zee said.

Van Zee didn't yet grasp what was truly driving the furious rate of overprescription. Sales-rep bonuses were growing exponentially, from $1 million in 1996, the year OxyContin hit the market, to $40 million in 2001. New patients were given OxyContin "starter coupons" for free prescriptions—redeemable for a thirty-day supply—and Purdue conducted more than forty national pain management and speaker-training conferences, luring doctors to resorts from Boca Raton, Florida, to Scottsdale, Arizona. The trips were free, including beach hats with the royal-blue OxyContin logo. More than five thousand doctors, nurses, and pharmacists attended the conferences during the drug's first five years—all expenses paid.

"The doctors started prostituting themselves for a few free trips to Florida," recalled lawyer Emmitt Yeary from nearby Abingdon, Virginia. As Van Zee delivered his message in meetings and letters, some desperate families hired Yeary to represent their loved ones for Oxy-related crimes. "The irony of it was, the victims were getting jail time instead of the people who caused it," Yeary recalled.

He remembered a dislocated coal miner from Grundy, Virginia, confessing that OxyContin had become more important to him than his family, his church, and his children. "It became my god," the man said.

By the end of 2000, Purdue had passed out fifteen thousand copies of an OxyContin video called "I Got My Life Back: Patients in Pain Tell Their Story," without submitting it to the FDA for review, as required by the agency.

The video, available for checkout from doctors' offices, lauded Oxy-Contin's effect on patients' quality of life and minimized its risks. The doctor-narrator heralded the new term "pseudo addiction," wherein opioid-seeking patients "look like a drug addict because they're pursuing pain relief... [when in reality] it's relief-seeking behavior mistaken as drug addiction." He then repeated Haddox's favorite sound bite: that opioid analgesics caused addiction in less than 1 percent of patients.

The source of this claim was a one-paragraph letter to the editor of the *New England Journal of Medicine* written in 1980. The letter was never intended as a conclusion on the risks of long-term opiate use, one of the authors would much later explain, yet it was trotted out repeatedly during OxyContin's first decade.

At Dine 'n' Dash gatherings and in doctors' offices from the coalfields to the California coast, this letter about an unrelated initiative was repeated and tweaked until its contents no longer resembled anything close to the authors' intention, like an old-fashioned game of telephone gone terribly awry.

A year after starring in the Purdue Pharma video, that same doctor, South Carolina pain specialist Dr. Alan Spanos, gave a lecture insisting that patients with chronic noncancer pain should be trusted to decide for themselves how many painkillers they could take without overdosing—just as the morphine-dispensing doctors had said of wounded Civil War veterans a century before. He reasoned that the patients would simply "go to sleep" before they stopped breathing.

*　　*　　*

By March 2001, Van Zee was as fed up with letter writing as the alarmed Richmond doctor had been in 1884, precisely two decades before his peers took up the cause and three decades before the government began regulating the drugs: *I have heard them, with tears in their eyes, say that they wished it had never been prescribed for them.*

Van Zee's neighbors were dying. The region had now buried forty-three people, dead of oxycodone overdose, since Purdue launched its drug. Addicted users had gone from snorting to routinely injecting the liquefied crushed-up powder with livestock syringes they bought (or stole) from local feed stores. At the Lee County jail, seventy-nine people were crammed into cells designed to hold thirty-four. "We were so overwhelmed, we were just stacking 'em on the floor," the sheriff, Gary Parsons, told me; one of the prisoners had bought four OxyContin tablets by trading away his family's mule.

While attempting to make a night deposit at the bank next door, the manager of Payless Supermarket in nearby Coeburn was gunned down by a masked robber trying to fund his next Oxy fix.

A half hour away in Clintwood, a man made the bold move of throwing a cement block through the front door of a pharmacy, even though it was across the street from the courthouse and the sheriff's department. "A deputy heard the alarm go off, and here's this guy running away and dropping pill bottles along the way, he's so high," Richard Stallard, the lieutenant, recalled.

In small towns where residents were used to leaving their doors unlocked, patrol officers were suddenly seeing people pushing stolen lawnmowers, four-wheelers, and even garden tillers down the street. "We called it 'spot and steal,'" recalled Rev. Clyde Hester, who joined Van Zee and Sue Ella in their Lee Coalition for Health, the grassroots group. "They'd look for things during the day—weed eaters were popular—and then at night they'd come back and pick them up," he said. To fuel his OxyContin habit, Hester's own son stole his gun, which the minister later retrieved from a local pawnshop.

A man in Dryden killed a young man attempting to break into

his house to steal his wife's prescription drugs, which he'd spotted above the kitchen-sink windowsill—down the road from Van Zee's house. And as metal prices rose, Sheriff Parsons reported thieves stealing everything from copper cemetery vases to wires plucked from a telephone pole that addicted users had chopped down. Parsons even had his stepson arrested for stealing his own personal checks to buy black-market OxyContin. "There is literally not a family in this county that has not been impacted by this drug," he told me in 2017, a statement I heard in every Appalachian county I visited.

In early 2001, Van Zee and the Lee County Coalition for Health launched a petition drive asking the FDA to order a recall of the potent painkiller, via a website called recalloxycontinnow.org.

Drawing deeper lines in the sand between Van Zee and the industry, and also between him and most of his physician peers, the petition received more than ten thousand signatures, most from Lee County and the result of a standing-room-only town-hall forum he organized at the high school in March 2001. "In a place where people barely have money for gas in their cars, by far this was the biggest crowd I'd ever seen gathered in Lee County," one organizer told me. Eight hundred people attended, some sitting in the auditorium aisles. Roanoke-based U.S. attorney Bob Crouch called OxyContin "the crack of Southwest Virginia," with Oxy overdose deaths now substantially surpassing those caused by cocaine and heroin.

The next month, the DEA developed a "national action plan" to monitor Purdue, asking the company to limit distribution of the drug, rethink its marketing strategy, and consider reformulating the drug to be abuse-resistant. This marked the first time in the agency's history that it targeted a specific drug to be policed by its manufacturer to prevent diversion and abuse.

In response, the company announced a ten-point plan to curb abuse, including the distribution of tamper-resistant prescription pads, an educational program aimed at alerting teens to the dangers of prescription drugs, and a $100,000 grant for the creation of a statewide prescription monitoring program, or PMP, to halt doctor-shopping. The company also stopped distributing its most potent form of OxyContin, the 160-milligram pill, and reduced shipments to Mexico in light of reports that the drug was being smuggled back into the United States—sometimes by people making the twenty-three-hour drive from Virginia's coalfields to the Mexican border or flying with pills taped to their back.

With great fanfare in July 2001, the FDA announced it had worked with Purdue to put a black-box warning on the drug, the strongest type of prescription-drug caution. The goal was to help prevent inappropriate prescriptions, misuse, and diversion.

But a company spokesman downplayed the black box, calling it "more of an exercise in graphic design" and pointing out that legitimate users didn't experience the high created by abusers who snorted or injected the drug. The real victims, executives said time and again, were their "legitimate patients," who would be denied OxyContin if its distribution were restricted.

That year, a former Purdue rep remembered, the salesperson attended one of the company's new seminars on diversion and abuse, meant to educate reps so they could inform authorities about suspected diversion. It was now possible for a rep who called on indiscriminate prescribers to earn as much as $100,000 a quarter in bonus pay alone, the rep told me. "It behooved them to have the pill mills writing high doses," the rep added. "The [diversion/abuse] seminar was just a cover-their-ass type of thing."

"Let's be clear," a Purdue Pharma spokesman said in August 2001, in a meeting with Virginia's attorney general. "The issue is drug abuse, not the drug." The product shouldn't be blamed for deaths, because in many cases the victims were also drinking alcohol and taking other drugs.

Van Zee scoffed, telling a *Roanoke Times* reporter: "To me, that's like somebody who was shot with a howitzer and a BB gun, and you walk up and say it's a little hard to tell what killed him. Was it the howitzer that took off half his chest, or was it the BB gun?"

Another set of scales fell from the doctor's eyes as a distinct possibility flashed before him: No one in federal government would take seriously the concerns of a country doctor until opioid abuse took hold in the cities and suburbs. "If it's a bunch of poor folks up in the mountains, it doesn't affect them personally," he said.

Purdue had tried in vain to quiet the Appalachian naysayers a few months before, in March 2001, by offering Stallard and other county leaders a $100,000 "grant" they could put toward drug treatment and law enforcement. The offer had come the day after a meeting Van Zee arranged between Purdue executives and concerned family members, including a prominent Pennington Gap banker, the one whose addicted son had already blown through $80,000 of his life savings. If Purdue wouldn't listen to local doctors and cops, Van Zee reasoned, maybe it would listen to someone whose son's addiction had nearly depleted his 401(k).

"We are an average family," the banker said in his appeal to the executives, showing them a picture of his son. The banker had grown up in the Monarch coal camp, putting himself through college one night-school class at a time. Before his son stole from the family to buy black-market OxyContin, he had been a good student and a burly outdoorsman. "Surely you have got enough patriotism to worry about this country?" the banker said. He pointed out that the company must have known Lee County (population twenty-three thousand) had an OxyContin problem before Lee County did, considering that it was sending as many pills to the region as it was to areas five times the size. "I'm sorry your family is having such a problem," Purdue's chief executive officer, Michael Friedman, said.

At the meeting's end, the executives stunned the group when they laid out an ad they planned to place in the local newspaper, a full-page "open letter" to the people of Lee County. In it, the company contended that Purdue had not targeted its marketing to areas like Appalachia with high disability or Medicaid rates, nor had the company known of the drug's abuse potential. Purdue Pharma also disputed suggestions that it could quickly or easily reformulate the drug.

The parent meeting had been a setup. Whereas Van Zee thought the company might finally be willing to make some compromises— "Art...really thought Purdue would feel some empathy" toward the banker, Sue Ella recalled—it was plain now that was not the case. The meeting had been brokered to shove the ad down the group's throat.

Sue Ella blew up, telling Haddox: "You have done more to hurt Appalachia than the coal industry has ever thought about doing."

Haddox said he resented the implication, and Sue Ella said she didn't give a damn if he did. "I said, 'Look, I'm an Appalachian scholar, and my family goes back here forever, and I take tremendous insult,'" she recalled.

She stormed out with the others, and the newspaper ad never ran.

The next day Friedman gathered with Richard Stallard and other law enforcement officers at Kathy's Country Kitchen in the Lee County seat. Sister Beth Davies, the pluckiest of the three nuns who had answered the War on Poverty call, was in attendance.

So was pharmacist Greg Stewart, a miner's son whose parents had personally helped build the St. Charles clinic. When Stewart filled OxyContin prescriptions, he begged his customers to lock their medication up. He'd already been the victim of two robbery attempts, including one by the son of a neighboring hair-salon owner who crawled in through the ceiling vents connecting the salon to Stewart's store.

When Purdue Pharma offered to put $100,000 toward expanding the county's drug treatment and law enforcement efforts, Stewart said he was inclined to accept the donation as partial payback, considering the fortune the company was making off the area's misery. Van Zee and

Sue Ella agreed, and even drafted a letter of acceptance after the meeting. Sue Ella explained that she was initially for accepting the money "because of my experience with the coal companies taking and taking and taking, and all the companies, they sit up north with their inherited wealth and leave nothing behind except broken bodies."

But Sister Beth, the five-foot-tall redheaded nun, was having none of it. The executives might be able to intimidate the people up north, where their philanthropy held sway in places like Harvard and Manhattan. But Beth was a formidable New Yorker herself, with a master's from Columbia. More important, she'd grown up under the tutelage of high-powered nuns who ran hospitals and colleges with a firm hand but a fair eye, and a mother who read a book every day.

A Staten Island native, Sister Beth had worked in Stamford, Connecticut, Purdue's hometown, where she ran a Catholic school before moving to Appalachia in 1971. A former student of hers from Connecticut had recently called to apologize, in fact; he was a reporter at the Stamford newspaper, which had been strongly encouraged not to write anything critical of the company, she said.

In 1996, the same year OxyContin was introduced, Sister Beth had stood up to a crowd of sixty coal miners and executives and their lawyers—all men—to demand the Lone Mountain coal company make reparations for the havoc caused by one of its faulty coal-slurry ponds. A liner had burst, sending wastewater screaming through the village of St. Charles. The water unloosed a boulder that rammed a resident's house, flooded other homes, scattered coal waste and litter for miles along the Powell River—endangering fish and mussel beds—and generally scared people half to death.

That event pitted company miners from other camps (forced to defend the company or lose their pay for the day) against local miners whose community had been devastated by the flood. Lone Mountain's defense, as articulated by one of the outsider miners: The town was already full of litter and "Pamper trees"; therefore, the flooding was simply another "act of nature" unleashed on an already diaper-scarred landscape.

Health care administrator Tony Lawson remembered the way Sister Beth stood up in that meeting — "this tiny little thin woman who was so angry the paper she was holding with her statement shook in her hands. But she spoke loud and clear to all those men in that audience. She was absolutely the most fearless, bravest person I've ever seen."

The executives glared, and the hired miners booed, but Sister Beth didn't waver. Though the coal company eventually paid to clean up the mess — not nearly enough, in the nun's opinion — the flood of slurry-pond waste was an ominous harbinger for St. Charles.

If the Purdue executives thought that people like Sue Ella and Sister Beth could be bought, they had not done their homework. Both had stood on the picket lines with strikers and their families for nine life-and-death months in 1989, when the Pittston Coal Company wanted such huge union-contract concessions as reduced pay-in to retired miners' health insurance and wage cuts. Sister Beth had literally lain on the ground, to block the coal trucks, while Sue Ella stood next to the striking miners with her six-month-old baby in a carrier.

Over the years, Sue Ella's and Sister Beth's lives had been threatened because of their social activism, including once when Beth convinced an illiterate coal miner not to sign away all company liability for a mining accident. ("Greed makes people violent," she told an interviewer in 1982. "When we stand with the least in the struggle for justice, there's a price to pay.")

The Purdue offer was just another page in an old story. This is what happens when wealthy people think they own you, Sister Beth told her Lee County friends. Since the first piece of coal was chiseled from the first mountainside rock by a large out-of-state corporation, the region had suffered from a pattern of exploitation, she said, ticking off all the mining-company executives who'd flown in over the years and spread their money around trying to buy peace, and then shut down unions, reduced black-lung benefits, and kept other industries out to maintain low labor costs.

Sister Beth thought about all the firsts she was starting to see at her Addiction Education Center in Pennington Gap, where she and Van Zee were now conferring daily over their mutual patients, among them young women now prostituting themselves for drug money. She thought about the high school senior, a cheerleader, snorting OxyContin in the school library. About the people having their teeth pulled for the sole purpose of eliciting an Oxy prescription from a dentist. About the middle-aged woman who'd ruefully remarked in the middle of being fingerprinted and photographed that she was wearing the same gray sweatpants she'd had on the last time she was arrested for distributing OxyContin. "I'd burn those if I were you," a sheriff's deputy quipped.

But it wasn't funny to Sister Beth.

She recalled the first phone call she'd taken about the drug, in the late 1990s. The informant had told the cop. The cop called the pharmacist. The pharmacist called Sister Beth. It was another game of telephone, only this message remained tragically on point:

"Beth, you wait," pharmacist Stewart had told her on the phone. "They're saying it's nonaddictive, but you mark my words: This is the beginning of a disaster for us."

The disaster was now in full bloom. And Sue Ella and Sister Beth guessed exactly where it was headed. Even if Big Pharma and the pill-mill doctors could be brought to justice, the morphine molecule was so deadly, its lure so intractable, that those who were already addicted were likely to be ruled by it for the rest of their lives.

Sister Beth threatened to quit the coalition if anyone accepted Purdue Pharma's $100,000 grant, and Van Zee's letter of acceptance was never sent. The grant was nothing more than "blood money," she said, and the coalition agreed.

Poff Federal Building, Roanoke, Virginia

Chapter Three
Message Board Memorial

While regional reporters from Boston and Roanoke were un-packing the damage done in their rural outposts, the story of the burgeoning OxyContin epidemic didn't hit the national media until February 9, 2001, when *New York Times* reporter Barry Meier and a colleague swooped in just north of Lee County for a front-page story on Operation OxyFest, a nine-month federal investigation that had produced the biggest drug-abuse raid in Kentucky history. "We caught 207" user-dealers, a federal prosecutor told Meier. Most of those arrested were patients who had coaxed pills out of doctors who were either busy, slipshod, or quietly cooperative in overprescribing the drug. "We didn't catch half of them; that's how pervasive this thing is."

That summer, it became clear that OxyContin abuse had seeped out of the western Virginia and Maine backwoods, creeping up and down the Appalachian range. The news was disseminating, finally, not just to big cities on the East Coast but also into the Deep South and parts of the Southwest. Overdose deaths and OxyContin-fueled crime grabbed headlines from Miami–Dade County to Bridgeport, Connecticut. Across the country, OxyContin was becoming a staple of suburban teenage "pharm parties," or "pharming," as the practice of passing random pills around in hats was known (ironically in farming communities).

It would fall, ultimately, to the parents of the dead to organize the first national response, specifically to a thirty-nine-year-old IT worker named Ed Bisch. In February 2001, Bisch had been summoned home to his working-class enclave of Philadelphia after taking a frantic call from his daughter. She'd found her eighteen-year-old brother incoherent in the bathroom the night before, and when she asked him what was wrong, he said he'd had too much to drink. The next morning she found him bluish and unresponsive.

Bisch arrived home to find a pair of emergency workers in front of his house. His son, Eddie, was a high school senior, a soccer player with decent grades and plans to attend a local culinary school. Eddie had complained of feeling ill recently, but it had not crossed his father's mind that he was deep into opioid withdrawal. Bisch had suspected Eddie was drinking and maybe smoking pot but hadn't considered pills. They had plans to fly to Florida for a father-son fishing vacation in just six days.

"I'm sorry," one of paramedics told Bisch. Eddie was dead.

As friends gathered, Bisch was still in shock and grappling for answers when he asked the first responders what his son had taken.

"Oxy," one said.

"What the hell's an Oxy?" Bisch wanted to know.

The first time Ed Bisch heard the word "OxyContin," his son was dead from it.

If parents were slow to catch on to the epidemic, experts weren't any quicker. The movement of OxyContin from the economically straitened hinterlands to the largely more affluent cities and suburbs in the early aughts reminded historian David Courtwright of the iatrogenic wave of opium and morphine addiction that stormed the nation exactly a century before. By the 1920s and 1930s, most of the small-town morphine addicts and Civil War veterans with soldier's disease had died out, not long after the national crackdown hastened by the Harrison Narcotics Act, which set the scene for drug prohibition and, later, the so-called War on Drugs.

"After the old-time addicts died out, narcotics were unheard of throughout the mid-twentieth century, unless you got cancer," Courtwright said.

For most of the previous century, opioid addiction was mainly relegated to big northeastern cities, where heroin had long been smuggled in through illicit channels, infiltrating the Harlem jazz scene of the 1940s and the beatnik subculture of the 1950s. The term "hipster," in fact, drew from the Chinese opium smoker of the 1800s, who'd spent much of his time smoking while reclining on one hip. The hipster counterculture took inspiration from heroin-addicted jazz greats like Charlie Parker and John Coltrane.

But where prescribed painkillers were concerned, the Harrison Act had effectively contained the earlier iatrogenic wave of addiction, and the small-town female morphine addict gave way to the image of the hustling, mainlining male junkie. Progressive doctors championed the carefully restricted use of narcotics and called out heavy prescribers for being behind the times. Pharmacists, too, upped the refill bar so high that in 1955 the heroin-addicted Beat writer and artist William Burroughs called them "sour, puritanical shits," unlikely to fill even a codeine prescription without checking with the doctor's office first.

When 20 percent of American soldiers came back from Vietnam with symptoms of heroin dependence, researchers were initially puzzled by the fact that most didn't go on to become heroin addicts—possibly, some theorized, because they returned to spread-out social networks in rural areas and small towns where heroin didn't exist. It may have helped, too, that many were detoxed in Vietnam before they came home, with the veterans who continued to struggle with addiction typically being the ones who already had drug problems before serving.

"In the early 1990s, probably ninety percent of the heroin market was still in cities like New York, Chicago, and Detroit," Courtwright explained. "There was this long-standing urban hierarchy of heroin that completely dominated the illicit opioid market in the United States." But when doctors started widely prescribing OxyContin for noncancer pain in the late 1990s, it effectively nationalized the supply, making opioids no longer only a big-city story. "So that any doctor in any small town, under the dispensation of a new FDA-approved prescription, could now suddenly provide opioids to people with low back issues and so on. You read a lot about economic depression and loss of morale, and I'm certain that fuels the epidemic.

"But the supply expansion [via OxyContin] came before anything else. And if it hadn't been for the supply expansion, then this [epidemic] would not have happened," Courtwright said.

If history was any indication, the moment OxyContin and other opioid pills became too expensive or too cumbersome to get, illegal drug peddlers would step in to fulfill the market demand, just as they had done a century earlier when heroin became illegal. For centuries, dealers of opium, morphine, and heroin understood that an addicted person's fear of running out—of becoming dopesick—portended one hell of a business model.

The author of several books on the history of drug addiction, Courtwright said he used to tell his students that "what most surprised me in my lifetime were things like the internet, or seeing tattoos on respectable women. But I've got to add this to the list of real shockers. I'm sixty-four years old, and I have to admit, I didn't think I would ever see another massive wave of iatrogenic opiate addiction in my lifetime."

Courtwright wasn't the only one. Though it took nearly a decade before police, the press, and drug-abuse experts fully understood what was happening, Ed Bisch watched the urbanization of the pill epidemic play out on his front lawn in 2001, as paramedics carried his son's body away.

He retreated to his computer, where he was shocked to learn that his son's death had been the region's thirtieth opioid overdose in *the past three months*.

How was that possible when he'd only just learned the word? "The internet was still new, and back then it was mostly message boards as opposed to websites," he said.

Bisch channeled his grief into computer code. Hoping to warn other families, he created his own message board, giving it the bluntest moniker he could think of—OxyKills.com. Within weeks it had morphed into a scrolling database of grief, warnings, and statistics. The website became a clearinghouse for the latest Oxy-related overdose numbers reported by local medical examiners and the DEA. Bisch promoted news stories about OxyContin, such as when the *New York Times* noted that the drug's sales in 2001 hit $1 billion, outselling even Viagra.

Parents from Florida to California joined Bisch in memorializing their dead children on his site, which became a running tally of dead athletes and young mothers and former beauty queens, many no more than twenty years old. "I was answering every email, and it was consuming me," Bisch recalled. "Probably ten deaths a day, sometimes a hundred emails a week."

Lee Nuss of Palm Coast, Florida, was too grief-stricken to reach out to Bisch initially, but her daughter, Monique, called him one night, begging him to talk to her mom. Turned out they had grown up in the same section of Philly, in the same working-class neighborhood of Fishtown, less than a mile apart. And the similarities didn't end there.

Nuss, too, had lost an eighteen-year-old son, Randy, who died of a single, crushed-up 80-milligram Oxy bought from a friend whose mother wanted him to sell it to pay their rent. "I had no idea he was using pills until this happened," Nuss said. She told herself that Randy hadn't been using long, because she still had opioid pills prescribed to her in the wake of dental surgery that were untouched at the time of his death.

The Fishtowners made an informal alliance with Van Zee and Sister Beth after reading Barry Meier's 2003 book, *Pain Killer*. If OxyContin nationalized the opioid supply chain, Nuss and Bisch nationalized the opposition to it, launching a grassroots nonprofit called Relatives Against Purdue Pharma (RAPP). It was Ed Bisch's message board sprung to life, a nonvirtual resistance party that would play out politically and in person over the next decade.

Together the parents-turned-activists would lobby for the creation of statewide prescription monitoring programs, or PMPs, so doctors could check a patient's prescription records and prevent themselves from being shopped. Members would sponsor drug-prevention workshops in schools and hold signs outside Purdue's corporate headquarters featuring poster-sized pictures of their dead kids. They would battle—online and at times in person—with chronic-pain patients who praised the drug for allowing them to function and to sleep through the night. Bisch suspected (correctly, in a few cases) that some were "paid advocates," hired by Purdue to troll his website and post contrary views.

From court cases to medical seminars, RAPP could be counted on to turn up whenever and wherever Purdue was in the news. In 2003, its members traveled from Rhode Island and New Jersey to rally outside a drug-abuse-prevention conference held in Orlando at the Caribe Royale resort—because Purdue was an exhibitor at the conference. The protesters were already battling the rain when Bisch began reading aloud the names of 260 people memorialized on his website—only to have an unidentified woman turn a sprinkler on them. (A hotel executive denied having anything to do with soaking the parents.)

A Purdue Pharma spokesman at the event told an *Orlando Sentinel* reporter: "We offer our sincere condolences to anyone who has suffered the loss of a loved one from a drug overdose" but insisted that Purdue's marketing of OxyContin had been "appropriate."

Raised Catholic and deeply religious, Lee Nuss began wearing a pair of rosary beads for protection at such events. As an added talisman, she carried a tiny bronze urn in which she'd tucked a portion of her son's remains. (As she explained it to me: "I leave the main urn at home on my mantel. But when I leave the house, I like to have Randy right there with me.")

The memorials kept flooding the message board. When Barbara Van Rooyan's twenty-four-year-old son, Patrick, died in 2004—after ingesting his first and only OxyContin, at a Fourth of July party—she reached out to Bisch, who put her in touch with Van Zee. "At the time, I knew very little about the drug, other than Rush Limbaugh had been addicted to it," she told me.

Van Rooyan, who lived in Folsom, California, had also read about Van Zee's battle with Purdue in *Pain Killer,* and she had one central question for the country doctor: "How the hell had such a strong drug come on the market to begin with?"

Van Zee walked her through the FDA's 1995 approval of the drug, led by its top examiner, Curtis Wright. Van Zee just happened to have a copy of the company's New Drug Application, or NDA, a document trove that had been a Christmas gift from Sue Ella in 2000. "It was all I wanted that year," Van Zee told me. Sue Ella admired the way her mild-mannered husband was stifling his hardwired passivity to stand up for the region, yet she increasingly resented the time it took away from their family life. "We used to try to go a day without saying the words 'addiction' or 'OxyContin,' but we never made it, not once," she said.

Though Purdue claimed it had no idea of the drug's abuse problems until February 2000, Wright had signed off on a 1995-filed NDA review that spelled out how crushing the tablets would lead to immediate, rather than controlled, release of the drug; that withdrawal symptoms had been witnessed in several patients during clinical trials; and that 68 percent of the oxycodone was in fact recoverable from one single, crushed-up pill when liquefied and injected.

In a summary of his approval, Wright had even urged caution in the product's marketing materials: "Care should be taken to limit competitive promotion." In fact, minimal care had been taken in the drug's promotion. Wright would go on to work as a consultant for Purdue Pharma two years later.

Van Zee told Van Rooyan, too, about the eight-hour drive to Maryland he'd made in January 2002 to testify before an FDA advisory committee convened to discuss the agency's role in approving and overseeing the management of narcotics. That meeting pitted Van Zee, wearing his only suit and a Jerry Garcia necktie his mother had given him, against Purdue executives and some of the nation's top pain-management experts, most of them acknowledging that they were or had been paid speakers for Purdue.

Van Zee found himself outnumbered nineteen to one, a harrowing experience for a loner not accustomed to public speaking.

"I get nervous," he told me. "It was intimidating, especially in front of my peers, all of whom had big reputations in the field. But this was my responsibility to do, and I did feel like I was speaking truth to power."

"He practiced and practiced and practiced," added Sue Ella, who accompanied him on the trip. "I tend to be emotional when I speak, but Art is so careful about saying only what he absolutely knows to be true. His ego is never invested."

The gist of Van Zee's opposition, as outlined by one Purdue-funded speaker: "We are allowing the abuse and the ignorance of the few to affect the potential health for the many.... Remember the biggest form of drug abuse today is under treatment, and this is a crime that we can all eradicate."

The next morning, in a ten-minute conversation with the country's elder statesman of pain management, Dr. Russell Portenoy, Van Zee asked Portenoy to describe what he believed to be an acceptable level of addiction risk from OxyContin. Given that the "less than 1 percent" figure, trotted out repeatedly from the 1980 medical-journal letter, was out of date and applied only to a hospital setting—rather than in the context of chronic pain treated at home—Van Zee asked Portenoy: Hadn't that been a meaningless calculator of long-term risk?

He showed Portenoy an OxyContin distribution map, highlighting the overlap between heightened crime and drug abuse in regions like Lee County, where OxyContin was prescribed at a rate 300 to 600 percent above the national average.

"That's good," Portenoy responded. The more opioids that were out there, the better to meet the needs of chronic-pain patients.

But what if the risk of addiction is 5 or 6 percent? Van Zee persisted. "What do you consider acceptable collateral damage? If you create fifty thousand patients that are opioid addicts?"

The country doctor's single-mindedness exasperated Portenoy, who walked away.

Although a decade later Portenoy conceded to *Wall Street Journal* reporters that he and other pain doctors had mistakenly overstated the benefits of opioids while discounting their risks, back then Van Zee was the doctor whose judgment was questioned and even mocked. "A lot of people discounted Art as a rabble-rouser and a kook," a prominent Virginia health care administrator explained. Another parent activist suggested that Van Zee's uncomfortable and slightly disheveled appearance helped Purdue cast him as a kook rather than the groundbreaking physician he was. "He should've gotten the Nobel Peace Prize," she said.

Van Zee pressed on, raising similar concerns at the end of the 2002 hearing with the FDA committee's chairman, Dr. Nathaniel Katz. He told Katz he'd spent months looking for studies that addressed the long-term-abuse risks to patients who used painkillers.

"There's a reason you didn't find any," Katz, also a prominent pain doctor, explained. "They don't exist."

This time it was Van Zee's turn to walk away. It dawned on him then that the only detailed study about potential abuse was the one that Purdue itself had undertaken in 1995 for its NDA—the one he'd read about in the gift from his wife. The one that noted that 68 percent of the drug could be extracted from a crushed tablet.

The FDA forum ended with experts urging the agency to closely monitor abuse and addiction as soon as new drugs went to market. But for Van Rooyan's son Patrick, the efforts were way too little, way too late. A year before his death, the FDA had missed another opportunity to help her son when it chose not to restrict the use of OxyContin to severe pain, a move that might have reduced addiction without compromising terminally ill or dying patients' access to the drug. Van Rooyan was never against the use of OxyContin for terminal pain but argued that it should not be used for chronic, noncancer pain unless all other treatments have first been explored. "To this day, I believe Oxy-Contin has a place for terminal, end-of-life care, and for acute pain when other, lesser opioids haven't worked," she told me. But it was clear as early as 2004 to Van Rooyan, then a researcher, professor, and college counselor, that the FDA failed to protect the public, her son included, not only when it approved the drug but also multiple times thereafter.

It would not come to light for nine more years that FDA regulators and Big Pharma executives had been quietly holding private meetings at expensive hotels at least annually since 2002, through a drug-industry-funded nonprofit, an ethical quandary a *Milwaukee Journal Sentinel* reporter shone the light on in 2013. The meetings led to the development of "enriched enrollment," an aptly named practice that allowed drug companies to weed out people from their studies who didn't respond well to their drugs, therefore tipping the balance toward FDA approval of new drugs—and away from science.

"Pay-for-play is just not the way the FDA operates," an FDA regulatory official claimed when the investigation broke. "That's not part of the culture of the FDA."

The same *Journal Sentinel* reporter, John Fauber, would also uncover how the American Pain Society and the American Academy of Pain Medicine pushed for expanded use of opioids for long-term chronic pain while taking in millions from the companies that made them. His articles prompted a 2012 Senate investigation, led by Senators Chuck Grassley and Max Baucus, that targeted both the American Pain Foundation and Purdue, among other nonprofits and pharmaceutical companies.

But the results of that investigation would end up sealed in the Senate Finance Committee's office, where they remain buried, despite periodic calls for their disclosure.

"A lot of us were very happy when they started the investigation, but nothing's come of it; it was never followed up on," said Dr. Steve Gelfand, a South Carolina addiction specialist and activist who helped Van Rooyan file a recall petition with the FDA.

"To me, it's all been just another political power play," he said.

Staffers at the FDA got used to hearing the name Barbara Van Rooyan. ("We all know who you are," an ombudsman told her.) She was burning up their phone lines, demanding a temporary recall of OxyContin until it could be reformulated in abuse-resistant form and relabeled for severe pain only. "The FDA's recall form is long and involved, designed to make you not want to do it," Van Rooyan remembered. A similar FDA petition to force Purdue to put stronger warning labels on OxyContin, detailing the risks of frequent prescribing, had been filed by the Connecticut attorney general in 2004—and was stalled in bureaucratic purgatory. (That initial application would be rejected four years later, in 2008.)

"But I'm a stubborn Dutchwoman with my degree from Berkeley, and I was used to doing research." And the words of the friend who'd given Patrick the OxyContin pill haunted her as she typed: "It's kind of like a muscle relaxant, and it's FDA-approved, so it's safe," he had told him.

If Van Zee's decade-long quest had begun to feel quixotic—now in his sixties, he wondered how much longer he could keep up the pace of thirteen-hour workdays, much of them spent treating addicted patients—Van Rooyan's focus was a balm. Whereas Van Zee's earlier recall petition with its ten thousand signatures was never formally submitted to the FDA—"we simply didn't have the time, energy, staff to do that," he said—Van Rooyan was unfazed by the paperwork, happily folding Van Zee's data into hers with her physician husband's help and filing it on February 1, 2005.

She testified alongside Van Zee at FDA hearings and organized a protest in her Northern California hometown outside a Purdue-funded continuing medical-education seminar taught by a well-known pain-clinic doctor.

She waited for an answer on her FDA recall petition. And she waited.

Following in her artist son's footsteps, she painted portraits of herself holding Patrick shortly after his birth, then another of his brother, Andrew, as she saw him in his grief at his brother's death: raw and naked, curled up in a fetal ball.

"I had a feeling that things would get a lot worse before they got better," she told me. "I knew that I might not see change in my lifetime, but I was going ahead with this battle anyway."

If the federal regulators weren't moved by memorials to dead Americans from their grieving mothers and fathers, maybe the country doctor and the nun and their growing team of mourning parents would finally get justice from the courts. At minimum, they hoped to amplify Purdue Pharma's negative press and raise awareness about the heroinlike drug.

Among RAPP's first courtroom targets was the 2003 civil lawsuit against Purdue brought by former Florida Purdue sales rep Karen White. She'd been fired in 2002 for allegedly having paperwork irregularities, poor communication skills, and declining sales, the company said. But White claimed in her legal filing that she was actually fired for refusing to sell to doctors who were illegally overprescribing OxyContin to their patients.

In the winter of 2003, the company bragged in a press release about all the civil suits it had won against people blaming their addictions on OxyContin under a headline that read like a football blowout: "65–0." "These dismissals strengthen our resolve to defend these cases vigorously and to the hilt," said general counsel Howard Udell. "We have not settled one of these cases—not one. Personal injury lawyers who bring them in the hopes of a quick payday will continue to be disappointed."

But the firm's legal bills were mounting—to the tune of $3 million a month—and Purdue still had 285 lawsuits pending against it, including another whistle-blower suit, filed by Marek Zakrzewski, an assistant research director who described raising safety concerns with seventeen different higher-ups about the "serious negative implications" of the drug, according to his complaint. His bosses banned him from undertaking additional research into the problems and even from informing the company's regulatory department about his concerns, his suit claimed. Fired in May 2003 after complaining to the FDA, Zakrzewski eventually dropped his lawsuit, citing illness, the following year. He'd had a heart attack from the stress of working at Purdue Pharma and was fired while on medical leave, according to his filing. A Purdue spokesman countered that the researcher dropped the suit after the firm refused to settle the case, calling the allegations "baseless."

To help burnish its image in the face of so many legal, financial, and public-relations problems, Purdue hired former New York mayor and Republican insider Rudy Giuliani and his consulting firm, Giuliani Partners. Just a few months after his lauded response to the 9/11 terrorist attacks, Giuliani's job was to convince "public officials they could trust Purdue because they could trust him," as Barry Meier and another writer at the *New York Times* put it.

The DEA was already investigating lax security standards at the company's manufacturing plants following the 2001 arrest of two Purdue employees accused of trying to steal thousands of pills. Giuliani brokered a behind-the-scenes negotiation of the fine paid by the Purdue affiliate that ran its New Jersey pill factory, including the condition that the firm pay a $2 million civil penalty—without admitting any wrongdoing. The DEA's diversion control manager, tasked with making sure drugs are lawfully used and not diverted into illicit trafficking, was left fuming; she had argued for a $10 million fine. She was sure Giuliani and company executives had gone over her head to her boss in an attempt to gain "access and insights into how to manage things politically." At a luncheon, Giuliani had helped raise $20,000 for a new DEA Museum historical exhibit.

Facing a growing number of lawsuits and investigations, Purdue Pharma heaped praise on its American hero and new political star: "We believe that government officials are more comfortable knowing that Giuliani is advising Purdue Pharma," Udell gushed in a promotional brochure. "It is clear to us, and we hope it is clear to the government, that Giuliani would not take an assignment with a company that he felt was acting in an improper way."

After all, not only was Giuliani old pals with the DEA director, but he also had just been named *Time* magazine's Person of the Year 2001.

The terrorist attacks had elevated Giuliani's stature, but in a boon moment for his future employer, they also temporarily diverted media attention from OxyContin. A sales executive said as much to Purdue employees on September 12, via voicemail, giving them the day off. The message the sales manager left, according to a former Purdue staffer: At least the tragedy for the nation would take OxyContin off the front pages of the nation's newspapers.

The RAPP parents believed White's wrongful-termination case would prove that Purdue's marketing practices had crossed a legal line. "We had such high hopes that she would be one of our saviors," Van Rooyan said.

Ed Bisch drove twelve hours from Philadelphia in 2005 so he could sit in a Tampa federal courtroom beside Lee Nuss at Karen White's civil trial, the first case against Purdue to progress beyond summary judgment. White was asking the jury to award her $138,000 in lost wages plus $690,000 for emotional pain. Depressed and anxious since her dismissal, she had never before been fired from a job.

"They were counting on us to run out of steam," Bisch recalled. "They were all lawyered up and Rudy Giuliani'd up." He counted ten lawyers on Purdue's side, not including staff, quarterbacked by the formidable Atlanta-based firm of King and Spalding, whose clients ranged from cigarette makers to Coca-Cola. White's lone attorney estimated Purdue spent $500,000 defending the case, an amount a Purdue spokesman declined to confirm.

White was tall and trim, a thirty-six-year-old brunet based in Lakeland, Florida. She'd been a champion of the drug's painkilling properties early on, having witnessed her mother's painful, premature death from cancer.

White argued that she was wrongly fired for refusing to participate in aggressive marketing of OxyContin that, in her opinion, several times crossed the line into breaking the law. White's attorney named two specific doctors she was urged to call on who were widely known for overprescribing. Both eventually lost their medical licenses for shoddy prescribing, including one who'd handed out prescription drugs in exchange for sex.

At the time, prescription drug abuse had become so rampant in White's Florida sales territory that one opioid-addicted Orange County veterinarian had recently been caught using the names of several pet owners' dogs—including Brutus, Cha Cha, and Lady—to forge more than a thousand OxyContin prescriptions.

White had a single lawyer and no staff, not unless you counted Bisch, Lee Nuss, and Nuss's late son, Randy, who was tucked inside her mini urn. Nuss also brought her rosary beads, loaning an extra set to White to hold during the proceedings.

A few days into the trial, Nuss realized she'd accidentally left the beads behind in her car. Excusing herself to retrieve them, she handed White her son's urn to hold during her absence at the plaintiff's table.

"Really?" White said, tearing up, as Nuss recalled it. "You would let me do that?"

When Nuss returned with the beads, she was surprised to see White coming out of the courtroom so soon. A recess had already been called. "Where's Ed?" she asked.

He had to leave the building, White told her, adding, "Lee, please, don't get upset."

"Why?" Nuss wanted to know.

"You're not gonna believe this, but Ed had to take your son out of the courthouse."

Purdue's lawyers had heard about the urn and asked the judge to have it removed from the building.

Bisch and White expected the grieving mom to blow up, but Nuss surprised them by laughing instead. She told her friends, "My son is not here in body, but he is definitely here in spirit.

"He might have left the building, but he *will* be back!"

Bisch was due back at work in Philly before the jury's decision came in—but he was not surprised when Nuss called with the verdict. "Ed, there's just too much money involved," she told him. "We really thought we were doing something, only to find out, nobody is gonna do anything."

The jury ruled in favor of Purdue, whose lawyer called the case a "personal disagreement with promoting the drug in an entirely legal way." While White believed calling on sleazy pill prescribers was illegal, her lawyer had not proved the illegality of the company's sales strategies.

"The court basically said, 'Don't tell us what you believe. Tell us what you know,'" explained University of Kentucky legal scholar Richard Ausness, who has written about the difficulty of winning civil cases against Purdue, citing among other reasons the company's hefty defense chest. At the request of a Purdue lawyer, the government's highly critical 2003 Government Accountability Office study of Purdue's marketing practices was ruled inadmissible in court.

During the first decade of the drug's existence, the legal system could not prove the makers of OxyContin had broken the law.

Back in western Virginia, a young U.S. attorney with political aspirations was secretly working on his own attempt to defeat Purdue in court as early as 2003. John L. Brownlee was brash, a little bit of a cowboy, and as a former paratrooper and Army Reserve JAG Corps captain, the thirty-six-year-old was not afraid of high-stakes drama.

Or the press. He was married to a local news anchor, Lee Ann Necessary, whom he'd met on the job a decade earlier. With a ruddy complexion and a mop of reddish-brown hair, he had a boyish appearance that belied his hard-charging demeanor. If *Law & Order* sold action figures, they would look like John Brownlee, down to the crisp creases in his trousers and his American-flag lapel pin.

Brownlee became so fond of calling press conferences that he traveled with a portable podium with fold-out legs. His prosecuting philosophy: If you're not losing sometimes, you're not going after the hard cases. By the time Karen White's case was dismissed, in 2003, Brownlee was still smarting over his own trial loss, via an acquittal, hung jury, and dismissal, in a multiple wrongful-death suit against Roanoke pain specialist Dr. Cecil Knox, whose office had been raided by federal agents, storm trooper–style. Knox and several of his office workers had been handcuffed and carted away—one of the women was carrying her groceries out of a store—even though defense attorneys had already arranged with federal authorities for their clients to turn themselves in. The showboating earned Brownlee a reputation as aggressive and, at times, overreaching.

On the heels of the Knox case and another high-profile case that generated equally fierce public criticism and ended similarly—with two hung juries—Brownlee needed a big legal win.

With plans to seek elected office—Brownlee would run for Virginia attorney general in 2008—he may have viewed prosecuting Purdue Pharma as "a vehicle for being in the national news," recalled Laurence

Hammack, a longtime *Roanoke Times* reporter (and my former colleague) who chronicled OxyContin's spread.

"Yes, he had self-serving motivations. But on the other hand, [OxyContin abuse] was happening everywhere in the country, and no one else took them on."

Brownlee did, almost immediately after being appointed U.S. attorney, though he didn't go public with the investigation until 2005. He had read Meier's *Pain Killer* and knew about Purdue's attempt to bully the journalist after its publication.

Purdue lawyer Howard Udell complained to Meier's *New York Times* editors, claiming that Meier had a conflict of interest in the story. His book, Purdue argued, gave him a financial stake in the newspaper's continued coverage of OxyContin. Udell wanted Meier taken off the beat.

"Their agenda was to shut me down, and to suppress as much news coverage of the company as possible," Meier recalled. "And he [the paper's public editor, Daniel Okrent] bit on it, not realizing that what they weren't telling him was that they were already under criminal investigation," which Meier suspected. (With two minor exceptions, Meier would not write about Purdue Pharma for the newspaper again for four years.)

Meier may have been temporarily silenced from writing about the company, but nothing prevented John Brownlee from poring over the footnotes of his book. Brownlee also relied on an eager fraud investigator in his office, Gregg Wood, to communicate with Van Zee and the RAPP parents. Since the epidemic's earliest days—long before Google Alerts—Wood had been sending out regular compilations of OxyContin-related news articles and overdose statistics via email to law enforcement agents, prosecutors, and other interested parties. Recipients who spotted any OxyContin news in their localities should "let me know," Wood urged at the top of every update, which Van Zee nicknamed the Wood Reports.

"Never assume I already know!" Wood enthused.

* * *

"Gregg Wood was very high energy," Van Zee recalled. "He would get up in the middle of the night checking for stories."

As health fraud investigator for the U.S. attorney's office in Roanoke, Wood was tasked with picking through the weeds of the civil cases against Purdue, most filed by small-town lawyers who were trying in vain to challenge the company for overpromoting the drug while ignoring its risks for addiction. Their clients ranged from miners and masonry workers who became addicted following work-related injuries to a factory worker so desperate to stop taking OxyContin that he'd flushed his pills down the toilet, telling his lawyer that trying to explain dopesickness to a nonaddict was "like describing an elephant to a blind man." The lawyers, the parents, Van Zee, and Sister Beth—all were happy to pass along every piece of dirt they'd collected on Purdue, from sales-rep call notes and depositions to Van Zee's Christmas gift from Sue Ella—the NDA.

"The Purdue lawyers were totally underestimating the work done by Wood," recalled Abingdon lawyer Emmitt Yeary, who lost his own civil case against the company. Arnold Fayne McCauley, seventy-one when his suit was filed in 2004, had spent decades stooped over and crawling through thirty-six-inch-high Lee County coal seams. In coal-mining parlance, he worked "low coal," the most strenuous of the coal-extracting jobs. "Now that's working hard, working in low coal," Van Zee said, pointing to a picture in one of his exam rooms of a miner crawling on his knees, in the dark, under a sagging mass of mountain. "Compared to that, all I do is move around a mouse."

When he wasn't working low coal, Fayne McCauley spent nights and weekends hauling and spreading lime from his truck for area farmers. Asked to describe the defining characteristic of her father, Lisa Nina McCauley Green said simply: "All I remember about him growing up is, he worked." As the Virginia writer John C. Tucker described it in *May God Have Mercy:* "For a miner who avoids being crippled, burned or buried alive, the usual question is which will give out first—his lungs, his back, or his knees."

In McCauley's case, it happened to be his shoulder, from a late-1990s injury caused by the snapping of an underground cable that slammed into his shoulder and back. Building his product-liability case against Purdue, Yeary collected some twenty boxes of documents arguing that Purdue overpromoted the prescription painkiller while ignoring its risks—rendering people like McCauley addicts while reaping billions in sales.

Yeary had gotten the idea for the lawsuit in 2000 after hearing Van Zee give a community college lecture on OxyContin. Yeary hadn't been particularly interested in the topic but went along to satisfy a schoolteacher he was dating at the time. As Van Zee went through his slides—ranging from overdose deaths to spikes in Oxy-related crime committed by addicted users, all of it meticulously sourced and footnoted—Yeary leaned over to a lawyer friend sitting on his other side and said, "*Damn,* they're putting the wrong people in jail!"

He remembered thinking Van Zee was not the "kind of guy you raised hell with in college." It occurred then to him that the country doctor was the perfect conduit for helping him identify plaintiffs to sue Purdue. In fact it was Van Zee who eventually connected Yeary to McCauley, a patient Van Zee was by then treating for OxyContin addiction.

But like most of the civil plaintiffs suing Purdue, Fayne McCauley was an imperfect client, because he admitted under oath that he had taken multiple drugs, gradually supplementing his original OxyContin prescriptions with OxyContin he'd bought on the streets. When his original doctor, Richard C. Norton, tried to wean him from the drug, cutting him back from 40 to 20 milligrams, it had made McCauley extremely nervous, crippling him with diarrhea, sweats, and a skin-crawling feeling he called gooseflesh. McCauley bought the black-market OxyContin, he told an opposing lawyer from Purdue in a series of depositions, for the same reason a century's worth of heroin addicts had kept returning to their dealers for more dope: to stave off dopesickness.

It didn't matter that the septuagenarian hadn't been stealing from his granddaughter before OxyContin came along, or cashing out his relatives' life-insurance policies, or borrowing guns for protection from his new pill-peddling associates. It didn't matter that he'd been treated with lower-strength opioids after losing two fingers to a 1980 coal-mining accident but did not develop a $300-a-day drug habit until 1999, shortly after his first bottle of OxyContin.

Nor did it matter that people like Van Zee had urged Dr. Norton not to fall for the Purdue reps' spiel about "the great epidemic of untreated severe pain." Van Zee had seen Norton's clinic in nearby Duffield, with its parking lot full of out-of-state cars, and confronted him about it at a hospital meeting. ("I said, 'You know, Rich, people are injecting this.' And he was astounded," Van Zee recalled.)

In 2000, Norton was sentenced to five years in federal prison, not for overprescribing OxyContin but for his role in an unrelated hospital corruption scheme. According to sales-rep notes subpoenaed in the McCauley case, federal prosecutors were also investigating Norton for operating a pill mill but opted to front-burner the wider and more urgent corruption case.

Stallard, the Big Stone Gap drug detective, remembered an informant unpacking the life of a Norton patient: "He told us, 'Dr. Norton wrote prescriptions for Lortab, forty-milligram OxyContins, and eighty-milligram Oxys all in the same visit.'" When Stallard subpoenaed the physician's records, he saw Norton had prescribed thousands of OxyContin pills in just thirty days.

Stallard turned the information over to Brownlee's assistant prosecutors, who said physician cases were difficult to prove, since there was always another paid physician expert willing to testify that such prescription dosages were necessary. Nonetheless, the prosecutors brought in DEA agents to help target the most egregious prescribers, and local detectives started feeding them information, Stallard said.

"We sent all kinds of information in to the feds but we never got anything back out of them. They told us nothing," he added, of Brownlee and his assistant prosecutors. "We started calling them the Shadow Company."

The federal investigation actually began when the Shadow Company realized Norton was simply following his Purdue rep's guidelines to a T, Stallard said.

But none of that counted in the civil cases against Purdue, wherein plaintiffs had to prove that a specific injury was directly tied to company wrongdoing with such specificity that a reasonable jury could assign the wrongdoing a dollar amount. Federal judge James P. Jones dismissed the McCauley case on the grounds that a jury would not have been able to divine whether OxyContin alone had caused the coal miner's suffering.

Though other judges across the country simply dismissed the Oxy-Contin lawsuits, Jones took the unusual step of inserting a personal opinion into his ruling: "Does the relief afforded by high-dosage opioids to those with severe, life-altering pain outweigh the risks of harm from addiction?" he wrote. McCauley's case did not answer that question, he said.

A God-fearing Baptist, Fayne McCauley had loved country music and the Atlanta Braves. Everyone in the town of Jonesville knew him because he had refereed home basketball games at Lee High School for many years. His family had sent him to rehab seven times, before and after the case. "Every time he'd come back and lie to us and say he's not taking the pills anymore when we knew he was," his daughter, Lisa Green, told me. McCauley ended up selling family heirlooms at a flea market. He stole credit cards to buy a four-wheeler that he sold for money to buy drugs. "He would say my mom was trying to kill him when my mom doesn't have a mean bone in her body," Green added. "That drug took over his brain."

Two years before her father's death, Green would drive to her parents' home to rescue her mom, bringing her back to Texas to live with her. Together they waited, cringing every time the phone rang late at night. Around dawn on October 22, 2009, it finally did.

When McCauley, seventy-five, died four years after his case was tried, police found him in his lime-hauling truck at 4 a.m. in the middle of a pasture—he'd crashed through a fence. Several near-empty bottles of pills, prescribed just two days earlier, were strewn on the seat next to him. A state trooper told McCauley's daughter and wife that he died of a heart attack, but his daughter believes he was murdered over a bad drug deal.

His head was blown apart, she said, as if from a gun.

The boxes of juicy sales-rep call notes and depositions that represented Fayne McCauley's case files did not molder in Yeary's law office attic. They were folded into Wood and Brownlee's trove of ammo for their case against Purdue. By the time Yeary lost the case, Brownlee's office was in the process of secretly logging millions of records on spreadsheets. The Wood Reports were coming out at a rate of four or five a week, and one employee was assigned to do nothing but catalog documents for the investigation—all of them buttressing Brownlee's belief that Purdue had knowingly concealed the drug's addictiveness.

When a *New York Post* reporter broke the news in 2005 that a federal grand jury was investigating Purdue, Van Rooyan told Bisch and the other RAPP parents, "They think they're going to run roughshod over a bunch of hillbilly lawyers." She recalled how Udell had gloated over the scores of legal wins against people like McCauley, and his pledge that the company would never settle such "absurd lawsuits."

But the company and its executives underestimated the U.S. attorney from Roanoke, who brought in prosecutors from neighboring jurisdictions and deputized them as special assistants to pick up the non-Purdue-case slack. To lead the Purdue investigation, he appointed assistant U.S. attorneys Randy Ramseyer and Rick Mountcastle, career government lawyers who were not given to drama and worked three hours west of Brownlee in the district's satellite office in Abingdon, closer to the coalfields.

It would never occur to either of them to tote around a podium—or to voluntarily talk to the press. When I interviewed Ramseyer almost a decade later, he deflected questions with a combination of press paranoia and aw-shucks humility: "Sometimes people get intimidated by big companies and high-dollar lawyers. You just have to avoid that." And: "It's not rocket science; it's just hard work."

But Ramseyer and Mountcastle had watched their caseloads shift dramatically since OxyContin's introduction. And they were well aware that the few federal prosecutors who'd earlier tried to bring Purdue to account for rising Oxy-related crime had fallen short, with only a handful of exceptions. Jay McCloskey, the U.S. attorney in Maine, had challenged the company's promotional techniques early on, with some success. He had pushed the company to drop the doctor junkets and the 160-milligram version of its pill, only to leave his post in 2001 to work as a consultant for—wait for it—Purdue Pharma.

But the Abingdon prosecutors were content doing government work. Ramseyer and Mountcastle had sent a host of pill-mill doctors to jail over the years—one of whom had been doling out prescriptions from the back seat of his car. Since OxyContin's introduction, the tiny Abingdon office had successfully prosecuted ten doctors, pharmacists, and dentists for overprescribing the drugs, including to nine-year-old kids. By the time their investigation was over, nine state and federal agencies would spend five years helping the stone-faced prosecutors build the case. Unlike the civil lawsuits that preceded them, Brownlee's team had to prove only that the company had "misbranded" the drug, a broad and somewhat technical charge that makes it a crime to mislabel a drug or fraudulently promote it, or market it for an unapproved use. The federal prosecutors didn't have to prove the misbranding was actually responsible for the overdoses and the addiction and misuse, just that Purdue Pharma had criminally misbranded the drug, according to Hammack, the *Roanoke Times* courts reporter. "So it was a very murky legal line, but Randy and Rick figured it out. But there was definitely this feeling by Purdue that this was a little bit of a backwoods, small-town outfit. I think they underestimated them to some degree," Hammack said.

The four-year run-up to what would eventually result in the company's plea agreement involved Purdue Pharma struggling to *understand* that the backwoods lawyers had in fact sussed out a crime inside their mound of documents. The company put a full-court press on Brownlee, first with multiple phone calls from Rudy Giuliani, who attempted to unnerve the much younger man during settlement negotiations on Purdue's behalf.

Brownlee had read Giuliani's book, *Leadership,* to get ready for his first meeting with him. "I wanted to be prepared," he said. "Look, my view of the case was, it didn't matter where we were or how small we were. To me, it demonstrated that a couple of good, smart prosecutors, working out of a strip mall in Abingdon, Virginia, if they work hard and they're tenacious, they can win one of the biggest cases in Virginia," he told me.

An assistant prosecutor in the case recalled that Giuliani put on a folksy front but was not intimately involved in the negotiation's details, possibly because he was pursuing what would prove to be a failed bid for the Republican presidential nomination. "His role was that his star power alone was supposed to intimidate us," said an assistant federal prosecutor involved in the negotiations who was not authorized to speak publicly about the case. "People say 'the government and all its resources,' but when you're in the middle of a case like this, you don't feel that sense because they always have way more people working on the case than you have."

In the fall of 2006, Purdue's lawyers began to sense that this case against them was different; that a full-court press meant nothing when the opposing counsel was the United States of America. Was it really possible the small-town lawyers had compiled enough evidence to indict both the company and its top executives on a host of felony charges, not just for misbranding the drug but also for mail fraud, wire fraud, and money laundering? It seemed so, according to a memo written by the federal prosecutors to Brownlee at the time.

"But it got watered down, as it went through the Department of Justice headquarters, and the folks working for Purdue, including Giuliani, lobbied hard for the executives not to be indicted on felony charges," said an observer connected to the case. The fines would get batted around, too, with Purdue initially offering to pay $10 million compared with the government's initial proposal of $1 billion.

The winnowing down of a settlement is a common part of plea agreements. Prosecutors typically threaten more serious charges while defense lawyers counter that they'll go to trial to prove their client's innocence. Meanwhile, Giuliani's lobbying efforts arrived with the timing and authority of a flagrant foul. In 2005, Purdue lawyers called then–deputy attorney general James Comey to question Brownlee's investigatory tactics, and Comey called Brownlee with concerns. The young attorney responded by personally driving to Washington to lay out his strategies.

"Brownlee, you are fine. Go back to Virginia and do your case," Comey told him.

But Purdue's boldest move came later, in October 2006, the night before the plea agreement was set to expire—after which the company would face charges—when a senior Justice Department officer phoned Brownlee at home (at a Purdue lawyer's request), urging him to extend the deadline to give Purdue more time. Brownlee was through being pressured. The lobbying and negotiations had gone on long enough. The clock had all but run out.

Rather than risk more serious charges or a jury trial in western Virginia, where the drug's problems were by now legend, the company accepted the plea agreement later that night. But Purdue wasn't quite finished negotiating. Eight days after it accepted the deal, Brownlee was stunned to see his name on a firing list, along with four other U.S. attorneys. Though he wasn't ultimately fired, the incident provided fresh criticism of then–attorney general Alberto Gonzales, accused of trying to sway the work of U.S. attorneys' offices.

And it only underscored the long reach of Purdue: Udell's defense lawyer Mary Jo White, a former Manhattan U.S. attorney, had been the one to press for more time in a call to a Department of Justice official. (Brownlee would break down how Purdue's attempted influence peddling worked—or didn't—in a later Senate hearing about the case.)

Brownlee weathered the heat. By the time the negotiations were complete, a Purdue-owned holding company, Purdue Frederick, would plead guilty to a single misbranding felony and the company's executives to misdemeanor charges of misbranding the drug. In a bit of legal-language parsing, the executives would not stipulate that they'd had direct knowledge of the misbranding, only that "the court may accept these facts in support of their guilty pleas." In other words, their only crime was that they headed up a firm wherein *other* people committed crimes.

Compared with the charges Ramseyer and Mountcastle had originally threatened, the final agreement was a mixed bag. Prosecutors initially wanted to impose the $1 billion corporate fine as well as multiple felony charges against both the company and the executives. "But we got what we could get," said a prosecutor involved in the case.

Purdue, for its part, had initially proposed paying $10 million and incurring no felony charges—"an insult," according to a government source involved in the negotiations. "It was clear they thought we'd take a very small sum of money and go away—because it would be a lot of money for a district of our size," the source said. "I will tell you, what we ended up with was far closer to where we started than where they started.

"Their lawyers were shocked," the negotiator added. "They did not expect the firmness with which we approached this.... Had they not agreed, we were fully prepared to take them to trial." The Sacklers, anyway, were convinced. Midway through the negotiations, following a Washington meeting of both sides, word filtered down from the Sackler family: "We can't buy our way out of this one. Make this case go away," the government negotiator recalled. If that meant throwing three executives under the bus, well, then, the men had been loyal employees for many years. But the Sacklers had to do what the Sacklers had to do.

The Sacklers understood that a federal jury convened in southwest Virginia, a region that had now seen as many as two hundred OxyContin-related deaths, could have awarded far harsher penalties. "We weren't just trying to get a little bit of money from them. The goal was to stop the criminal behavior, punish it, and to strip them of their profits," the negotiator said.

On a clear day in May 2007, in the atrium of a downtown Roanoke office building, Brownlee unveiled the news of the settlement: The company and its top executives would plead guilty to their role in a marketing blitz that hyped OxyContin's strengths while downplaying its propensity for addiction and abuse. To resolve the federal criminal and civil misbranding charges, Purdue would pay $600 million in fines and admit that for six years it had fraudulently marketed OxyContin as being less prone to abuse and having fewer narcotic side effects than instant-release versions of the drug—a felony misbranding charge. Top executives Paul Goldenheim, Michael Friedman, and Udell would pony up $34.5 million (or, rather, the firm would, on their behalf) and plead guilty to misdemeanor versions of the crime. The fines against Purdue and its executives accounted for about 90 percent of the company's profits from the time the drug went on the market, in 1996, until 2001, when Purdue dropped the insert language about the timed-lapse mechanism's ability to "reduce the abuse liability of a drug,"

Brownlee explained. It was the eleventh-largest fine paid by a pharmaceutical firm in the Justice Department's history.

Best of all for people like Bisch, Van Rooyan, and Nuss: An Abingdon sentencing hearing was planned for mid-July that would bring the Connecticut executives face-to-face with grieving parents, who were invited to discuss—on record, in court—the damage OxyContin had wrought. The executives would not serve any jail time, per the plea agreement, though it was ultimately up to the judge, at their court appearance, to sign off on the deal and outline the exact terms of their probation and community service.

Brownlee enjoyed presenting his evidence at the press conference, unfolding his podium against a staggering backdrop of documents amassed by Gregg Wood, the stoic prosecutors Randy Ramseyer and Rick Mountcastle, and scores of others recruited to the team—all of whom stood to his right. To his left sat an assortment of evidence culled from the two thousand cardboard containers they'd filled with documents, depositions, and data. The boxes were lined up in columns four to five feet high.

For added visual effect, Brownlee displayed falsified charts created by Purdue that had claimed "smooth and sustained blood levels" and "fewer peaks and valleys" for patients on OxyContin. The ginned-up graphs were meant to buttress the drugmaker's claim that OxyContin had less potential for abuse. An adjacent easel featured actual clinical data that the prosecutors had culled from Purdue's own studies. The real data looked like a map of steep mountains, the faked data like a single gentle slope.

The fluctuations measured, in hours and milligrams, the difference between truth and lies. These charts represented two of forty-six assertions in a "statement of facts" drawn up by Brownlee's team and agreed to by Purdue, underscoring that the company had knowingly falsified several claims about the drug. Among them were numerous instances of Purdue quashing data critical of the drug, such as early reports of patients complaining of withdrawal symptoms ("I would not write it up at this point," one supervisor advised an employee, saying it might "add to the negative press"). Another fact highlighted the claim sales reps made to some doctors that oxycodone was harder to extract from OxyContin for IV use than other pain medications—when Purdue's own study showed that a drug abuser could recover 68 percent of the drug from a single pill. Likewise, the company conceded that some reps falsely claimed OxyContin caused less euphoria and was less likely to be diverted than Percocet and other immediate-release opioids and could therefore be used to "weed out" addicts and drug seekers.

It had all come from the Shadow Company's "Warehouse," as the prosecutors called it. The hillbilly lawyers had filled so many boxes with evidence that Brownlee had to rent extra space in an Abingdon strip mall to hold them all.

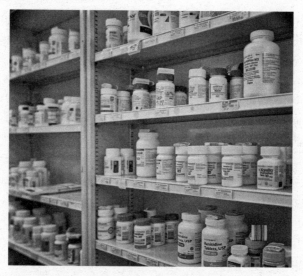

The Pennington Pharmacy, Pennington Gap, Virginia

Chapter Four
"The Corporation Feels No Pain"

Abingdon is the legal and artistic hub of far southwest Virginia, a quaint town full of restored colonial-era brick buildings. By the time Purdue executives turned up there to be sentenced in 2007, it was better known for upscale boutiques, arts, and crafts than for its twentieth-century role as a way station for coal trains hauling the prosperity out of places like St. Charles, some eighty miles west. That summer, the novelist Barbara Kingsolver was about to launch a trendy farm-to-table restaurant, the Harvest Table, in nearby Meadowview, an outgrowth of her memoir, *Animal, Vegetable, Miracle: A Year of Food Life*, then on the bestseller list.

Abingdon had nurtured the early acting talents of Ernest Borgnine and Gregory Peck in its storied Barter Theatre, named for

Depression-era theatergoers' practice of trading a live chicken for the privilege of watching a play. Just a few months before the Purdue sentencing, in the spring of 2007, the Barter stage featured a homegrown comedy about the widow of a moonshiner who, fallen on destitute times, goes into the business of selling OxyContin, supplying her enterprise with stolen pills and those from her own prescribed stash.

When Sister Beth Davies saw the play, she alternately cried at the ruined lives, marveled at the Appalachian resourcefulness, and laughed at the snappy dialogue. "If you don't laugh sometimes, you'll go crazy," she said.

For a town with a population of just eight thousand, Abingdon had also nurtured a surplus of lawyers over the years, who were able to walk from their historic homes to both the federal and the state courthouse, passing statues of Confederate soldiers and historical Daniel Boone markers along the way.

The lawyers and coal-mine operators who lived here were more accustomed to fine dining and theater than rallies or protests. But in a steady rain that fell over the small mountain town, families who'd lost relatives to OxyContin converged on July 20, 2007, to speak their piece and to watch Udell, Friedman, and Goldenheim squirm in their federal courthouse seats.

Barbara Van Rooyan had flown in from her home in California. She wore the same blue floral sundress and white sandals that she'd worn to her son's celebration of life and carried a sign she'd made that read ONE PILL KILLS.

Sister Beth Davies had driven in from Pennington Gap and marched, in her raincoat, with a sign of her own. It featured a picture of Ed Bisch's ruddy-cheeked son, Eddie, in his prom tux.

Van Zee had an out-of-state family commitment (his octogenarian father's birthday) and couldn't make it to Abingdon. But he left behind detailed notes for Sister Beth about everything from the sound system for the rally to bottled water for participants, plus talking points for follow-up letters to the editor.

He and Sue Ella were now attending funerals weekly, many of them his former patients', sometimes at a rate of two a day. He had even written a poem about one, titled "OxyContin," published in *Annals of Internal Medicine*:

> *It might have been easier*
> *If OxyContin swallowed the mountains,*
> *and took*
> *The promises of tens of thousands*
> *of young lives*
> *Slowly, like ever-encroaching kudzu.*
> *Instead,*
> *It engulfed us,*
> *Gently as napalm*
> *Would a school-yard.*
>
> *Mama said*
> *As hard as it was to bury Papa*
> *after the top fell*
> *in the mine up Caney Creek,*
> *it was harder yet*
> *to find Sis that morning*
> *cold and blue,*
> *with a needle stuck up her arm.*
>
> *Top of her class,*
> *with nothing but promise ahead*
> *until hi-jacked by*
> *the torment of needle and spoon.*

* * *

Ed Bisch and Lee Nuss had driven up together from her home in Florida, recycling the same signs they'd carried to the Orlando protest, only a little rumpled from the Caribe Royale sprinkler assault.

It fell to Bisch to lead the parade of fifty grieving relatives from a small park to the courthouse. His sign read OXY KILL$ in big block letters.

Nuss, a tiny redhead, was dwarfed by a larger-than-life photograph of her son, Randy, handsome and olive-skinned. It matched the giant magnet she'd plastered on her car—at the suggestion of her grief counselor—meant to warn other families wherever she drove: IN LOVE AND MEMORY OF RANDALL NUSS AND OTHERS.

More than a decade later, as journalists and policy makers tried to pinpoint where and how the opioid crisis began, images from the rainy rally in Abingdon would get recycled in news accounts, the prescient parents marching with their signs, and next to them Sister Beth standing defiant, a look on her face that projected equal parts anger for what had happened and worry for what was coming next.

The Purdue executives had flown in on a private jet from Connecticut the night before for the sentencing hearing, staying at the elegant, historic Martha Washington Inn, conveniently located next to the courthouse. To avoid the protesters, their attorneys had asked the judge for permission to enter the two-story courthouse by a back door.

But Judge James Jones, a straight shooter with a booming voice, had watched his docket be overtaken by OxyContin-related crime.

No, Judge Jones ordered, the executives would enter through the front door of the courthouse just like everyone else.

Barry Meier stood off to the side, taking it all in. He'd been to Abingdon once before, in May, when Udell, Goldenheim, and Friedman made their first visit, to deliver their guilty pleas. Meier wanted to witness that occasion so badly that he'd arrived the night before, staying in a motel on the outskirts of Abingdon. And he wanted his appearance to be a surprise. He and a freelance photographer the *New*

York Times hired from Roanoke would hide out near the front of the hotel, ducked between parked cars, staking out the executives.

Meier had interviewed the men many times before in their corporate offices and on the phone, but he wanted to witness their Appalachian reckoning firsthand.

It was his fifty-eighth birthday, and the veteran journalist could not have been happier with his gift.

"Everything I'd written was now justified," he told me.

As he and the photographer stood up, Udell, Goldenheim, and Friedman seemed stunned to see them, Meier recalled. Goldenheim, the scientist, stared steely-eyed toward the camera while Udell and Friedman glanced quickly away.

In a rally before the sentencing hearing, the parents took turns reading the names of the dead. Bisch had printed them out from his message board memorials, now so numerous that the document was more than fifty pages long. Their voices broke periodically as they choked out the names.

> *Bobby Lee Ashcraft Jr., aged nineteen*
> *Paul Aboata, twenty-two*
> *Heather Marie Goslinowski, fifteen*
> *Nicole Notaro, nineteen*

They got through only ten pages before the hearing began.

In a photograph that ran in the next day's *New York Times,* two moms in matching rain scarves held each other, one clutching a poster of her seventeen-year-old daughter: IN LOVING MEMORY OF SARAH NICOLE. HER LIFE WAS A LIFE WORTH LIVING. Behind them stood Van Rooyan in her sundress—blue, for her son's favorite color—holding her prepared remarks.

Before the day was over, the executives would hear themselves described as corporate drug lords and marketing tricksters, on a par with

Colombian cartels and P. T. Barnum. They would be asked to imagine themselves in the shoes of a parent of a college junior: "What if it was your son or daughter you saw in the morgue when we went there, and he was autopsied, sliced and diced?"

The executives would have their integrity questioned and their futures threatened. "I will reach out to any organization that Mr. Friedman speaks to about having a member of his family survive the Holocaust, and contact that group and say to them that Friedman is no better than Adolf Hitler, who killed and destroyed countless lives; Hitler through death and torture, Friedman through death and addiction," said Marianne Skolek, who lost her twenty-nine-year-old daughter, Jill. Skolek brought along her grandson, Brian, who was six years old when his mother died of an overdose of prescribed OxyContin in 2002.

"Brian is here in the courtroom with me today because he needed to see that bad things do happen to bad people," Skolek said.

But not bad enough, the parents told the judge. The plea agreement called for no jail time, and many beseeched Judge Jones to reconsider incarceration for the three.

"I think jail is too good for you guys," said Lynn Locascio from Palm Harbor, Florida. Her son was still struggling with addiction, having been prescribed OxyContin after surgery resulting from a car accident. "I think you should go spend some time in a rehab facility like my son did and watch that. Maybe you'll change your minds."

Lawyers for the executives argued that the shame of criminal charges was punishment enough. They reiterated, over and over, that the men—the top corporate executives who had directed the company's legal, financial, and pharmaceutical divisions—had personally done nothing wrong. Representing Udell, attorney Mary Jo White called the company's head lawyer "the moral compass of the company," pointing out that Purdue, at Udell's urging, had voluntarily taken the 160-milligram pill off the market after safety concerns became known.

Udell had championed prescription monitoring programs when most others in the industry were opposed, and he was behind the suspension of shipments of OxyContin to Mexico when it became clear Americans were traveling there to bring back the drug.

Calling the case "a personal tragedy for Mr. Udell," White said most people would wrongly equate the strict liability misdemeanor he pleaded guilty to with criminal wrongdoing. Jail time, she added, "would unjustifiably and needlessly compound the stigma and punishment for an offense and facts that are without personal wrongdoing."

Likewise, Goldenheim, the firm's former chief scientist and medical director, was in "agony" about the charge, his lawyer said. He'd been labeled "a criminal, and that is horrendously harsh punishment for someone who has done so much good, and under the agreed statement of facts has done nothing wrong."

Friedman's lawyer pointed out that the company distributed antidiversion brochures and antifraud prescription pads; created a law enforcement liaison unit within Purdue; funded local law enforcement programs; and, eventually, altered sales-representative compensation so the system would not lend itself to abuse. While other Purdue employees "made statements about OxyContin that were inconsistent with company policy and that should not have been made...Michael Friedman did not participate in that misconduct." Without proof that he committed a criminal act, to jail him would be virtually unprecedented under American law, his lawyer said.

In other words, the lawyers did exactly what Ramseyer predicted they would do in his remarks: They refused to take responsibility for the death and destruction caused by the drug—to the point of reiterating, again in court, that "the enormous benefits of OxyContin far outweigh its risks, even taking into account the grief from those we've heard about today."

Calling it "unprecedented" to hold pharmaceutical corporate officers criminally liable in such a case, Ramseyer noted that Udell,

Friedman, and Goldenheim, in accepting the plea, were conceding that they had not been "powerless to prevent the crime. As corporate officers, these men had a duty to ensure that misbranding did not occur." He predicted that Purdue's next public-relations campaign would begin the moment he sat down from making his remarks: "They will attempt to minimize the crimes to which they pled guilty."

And while that is exactly what their lawyers did, Ramseyer later said the men seemed distressed throughout the proceedings. "They were very unhappy," he told me. "We do cases in court where people get sentenced to twenty or thirty years in prison, and they didn't seem as unhappy as those three guys."

Ramseyer remained loath to say much more about the case, although the fact that he'd been diagnosed with cancer while working on it—and had to take a break midway through the case for treatment—seemed to sear it in his mind as both a personal challenge and a professional high mark. He hoped the case had a chilling effect on pharmaceutical companies and overprescribing doctors alike, but he wasn't sure. He'd read recently that enough opioid painkillers had been prescribed in 2010 to medicate every American adult around the clock for a month. "And it's worse now," he told me in 2016.

The problem was so widespread that Super Bowl ads now targeted relievers of opioid-caused constipation. "Purdue had a laxative they marketed, too," Ramseyer said, of Senokot. In fact, according to the rep-call notes subpoenaed for the case, OxyContin and Senokot were routinely recommended hand in hand. "So they got you on both ends!" Ramseyer said.

Conspicuously absent from the courthouse drama was the family that owned the company and its 214 affiliates worldwide—and benefited the most from the drug's sale. Purdue had earned over $2.8 billion from the drug by 2007, including $595 million in earnings in 2006 alone. Unlike a public company that answers to shareholders, privately held Purdue answered only to the Sacklers.

In 2015, the family would earn its way onto *Forbes*'s "America's Richest Families" list. With an estimated net worth of $14 billion, the OxyContin clan would edge out such storied families as the Busches, Mellons, and Rockefellers. Having gone from selling earwax remover and laxatives to the most lucrative drug in the world, the family had museum wings and college institutes named for it from Boston to Tel Aviv.

Mortimer Sackler even had a pink climbing rose named after him, courtesy of his gardener wife. The official description of this flower, the Rosa Mortimer Sackler, reminded her of her husband, she said: "The blooms give the impression of delicacy and softness but are, in fact, very tough and little affected by bad weather."

Mortimer may have inherited his toughness from his older brother, Arthur, who'd put himself and his two brothers through medical school by selling student newspaper ads and delivering flowers, sometimes with holes in his shoes.

The Don Draper of American pharmaceutical marketing, Arthur pioneered the idea of showering doctors with favors and funding experts to back drugmakers' claims in the 1960s. It was his marketing genius that fueled the emergence of pills as a quick fix, his marketing prowess that delivered Valium and Librium, dubbed Mother's Little Helper by the Rolling Stones, to countless nightstands.

Realizing the importance of controlling his company's message, Arthur had launched both a medical advertising agency and a medical newsmagazine before buying Purdue Frederick with his brothers. It was under his direction that preliminary and inevitably flawed scientific studies were first used to buttress the wonders of whatever drug he was hawking; no wonder his brothers thought nothing of excavating the flimsy and outdated letter heralding the "less than 1 percent" addiction rate nearly a decade after Arthur's death.

What in fact *was* the addiction rate among those prescribed opioids for chronic nonmalignant pain? More recent studies—not letters to the editor penned in 1980—put the figure as high as 56 percent. At the time of his death, in 1987, Arthur was lionized for his entrepreneurial vision and boundless obsession for collecting things. Especially art. He once talked the Met into letting him reimburse the museum for four major works that the museum already owned just so he could have them displayed with his name as the donor.

Still, he had not been fully embraced by the Upper East Side society to which he aspired—not until his memorial service, held at the storied Temple of Dendur, inside the Met's Sackler Wing, at which New York mayor Ed Koch remarked: "I don't know why, but Jews aren't buried in synagogues. Well, Arthur built his own temple."

Arthur Sackler hated not just bad press but *any* press that was not of his own directing, a *Vanity Fair* writer observed shortly after his death. As obsessive about secrecy as he was about moneymaking and art, he would have abhorred everything about the Abingdon hearing.

At the courthouse, testifying before the judge, the relatives of the dead argued repeatedly for jail time. As did Public Citizen, a consumer advocacy group that vented: "Why have three wealthy Purdue executives, who have pleaded guilty to orchestrating this dangerous promotional campaign, escaped jail time, and why are they paying merely $34.5 million in penalties?" Even a fellow prosecutor in Brownlee's office felt Purdue's punishment was too light: "The dividends may go slightly down, but nobody cares because nobody who made the product goes to jail. If the government were serious, they'd put people in jail, and [others would be] fearful," said Assistant U.S. Attorney Andrew Bassford, who would spend most of the next decade prosecuting heroin dealers as a direct consequence of the OxyContin epidemic, down the hall from the office where Brownlee worked. "But you can't put a corporation in jail; you just take their money, and it's not really their money anyway.

"The corporation feels no pain."

Van Zee and Sister Beth viewed the settlement with both satisfaction and regret. Though the executives were placed on probation for three years and ordered to perform four hundred hours of community service in a drug abuse or drug treatment program, Van Zee and Sister Beth were furious that the Purdue fine would not be allocated to provide drug treatment in the medically underserved region. "This little county was left with nothing, even though we've been disproportionately impacted" by the drug, Sister Beth said.

The $634.5 million fine was instead divided among law enforcement, state, and federal Medicaid programs (to reimburse it for claims resulting from the misbranding); to create Virginia's Prescription Monitoring Program; and to settle $130 million in civil claims.

The only thing the Lee County sheriff's office got from Purdue was placebo OxyContin pills for use in drug stings.

Many anti-opioid activists were mad, too, that technically it was Purdue Frederick, Purdue Pharma's holding company, that was banned from participating in the federal insurance programs Medicaid, Medicare, and Tricare as part of its five-year probation—rather than Purdue Pharma itself, which was still permitted to participate, and therefore to continue selling OxyContin. ("They are independent, associated companies," a spokesman explained.) The executives were likewise banned from doing business with federal health programs, a decision they repeatedly appealed in intervening years and lost, leading one federal district judge to scold: "Plaintiffs appear to misunderstand or misstate the basic elements of their conviction."

"It's very typical for these companies to have an entity that is a shell company, basically, set up to plead guilty to the crime, rather than the actual corporate entity taking the fall," Meier said.

Flanked by state and federal flags, Judge Jones admitted that the lack of jail time frustrated him. But the Abingdon federal judge's hands were tied by the plea agreement struck between Purdue and the prosecutors, he said. He would have preferred that parts of the fine be funneled into treatment, adding that prosecutors were reluctant to "direct treatment funds in a manner beyond their expertise and possibly contrary to national policy."

Asked nearly a decade later about the aftermath of the Purdue Pharma settlement on the communities his court covers, Judge Jones told me: "Opioid addiction continues to be, frankly, a terrible concern.... It's rare that I don't have a case today involving substance abuse."

He declined to divulge the details of the executives' probation, citing privacy concerns, other than to say they completed it, to his satisfaction, in their home state of Connecticut.

When Howard Udell died unexpectedly of a stroke, in 2013, at the age of seventy-two, a local newspaper heralded him for having turned his community service into a redemptive experience. After counseling veterans at a Veterans Administration hospital on job skills, Udell went on to found the Connecticut Veterans Legal Center, helping hundreds of veterans navigate problems including evictions, dishonorable discharges, and substance-abuse-related crimes. Even after his community service hours were completed, Udell stayed on to assist the legal center. "It was very unpleasant for Howard, who was scrupulously honest and careful, but we endeavored to make the most out of it," said Friedman, who also performed his community service at the site, according to the newspaper, which described the executives' initial service there, euphemistically, as "volunteer."

A lesser person would have crawled into the basement, said Udell's son, Jeffrey, himself a former federal prosecutor. His dad's fingerprinting at the guilty plea, his three years of supervised release, the fact that Udell had to check in with his probation officer before he visited his grandchildren across state lines—the younger Udell was still incensed that his late father had been forced to endure such indignities. He pointed out repeatedly in an hour-long phone call that the government presented zero proof of his father's wrongdoing.

"The idea that someone of his caliber and his integrity could have the ignominy of a federal crime is so outrageous and unjust," said Jeffrey Udell, describing his dad as a humanitarian and a law-and-order saint, the kind of restaurant patron who would correct a waiter when presented with a mistakenly small bill.

"I know there are unfortunately some very sad and unfortunate people who are parents of kids who abused drugs and overdosed. I feel horrible for those people, as my father did, and for the loss they've suffered."

But again, he insisted, Team Brownlee presented no evidence that Howard Udell had any knowledge of what was happening in the company "some twenty-five levels below him amid a [sales] hierarchy that was not remotely within his purview."

Jones said the case was not only the largest he'd ever presided over, in terms of the fine, but also the most dramatic. There was a hard rain that day, he recalled, and yet there were so many people in attendance that the court set up a separate overflow room for observers to watch via video.

Nor would he ever forget the most heart-wrenching portion of the parent testimony—that of Fishtown native Lee Nuss, who described how her only son, Randy, died as he was getting ready to leave for culinary school in 2003. "His prepaid college ended up paying for his funeral," Nuss said.

Nuss had begged the judge to reject the terms of the plea agreement, imploring him, "Money means nothing to them. Let the punishment fit the crime."

Then she brandished the tiny brass urn she carried whenever she traveled, the one Purdue lawyers had gotten ejected from Karen White's whistle-blower trial. Randy had begun as dust, in her belief, and unto dust he had prematurely returned. She clutched his ashes as she stepped down from the stand.

"This is from your drug, OxyContin, and here he is in this courtroom," Nuss said, staring steely-eyed at Udell, Friedman, and Goldenheim.

A reporter sitting in the courtroom thought for a moment she was going to throw the urn at the men. But Nuss waved it instead and returned to her seat.

She had wanted the men to apologize, to admit that they had understood all along that OxyContin wasn't a novel way of fighting pain but simply a different and more potent way of dispensing nature's oldest drug.

If the Sacklers' lieutenants had legitimately not known about the flood of pills unleashed by sales reps toting around bad data and free shrubbery twenty-five rungs down the corporate ladder from them, maybe it was because they had not cared to look.

PART TWO

Objects in Mirror Are Closer Than They Appear

Hidden Valley, Roanoke County, Virginia

Strasburg High School, Strasburg, Virginia

Chapter Five
Suburban Sprawl

Awareness of the opioid crisis has typically come in waves, often celebrity-studded and well covered by the media: the death by overdose of Philip Seymour Hoffman, in 2014, then two years later the death of Prince. But for ordinary citizens, the news that opioids had crossed over from *Not me and not anyone I know* to mainstream traveled more slowly, in dribs and drabs, maybe when the *Cincinnati Enquirer* became the first newspaper in the country to dedicate a reporter solely to the heroin beat.

Four hours east of Lee County, in a southern city that counts the local TV weathermen among its biggest celebrities, the February 2006 news that meteorologists Jamey Singleton and Marc Lamarre had been shooting up heroin stunned viewers of the NBC affiliate station in

Roanoke, where I live. The story broke after Lamarre suffered a near-fatal overdose at a party, an event that drew local police and, eventually, the attention of federal authorities.

Viewers loved watching them both, especially the stylish, tanned Lamarre, poised and confident, his hands gesturing fluidly in front of the weather map's green screen. Back then, it was still hard to picture a thirty-six-year-old collapsed on an apartment floor in an affluent Roanoke suburb, harder still to imagine a world where educated, well-paid white guys felt the need to disappear into bathrooms at parties or, worse, as in Lamarre's case, end up being tossed into a bathtub and doused with cold water and ice in the hope of waking him up.

"The weathermen were skin popping," recalled police chief Chris Perkins, then an undercover Roanoke detective. The term referred to the practice of injecting the heroin under the skin, rather than directly into a vein, for a milder high—the idea being that skin popping gave you a better high than snorting heroin but wasn't as potent or dangerous as intravenously injecting it.

But the weathermen were soon outed, as most users are, the sweat circles under the guys' sport coats the first in a progressively sad series of giveaways.

"They'd been running around in eighty-degree weather in long sleeves," Perkins said. "Young people were already starting to snort heroin, but then when the weathermen made the news, it started to become almost vogue, this notion that you could inject heroin and somehow still be functional."

Perkins was working the city's drug unit when the overdose call came in. He remembered finding Lamarre unconscious in the bathroom of his well-appointed apartment, before rescue squad workers arrived. Lamarre survived, barely, moving away from the region soon after.

Friends of overdosing users commonly chuck them into the bathtub and try to revive them with ice or cold water, to avoid having to call 911, which could draw police to the scene, along with criminal charges. One police officer I know showed up to an overdose call to find an unconscious man on the floor, a frozen fish on his neck, a frozen bottle of soda shoved into his pants, ice all over the floor—and the user's friends long gone from the scene.

In a region of just over a quarter-million people, a blue-dot Democratic stronghold in the center of a hilly rural red, Roanoke is a smallish city, transformed in the mid-1880s into a gritty railroad town and now, more than a century later, striving to become a health care, neuroscience, and medical-research hub. "We're really going from Train City to Brain City," a city manager recently enthused.

But Roanoke retains its safe, small-town feel with an almost Mayberry level of friendliness. Shortly after I moved here in 1989, a grocery store clerk picked up my bag of shiitakes and cheerfully wanted to know, "Lordy, what are you fixing with these?" A neighbor and journalist friend who spent the bulk of her career in Philadelphia still chuckles when I lock my doors. She used to lock her doors in Philly, but here in Roanoke she travels for days at a time and leaves her house wide open.

"The opioid epidemic is an urban story, a suburban story, and a rural story," said Dr. Jennifer Wells, a Roanoke addiction specialist who has patients from each of these demographics, including one mom with five kids in a countryside trailer and no running water who somehow manages to make it to her group therapy meetings every week.

"Roanoke is just big enough where all the stories meet."

The skin-popping weathermen represented Roanoke's first wake-up call. But it was wrongly viewed, by myself and other area journalists, as an anomaly. The story was so tawdry that the *Roanoke Times* assigned two beat reporters to track it, one from courts and the other from media and entertainment. It received much more attention, for instance, than the national story that broke in our backyard when Purdue Pharma settled with the feds a year later.

Before the weathermen incident, heroin had been the domain of police and court reporters in Roanoke, widely believed to be an inner-city (read: black) drug. "In the '80s and '90s, maybe a few dozen people were doing heroin here," said Don Wolthuis, the assistant U.S. attorney who became one of the federal government's top heroin prosecutors in the state's western half. "Because heroin is a depressant, people kind of withdraw; they go in a corner, shoot up, and sit there in the dark, in a fetal position. They weren't out there committing crimes like with crack or meth. It was a largely invisible and isolated group."

It was common knowledge back then, among the handful of mostly African-American heroin users and dealers in Roanoke, "that you don't sell heroin to white people because they'll turn you in," as Wolthuis put it. In the mid-2000s, it was also common knowledge that the stronger and more dangerous the heroin, the more users yearned to have it, as Roanoke addiction researcher Warren Bickel, then working in Baltimore, described it.

"Herr-on is my girlfriend," one of his patients told him, adopting the street pronunciation for the drug popular among African-American users. He'd come to Bickel's lab with track marks on his neck—all his other veins were spent.

And what this patient wanted Bickel to know was no different than what the Lee County farmer meant when he told his doctor how OxyContin had stolen everything from him: Nothing's more powerful than the morphine molecule, and once it has its hooks in you, nothing matters more.

Not love. Not family. Not sex. Not shelter. The only relationship that matters is between you and the drug.

Bickel went on to scientifically quantify the indifference of the typical opioid user, comparing the average nonaddicted person's perception of the future—calculated to be 4.7 years—against an addicted user's idea of the future, which is just nine days.

The first time I interviewed him, in 2016, Bickel said he hoped to design treatment methods that would not only predict future addictive behavior among children but might also help those at risk of becoming addicted improve and extend their temporal views, therefore arming themselves against the scourge.

Though he'd won prestigious grants and awards for his ground-breaking work—he was often touted as a star of the growing Brain City constellation—I struggled to understand how Bickel's research applied to the real-life heroin users I knew, some of whom were now trading sex for drug money a few blocks from his office.

Could a Bickel-designed app have prevented Jesse Bolstridge's death? Where was the hope? When I asked him those questions, he pointed to a framed Chinese proverb that he takes inspiration from: "It is better to light one candle than to curse the darkness."

But the larger question about hope continued to reverberate wherever I went. I heard a version of it from an overwhelmed family friend, who pulled me aside at a wedding party to tell me about her thirty-four-year-old addicted daughter and pleaded with me through tears: "Just tell me one thing, what can your book do to help me keep my daughter alive?"

My friend was discovering the same thing through experience that I was through my interviews: that the legal and medical structures meant to combat America's heroin epidemic were woefully disconnected, often at odds with one another, and full of unintended consequences.

A crack-turned-heroin-dealer with Philadelphia roots landed in Roanoke in 2006, the same time the weathermen began sweating through their long-sleeved shirts. Clifton "Lite" Lee made heroin an equal-opportunity drug, connecting with drug users, black and white, and figuring—correctly—that he could easily double his profit margin if he imported the drug to comparatively staid Roanoke rather than continue selling it solely in New Jersey and New York. When police caught two suburban teenagers middlemanning for Lee—selling heroin to their friends and keeping some for their own use—they were stunned by what their cellphones revealed: evidence implicating fifty other kids they'd been selling heroin to. Most attended Hidden Valley

High School, in outlying Roanoke County's wealthiest neighborhood, home to insurance agents and doctors and lawyers.

"Lee was the guy willing to get the kids involved," Wolthuis said, pulling out a handwritten organizational chart he'd put together to help him keep visual track. At the top of the pyramid were the nonusers like Lee, who were in it just for the money, and at the bottom were the addicted, including some whose names were crossed out—dead of overdose.

By the time Lee was sentenced to eleven years in prison, in 2008, prosecutors had pinned him with bringing a thousand bags of heroin into the region two to three times a week, paying $5,000 for twenty bricks of heroin that his network then sold for $30,000.

The growth in heroin users was as exponential as its 600 percent profit margin. The first bags sold in Roanoke were stamped with the names Funeral and Green Frog, and some had a purity of 90 percent, a concentration that addicted users quickly and made the dosages deadlier.

"I can remember lying in bed awake at night, thinking, how far is this thing gonna go?" Wolthuis said. "If you have a guy doing a chain of bank robberies, you catch him and the robberies stop." But the problem with heroin is the lure of the morphine molecule. *Herr-on is my girlfriend.* Even as Wolthuis locked up the perpetrators, he suspected that the demand for heroin was already too entrenched. There were still plenty of user-sellers eager to get on the nearest heroin highway to fetch a new batch from Baltimore or Richmond or Paterson, New Jersey. Unlike Ronnie Jones and Clifton Lee, they didn't aspire to get rich dealing dope. They just wanted to keep from getting dopesick.

The story of Clifton Lee and the addicts he serviced and created didn't trickle down to me at the newspaper, where I wrote about family issues, until 2010. That year, the region's only heroin-overdose death made headlines, not because it was unique but because it involved the twenty-one-year-old son of a prominent white businesswoman.

No one was paying attention to heroin arrests when they only concerned the children of inner-city black families. A 2009 *Roanoke Times* story suggesting that heroin was now closing in on the illicit use of OxyContin and prescribed fentanyl patches in popularity seemed to draw shrugs, even as one prosecutor publicly warned, "They're skipping over pot and going straight to heroin."

Wolthuis may have been lying in bed worrying about Spencer Mumpower's role in his classmate Scott Roth's death, but no one, not even the do-gooders giving drug-prevention lectures in local high schools, talked about the kids left behind who were still using. It was as if heroin had settled peaceably into Hidden Valley, with its manicured lawns and attached multiple-car garages, and Scott and Spencer were the only two exposed. Hidden Valley was the perfect name.

Scott Roth bought the heroin that ended his life in an apartment in Roanoke's Grandin Village, a retail hub fifteen minutes from the Hidden Valley split-level where he was raised. A neighborhood where locals dine on regionally sourced produce, take yoga classes, watch subtitled movies, spend thousands on Stickley sofas, and crowd the weekly farmer's market, the village is full of tree-lined streets and solid 1920s-era brick homes with expansive carports.

As Spencer Mumpower prepared for prison for handing Scott Roth the heroin that resulted in his life-ending overdose, I spent the summer of 2012 trying to make sense of how two young men with educated, caring mothers and movie-star good looks could keep the severity of their drug habits hidden for so long. I wanted to alert readers to the growing scourge of heroin in our community, and with two teenage sons still at home, I hoped to inoculate my own family, too.

After all, information is power, I told myself. I talked to my older son about heroin so much that one of the last things he said to me when we dropped him off at college that fall was "I know! Don't do heroin!" He rolled his eyes with an annoyance reserved for the exceedingly daft.

* * *

In the photo Robin Roth chose for her only child's obituary, Scott Roth looked like one of the Backstreet Boys. Blond and breezy, he called his mom Rob and wore madras shorts and Izod shirts. He went by the nickname Vanilla Rice, from a cooking job he had at a Japanese steakhouse where he stunt-cooked tableside, juggling knives and shrimp, rapping as he chopped.

He was a likable young man, polite to strangers, nice to his single mom. He loved the sunflowers she grew on their spacious lawn. She was only mildly annoyed when he invited his friends home to cook for them, using up all the food she'd bought to last them the week.

He'd been using drugs off and on roughly since the age of seventeen, in 2006. The first time he came home clearly impaired, his mom decided to respond boldly. A registered nurse, she wanted to scare him a little, so rather than give him a take-home drug test from CVS, she took him to the emergency room.

Her plan backfired when the emergency-room doctor returned with Scott's test results. "It's only marijuana, Mrs. Roth," he said, a response that still sends her into a fury.

It was all the ammunition Scott needed, over the course of his remaining short life, to dismiss his mom's warnings.

"Lighten up, Rob," he told her.

But there was reason for Robin's concern. Later, Scott admitted that he'd smoked his first heroin in 2006, around the time the news broke about the skin-popping weathermen. He was at a high school party when someone handed him a joint laced with heroin, and the high was so soothing, so enveloping, that he realized right away this was something special, something new.

"You think of heroin as seedy street slums, but that's not at all how it started," Robin told me. About a year after their ER visit, she found a needle and a syringe in Scott's room and, figuring he was already in too deep, she left them there. Afraid he'd resort to sharing needles, she put him in rehab instead.

She tried everything she could think of to help her son, from attending Families Anonymous twelve-step meetings for relatives of people suffering from addiction to driving him to weekly drug tests at a doctor's office. She took away his car after an alcohol-fueled fender bender in her driveway, and after he turned eighteen, she kicked him out of the house whenever she found him drinking or doing drugs. She had every door inside the house removed—including the ones to the bathrooms—so he could not hide his drug use inside her home.

When I met her, two years after her son's death, she still had not gotten around to putting the doors back on. Racked with guilt and grief, she could no longer work. At Scott's funeral Mass, friends had arrived with sunflowers, his favorite, placing them on the altar. Robin dried them and saved the seeds, and though she was too depressed to plant them the next year, a neighbor tilled up a garden plot in her side yard the following spring.

There she planted sunflowers by the hundreds. They grew so tall that they dwarfed her when she stood among them. It became her favorite place, her favorite thing to do, standing in the sunflower grove, listening to the wind chimes on a nearby apple tree that Scott had planted for her one long-ago Mother's Day. She felt closest to him there, especially when the wind whipped down Sugar Loaf Mountain and through her subdivision, the chimes banging out their bittersweet tune.

That summer, Robin brought a cardboard box full of sunflower seeds for me to our first interview, wrapped up in a bow. Sunflowers were her touchstone, not unlike the 55 on Jesse Bolstridge's football jersey. She texted me pictures of them repeatedly, along with snapshots of her very happy and very silly knife-wielding Vanilla Rice. She shared her favorite-ever picture, of a ten-year-old Scotty, the classic headless-at-the-beach trick where he's buried in sand up to his neck.

In Roanoke, 2012 was the tail end of the epidemic's stealth phase. Two hours up I-81 in the rolling farming country of the northern Shenandoah Valley, the epidemic was now rearing its head, too—though mostly still in pill form—and the news of its presence was even slower to emerge.

Jesse Bolstridge was now in high school and trading his ADHD medication Adderall to classmates who liked the way it allowed them to drink all night without passing out. In exchange, they plied him with painkillers, either bought on the black market or pilfered from their parents' or grandparents' medicine cabinets.

Like most parents of the addicted, Kristi Fernandez can't pinpoint the moment when her son's life became hostage to prescription pills. It was sometime after Jesse was diagnosed with Lyme meningitis at fifteen, sometime in between the half dozen high school football and snowboarding injuries that landed him in doctors' offices and emergency rooms, where he was prescribed opioid painkillers including Oxycodone, Vicodin, and Percocet "thirties," as he later referred to the 30-milligram pills, his drug of choice.

"The boy had so many rounds of stitches, so many concussions and broken bones from playing football, I lost track," Kristi said. By his junior year, Jesse had sustained so many concussions that a neurologist told her he'd have to quit football if he got injured again.

What Kristi didn't understand then was how much the drugs calmed him, dulled the purr of his motor, made him feel "normal," as he would later confide. She didn't know then, either, that Jesse and his friends were trading the bought and stolen pills around widely at so-called pharm parties.

Kristi remembers the first time someone in town suggested her son had a pill problem. Jesse had spent the night at a friend's, and the friend's mother called to accuse him of stealing Percocet from her bathroom cabinet. Kristi defended her son, even suggesting that it had been the woman's son, not Jesse, who swiped the pills.

The manager of a temp agency, Kristi is a businesswoman. Civic-minded, she has always followed the news about nearby towns Strasburg and Woodstock. But the only 2010 stories that would have been of relevance to her son's story had been occluded by bigger, headline-making news: the attempted bank robbery by a local young man, someone she didn't then know. One among a small but growing group of area heroin users, Brandon Perullo had become so desperate in his dopesickness that he tried to rob a bank, donning a bandana and a black hoodie. He entered the bank twice before demanding cash by handing the teller a threatening note, but his jittery demeanor had already given him away. Brandon was arrested, unarmed, as he exited the building with $1,860 in cash.

At his February 2011 sentencing hearing, the twenty-seven-year-old described the growing problem in the region, offering to tell his story to teenagers to warn them away from the drug. "No mistake is too big that I can't bounce back from," Brandon told the judge, who sentenced him to three and a half years in prison.

In a quaint town full of historical markers and pricey antiques, the bank robbery in Woodstock made headlines across the Shenandoah Valley. Brandon's mother, Laura Hadden, begged the local newspaper to write about the growing heroin scourge. Her son wasn't the only one buying pills and heroin from mules and commuter dealers driving to Baltimore, she told an editor. "But they blew me off. It was more interesting to write about my son being arrested for robbing a bank!" she said.

Just before Brandon left for prison, in 2011, the local sheriff teamed with school prevention workers to hold the first community-wide meeting about opioid addiction.

Stigma was the real enemy of hope for the drug-addicted, Hadden decided. So to tamp it down, she decided her job was to explain the misunderstood science of addiction: Once a person becomes addicted, he loses his power of choice; his free will becomes hijacked along with the opioid receptors in his brain. When a person's natural opioids are shut down by the deluge of synthetic ones, she told the audience at the community meeting, it creates a growing tolerance to the drug, making the brain crave ever-larger quantities of opioids just to keep from being violently ill.

Hadden asked the parents to imagine this: You haven't been able to eat for three days, and you're starving. Then someone shoves a plate of delicious food in front of you and leaves you alone with it—but it's strictly off-limits.

Because of the urge to quell that insatiable hunger, she told them, young people in their midst were now "driving up to Baltimore, bringing the heroin back here, and selling it like crazy. People you don't even think would be using heroin are using it."

But Hadden's lesson about dopamine-overloaded neurons and Baltimore drug deals fell on the deaf ears of the select attendees. No one wants to believe that heroin will ever touch the veins of their children.

"Maybe ten people showed up, and no one asked me a single question," she recalled. "The response was a joke."

Years later, not long after her son was released from prison, Hadden began a second, more urgent round of drug-prevention advocacy. Soon after Brandon got out, he moved to New York, to live near his father and his tight-knit extended Italian family, because it was almost impossible to get hired anywhere around Woodstock with a felony record.

Brandon was doing well at first, working for his dad and teaching bodybuilding on the side. But seven months after his release from prison, he relapsed. His family encouraged him to seek treatment, Hadden said, but it was as if some remote dictator had claimed eminent domain on his brain. He died two weeks later from an overdose of cocaine and heroin.

His mother believes her son died by suicide, driven by his outsized fear of becoming dopesick. "I wonder, to this day, whether he just couldn't do it anymore," she told me.

Two days before his death, Brandon posted on Facebook: "I hope people remember all the good I've done."

Kristi had not been among those Brandon's mom tried to warn in 2011. If Jesse had any problem at all, she told herself, it had to do with pills, not heroin. But over the next year, her own mother's wedding ring would turn up missing along with some cash and more pills. And Kristi could deny the severity of her son's addiction no longer. Her husband, Jesse's stepdad, insisted she install a lock on their bedroom door.

And though she still feels guilty about it, she did.

In 2012 there weren't yet Facebook groups to connect the suffering parents in different parts of the state, to share tips about rehab and coping strategies, or to offer physical and monetary support.

Back then Robin Roth felt as if she walked around Roanoke with a giant *F* on her forehead, branded as a parenting failure. She suffered in silence and anger, much of it directed toward the young man she held responsible for the death of her only child. At Spencer Mumpower's 2012 federal court sentencing, Robin carried a framed portrait of Scott to the witness stand. She looked directly at Spencer, his dark mass of curly hair now neatly shorn, and leveled a litany of questions designed to make him understand the pain his actions had caused:

"Spencer, will you be there to visit me when I am old and lonely? Neither will Scott.

"Spencer, will you be there to eat dinner with me, mow my lawn, and wish me a happy birthday? Neither will Scott.

"Spencer, will you be there to hold my hand when I am sick and dying? Neither will Scott."

Her anger was so palpable that U.S. District Court Judge James Turk, an affable octogenarian who shook every defendant's hand and brought his dachshund mix, Baby Girl, to court, encouraged her to meet with Spencer before he left for prison. Turk had already sentenced the dealer who supplied the drugs to twenty years; Spencer had played middle man in the deal, pleading guilty and helping prosecutors nab his roommate dealer in exchange for a lighter, eight-year sentence.

"I think it would help you," Turk told Robin, gently, from the bench, as Spencer sat.

But Robin declined, saying she wasn't ready.

*   *   *

In the summer of 2012, I followed Robin and Spencer as Spencer prepared for prison. I gave Spencer rides to karate classes, recording our conversations with his permission as I drove. At a KFC lunch buffet, I watched him cheerfully demonstrate a recipe he'd picked up during his earlier jail stint on state charges: blending packets of ketchup, Tabasco, and barbecue sauce.

I sat near his relatives as he graduated from drug court, looking childlike in his too-big suit. I spent a Saturday with him while he volunteered his time teaching first-time teenage drug offenders and their worried parents, who leaned in intently, trying to divine where Spencer's parents had gone wrong. I found it impossible not to like the kid, honestly. I could ask him anything my mind conjured up, and he would answer me warmly and enthusiastically. He seemed more concerned about being honest than trying to control the narrative.

In a freewheeling talk full of advice and drug-detecting techniques that was half *Scared Straight* and half *American Gangster*, Spencer had parents alternately laughing, wincing, and crying as he displayed the needle-mark scars on his arms and the teeth once ruined by amphetamines, now restored by forty hours of dental work. He showed off his jailhouse tattoos, fashioned by burning Vaseline mixed with VO5 Shampoo and a contraband staple, though he'd since had those neatened up, too.

He discussed the dangers of black-market Adderall, an ADHD medicine and amphetamine he once took hourly for eight days straight. He recited a list of places where he'd hidden his stash as a teenager—inside computers, emptied Sharpie markers, and socks, and in the pockets of gym shorts he secretly wore under his jeans. "My mom made me empty the pockets of my jeans, but she didn't know about the shorts," he said.

He shared tips that, in my view, remain among the best prevention advice I've seen dispensed to parents of at-risk teens: Rid your medicine cabinets of anything that has *codone,* indicative of morphine components, in the name. Set rules and hold kids accountable when they break them, even if it means they go to jail. "The problem with me was, the trouble had to outweigh the fun," he said. Though his mother, Ginger Mumpower, had sent him to fifteen different rehab facilities, for eight years Spencer managed to use and sell drugs before his name ever entered a police blotter.

He described what led to his decision to quit selling drugs after being targeted by local police in a catch-and-release drug bust in 2009. Hoping to convert him into a confidential informant, police had taken his drugs and told him, "We're gonna wait for you to mess up again so we can catch you again and get you for more things," Spencer recounted, an oversimplification that police only partially confirmed. The threat was enough to make him give up dealing, but in a case of warped reasoning he believed he could still keep using heroin without getting caught. He allowed his dealer to live with him in exchange for drugs.

When Scott Roth showed up at Spencer's apartment to buy heroin, the two hadn't seen each other since high school at Hidden Valley, some three years before. They were never best friends, just drug buddies who hung out in the basement of the home of a fellow partyer whose dad gave them space to get high and routinely shot up heroin in front of them, according to both Spencer and Robin Roth.

Spencer played go-between in the deal, a move that resulted in death by overdose for Scott in April 2010 and prison for Spencer and his roommate dealer.

When Scott showed up on his doorstep that night, Spencer was already a full-blown heroin junkie. In his jailhouse mug shot, his eyes are bruised and sunken, and there are chicken-pox-like scabs on his face—from the itch of amphetamines, to which he was also addicted. He weighed 135 pounds.

"One day in jail I realized I could touch these two fingers around my forearm," he told me, making a *C* out of his thumb and middle finger. "It meant I was a junkie." When fellow inmates teased him about how skinny he was, he started lifting weights in his cell. He fashioned them out of trash bags he filled with water, tying them with bedsheets ripped into strips. He used the money his mom put on his jail commissary account to amass multiple cartons of milk, to help build up his muscles—by trading ramen noodles and bags of coffee for his cellmates' quarts of milk.

For eleven months, his mother refused to bail him out, and even though she knew that jails and prisons could be rife with drugs, she also believed that jail was her best chance for keeping Spencer alive while he awaited federal sentencing. She encouraged church friends and relatives to write to him. His sister, Paris, an art student, mailed poems and drawings. Ginger sent him inspirational song lyrics, copies of pages she'd marked from the Bible and *The Purpose Driven Life*.

His lawyer, Tony Anderson, recalled his transformation: "After six months of begging for his mother to bail him out, he finally hit bottom and accepted he had nowhere to go but up." Spencer soon realized, "I like being clean. I like being sober. I like being able to talk to my mother and she talks to me, and I get what's going on here."

As his counselor Vinnie Dabney remembered it, "Fifteen rehabs had not convinced Spencer that it was not in his best interests to get high. It took time in jail and a friend dying before he could decide he wanted to change."

In our interviews, Spencer was alternately immature and wise. His goal, he told me, was to get in shape, physically and mentally; to earn some karma before he went away to federal prison. "God knows, I've got a lot I need to build back up," he said.

He was happy to school me on drug culture—how he'd once saved his lunch money to buy weed and cocaine, the way he extracted the gel out of a fentanyl pain patch and smoked it, where the best places were to find drug dealers (loitering outside Narcotics Anonymous meetings). Driving by a diabetes-supply pharmacy, he recalled once buying

OxyContin off a pharmacy delivery driver. The driver was eventually arrested. "But somehow he had another six hundred or seven hundred pills the next day. That's a shitload of dope." he said.

Spencer talked about his drug counselor, Dabney, who years before had been a mostly functioning heroin user for three decades, snorting a much less potent form. "It's hard to explain, but some people can manage it. Like if I knew that none was gonna be in till Friday, and it's Tuesday, and I normally do ten bags a day but I only have thirty left, I would do the math and make sure I had enough to last till Sunday...because you'll do anything to make sure you're not dopesick."

He even offered parenting advice for one of my friends, whose son had already been busted for smoking weed, once in a northern city, where it was deemed a misdemeanor, and once on a Blue Ridge Parkway overlook—where it was on federal property and therefore a federal offense. "When he's eighteen, tell him to move to a state where [marijuana] is legal. Until then, tell him he'd better start lifting weights because he's not gonna do well in jail. Scare the hell out of him, if you can. But honestly, there's only a small percentage of kids you can get through to. When I was that age, I didn't want to hear it either."

Spencer was making amends to his mother, apologizing almost daily for the hell he'd put her through and helping with her latest jewelry-store opening. As she recalled committing him to a psychiatric facility after he'd busted himself out of a Christian rehab in West Virginia, Spencer immediately stood up and walked over to hug her for maybe the fourth time that day.

"I'm sorry," he said.

"I know," she said.

With his mom's help, he drafted a letter of apology to Robin Roth and mailed it to her therapist, who would decide when she was strong enough to read it. In it, Spencer offered, when he got out of prison, to mow her grass. From his prison cell, he would even donate to her the inheritance he received following his grandmother's death.

All told, Spencer had already lost twelve friends from Hidden Valley to drug-involved deaths, and every dealer he knew was either dead now or in jail. And he would soon lose several more.

He was hale and hearty by the time his mother drove him to a minimum-security federal prison in Petersburg, Virginia, in August 2012. Drug-free for more than two years, Spencer admitted that he'd replaced his opioid addiction with kenpo karate, taking classes almost daily and learning breathing techniques to deal with the anxiety of going to prison. His karate instructor, Rikk Perez, had become a father figure to him; Spencer was estranged, off and on, from his own dad. Perez taught Spencer exercises he could practice in his cell, like slow foot taps that progress up a cinder-block wall.

Being fit brought Spencer a feeling of confidence as he left for prison, where he hoped to finish his bachelor's degree. After his release, he planned to dedicate himself to helping young people with addiction, in memory of Scott Roth.

I called Robin the day Spencer's mom helped him report to prison. She said knowing that Spencer was behind bars again brought her no comfort.

"I hurt as much today as the day my son died," she said, choking up. "I pray for Spencer every day, that he'll be strong. My heart's breaking for that kid. But it's the only shot he has at a normal life—to get some accountability."

As the months wore on, Robin began to soften toward Spencer. That fall, she started spending her Friday nights with troubled teenagers and their worried parents in a setting similar to the court-ordered Saturday sessions where Spencer had spoken.

She was learning that in her loss, she was far from alone. She and Ginger both were beginning to see that all the sunflowers and speeches in the world would not slow the epidemic's spread. Ginger, a minor celebrity in town from her own ads for her business as well as from a failed campaign for state delegate, was recognized as a friendly face.

At her new Ginger's Jewelry store, a day rarely passed when someone didn't show up at her counter wanting advice on something other than gold. Distraught parents might pretend to shop for a few minutes, but before long they'd mention the newspaper articles, and the tear-filled stories would tumble out.

A pastor's wife with two addicted sons drove from two hours away to search her out. A sixty-three-year-old nurse was struggling to take care of her infant grandson because her twenty-five-year-old heroin-addicted daughter could not.

While Ronnie Jones was establishing his clientele in the northern Shenandoah Valley, young people in Roanoke were driving right past Woodstock on their way to Baltimore, Philadelphia, or Newark, or taking the Chinatown bus to New York, where they could pay $100 for fifty bags of heroin, stamped with names like Blue Magic or Gucci, then resell them in Roanoke for six to eight times their investment.

A drug-use survey of Roanoke-area high school students bore out the trend. In the fall of 2012, 6.4 percent reported using heroin one or more times, and almost 10 percent said they'd tried illicit prescription drugs. A local prevention counselor warned that the two percentages were in the process of flipping because heroin was becoming so much cheaper and easier to get.

The Families Anonymous meetings in town were filling up. Six years had passed since the weathermen's final forecast, and the storm had settled in.

While Robin Roth searched for solace in sunflowers and Ginger Mumpower relaxed for the first time in years—knowing that in prison, at least, her son would likely not die of a drug overdose—parents up and down America's heroin highways struggled to find the right culprit, or set of culprits, to blame.

But mostly they kept quiet about it, shut down in their grief and their shame.

Hidden Valley High School, Roanoke County, Virginia

Chapter Six
"Like Shooting Jesus"

An hour south of Roanoke, in a part of the state once dominated by unfettered industry, Martinsville, Virginia, was stuck in an economic morass. In 2012 the small city of thirteen thousand laid claim to having the highest unemployment rate in Virginia for twelve years. For most of the twentieth century, it had been the state's industrial powerhouse, packed with textile and furniture factories, home to more millionaires per capita than any other city in the nation. But nearly half its jobs went away when the millionaires sent the textile work to Honduras and Mexico in the wake of NAFTA in 1994, and the furniture jobs to China after that.

Bill Clinton had predicted that China's 2001 entry into the World Trade Organization would eventually create a "win-win" for workers.

American companies would theoretically be able to export products to China's growing consumer class, an argument Wall Street championed when stock prices climbed with every new plant-closing announcement. Corporate shareholders and CEOs ate up Clinton's prediction, a cheery best-case version of Adam Smith's eighteenth-century "invisible hand." As the economists described it, Chinese peasants would better their lot by making chairs in factories, while dislocated American workers would retrain for more fulfilling, advanced jobs.

But with ill-designed training for displaced Americans based on a lumbering federal program created in the 1960s, the second part of that equation very rarely came to pass. Only a third of workers who qualified for Trade Adjustment Assistance even went back to school, and the majority of those who did found themselves with new certifications and associate's degrees yet earning much less than they had in the factories, if they were working at all. The ones I met who were coping the best worked part-time at Walmart, supplementing their pay with food stamps, food pantry donations, and small vegetable gardens.

Consumers all got cheaper jeans, yes, but what did that matter to the people who had once stitched them if they were now out of work and couldn't afford new clothes? The global economy created winners and losers, Bassett Furniture CEO Rob Spilman told me, explaining the dismissal of some eight thousand furniture workers from his payroll. "It was that or perish," he said. "At the end of the day, we are not a social experiment."

In rural counties decimated by globalization, automation, and the decline of coal, the invisible hand manifested in soaring crime, food insecurity, and disability claims. In Martinsville and surrounding Henry County, unemployment rates rose to above 20 percent, food stamp claims more than tripled, and disability rates went up 60.4 percent.

What those numbers looked like on the ground, as I began reporting on the recession in 2008 for the *Roanoke Times* and later for my first book, *Factory Man* (published in 2014), could be distilled in two images I observed but did not fully, at the time, comprehend:

The first was of adults—black and white, old and young—arriving at area food pantries two hours before the doors opened, the older among them clutching canes or leaning on walkers. The second was the smoldering remains of an abandoned furniture factory in the town of Bassett, near Martinsville. An unemployed thirty-four-year-old was attempting to rip out copper electrical wires to resell on the black market when he inadvertently sparked a fire that burned the shuttered factory down. In his police mug shot, you could see the burns on his face.

It was easy to understand the connection between joblessness and hunger, to get that hunger fueled some of the crime. It was growing clearer, too, that the federal disability program was becoming a de facto safety net for the formerly employed, a well-intentioned but ultimately disastrous way of incentivizing poor people to stay sick, with mental illness and chronic pain—conditions that are hard to prove and frequently associated with mental health and substance use disorders—prompting the majority of disability awards.

That same pattern was playing out in the Lee County coalfields, where some parents coaxed their children's doctors toward ADHD diagnoses, knowing that such behavioral problems could help make them eligible for Social Security disability when they became adults. "Ritalin is a pipeline to disability here," one Lee County health care manager told me, describing the federal program as a coping mechanism for poverty and workplace uncertainties.

A hospital administrator I know from nearby eastern Kentucky recalled a Drug Abuse Resistance Education officer asking her high school classmates what they wanted to be when they grew up.

"A drawer," one young man said.

"You mean an artist?"

"No, a *draw-er.*"

Someone who draws disability checks. It was the only avenue he could imagine for himself, the only way to get himself and his family fed. Well over half of Lee County's working-age men—a staggering 57.26 percent—didn't work. (The trend line was somewhat better among women, around 44 percent.)

If OxyContin was the new moonshine in rural America, disability was the new factory work. By 2016, for every unemployed American man between the ages of twenty-two and fifty-five, an additional three were neither working nor looking for work. Having dropped out of the workforce entirely, they had numerically vanished from the kind of monthly jobs reports touted by politicians and reporters.

Many turned up instead in disability statistics, which were largely ignored in headline-grabbing economic reports. Disability claims nearly doubled from 1996 to 2015. The federal government spent an estimated $192 billion on disability payments in 2017 alone, more than the combined total for food stamps, welfare, housing subsidies, and unemployment assistance.

For people who have not ventured recently into rural America, the jaw-dropping and visible decline of work comes as a shocker, an outgrowth of the nation's widening political and cultural divide. Before the 2016 election of Donald Trump, that disconnect was maintained by a national media that paid little attention to rural, predominantly white places like St. Charles or Bassett, where the country's much-hailed economic recovery had definitely not trickled down.

At the same time, it had never been within the purview of local papers like the *Martinsville Bulletin* to investigate what was happening with international trade in Washington or New York, much less the latest push by Big Pharma or global drug cartels. And regional newspapers like my own *Roanoke Times* had drastically shrunk their coverage to a mainly urban and suburban core, ignoring the increasingly distressed communities in our hinterlands just when reporting on those places was needed the most.

Those of us living highly curated and time-strapped lives in cities across America—predominantly mixing virtually and physically with people whose views echoed our own—had no idea how politically and economically splintered our nation had become. And also how much poorer and sicker and work-starved the already struggling parts of the nation truly were—because we didn't follow that story.

We may feel more connected by our cellphones and computers, but in reality we are more divided than ever before.

In the midsized city where I live, OxyContin continued to be viewed as a rural problem into the early 2010s—a problem in the coalfields, some four hours to the west. While the *Roanoke Times* covered the 2007 sentencing hearing of Purdue Pharma executives, it rarely mentioned OxyContin after that. We in Roanoke had heard opioid abuse was seeping into distressed factory towns like those in Henry County, but very rarely did our newspaper report on it.

We were safe in our ignorance, or so we thought—content to stereotype drug addiction as the affliction of jobless hillbillies, a small group of inner-city blacks, and a few misguided suburban kids.

But another invisible hand was upon us.

Heinrich Dreser's drug moved seamlessly across city and county lines, with zero regard for politics, race, neighborhood, or class.

I didn't understand the connection between rural poverty, disability, and opioid addiction until I learned more about the accidental Bassett Furniture arsonist. Turned out he'd arrived at his copper heist on the outskirts of Bassett on his bicycle—a rare sight in the rolling foothills of the Blue Ridge Mountains.

"He was one of the unemployed masses; he did not have a paying job," said the prosecutor (now a judge) in his case. "But his crime actually required work, so he wasn't lazy so much as he was desperate." Like so many of the region's petty thieves, the arsonist was propelled by fear of becoming dopesick, added another local prosecutor, who told me that 75 percent of all police calls in the county now involved heroin or methamphetamine, or, increasingly, a combination of both.

Not only were rates of unemployment, disability, and opioid addiction soaring, but there was also renewed interested in methamphetamines and the practice of switching between opioids (in the form of either pills or their much cheaper cousin, heroin) and meth. "Crystal meth controls all the dockets now" in rural Virginia, a local drug task force officer told me. "If you're addicted to painkillers, you become so lethargic you can hardly function. But meth keeps you going if you need to run the streets to go get your next dose of heroin or pills, to keep you from getting sick. It allows you to function. There's a reason they call it 'high-speed chicken feed.'"

I thought immediately of Spencer Mumpower's 2010 jail mug shot. So much separated Spencer, whose mother had sent him to private school and then paid for fifteen different rehabs, from the young man who stripped copper wire out of the abandoned furniture factory. A scrawny junkie with sunken eyes and sticky-out collarbones, as Spencer described himself to me in 2012, "I looked ridiculous, like I had chicken pox. Like I'd stuck my head down a groundhog's lair."

But I had failed, just as the police and parents had, to connect young adults like Spencer to the rural addicted, even though Spencer told me he'd come to his heroin addiction the same way they had—through prescription opioid pills.

Our culture seems to excuse drug- and other risk-taking in white middle- and upper-middle-class kids, especially young men. The same liberties, when taken by rural poor whites or people of color— wherever they live—come across as more desperate, born of funda- mental wants or needs that can't be satisfied. But as I've come to learn, gauged strictly by drug use, there is no less urgency and desperation in America's middle and upper classes today.

Drug epidemics unfold "like a vector phenomenon, where you have one individual who seeds that community and then the spread begins," said Dr. Anna Lembke, an addiction-medicine specialist at the Stan- ford University School of Medicine and the author of *Drug Dealer, MD.* People whose parents or grandparents were drug- or alcohol- addicted have dramatically increased odds of becoming addicted them- selves, with genetics accounting for 50 to 60 percent of that risk,

Lembke explained; she noted that the correlation between family history and depression is much lower, 30 percent. Other risk factors for addiction include poverty, unemployment, multigenerational trauma, and access to drugs.

"It's important to note, it's really not just the unemployed and the poor who are vulnerable today; it's really everybody, especially underchallenged youths or youths who aren't engaged in school or other meaningful activities," Lembke said.

At the age of thirteen, Spencer had stolen five bottles of painkillers more than halfway full—leftovers prescribed to different relatives in the aftermath of routine outpatient surgeries. By fourteen, he was taking pills regularly. Back then he used saved-up lunch money to buy weed, which he then traded for ADHD medications prescribed to his friends, or for OxyContin pilfered from their parents' medicine chests.

"I did my first bag of heroin before I drank my first bottle of beer," Spencer said.

In his Hidden Valley subdivision, full of sprawling ranches, trim colonial two-stories, and Arts and Crafts bungalows that were new but meant to look old, heroin was easier to get. "When we first started doing it, we didn't worry about getting caught because cops didn't know what heroin even looked like.

"One time I got pulled over, I had ten bags at my feet, and they didn't know what it was so they didn't look at it."

In rural America, the opioid epidemic aged into a wily adolescence in the aughts. In the hinterlands of Virginia, it had tended to pool in families. "We'd sometimes have one overdose where the son would die, then the next day the father would die, then the next day the mother would die," the Roanoke-based medical examiner said. "If it had been an infectious disease, there would have been widespread panic."

Then–Virginia Tech researcher Martha Wunsch remembered the moment she went from studying overdose deaths in rural counties, funded by a National Institutes of Health grant, to hearing about it from her own teenagers, who went to high school with Spencer and Scott Roth. State health officials in Richmond had originally dismissed her research, telling her the same thing they'd said to Sue Cantrell, the rural health-department director: "This is a regional problem."

"The issue is Interstate 81," Wunsch told me. "The OxyContin epidemic spread from East Nowhere Jesus all up and down the Appalachian chain by way of the interstate, and suddenly my own kids were coming home from parties," talking about pills being passed around in bowls.

Opioids infiltrated the toniest suburbs not by way of families but by peer groups. The new suburban users didn't come to the attention of police until roughly around the time Purdue Pharma launched its 2010 abuse-resistant version of the drug, at the same time Spencer handed Scott Roth the heroin that led to his death—fourteen years after OxyContin was introduced.

In Roanoke, the urban hub for the western half of the state, I-81 perches at the edge of the northern suburbs. It rolls and undulates, connecting western Appalachian communities from Tennessee to Virginia as it travels northeast around Roanoke and up through the northern Shenandoah Valley, intersecting with other interstates leading to Baltimore and Washington, New Jersey and New York.

One of the most segregated cities in the South, Roanoke had long had a steady but largely quiet group of heroin users in its urban core, which positioned it to become an ideal transfer station for the region's transition from dope to pills, then back to dope. It was the perfect incubator for the opioid epidemic—a cultural and geographic crossroads. It was big enough for users to easily forge drug connections and yet small enough for the drug dealers to hide out.

Some dealers, traditionally ensconced in the city's poorest, northwest quadrant, were beginning to migrate to the more affluent neighborhoods of Hidden Valley and Cave Spring, one heroin task officer told me—to avoid robberies and home invasions.

"As long as it was in the lower economic classes and marginalized groups, like musicians and people of ethnic minorities, it was OK because it was with *those people*," said Spencer's counselor, Vinnie Dabney, an African American who took his first sniff from a bag of heroin his sophomore year of high school, in 1968, and was a mostly functional user for thirty years. (Needle-phobic, he never once shot up.) Back then you could maintain that way because the drug's potency was low—3 to 7 percent, compared with 40 to 60 percent today—and the police paid little attention, since white kids in the suburbs weren't dying or nodding out in the football bleachers.

"But the moment it crossed those boundary lines from the inner city into the suburbs, it became an 'epidemic,'" said Dabney, shaking his head. After two drug-related jail stints, he left court-ordered treatment in the late 1990s to get a master's in counseling and now works as a mental health and substance abuse counselor who leads support groups for users taking the maintenance drug buprenorphine, or bupe (more commonly known by the brand name Suboxone). "It's ludicrous, this thing that's been knocking on your door for over a hundred years, and you've ignored it until finally it's like a battering ram taking your doors off the hinges.

"It's a monster now, but nobody paid any attention to it until their cars were getting robbed, and their kids were stealing their credit cards." The worst of it, Dabney warned, was that people were getting hooked at even younger ages, and making the switch faster from pills to heroin.

It took a while for the force of the battering ram to register. Unlike in the coalfields, where addicted users quickly resorted to thievery to fund their next fix, in the suburbs the epidemic spread stealthily because users had ready access to money. Many of them were teenagers selling electronic devices (then telling their parents they'd been stolen), or raiding their college savings accounts, or simply using their allowance. They were not engaging in "spot and steal," not trading a mule for four pills, not wheeling stolen garden tillers down the street for everyone to see.

In the wealthiest Roanoke County suburbs, illicit pill-taking commenced, shared on TruGreened lawns, next to school lockers, and in carpeted basements while clueless parents in Cave Spring and Hidden Valley were making family dinners upstairs.

There was no widespread panic, because the teenagers and young adults had the money to keep their addictions at a low boil, and those parents who were in on the dirty little secret were too ashamed to let the neighbors know.

From California to Florida, the parents behind Relatives Against Purdue Pharma already knew that OxyContin stood out more in rural America's distressed hollows and towns, where reps could easily target the lowest-hanging fruit—the injured jobless and people on disability, with Medicaid cards. But OxyContin was everywhere, of course, and it had been almost since the beginning, even if the crimes associated with it hadn't dominated the urban news.

"The early suburban wave mostly stayed hidden...because parents there could afford to put their kids in a thirty- or sixty-day program," said Dr. Hughes Melton, an addiction specialist and now the Virginia Department of Health's chief deputy commissioner overseeing much of the state's response to the crisis. "You really didn't hear much about it until young people started dying."

It was the death of the funny young rapping chef, Scott Roth, with his mop of blond hair and life-of-the-party disposition, that should have put the Roanoke region on notice.

The weekend when most of his friends were going off to college, his mother had driven him to a rehab program at the local rescue mission. She remembers leaving him by the mission door in the rain, in his plaid shorts and Nautica shirt.

Spencer Mumpower helped me unpack the epidemic as it unfolded behind mall movie theaters and in wooded cul-de-sacs in the late aughts. But even though high school surveys showed suburban heroin use was growing in 2012 (it was then 3 percent higher in Roanoke County schools than the national average), parents and prevention workers alike underestimated Spencer's warnings, viewing his crime as an anomaly, maybe even an outlier case of bad parenting.

"We didn't understand the connection between heroin and pills at least until 2014," admitted Nancy Hans, an area drug-prevention coordinator. In 2010, her Prevention Council of Roanoke County initiated drug take-backs, events where citizens were encouraged to safely dispose of unused medications, but she wishes now that she had singled out opioids.

At the urging of local police, Hans instead launched a campaign to warn parents about synthetic bath salts in 2012, then in the public eye because they had caused bizarre behavior, including physical scuffles with police as well as the overdose deaths of two local young women. Shortly after President Obama signed a law banning the sale of the products, *Vice* magazine swooped into Roanoke for a scoop. Looking back, the bath-salts blight was a red herring, problematic but short-lived—and a distraction from a much quieter, even deadlier drug.

"That's how it got way out in front of us," Hans said. "And the doctors didn't see their role in it, either. When a doctor prescribed our teenagers thirty Percocet pills for a pulled wisdom tooth, we didn't know to complain. It was like we were all in a big fog of denial."

Within five years, Hans would have the numbers of multiple mothers of addicted kids programmed into her cellphone. She would find herself rushing from the funerals of heroin-overdosed twentysomethings to giving prevention talks in the auditoriums of the high schools they once attended. Spencer's master class in drug abuse had gone unheeded, boxed away into a category of Things That Happen to Other Families.

Andrew Bassford, the assistant U.S. attorney who prosecuted Spencer's case, took an angry phone call from the Roanoke County school superintendent, who was mad that he'd openly addressed the accessibility of heroin and OxyContin in her schools.

"How dare you tell the newspaper these things?" the superintendent seethed.

Bassford, who also works as a brigadier general in the U.S. Army Reserve, was unmoved by the scolding.

"I say these things because I know them to be true," he said. "Your schools are a pit because your students have money, and money attracts drugs."

The Hidden Valley teenagers called the green 80-milligram Oxys Green Goblins. They scored them from an array of sources: a restaurant co-worker, a brother who'd had them prescribed in the wake of wisdom-tooth surgery, an Iraq war veteran who had legitimate pain but was prescribed twice as many pills as he needed and funneled the rest to the kids down the street in exchange for cash.

"Parents didn't really know what was going on when it was just pills," recalled Victoria (not her real name), who tried her first Oxy-Contin pill her senior year after a friend ratted her out to school officials for smoking weed.

Victoria remembered the first time she tried to crush an abuse-resistant Oxy, following Purdue's long-awaited reformulation in 2010, and it worked exactly as Barbara Van Rooyan envisioned it would when she petitioned the FDA, demanding an opioid blocker, or antagonist, be added to the drug: "If you tried to crunch 'em, they'd gel up on you. You couldn't even snort 'em, let alone shoot 'em. After that, the pills either went dry or were just too expensive to get. And everybody who used to deal pills starting dealing heroin instead."

I noticed another, lesser-known pattern among the addicted suburbanites I interviewed: The Green Goblins were typically preceded by a starter pack of a very different drug. Almost to a person, the addicted twentysomethings I met had taken attention-deficit medication as children, prescribed pills that as they entered adolescence morphed from study aid to party aid. On college campuses, Ritalin and Adderall were not just a way to pull an all-nighter for the physics exam, never mind that they were prescribed to your roommate, not you; they also allowed a person to drink alcohol for hours on end without passing out. That made them a valuable currency, tradable for money and/or other drugs.

Between 1991 and 2010, the number of prescribed stimulants increased tenfold among all ages, with prescriptions for attention-deficit-disorder drugs tripling among school-age children between 1990 and 1995 alone. "And we're prescribing to ever- and ever-younger children, some kids as young as two years old," said Lembke, the addiction researcher.

"It's just nuts. Because if we really believe that addiction is a result of changes in the brain due to chronic heavy drug exposure, how can we believe that stimulant exposure isn't going to change these kids' brains in a way that makes them more vulnerable to harder drugs?" she added.

The science is far from clear, according to a 2014 data review. Some studies show that ADHD-diagnosed children treated with stimulants have lower rates of addiction to some substances than those who weren't medicated, while other studies suggest that exposure to stimulants in childhood can lead to addiction in adulthood.

"A lot of us think that doctors have overdiagnosed children with ADHD, so a diagnosis is something to very carefully discern, and parents should always monitor the medicines their children and teenagers are on," said Cheri Hartman, a Roanoke psychologist.

Lembke pins the opioid epidemic not just on physician overprescribing fueled by Big Pharma but also on the broader American narrative that promotes all pills as a quick fix. Between 1998 and 2005, the abuse of prescription drugs increased a staggering 76 percent.

While opioids have resulted in the direst consequences, Lembke is equally leery of benzodiazepines (prescribed for anxiety) and stimulants, both of which make teenagers—especially underchallenged kids who aren't engaged in meaningful activities—dangerously comfortable with the notion of taking pills. Any pills. Whether the pills originated in a bottle with their name on it or came from a bowl at a so-called pharm party.

Emergency-room administrator Dr. John Burton watched the cultural shift play out at the North Carolina YMCA summer camp he attended as a kid and returned to later as the camp doctor. Whereas very few campers took prescribed medications in the 1970s, by the mid-1990s 10 percent were taking a pill at some point during the day—most for asthma or allergy conditions, followed by a small subset of kids on behavioral medications, usually for ADHD.

By 2012, fully one-third of his campers were on meds, mostly ADHD medications, antidepressants, and antipsychotics. "What happens is, we've changed our whole culture, from one where kids don't take pills at all to one where you've got a third or more of kids who are on pills to stay well because of what are believed to be chronic health conditions," Burton said. "They get so used to taking pills that eventually they end up using them for a recreational high."

So it went that young people barely flinched at the thought of taking Adderall to get them going in the morning, an opioid painkiller for a sports injury in the afternoon, and a Xanax to help them sleep at night, many of the pills doctor-prescribed. So it went that two-thirds of college seniors reported being offered prescription stimulants for nonmedical use by 2012—from friends, relatives, and drug dealers.

"In the short term, kids and parents and even teachers may feel better" about Adderall's ability to enhance memory and attention, Lembke said. "But studies show that over the long term those kids don't do any better in school than people who don't receive stimulants."

And among those whose stimulant usage becomes a gateway to harder drugs, they're doing much worse. That was true for Spencer Mumpower, who routinely traded Adderall for marijuana, and Ritalin for cocaine. That was true for almost every addicted young adult I interviewed for this book.

*   *   *

As Spencer prepared for prison in the fall of 2012, the remainder of the Hidden Valley group with whom he'd abused drugs kept on as usual to avoid becoming dopesick. Whether that meant recruiting new users at parties or taking jobs at senior moving companies with the express intent of stealing opioids from retirees, targeting the expired or leftover prescriptions so the client wouldn't notice.

"If it was a current medication, I'd take just a couple," recalled a recovering heroin user I'll call Brian, then a Hidden Valley High School student, a doctor's son, and a member of the marching band. "If it was an old prescription, I'd take the whole bottle. Some old people would tell me, 'Just throw it away,' and I'd definitely take those."

Dependent on pills by age seventeen, Brian was twenty when a co-worker introduced him to heroin. He snorted it first from waxed-paper bags marked COLOMBIAN COFFEE and BLUE MAGIC, in wrappers so small he could hide them inside his phone case. "From the moment I did that first bag, I can tell you, looking back now, it was destined," he said. After snorting the crushed-up Oxys, inhaling the heroin powder was easy—and the heroin was cheaper, more intense, and, increasingly, it was everywhere he went. Though he was deeply troubled by Scott Roth's death, little else but drugs mattered anymore. Another friend taught him how to inject himself; he bought the needles at a local drugstore, telling the pharmacist he needed them for insulin.

"It was like shooting Jesus up in your arm," Brian said of his first IV injection. "It's like this white explosion of light in your head. You're floating on a cloud. You don't yet know that the first time is the best. After that, you're just chasing that first high."

Within six months, Brian had blown through the $8,000 he'd put aside for college and pawned his Xbox and video games, all without his parents' knowledge. "I would spend six hours a day driving around Roanoke picking up drugs, waiting for phone calls, going to ATMs."

His parents noticed he was moodier than usual and worried about his weight loss; he'd dropped from 150 to 125 pounds. They asked him if he was anorexic.

A counselor he was seeing for anxiety set up an intervention of sorts in his office, inviting Brian's parents to attend and beginning with "Brian wants to tell you about a problem he's having."

By then he was shooting up twenty bags a day, buying them from a host of user-dealers that had once included Spencer and Scott.

"I'm addicted to heroin," he told his parents.

And while they were relieved to finally know why he'd lost so much weight—and why he sometimes stayed out until 3 or 4 a.m.—they were also gobsmacked.

They sent him to a local hospital to detox, then to intensive outpatient treatment, where he was prescribed the opioid-maintenance drug Suboxone, with mandatory urine screenings, one-on-one counseling, and support group meetings.

Brian was twenty-three years old and beginning to wean off Suboxone when I first interviewed him, in 2012.

"It's been seven days today" since his last dose of Suboxone, he said. "I have pinprickly skin, and I'm restless. It's hard to sit still." Still mourning Scott's death, he noted that none of his other user-dealer friends, with the exception of Spencer, had been caught.

"The cellphone is the glue that holds it all together for the modern drug user," Brian told me. "In high school, I snuck out of the house a number of times to meet people at the bottom of the driveway, and my parents had no clue. Aside from taking my cellphone away, my parents also could have looked at my text message logs and gotten a sense of what was going on."

At a Lutheran church on the outskirts of Hidden Valley, two moms of opioid-addicted young men met at a Families Anonymous meeting, where worried parents go for peer support. Not only would their chance meeting have lasting implications for families of the addicted in the region, but their stories would also expose how families operate inside the sizable gaps that have opened up between the two institutions tasked with addressing the opioid epidemic: the criminal justice and health care systems. While shame too often cloaks these gaps in secrecy, some doctors, drug dealers, and pharmaceutical companies continue to profit mightily from them. The addicted work to survive and stave off dopesickness while desperate family members and volunteers work to keep them alive.

Jamie Waldrop was a civic leader, the wife of a prominent surgeon. Drenna Banks and her husband ran a successful insurance agency. Their sons had been friends and used drugs together, crossing paths briefly through friends at North Cross, a private suburban school that Jamie's son Christopher attended.

"I just knew [Jamie] was this cool blond-haired chick who was making me laugh at a time when I needed to laugh," Drenna recalled. Jamie had not one but two children who'd become addicted, first to pills, then heroin. She hadn't realized the depth of their addiction until she found them both passed out in separate incidents in her home—her oldest, breathing but slumped over in a chair from a combo of Xanax and painkillers, his cellphone fallen to the ground; her youngest, passed out on the bathroom floor, heroin needles and blood sprawled around him.

Between the outpatient Suboxone programs (none of which worked, the family said) and multiple residential rehabs and aftercare sober-house programs (two of which, eventually, did), the Waldrops would spend more than $300,000 on treatment—not counting the drug-related legal fees or the thousands in stolen checks and credit-card bills for gift cards, which were traded to dealers for drugs. (A $200 gift card goes for $120 worth of pills, Jamie explained.) "I was a pretty bad robber," Christopher, her youngest, said.

Jamie and her husband can't pinpoint the most frenzied moment in their journey. Maybe it was when they were scheduled to attend a medical conference at the Greenbrier, a storied five-star resort, but had to bring their grown sons along because they couldn't trust them to stay home alone. Before the conference was over, they discovered a sizable drug stash hidden in a potted plant in their room.

Maybe it was when Jamie's surgeon husband had to drive to the roughest part of the city to pay off one son's drug-dealer debt. Or maybe it was the daily jewelry shuffle Jamie initiated in the wake of discovering her diamond necklace gone, along with her husband's Rolex: She'd take what remained of her best jewelry, "the handed-down stuff," and rotate it between an oatmeal container, the freezer, and the dirty-laundry hamper—the last places her children would look. "We lived like that for years; it was our new normal. Until they go off to rehab, you don't realize just how dysfunctional your life has become."

In the beginning, Jamie and Drenna had, like most parents, isolated themselves—until it dawned on them, at the Families Anonymous meeting, that they were living a very similar nightmare. "I stayed away from my other friends because what do you say when people ask you, 'How are your kids doing?'" Jamie said.

Christopher was two weeks into his first residential-treatment stay when word reached him that a good friend had fatally overdosed on 30-milligram oxycodone pills and other narcotics. It was Colton Banks, Drenna's son.

"It tore me up pretty good," Christopher remembered. "Colton was the nicest guy ever. You could call him up in the middle of the night and ask him for a ride, and he'd get out of bed and come and get you."

Christopher recognized the location of his friend's death immediately. His body was found at the home of a middle-aged man, an opioid addict who'd been prescribed hundreds of the pills from a Roanoke pain clinic three days before. All but twelve of the pills were missing, a police search warrant confirmed, in a painkiller-selling scheme that placed Colton, nineteen, on the campus of Radford University, where he was selling the pills to pay back a drug debt from the day before.

"We got most of our pills from him," Christopher said of the middle-aged addict. "He'd get four hundred thirties [Roxicodone], then some fifteens [Roxicodone], Xanax, and Klonopin all prescribed to him at once by the same crooked doctor. You can use a lot and still make five thousand dollars a month off that, if not more."

The weekend of Colton's death was supposed to be his last hurrah before getting clean. He had an appointment with an addiction specialist lined up for Monday—he'd stuck not one but two Post-it notes on the dashboard of his car reminding him to go.

Colton died at eleven-thirty on the morning of November 4, 2012, All Saints Sunday, while his parents were in church. A few hours later, when a policeman showed up on their stoop to say that Colton had "expired," they were initially confused. Expired? No, their younger son was dead.

To add insult, no charges were filed against the middle-aged dealer, because it's impossible to pin blame on a single batch of pills when an autopsy rules "multiple toxicity," as it did in Colton's case, the police chief confirmed.

The Bankses fumed, then and now, about that. "I want to go kill the bastard," Drenna told her husband, but he persuaded her to stop and think about their other son.

And she did, though she sometimes sat outside the man's house in her car, her gun on the seat next to her, anguishing and hating and praying for her son.

Two years before Colton's death, a family friend in Fredericksburg, Virginia, lost his son to a heroin overdose, and Drenna remembered thinking, "Why can't you control your kid?" She apologized, later, for having judged. She had monitored Colton's Adderall when she learned he was abusing it at age seventeen. She'd grounded him soon after, when she found pot hidden in a briefcase under his bed. She'd sent him to a twenty-eight-day rehab at nineteen after he progressed to pills.

"At first you're just so embarrassed," Drenna said. "You think you're doing right as a parent, but then these drugs take over their life, and nobody talks about it because it's this dark, hidden secret."

At the funeral-home visitation, Drenna had Colton presented in an open casket, wearing a flannel shirt she'd just bought him from Kohl's, pants, hat, and his favorite boots, the ones he wore four-wheeling. His hands were arranged so they clutched a necklace he'd recently borrowed from his older brother, a silver fish medallion with the inscription WWJD.

She remembered her handsome bearded boy borrowing it from his brother's nightstand, telling her, "I may not be as good-looking as Kevin, but I do pretty well with the girls." And they both laughed.

She would remember that moment every day for the rest of her life—especially when she stopped by Burger King on his birthday to order his favorite meal (a cheeseburger with fries and sweet tea), and when she poured dressing on her salad ("He'd use ranch, and he'd think the bottle had a small hole when it didn't, and invariably it'd go all over the place").

"I wanted his friends to see this person they knew who was no longer here. This was the star athlete, the kid who stood up to bullies. Colton was everybody's protector, everybody's friend. He had a good home life. He really had it all," she recalled, tearing up.

"They think they're invincible."

Three months after Spencer left for prison and two years after Scott Roth's death, the Bankses used their nineteen-year-old son's funeral to send a message to his opioid-addicted friends and their parents.

Though Christopher Waldrop was away at rehab and not allowed to come home, Jamie made a point of sitting next to one of his high school friends at the service, in an increasingly familiar role.

She and a handful of other local moms were preparing to out themselves and their families, understanding, finally, that survival had to trump shame. Jamie pledged to help her son's friend find a bed at a treatment facility the moment he was ready to go. "His parents were in total denial," she said.

She would tell Christopher later how Drenna Banks stood at her son's funeral, her voice quavering, and begged her audience to let Colton's death be the last:

"For the longest time, I didn't know what God wanted me to do, but now I know," she told the mourners, chucking her prepared remarks in favor of an impromptu call for treatment. "There are so many families struggling with the same thing Colton has been struggling with. It's insidious, and it's evil, and it's not just pot....And I know there's a social stigma attached to this, but don't hide. Don't hide from it.

"I know there are at least three other boys here that I know Colton wants me to help. And you know who you are....I know now that I'm supposed to be here for you boys, and we're gonna make it through."

The following Mother's Day, Jamie called Drenna and asked her to come over because her husband was out of the country, and she didn't know what else to do. Christopher was close to relapsing, Jamie suspected, if he hadn't already. He was at home visiting her, having checked himself out of an Asheville, North Carolina, aftercare program—against his counselor's advice. After four months of sobriety, "I was tired of all the rules," Christopher told me later. "I wanted to drink again."

Jamie begged Drenna to talk some sense into her son. And Drenna tried, telling him that Colton would not want him to be using again; that it wasn't fair for his mom to have to wonder every second of every day if she would be going to his funeral as she did Colton's. He insisted that he wasn't using heroin and that he hoped, eventually, to make Colton proud.

But the drinking would lead to poor choices, as it usually did, and before long the usual signs presented themselves in the form of stolen checks and pawned laptops; in Christopher continuing to lie through his teeth to his mom, over the phone from Asheville, that he was not doing drugs.

Drenna advised Jamie to drive the four hours to her son's apartment and show up on his doorstep, unannounced. "You've got to go down there," she implored her friend. "You've got to go look at him and pull up his sleeves!"

Jamie arrived at her son's apartment to find cases of beer and a bong in the middle of the living room.

"Hand me your phone," she said.

Her stomach sank the moment she clicked on his text log and found scores of messages to and from drug dealers. There was no need to pull up Christopher's sleeves—the needles and bags of heroin were right there near the beer, tucked into his shoes.

"I was like, shit, here we go again," Christopher remembered.

What he needed, said his counselor, whom Jamie had called in for advice, was "another fucking spiritual experience, and I have the perfect place": an abstinence-based rehab in the Montana wilderness.

"I'm not going anywhere," said Christopher. "I hate the wilderness."

"Then you can join the Asheville transient society," the counselor said.

Christopher pleaded for help from his mom. Surely she could not abide him becoming homeless.

But Jamie said she would no longer help Christopher finance an apartment, a car, a cellphone, or even food. "We're not enabling you anymore," she said.

Instead, she spent a week in an Asheville hotel room with her dopesick son as he detoxed, toggling between a hot shower and the toilet, prepping for his return to rehab.

A day into the detox, Christopher decided he was ready for another fucking spiritual experience. He was twenty years old.

"I felt terrible," he remembered. "From Colton dying, and I knew I'd hurt my family a ton." He was tired of trawling for purses in mall parking lots when most of the car doors were locked. "I was not having enough money to get high, I'd been stealing too much, and I hated it. This time, I wanted it [sobriety] for myself."

As of this writing, Christopher has remained sober four years. At twenty-four, he's back in college, this time in Dallas, the city where he landed after Montana to live in a sober house for young men transitioning from rehab to recovery. Offered a drink on his twenty-first birthday, Christopher told a waitress, "I'm allergic to alcohol."

He was spending a lot of time "giving back" to the recovery community, mentoring young people who are newly sober, helping them work the twelve steps—and worrying about his mom as she increasingly devoted herself to helping other addicted people access treatment, calling rehabs, picking them up off the streets, and taking them to homeless shelters. His surgeon dad has even been known to give Jamie's cellphone number out to addicted patients he meets in the ER.

"There's a lot of emotional investment in it for her, but she's not an addict and doesn't totally understand, still, that some of the people she deals with are going to die. And the small percentage of people who do end up getting better may end up" relapsing, Christopher said, especially those who can't afford multiple rehabs and aftercare.

How many addicts, after all, have moms who can afford not just to send their dopesick son to a second $30,000 rehab but also to accompany him on his flight to Montana so he won't, at the last minute, back out?

Christopher knows he's in a rarefied position: Fewer than one-quarter of heroin addicts who receive abstinence-only counseling and support remain clean two or more years. The recovery rate is higher, roughly 40 to 60 percent, among those who get counseling, support group, *and* medication-assisted treatment such as methadone, buprenorphine, or naltrexone.

"We know from other countries that when people stick with treatment, outcomes can be even better than fifty percent," Lembke, the addiction specialist, told me. But most people in the United States don't have access to good opioid-addiction treatment, she said, acknowledging the plethora of cash-only MAT clinics that resemble pill-mill pain clinics as well as rehabs that remain staunchly anti-MAT.

All told, Christopher had lost four close friends to opioid overdose, including Colton Banks and Scott Roth. For Brian, the number was also four.

None of the recovering users I interviewed had been in the military, but they tallied their losses with the sorrowful stoicism of veterans who'd been to war.

Near the tail end of Spencer Mumpower's prison sentence, he had lost twelve friends, and five others were now in prison or jail. "He's had very few friends get clean, either through going to rehab or jail, but the ones who didn't are either dead, or they have parents who enable them, and they continue to do drugs," Ginger Mumpower said. "Most of his friends have never seen jail; they either talk their way out, or their parents buy their way out."

When Colton Banks died, in 2012, for every one opioid-overdose death, there were 130 opioid-dependent Americans who were still out there, still using the drugs.

George's Chicken, Edinburg, Virginia

Chapter Seven
FUBI

In the picturesque Shenandoah Valley town of Woodstock, more than two hours north of Roanoke, bulk heroin cut in a Harlem lab had just made its way down I-81. It was the last thing Shenandoah County sergeant Brent Lutz, a Woodstock native, would have expected to find himself doing: stalking a major heroin dealer. But here he was, at all hours of the day and night, clutching a pair of binoculars while crouched in the upstairs bedroom of his cousin's house a few miles outside of town. He'd spent so much time there in recent days that the mile-wide stench of chicken entrails coming from George's Chicken across the road no longer bothered him.

Lutz was tracking the movements of Charles Smith and Pete Butler, suspected dealers in a newly arrived drug ring. Butler lived in a marigold-colored boardinghouse called Alma's, full of chicken-processing-plant employees, while Smith lived in a trailer park with his girlfriend behind the giant plant. Confidential informants had told Lutz that the men, former drug offenders who'd landed in town a year earlier to work at the plant via the Virginia prison system's work-release program, were responsible for the recent surge in heroin-related crime in Shenandoah County. Not only did Smith and Butler have dozens of people working under them, many of them addicted, they also had a boss.

Over the next year, the story of that boss and his underlings would allow the young sergeant and his peers to pull the curtain back on the inner workings of a large-scale heroin ring for the first time.

Across the nation, police chiefs and sheriffs were beginning to lament, "We can't arrest our way out of this epidemic." That sentiment illuminated the folly of the decades-long War on Drugs, in which drug users are arrested four times more often than those who sell the drugs.

Sergeant Lutz's government-financed odyssey would also illustrate just how expensive, difficult, and time-consuming enforcement strategies are—with $7.6 billion spent nationwide combating opioid-related crime in 2013 alone—compared with treating the addicted people who drive the demand.

It was late 2012, and Lutz, thirty, had just returned to his job as lead narcotics investigator from a temporary assignment elsewhere in the sheriff's department. Before he left, drug arrests in Woodstock, the county seat, were mostly related to black-market opioid pills: Roxicodone, or Roxy; Dilaudid; Percocet; and the like. His mother, a pharmacy assistant in the storied uptown drugstore with turquoise soda fountain counters and a handwritten charge-account ledger like something out of *Happy Days,* had first warned him about pill abuse more than a decade before, sharing stories of customers who claimed they'd accidentally spilled their prescription down the bathroom sink. The local emergency room was by now accustomed to the classic fake and fraud: a moaning patient claiming kidney stone pain and pleading for Dilaudid, also known as "that one that starts with a D." Drug-seeking behavior was so common that it had spawned an *Onion*-style medical parody on a website called GomerBlog, which punchy health care workers across the state had gleefully called to my attention: "To kick off their new labeling, [the Dilaudid-making] company hopes to change the pain scale from a 0–10 to Tylenol-to–That One That Starts with a D," the satirist wrote. ("You go crazy if you can't laugh every now and then," a nurse-practitioner told me.)

Farther out, in the foothills of the George Washington National Forest, people were still making methamphetamine, Lutz knew. In 2008, he had worked a notorious case, arresting some twenty locals and diversion-program inmates for smuggling meth-making materials out of George's Chicken via an elaborate pulley system dangling from the plant's roof.

Lutz thought he had seen everything at George's Chicken, a plant manned by dislocated factory workers, young locals who lived just north of the poverty line, immigrants who'd managed to land a work visa (or a passable version of one), and an increasing number of workers whom Lutz referred to simply as "diversion," as in: "Most of the trouble we get around here is from diversion." A Virginia Department of Corrections initiative, the program aims to divert nonviolent felons from prison to employment, and to help them gain work experience that will ease the transition back to their communities after their sentences are complete. Most divertees hail from the urban centers of Roanoke, Richmond, and the Tidewater region, or outside Washington.

Lutz had met with managers at George's Chicken numerous times. "We're out there once a week at least—fights, drug-related stuff, overdoses in the company parking lot," the sergeant said. "You ask them if they drug-test, and they say they do, but I doubt they watch 'em, so they can still bring in [clean] urine. As long as they got people coming and going to work, they don't care."

Lutz's boss, Shenandoah County sheriff Tim Carter, told me the Department of Corrections was equally lax. "They put these people in this program, but they don't put the resources to monitor them," he said. A local probation officer, one of two overseeing the diversion workers at George's, told me she was lucky to check in with them once a month. Among the divertees who stay after their sentences are complete, "very few of them earn enough money on their own to make expenses. So, they either commit new crimes, or they decide to give up and return back home. Or they abscond. They run."

The plant had become such a sore point among local police that Lutz and his colleagues joked: "Forget building a Mexican border wall. What they should really build is a wall around George's Chicken."

But the arrival of bulk heroin in Woodstock was more proof that borders were impotent in the face of the drug. The weed-killer Roundup may cure your front yard of crabgrass, but if your next-door neighbor's lawn is infested with it, those weeds will eventually creep back into your turf.

During the six months Lutz was away from his usual drug beat, heroin exploded in his tiny, bucolic community—three people died of overdose, and the hospital would soon report its first opioid-dependent baby. "How it transformed from a pill problem to a heroin problem here, it was like cutting off and on a light switch," Lutz recalled.

Local deputies had yet to identify the supplier of the dope. But an informant helped them zero in on people close to the dealer, including Smith and Butler, who were the eyes and ears of a major heroin supplier Lutz knew only by his nickname: D.C.

In late 2012, D.C. was more rumor than reality, a malignant but murky force. A few counties to the east, an associate of D.C.'s selling heroin in Stafford County went by the nicknames Sunny and New York. In between the new heroin hot spots, local police were also noticing a spike in drug arrests and shoplifting.

Lutz called in federal reinforcements when he heard that D.C., whoever he was, was in the habit of demanding sex from female addicts before he'd sell them their dope. Informants said at least one was a teenager. Lutz was also beginning to see former classmates hijacked by the drug—farmer's kids, football stars, many of them still managing, somehow, to get up and go to work. One woman he knew was in the habit of kissing her husband goodbye in the morning, putting her kids on the school bus, then driving to Baltimore to buy enough to last the day before returning to Woodstock just as the school bus brought her kids home.

Though Lutz had made his first undercover heroin buy in 2010—at a price twice the current going rate—Woodstock was now, three years later, beginning to fall prey to what economists would label the diseases of despair. Whereas central Appalachian communities like Lee County—victims of factory and coal-mine shutdowns, followed by skyrocketing disability claims that made them prime sales targets for Big Pharma—had been battling opioid addiction since OxyContin's 1996 release, Woodstock and similar small towns were slower to experience deaths related to opioid addiction, alcohol-related liver disease, and suicide. They seemed to be somewhat shielded because their economies, while not exactly robust, had maintained a centuries-old agricultural base and were never dominated by a single industry or two like so many smaller Appalachian counties where pill abuse first took root.

"The places with the lowest overdose mortality rates tend to be in farming-dependent counties" with a more diversified economy, said Shannon Monnat, a Syracuse University professor. She likened Woodstock to her hometown of Lowville, New York, a village near the Adirondacks that's economically dependent on dairy farming, wood products, and a wind farm that generates about $3.5 million a year for the local school district.

Compared with Lee County at the western tip of Virginia, Woodstock and other rural communities like it displayed far better indicators of health: Fewer residents smoked, fewer were uninsured, and drug-related mortality rates were much lower than in places where single, labor-heavy industries like coal and furniture once dominated.

More significantly: The opioid-prescribing rate in the Woodstock region was almost half the state's rate—and less than one-third the rate of opioid prescriptions in the coalfield counties. On average, every person enrolled in Medicare Part D in Lee County had been handed a whopping 10.23 opioid prescriptions in 2013, compared with just 2.96 in Shenandoah County.

As the epidemic spread from rural enclaves to cities and suburbs in the early aughts, police in Monnat's upstate New York hometown began seeing the same trends as Sergeant Lutz: "They were saying, 'It's coming, we see traces, but it isn't yet here,'" she said. "That doesn't mean people weren't self-medicating in other ways. It's just that alcohol doesn't kill you instantly like heroin and fentanyl can."

As journalist Sam Quinones theorized in his 2015 book, *Dreamland,* maybe the addiction-prone people who would have succumbed to alcohol addiction in late middle age—had opiates not appeared—were the same people who were now prematurely dying of heroin in their early adulthood.

Monnat's deep dive into rural wellness data underscored that hunch: Binge-drinking rates in the northern Shenandoah Valley were roughly the same, even a little higher, than rates for rural dwellers living in the nation's most distressed counties and towns. But people in their late teens and twenties didn't often die from booze.

The real perfect storm fueling the opioid epidemic had been the collapse of work, followed by the rise in disability and its parallel, pernicious twin: the flood of painkillers pushed by rapacious pharma companies and regulators who approved one opioid pill after another. Declining workforce participation wasn't just a rural problem anymore; it was everywhere, albeit to a lesser degree in areas with physicians who prescribed fewer opioids and higher rates of college graduates. As Monnat put it: "When work no longer becomes an option for people, what you have at the base is a structural problem, where the American dream becomes a scam."

She likened the epidemic's spread not to crabgrass but to a wildfire: "If the economic collapse was the kindling in this epidemic, the opiates were the spark that lit the fire."

And the helicopters were nowhere in sight.

By the spring of 2013, Lutz still didn't know D.C.'s real name or what he looked like. But he had pieced together an impressive dossier of details: D.C. was African American, in his midthirties, with no tattoos. He drove a silver, older-model Mercedes SUV, nice but not too flashy, no custom rims. His heroin was said to enter Virginia's I-81 corridor in plastic Walmart bags, tucked inside snack containers carried by young women riding the Chinatown bus from New York, earning $300 to $500 per round trip.

Packaged in Harlem, the heroin was shaped into uniform, four-ounce hockey-puck-shaped disks that nestled snugly inside a Pringle's can. Whoever was coordinating the production seemed to have a craving for a single flavor, cheddar cheese. And they were methodical, emptying the cans, then repacking them with four pucks and stacking a few Pringles at the end before resealing the tubes with a hot-glue gun. The mystery source also seemed to crave Nilla Wafers and Pepperidge Farm chocolate chip cookies, using those empty packages to transport powder cocaine, which Butler and Smith cooked into crack, Lutz later learned.

An ex-offender who had long dealt in crack and marijuana, D.C. at first had no idea what to do with the Pringles pucks when they landed in Woodstock. So he hired Smith and Butler to break them down into dosage-sized units, or tenths of a gram. In fact, D.C. was so afraid of the drug that he wore rubber gloves, goggles, and a face mask while Smith and Butler cut and packaged the heroin into bags, called points or tenths—on the other side of his living room.

"He looked like he was doing surgery," one of his subordinate dealers told me. "He was way too scared of heroin to ever use it." Like many black heroin users and dealers, D.C. pronounced his product "*herr*-on," as in: *None of my friends or close associates does herr-on. I wouldn't even know where to put the needle.*

But from the first moment he sent one of his subordinate dealers out in Woodstock to sell a gram's worth of heroin he'd paid $65 for in Harlem—and the dealer returned with $800 in cash—D.C. was hooked on another drug.

"What you sell up in the city, you can double down [your profits] here," said an investigator on the case. "You don't have the competition in the small towns, and you don't have people shooting at you."

Whereas commuter dealers running to Baltimore were bringing in 20 grams—at most—D.C.'s Pringles haul routinely contained 200 grams.

Lutz crouched beneath the window, waiting for the Mercedes and thinking about his fiancée back home, still pissed that he'd been called out to work on Christmas Day. At a family wedding in Florida, he'd spent most of his time on his cellphone, monitoring an investigation of the latest overdose. When his cellphone rang at night, his fiancée's kids moaned loudly about him leaving, again, for work. As the county's point man for drug activity, he was now getting, on average, one phone call a night.

Ever since the 2010 reformulation of OxyContin, Lutz had been tracking a small cluster of heroin users, most of them young white men who made the two-hour drive to Baltimore, a longtime heroin stronghold, on a near-daily basis. They'd buy enough to use, plus extra to sell to friends, making enough to fund both their next fix and gas for the trip to get the fix after that. Police classified them as commuter-dealers, and they were becoming an important subset of the drug trade in Baltimore, where heroin sales were estimated at $1.5 million every day.

For forty years, Baltimore had been a prime staging area for dealers moving drugs, especially heroin, along the East Coast. Its port was an entryway for international drug smuggling. Another trafficking artery was Interstate 95, which connected Baltimore to cities from Miami to Bangor, Maine, with nicknames that transitioned over time, depending on the drug of choice, from Reefer Express to Cocaine Lane to the Heroin Highway, also called the Highway to Hell.

With the highest per capita rate of heroin use in the country, Baltimore residents were six times more likely to die from an opioid overdose than the national average.

Commuter-dealers weren't making the trek just from Woodstock but from nearby towns, too, including Martinsburg, West Virginia, and Hagerstown, Maryland, localities that would both earn the nickname Little Baltimore for their explosions in heroin-overdose deaths. A 2017 *New Yorker* profile of Martinsburg by Margaret Talbot opened with the synchronous thud of two Little League parents who had fallen from the bleachers after overdosing at their daughter's softball practice, their younger children running around and frantically screaming, "Wake up! Wake up!"

Twentysomething Roanokers were drawing on drug-dealing connections for their daylong northern treks up I-81 to New Jersey and New York. But in wide-open Baltimore, commuter-dealers needed no such connection.

When Shenandoah County native Dennis Painter made his first trip to Baltimore to buy heroin, in 2012, he'd been advised simply to look for the blinking blue lights. Intended to aid police surveillance of high-crime neighborhoods, the lights also functioned as beacons for drug seekers with out-of-state plates. "Sometimes the dealers will flash their lights at you when they see your plates, it's just crazy," he explained in a phone interview from a Nashville rehab facility in 2016.

"Then, once you know somebody [to buy from], you just keep going back. And when the police arrest someone, there are four more people waiting to take that person's place."

Dennis usually drove to Baltimore with his best friend, Jesse

Bolstridge, Kristi's son. Sometimes the pair stopped by the city health department's syringe-exchange van to pick up clean needles. Once when Jesse was away at rehab, Dennis made the trek to Baltimore with friends of friends, only to be robbed and ultimately abandoned by the people in his car pool. His girlfriend had to pick him up late that night, fuming, their toddler twins asleep in the back seat.

Jesse and Dennis had been best friends since they were toddlers—"I have pictures of us together as three-year-olds playing in a sandbox," Dennis told me. They'd been partying together since the age of sixteen, when Jesse began trading his ADHD medication for painkillers.

Whereas at the start of D.C.'s heroin ring in late 2012, Jesse still preferred injecting crushed-up Roxys, Dennis said, his friend's drug of choice soon became IV heroin, because it was cheaper and stronger, and suddenly it had become much easier to get. As their cravings grew in 2013, their parents paid for them to get residential treatment in separate out-of-state facilities, only to watch them fall back into using shortly after they returned and reunited. The first time Jesse shot up heroin, his mother told me, it was with drugs Dennis bought from one of D.C.'s subdealers.

Police officers and prosecutors working the case told me they could count on one hand the number of heroin users in the region before D.C. arrived. But Dennis and others familiar with heroin in Woodstock contend there were more. Dozens of young twentysomethings from Woodstock had already been driving to Baltimore to buy heroin, some making the trip twice a day.

One night in late March 2013, Sergeant Lutz got a lucky break from an unlikely source—a minor traffic stop in neighboring Middletown (population 1,320). A traffic cop had pulled over the driver of a 2008 Hyundai Elantra for a broken license-plate light and smelled marijuana wafting from his car.

The moment the officer returned to his cruiser, Devon Gray floored the Hyundai—before the policeman could piece together that Gray was driving on a suspended license or that he was an armed career criminal who went by the street name D, with several felonies on his record, including multiple convictions for assault and battery, smuggling drugs into a prison, and felony cocaine trafficking. In the course of Gray's forty-two years, his only legitimate employment, police later learned, had been a stint at George's Chicken that ended a few months before. And he was one of D.C.'s and New York's key distributors.

Neither did the Middletown cop know that Bill Metcalf, an agent for the Bureau of Alcohol, Tobacco, Firearms and Explosives, had already been pursuing Gray for the past three weeks, arranging undercover buys from him in the parking lots of Pizza Hut, Target, 7-Eleven, and Petco in several northern Shenandoah Valley towns. (During the Petco buy, Gray had ridden shotgun with a girlfriend who had her two-year-old in the back seat.) Metcalf surreptitiously captured the buys on video from his vehicle and supplemented the visual record with an audio wire he'd tucked into the clothes of his confidential informant. Metcalf had been called into the case a month earlier by a detective buddy in Front Royal, a half hour east of Woodstock, who explained that Gray was carrying guns, in violation of his probation terms.

Lutz had teamed with Metcalf before on cases and admired his ability to work all night and keep going the next day. "ATF agents are the street cops of the federal world; they're a different breed and very much more gung ho than we're allowed to be," Lutz told me in early 2016. "The [Obama] administration is trying to rein 'em in a little; if there aren't guns connected to a case, they want 'em to pull back. But ATF agents want to work. They're like, 'Call us, call us, call us.'"

Every officer and prosecutor involved in the sprawling D.C. investigation used the same word to describe Metcalf: "relentless." Frequently they used the same phrase: "He can be a pain in the ass." "We've almost come to blows a couple times," said Sergeant Kevin Coffman, the Front Royal officer who alerted Metcalf to Gray's guns.

*   *   *

The two cars screamed as fast as ninety miles an hour. Gray led the local officer on a squealing chase through Middletown, a one-stoplight hamlet, down a scenic byway across I-81, and into neighboring Strasburg. On the southern edge of Strasburg, Gray abruptly stomped his brakes, causing the cruiser to ram the tail of the Hyundai and veer into an embankment before skidding and coming to rest on its side. The wreck left the officer with minor injuries. His police dog, a black Lab named Trooper, broke loose and ran frantically around the totaled car, his training toys strewn across the street.

While the officer extricated himself from the vehicle, Gray drove away, then abandoned his Hyundai and took off on foot—less than a mile from the field where Jesse Bolstridge had made his hometown football fans stand and roar.

The case was sprouting new tentacles by the day. As it stretched across state and county lines, Metcalf called in a federal prosecutor from Roanoke who specialized in heroin cases, and a grand jury was eventually convened. The prosecutor's Obama-era marching orders, according to a road map written by then–attorney general Eric H. Holder Jr., was to use discretion in filing criminal charges, reserving the harshest penalties for serious, high-level, and/or violent drug traffickers. Responding to a nearly sixfold increase in the national prison population between 1972 and 2008, Holder wrote: "Too many Americans go to too many prisons for far too long and for truly no good law enforcement reason."

This case seemed to fit all the criteria. It targeted the biggest dealers.

But to get the worst offenders off the streets, investigators typically need witnesses in the form of user-dealers. It's a messy and often dangerous business, in which police try to glean evidence and witness testimony from lower-level offenders in exchange for what's called substantial assistance. The unofficial interviews are not typically part of the public record, giving prosecutors and law enforcement officers alike a great deal of discretion over which witnesses to believe and which to target for the harshest punishment.

*　　*　　*

With a fugitive hit-and-run now among his list of offenses, Gray was definitely in the mid-level category. The day after the high-speed chase, he reached out from his hideout—in a tiny town near the base of Shenandoah Mountain—to the same informant Metcalf used for the earlier drug buys. Gray was desperate to buy a gun. (On the day of the chase, he had left the house without his usual complement of weaponry.) Metcalf was eager to do the undercover deal.

Within a week, a new setup was arranged to focus on Gray, a Florida native with a history of evading police. Metcalf arranged to meet Gray and trade him a gun for heroin. The deal would take place in a local storage facility, a public space with long rows of buildings and surrounding fences—easy to surround at a moment's notice by throngs of federal and local police.

"My story was, I was recently out of jail and cleaning out my storage bin," Metcalf recalled. "I had some guns there, and I was trying to get back on my feet by trading guns for dope."

A stocky guy with graying temples and piercing eyes, Metcalf grew out his trim beard for the occasion and wore a wire to capture the quick exchange. As soon as it was finished and Metcalf walked away, federal agents swarmed in to place Gray under arrest.

From the moment he was in handcuffs, he cooperated with authorities.

"I can give you the name of the guy who controls everything," Gray offered, according to Metcalf and other officers working the case.

It was a huge moment, albeit a messy one, relying as it usually did on joining forces with one criminal to nab another. "In the end, they all sing" is how Metcalf told the story. But desperate people often lied to reduce their prison time, and there were a lot of people crooning some discordant, self-interested tunes.

*　　*　　*

He went by the nickname D.C., Gray told Metcalf, but his real name was Ronnie Jones.

While Jones controlled the heroin supply in the northern Shenandoah Valley, Metcalf would later learn, Kareem Shaw—aka New York—controlled the supply east toward the northern Virginia bedroom communities closer to Washington. Their dope was Mexican, trafficked by a Dominican dealer who ran a lab somewhere in Harlem.

Agent Metcalf and Sergeant Lutz now knew not only D.C.'s name but also where he lived—in a low-income apartment on the outskirts of Woodstock. His drug ring trafficked in seven counties, and federal authorities were on their way to proving he was the largest heroin trafficker along Virginia's I-81 corridor and possibly in the state. In the small towns that dotted the region, Jones's business model was wholly new. "When you get someone like Ronnie coming in here with real weight, that's far beyond a bunch of users piling into a car to go to Baltimore for the day," Metcalf said.

But a black man in an almost entirely white town driving a Mercedes SUV, even if it wasn't flashy? That was harder to camouflage than the smell of the chicken plant.

"When big dealers come into small towns, they don't last long, because they get talked about a lot," said Don Wolthuis, the assistant U.S. attorney who directed the prosecution of the case. Not much time elapses before their customers become involved with police, who catch the addicted users stealing stuff—or robbing banks—to afford their next buy. "They get dimed out quick," he said.

"The drug dealer's dilemma is always: How do I market myself and remain invisible simultaneously?"

Metcalf alerted Lutz to Jones's identity, only to learn that Lutz had just identified him through another George's Chicken diversion worker, Logan "Low" Rose, who sold Jones's heroin from a Honda Civic with gold rims that really did stand out. He had been Jones's "stick man," or driver, on occasions when he couldn't find a mule and had to personally replenish his Harlem supply. Jones wasn't allowed to leave the state without his probation officer's permission.

Before Lutz could move in for the arrest, Rose fled to his native Puerto Rico, where federal marshals caught up with him a few days later. They found him sitting on a wall in front of his mother's tiny shack, eating a bowl of cereal.

When the marshals phoned with news of Rose's arrest, Lutz was stunned. "We're like, 'Puerto Rico? You're kidding me. But that's so far away!'"

It was so far away, in fact, that Rose had forgotten it was a territory of the United States, complete with its own federal law enforcement offices.

While Brent Lutz was memorizing Jones's driver's-license photo and Bill Metcalf was learning about his gun—a Taurus .357 revolver, nicknamed the Decapitator—Ronnie "D.C." Jones confided in his neighbor, Marie, one of his user-dealers and one of the many women with whom he kept company. When Jones or his runners went to New York to resupply, Marie later told investigators, "two hundred people I know of would get sick [go into withdrawals]. They could not wait for Jones to get back, and when he got back, everybody was better."

"You can't blame Ronnie for everything," Marie told me. "We're the ones who stuck the needle in our arms. But we didn't have heroin available to buy here in town till Ronnie came. What he did ruined a lot of people's lives," she said, ticking off a long list of names.

By importing heroin to a small town in bulk, Jones was able to make twice what the dealers in Baltimore and other cities were making. He made so much that he stockpiled new clothes in his new apartment, discarding them after a single wearing. He had a security system installed so that when he opened his front door, a woman's chipper recorded voice intoned, "Front door. Open." He kept a personal trainer on call for workouts. He hired a designer to create a logo for an all-natural skin-care line he hoped to sell. He wore gold chains, outfitted his girlfriends in new clothes—one kept her own stacks of new Lucky jeans in his apartment—and told people he followed the motto of rapper Biggie Smalls: "Never get high on your own supply."

As the task force charted out Jones's ring, pinning photographs on police department walls, with street names to keep everybody straight, Metcalf turned to Lutz. The goal before had always been to stop the small-town dealers. This case was larger and more complex than any conspiracy they'd worked before. Maybe it was possible this time, even, to bring down the source.

"Man, this reminds me of *The Wire*," Metcalf said.

Lutz hadn't heard of the show. But watching it later with his fiancée, he agreed. Thinking about the exponential scope of Jones's impact—a trail of addiction that would not be contained, in all likelihood, for many years—both men seethed. "We were starting to have eighteen-year-olds overdose," Lutz remembered. "We were disgusted with what he was doing to our town." Before 2013 was over, overdose deaths in the region would surge to twenty-one, up from a single death in 2012.

Heroin was so wildly lucrative that even mid-level dealers in the ring could make $15,000 in a single weekend. Metcalf and Lutz interviewed an addicted user-dealer from Stafford County, thirty-one-year-old Kimberle Hodsden, who was dating Kareem Shaw and going on regular trips with him to Harlem to test the potency of the heroin before he bought it. On one trip, Shaw got mad at Hodsden when she declined his initial offer to buy her a $400 pair of pants from a swanky Manhattan store. It was heady stuff for a local girl, a high school dropout who'd been shuffled among her mother, grandmother, and a local shelter.

Hodsden's name and picture were pinned halfway down the growing chart, the words "Crash Test Dummy"—Shaw's pet name for her—inked beneath her mug shot. And Hodsden had a tiny clue about the New York supplier to share: He went by the nickname Mack.

Jones controlled the left, or western, side of the chart while Shaw's name went on the eastern side of the ring, on the right. Low-level informants dealing only to support their habit were at the bottom of the pyramid, including some whose names would eventually get crossed out due to overdose death.

The chart eventually earned an unusual nickname, thanks to an interview between Metcalf and one of Shaw's lieutenants, Keith Marshall, in jail for possession of illicit pills. Addicted to opioids since the age of sixteen, Marshall was a functioning heroin addict from Baltimore who'd managed to keep a job for fifteen years—as a worker for Payne's Tree Service in Stafford—before getting ensnared in the Jones/Shaw ring. His lawyer told me he'd overdosed five times, and had been in and out of jail for petty theft and possession charges most of his adult life.

In a letter from a North Carolina prison, Marshall himself wrote: "I've done tree work, tended bar, did graphic design for a studio up in Manhattan, among other jobs. I've had 20 grand stashed in my house for the re-up, and I've lived in a tent in the woods because I was so far gone on dope."

Scheduled to be jailed on possession charges in mid-2013 (stemming from an earlier state charge), Marshall said he returned to dealing because he wanted to make extra money in preparation for going to jail. He had debts to pay off, and he wanted to have money on his jail account for toiletries and food. "He started dealing for Kareem Shaw to take care of business, before he went away for a year" for the possession conviction, his lawyer, Dana Cormier, said. "Jones and Shaw were living the life, but almost everyone underneath them, Keith Marshall included, were junkies distributing just to supply their own habit."

Metcalf waited until Marshall went to jail for the 2013 state charges to interview him, carefully, about his role in Shaw's network. "You don't want to reveal too much of your case," Metcalf explained. "You just wanna poke around and see if they'll talk."

But Marshall refused, steadfastly and defiantly.

"Guys, I could've given you the biggest dealer supplying Stafford County, but I'm not giving you shit," Marshall told him.

Already surveilling Marshall's dealer, Kareem Shaw, now operating out of cheap motels along Route 11, Metcalf was fishing, trying to see if Marshall knew anything that would help him peel another layer from the onion, maybe a detail about the New York source. He challenged Marshall to tell him everything he knew, but Marshall refused.

"What if we have proof you're already involved [in the federal case], and we come back here with a warrant?" Metcalf challenged.

Marshall was sure Metcalf was bluffing, convinced he would have already indicted him if he had the evidence, Marshall later told me from prison. "Mr. Metcalf unfortunately is a man of his word," he said, referring to the additional federal distribution charges Metcalf returned with six months later, which resulted in another sentence for five years.

But at the time, Marshall leveled a cold stare at his interviewer and ended the conversation with a clipped "Fuck. You. Bring it."

Back at the prosecutor's office, Wolthuis now had a name for the worst drug ring in the region's history. Above his chart, topped with the names of Ronnie Jones and Kareem Shaw, he took out a Sharpie and wrote in black capital letters: FUBI.

"It just resonated," he said.

Jesse Bolstridge's grave, Strasburg, Virginia

Chapter Eight
"Shit Don't Stop"

The Ronnie Jones arrest, when it finally came in June 2013, was almost anticlimactic. Poetic, just about, the way it featured the usual cascade of drug-bust interactions: an informant tip, followed by a recorded buy that led to one of Jones's main subdealers, a former Marine who'd been kicked out of the Corps for alcohol-related charges before spiraling into heroin addiction. In the end, all Bill Metcalf had to do was track the movements of Joshua Pettyjohn, the ex-Marine, as he bought 20 grams of heroin from Jones and then drove away. Pettyjohn would warble a detailed tune, confessing immediately after police arrested him in possession of heroin.

Jones had known he was "hot," a police target. A month earlier, Brent Lutz and other task force officers swooped in on his Woodstock apartment complex on Lakeview Drive, only to find that he'd de-camped to one of the two other apartments he was also keeping, one with a girlfriend in Dumfries and the other in Front Royal, closer to Kareem Shaw. He drove a decidedly less flashy Chevy Impala when he drove to Woodstock, reserving the Mercedes for nondope activities. Police called the Front Royal apartment they'd been surveilling—a vinyl-sided three-floor unit just off Main Street—the man cave. They suspected it was where the Pringles pucks were now being "re-rocked," or broken down.

To lower his profile even more, Jones changed cellphone numbers and started parking several blocks away from his apartments. He also transitioned his operation from a "brew-thru," as Don Wolthuis called it—selling at his apartment, to just about any buyer who showed up—to dealing only with a handful of subdealers. He was trying to distance himself from his buyers and therefore, he hoped, from arrest.

At the Lakeview raid, Lutz and his colleagues arrested Marie instead, along with four others near the bottom of the FUBI chart. Marie spent seven months in the county jail on charges of heroin possession, a probation violation from an earlier, Suboxone-distribution charge, and child endangerment. "My daughter, she's seven now, and she still has bad dreams about the night the cops kicked in our door," she told me in 2016.

"We spooked him," Lutz recalled of Jones.

Jones had been so positive that Marie would sing that his expression barely changed six weeks later, when more than two dozen state, federal, and local officers descended to place him under arrest. Lutz would never forget the moment he first eyed, through binoculars from the Chinese restaurant next door, the guy whose picture he'd fixated on for months. "He had the look like he wasn't surprised," Lutz said, an assessment Marie echoed when she remembered Jones telling her months before: "If I have a good run, it'll last three months. If I have a great run, I can make it six."

Jones had been bringing bulk heroin to Woodstock for exactly six months. During that time, not only had overdose deaths surged but so had nonfatal overdoses, the number of children entering foster care due to parental opioid abuse, and the cases of children born with neonatal abstinence syndrome—all at roughly five times the previous year's rate.

Once they had Jones in handcuffs, Metcalf wanted to pounce; he gathered as much evidence as possible from Jones's apartments before word of his arrest reached the other dealers in the ring. The day was filled with hurry up and wait—too much waiting and not enough hurrying, in Metcalf's view—as search warrant requests slogged their way out to local judges in several localities for everything from Jones's residences to his vehicles to the homes of other members in the ring. Jones stonewalled throughout, initially telling Metcalf he didn't have an address and then giving him the wrong apartment number when he did. (Judges require police to offer an exact address before issuing a warrant.)

Lutz arrested Pete Butler and Charles Smith in their respective homes near George's Chicken while Kevin Coffman and Metcalf surveyed Jones's apartments, where they confiscated copious amounts of heroin, crack, firearms, and cash. They finally located his Dumfries apartment after finding an estimate for a repair bill in his name at the apartment in Front Royal.

Later that day, when Metcalf finally got his first close-up look at Ronnie Jones in a county jail interviewing room in Front Royal, he found him to be "very smug, very arrogant."

The feeling was mutual. "He was very aggressive; he harassed people," Jones said of Metcalf. Jones hated him for delivering a subpoena to the mother of his oldest child—at work, embarrassing and intimidating her, he said—and for interviewing Jones's mom.

His younger brother, Thomas Jones, told me the family had no idea Ronnie was a big-time heroin dealer until they heard about it on the news. Their mother was deeply embarrassed by it and did not wish to be interviewed, he said. She had seen him only a week before his arrest. Ronnie stopped by her house in the northern Virginia suburbs to chat after delivering cupcakes to his daughter's school.

Ronnie told his family he'd been running his own computer repair shop, fixing broken laptops, iPads, and cellphones. He even showed them a logo he'd had prepared for the business, called Nu2U.

Metcalf and Jones hated each other instantly. But they had more in common than either of them knew.

Metcalf, forty-four in mid-2013, had worked gang cases in L.A. and drugs in Washington. "From my perspective, in the cities, you take off one drug dealer, and they're not even missed, there's so many," he said.

"But this, this was truly the front lines. You shut down somebody like Ronnie Jones, somebody who's making the whole town dopesick, and you're really making an impact." If he could get Jones or the other FUBI consorts to give up their Harlem source, the effects would be more widespread.

The quest had become deeply personal. The worst event in Bill Metcalf's life had taken place almost four decades earlier on a hot summer night when he was seven years old. He was seated at the dinner table with his parents and older sister when he noticed a police officer running outside the window with his gun drawn.

"Go to your room," Bill's mother told the kids. What Bill didn't know then was that his father was a heroin-addicted drug trafficker, and that his mother felt she had no option other than cooperating with police to have him arrested.

Metcalf remembered running down the stairs the night of the arrest, in time to see officers slam his father against a wall and handcuff him. His father looked at him, his head still pressed against the wall, and told him: "You're the man of the family now. Take care of your mother and your sister." Metcalf said he was more confused than intimidated by the order. He wondered: "How am I going to do this when everyone's so much taller than me?" His mom hustled him and his sister into her car and fled to her mother's house in Chapmanville, West Virginia, with just the clothes on their backs.

His parents had met in the 1970s, after his mother migrated from West Virginia to Baltimore for factory work; the family moved to Cleveland, chasing better factory jobs, a few years later. His mom did piecework in a Cleveland textile factory while his dad worked sporadically, constantly feeling the tug of his Baltimore hometown.

His father and uncles were in and out of jail, and only the oldest brother of the five, his uncle Bill (for whom Metcalf is named), was not a heroin user. "There were always guys just out of prison showing up at our house. And when my dad's brothers moved to Cleveland, it got progressively out of control," he said. His father sometimes beat his mother, who felt so trapped that she ultimately informed on him to the police. It was her kids' one shot, Georgia Metcalf believed, for a peaceful life.

As a child, Metcalf knew his father loved him. Even then he understood that drugs were the primary driver of his family's instability. "I had seen my father nodding out into the spaghetti, and Mom was like, 'Daddy's sick,'" he recalled. When the antidrug rhetoric of the mid-1980s emerged, he was an immediate convert, buying into the "This is your brain on drugs" ad campaign that featured the searing egg in the iron skillet. To this day, a six-pack of beer would expire in his refrigerator before it would occur to him to drink all six.

"We stood in the cheese line," Metcalf recalled of growing up in Chapmanville, where his mother worked two, sometimes three jobs before becoming one of the county's first female coal miners. The Salvation Army Santa Claus came to their house with Christmas gifts. When his mom died, in 2015, mourners recalled how she had always stood up for the little guy, filling out black-lung benefit forms for her co-workers and threatening to sue the company when she caught a coal-mine manager throwing her and another woman's job applications in the trash.

Asked if he was made fun of as a kid, Metcalf laughed. "Are you kidding? My grandmother chewed tobacco! Everyone at my school was in the same boat. No one had any money."

Chapmanville was, in retrospect, another perfect breeding ground for the opioid epidemic, with OxyContin moving in just as most of the mines were shutting down in the late 1990s, and the only viable economic option—beyond disability and illicit drug sales—was joining the military, one that Metcalf took. He chose the Air Force because the recruiter promised he'd have a job in law enforcement waiting for him when he got out. Playing cops and robbers as a kid, he'd always insisted on being the cop.

"I distinctly remember teachers skipping entire chapters in textbooks because 'you will not need this when you are working in the mines,'" he told me in late 2016. It took precisely one visit to an active low-coal mine for Metcalf to understand that his future wasn't at the bottom of one.

The next county over, in tiny Kermit, West Virginia, *Charleston Gazette-Mail* reporter Eric Eyre had just won a Pulitzer for pointing out that Big Pharma shipped nearly nine million hydrocodone pills to a single pharmacy in a town of just 392 people, giving Mingo County the fourth-highest prescription opioid death rate of any county in America. Metcalf had seen it coming as early as 1997. Out of the country at the time, he was serving in the Air Force and hated the thought of missing his ten-year high school reunion, though the turnout was dismal.

The chief organizer, a drug user, had absconded with the class-reunion funds.

"When everybody showed up, she wasn't there, and neither was the party," he said.

By arresting Jones, Metcalf was not only doing his job; he was atoning for the sins of his father. His wife, though, was starting to complain about his obsession with Jones—he routinely worked till midnight or later, leaving her stranded at home with their four kids. With every new conspiracy chart, he promised he'd request a desk job "after this case."

"I spent one Thanksgiving on the hood of a car," doing surveillance work, he said. He did not want to end up like Lutz, who'd recently split with his fiancée, partly due to conflicts over work.

A former Air Force military police officer, his wife, Jessica, understood the life. She'd witnessed how enraged Metcalf had been after arresting a user-dealer in a traffic stop and finding heroin tucked into his baby girl's shoe, the smell of marijuana blanketing the inside of the car.

But their kids were another story. One night in the middle of the FUBI case, Jessica drove them to the task force headquarters to see Metcalf, and his youngest daughter asked him plaintively, "Daddy, is this where you live?"

He renewed his promise to his wife: *After this case . . .*

"Ronnie Jones was a predator, and the people in Woodstock were sheep to him," Metcalf said. His desire wasn't just to be a big-time heroin dealer, Metcalf believed. It was also "about money. Control. Manipulation. He created a market that didn't exist before, then he manipulated it to increase his profits. And that's the problem with heroin, and why I don't think it's going away: The money is insane, and the customers are always there."

Bulk dealers like Mack, the New York supplier, manipulated Jones by adding their own diabolical spin to the scheme, designed to keep him returning for more: When Jones sent a runner up to Harlem to buy 200 grams of heroin for $13,000, rather than just give the mule what Jones paid for, Mack typically sent the runner home with double what Jones had ordered—400 grams—plus a bill for an additional $14,000, amounting to $5 extra per gram on the fronted drugs. It was double the Pringles at a bargain interest rate, and Jones had no trouble selling the dope.

The rule was: The money had to be paid back to Mack, via Western

Union or MoneyGram, before the next order could be placed. The arrangement not only contributed to the exponential growth in heroin in Woodstock and bigger profits for both Mack and Jones, it also created a paper trail that Metcalf could follow. "They thought, 'These country bumpkins will never figure this out,'" Metcalf said.

With Shaw's supply side of the ring still operating, dozens more low- and mid-level user-dealer arrests were made as the summer of 2013 wore on, including in an EconoLodge motel in Dumfries, where police found dealers setting up shop in a room and selling heroin stuffed into the false bottom of a can of Red Bull. As local task force officers staked out more deal-making hot spots, Metcalf tried to home in on Mack.

Wolthuis plotted out the officers' progress on the FUBI chart as one arrest led to another. Every time another person was jailed, Wolthuis tallied the offense by the weight of the drugs sold in grams and by the dosage unit: the number of times someone stuck a needle in his or her arm. One low- to mid-level dealer ended up with a five-year sentence for selling the equivalent of between 6,400 and 14,400 needles' worth of dope.

Metcalf wanted badly to arrest Jones's main girlfriend, in Dumfries—he'd found the Decapitator loaded in a safe in her apartment next to a concealed-carry permit in her name. Surely she was also complicit and not just going to the movies, as she claimed, as Jones's heroin made its way to farmers' kids and high school football stars. Did she really buy Jones's story about fixing computers at the local library? Didn't she realize what paid for all those new Lucky jeans?

Wolthuis, the prosecutor, had to keep reminding Metcalf: "There's this thing the courts require, Bill. It's called evidence."

The E-word became part of their banter, with Wolthuis drawing a giant *E* on a piece of paper and telling Metcalf to stick it to the ceiling above his bed. By the time the case wrapped up the following year, with sixty-six people prosecuted in state courts and eighteen convicted federally, Metcalf presented Wolthuis with a homemade award: a glass-encased can of cheddar cheese Pringles, with a single word on the trophy nameplate: EVIDENCE.

In a corner of Wolthuis's desk, not far from the trophy, he still keeps an old case file open. Experience tells him that the September 2013 death of Jesse Bolstridge, once the Strasburg Rams' defensive star, was connected to the FUBI ring, but the shards of evidence have never fully formed into a whole. "I don't forget this one," he said.

Wolthuis, sixty-one, is known for litigating "death cases," prosecutions of suppliers in which a person has died as a direct result of that dealer's drug. From his perch in the U.S. attorney's office in Roanoke, the same office that prosecuted Purdue Pharma, he's indicted heroin dealers for decades, long enough to witness the transition from a small, fairly quiet group of mostly black and middle-aged users in the mid-1990s to a much larger, younger, and whiter group. One of his first death cases involved a thirteen-person conspiracy brought to his attention when police found a middle-aged woman slumped over on a chair inside her apartment door, shortly after she'd shot up in the bathroom of a Kentucky Fried Chicken. "She was sitting on a claw hammer when [the officers] found her; they'd just left her there all alone to die." Her friends had propped her up in the chair, he remembered, placed atop the randomly discarded tool.

Another woman prosecuted in that same heroin conspiracy sent her child to the door to deliver the heroin because she was nodding out in her bedroom and couldn't get up. "There's just something so fundamentally soul-sucking about heroin," Wolthuis said.

He said he was still "just waiting for something to fall from the sky" in the Jesse Bolstridge case. The timeline between the point of sale and his death was not airtight: Too much time elapsed between the time Jesse's best friend, Dennis Painter, bought the heroin and the moment Jessie died, some eighteen hours later, and there were too many people with Jesse in the interim and too many other unknowns.

Metcalf and Lutz believe Dennis bought the heroin from a local user-dealer originally supplied by people in the Jones/Shaw ring, but such death cases are hard to prove in the fluid realm where most overdoses occur, and resources are limited. "We don't have the capacity to try everyone involved in a ring of hundreds of people," Wolthuis said. "But we do try to cut the heart out of the monster."

Kristi Fernandez was already scared when a homesick Jesse begged to come home for the weekend from an Asheville sober house in May 2013 against his counselor's advice. She worried that weekend, too, when he disappeared for hours at a stretch with Dennis. She liked Dennis—and still has pictures of the two of them together playing in the sandbox at their preschool, Grasshopper Green—but she knew full well that Dennis had been in and out of drug rehab for heroin. And as far as she knew, Jesse's problem hadn't progressed to that.

When Jesse returned to Asheville that Sunday night, he tested positive for marijuana and, per the contract he signed when entering the program, counselors booted him out. He had loved living there, telling his Facebook friends a month earlier: "I'm grateful to have such a big support group, I love all of my family & friends. They're the best."

And: "So glad to be sober on this date. 93 days!"

Those same supportive counselors advised Kristi not to welcome Jesse home after his dismissal, but she took him in anyway. "I don't regret that," she says. "I was not going to leave my eighteen-year-old son in a different state with nowhere to live."

And unlike Jamie Waldrop, the Roanoke mother and surgeon's wife, Kristi could not afford to spend thousands sending her son immediately to another rehab, or flying with him to make sure the transfer stuck. Kristi had already sent Jesse to a rehab in Jacksonville once, in January 2013, a ten-week treatment regimen that began with intensive counseling and medical detox, during which Jesse briefly took buprenorphine (more commonly known by the brand name Suboxone), a partial-opioid agonist designed to stem cravings. Jesse still owed $25,000 for that earlier rehab stint, even though he was on his mother's insurance, paying $25 a week that he had autodeducted from his checking account.

He was weaned off Suboxone after three weeks, a not-uncommon practice that would become increasingly controversial as the treatment became more prominent. As National Institute on Drug Abuse (NIDA) director Nora Volkow told me in January 2016: "To be clear, the evidence supports long-term maintenance with these medicines in the context of behavioral treatment and recovery support, not short-term detoxification programs aimed at abstinence."

NIDA, the Institute of Medicine, the World Health Organization, and the White House drug czar's office would all agree that indefinite (and maybe even lifelong) maintenance treatment is superior to abstinence-based rehab for opioid-use disorder. And even Hazelden, the Betty Ford–affiliated center that originated the concept of the twenty-eight-day rehab, changed its stance on medication-assisted treatment, or MAT, offering Suboxone to some patients in 2012.

But the rehab Jesse went to was aimed at abstinence, as most were, then and now.

"The whole system needs revamped," said Tracey Helton Mitchell, a recovering heroin user, author, and activist. "In the United States, we are very attached to our twelve-step rehabs, which are not affordable, not standardized from one place to another, and not necessarily effective" for the opioid-addicted.

Clearly, more recent data supports ongoing MAT, but there is a catch: "One of the reasons people stay so hopeless about the epidemic is that, in any given episode, they only see a small proportion of people get into remission," Harvard researcher John Kelly told me.

"What happens is, it takes about eight years on average, after people start treatment, to get one year of sobriety...and four to five different episodes of treatment" for that sobriety to stick.

And many people simply don't have eight years.

*   *   *

After being kicked out of the sober-living house in Asheville, Jesse moved back home and took a construction job with his father, commuting ninety miles one way to the D.C. suburbs, where they worked on a government contract and Jesse earned $1,000 a week.

He was a good worker. He was pleasant to be around. And he lived rent-free with his mom. And so Kristi was stymied, later that summer, when the overdraft notices from Jesse's bank started piling up.

"I can't stop," he finally admitted to his mom. He was spending $200 a day on black-market opiates, he told her, and asked for help returning to rehab in Florida. He was so high then that she refused to allow him to come home, to protect his younger sisters. But she arranged for him to stay in a nearby town with her sister, who made him hamburgers that night and let him sleep on her couch. He used what she believed was the last of his money to buy an airline ticket to Jacksonville. He was forty-eight hours away from a do-over, the insurance and admissions paperwork already arranged.

And yet Kristi still didn't comprehend the depth of her son's addiction. "I hate to even say it, but I thought he was going back to rehab for 'just pills.'" Jesse still looked like a linebacker, after all. He was handsome and tanned. He hadn't missed a day of work at his construction job. "They'd leave at four a.m., and that's not easy work," she said. He had plans to start community college in January 2014, then transfer to a four-year university. His goal was to become a phys-ed teacher, coach, or sports medicine trainer. He hungered still for the football field.

The idea that her son was shooting up heroin hadn't crossed her mind, she said, then corrected herself: The truth was, the thought had crossed her mind; she just hadn't let it roost. Despite evidence to the contrary. Despite having already padlocked her bedroom door, to keep Jesse from stealing money for drugs.

Only later would she learn about the spent syringes found on the

Porta-John floor at the construction site where Jesse worked. Only later would she understand that Jesse lied about his dismissal from a warehouse job a year earlier. He swore he had nothing to do with the syringes his boss found in the bathroom, and Kristi believed him. How could someone who looked that robust be addicted to heroin?

It was late September 2013, and news of Jones's heroin ring hadn't yet appeared in the local press, though several arrests had already been made, and federal agents were working with local police from seven counties to target the leaders of what they were privately calling one of the largest heroin rings in the state. The region's pill problem had become a full-fledged heroin epidemic in the span of just a few months.

But the only ones to know about it—other than the addicted— were a handful of cops.

That Friday night, two days before Jesse was scheduled to fly to a Jacksonville treatment center for his do-over, Dennis was deep in the throes of dopesickness when he and Jesse stole insulin needles from Jesse's grandmother and bought heroin.

"I was puking," Dennis recalled of their last day together. "I told him, I was like, 'I gotta gotta get this dope.'"

"I'm not trying to do dope," said Jesse, who'd spent the summer injecting black-market Roxys. But the pills had worn off, and he, too, had been throwing up off and on all day. He tried eating his two favorite foods—McDonald's chicken nuggets and macaroni and cheese—but couldn't keep them down.

As soon as Dennis made the buy, Jesse relented, deciding it would be his final hurrah before returning to rehab. They hosted a going-away party at a friend's house. Late that night, a mutual friend broke down crying when she saw Jesse shoot up in front of people; he'd never before been so open about his heroin use, she told me.

But Jesse assured his friends that he liked the rehab he was returning to. Even though he missed his mom and twin teenage sisters, Jesse said, he liked being with people his age going through the same struggle as he was. He hugged Dennis's girlfriend, Courtney Fletcher, and told her, "I promise, I'm gonna be OK."

The next morning, as several friends left to go four-wheeling, Jesse came out of the spare bedroom complaining of a headache. Courtney offered him Tylenol from her purse, but Jesse declined and returned to the bedroom, she said.

Two hours later, Dennis saw that Jesse's door was cracked open and went in to bum a cigarette. His bed was empty.

A few steps away, Dennis found his best friend unconscious in the bathroom, slumped over the vanity, a needle stuck in his arm and the belt he'd used to tie off with in a perfect circle on the floor.

"What do I do?" he shouted, running back and forth between the living room and the bathroom, screaming and crying and grabbing his hair. Some friends quickly fled, chucking the drugs and the paraphernalia into the woods beside the house.

Courtney was one of them. She said she ran because she feared her children would be removed by social service workers. (She does not do drugs, she said, and her kids had been asleep in an upstairs bedroom throughout the party and were not exposed.)

Dennis called 911 and waited for police.

By the time Lutz arrived—between two and six hours later—rigor mortis had set in. "I think there's still something they're not telling me," Kristi says about why Jesse's friends waited so long to call 911. "Jesse usually used pills instead of heroin, and I don't think he'd use alone. I'd feel better knowing that he was not alone when he died."

Lutz remembered thinking how strange it was: Here was a fit, burly construction worker, a guy who'd just put in forty hours of work that week, felled to his core by the diabolical drug.

When a cellphone atop the bathroom vanity rang that morning, Lutz picked it up. It was a counselor, calling Jesse to confirm his Sunday arrival time at the Jacksonville rehab.

* * *

Over the next several weeks, Metcalf pounded Ronnie Jones with questions, trying to get him to reveal his source. But Jones denied being a drug dealer, denied that the confiscated guns and drugs belonged to him. And who the hell was Mack?

It didn't help Jones's case that his gun, recovered from the Dumfries apartment, had Jones's DNA on it, as did another gun, reported stolen from a car in Woodstock. Or that Metcalf had multiple witnesses claiming that Jones threatened to kill them with it if they didn't pay off their drug debts.

Police even recorded phone calls from Jones trying to coordinate drug pickups and sales—from inside the jail.

"Shit don't stop," he told one of his girlfriends.

He wrote angry letters to people, telling Marie he still loved her but was mad that she'd dimed him to police. Above all, he wanted people to know, he was not a snitch.

"Arthur, I have been hearing a lot of foul shit lately from people who you have spoke to," began one of Jones's letters from jail. "I want to set the record straight...I never told/snitch on you. NEVER....After that nigga Logan [Rose] gave all that info to the [feds] they still told him he would be charged, and he ran to Puerto Rico with his girl that he met at George's. Do you see me putting a bad bone out there on you for that shit? Hell no, because I'm going to wait until I see you face to face to ask you about it like a man....I don't want nobody fucking up my name or character in these streets or jails. If you got questions just holla at me."

Though most of the user-dealers were happy to sing, it was code among the people at Jones's level to behave as if not only their dignity was at stake but also their lives, which quite possibly they were.

Not so with dealer Kareem Shaw, who was happy to pull back the curtain on the FUBI ring when the task force arrested him four months after Jesse's death. Best of all, he led Metcalf to a key piece of information: a face.

"You saw the video, right?" he asked Metcalf.

What video?

An eighty-minute production, *Hell Up in East Harlem* was a gritty, street-level documentary about a Harlem block plagued by gang violence during the crack epidemic of the late 1980s and '90s. It was all available on YouTube and so, around minute thirty, was the source of the tsunami of misery that descended on Woodstock a decade after the film was made.

Seated on a bench for the camera, Mack wore a red hoodie. He bemoaned the fact that death and prison seemed too often to be the only avenues out of the loop of poverty and drugs.

Appearing on camera had been a rookie mistake for the young, then-low-level dealer, who described walking the block and seeing "guts and brains....That shit be like some real walkin' hell shit," he said. "N—s gettin' laid out."

Shaw watched the video with Metcalf and, dutifully—in exchange for substantial assistance at sentencing time—he pointed out Mack. Though the filmmakers identified him only as Matt Doogie, Metcalf was thrilled to have a visual of his target.

"Now I could hear his voice and see his mannerisms," he said.

Still, not even Shaw, who was from New York City and forged the initial connection to Mack through a cousin, knew Mack's real name. He could, however, describe the general vicinity of the Harlem heroin mill where Mack "stepped on," or cut, the pure tan powder, diluting it to extend their profits before re-rocking it into pucks.

Metcalf now had more than enough proof to arrest Mack based on witness testimony and scores of cellphone exchanges among Jones, Shaw, and Mack. But where exactly was the apartment, and who exactly was Mack? He felt as if he were being taunted by a ghost.

"Most agents would have written it off, but Metcalf was not gonna leave it alone," Wolthuis said.

In a city of almost eight and a half million people, now all Metcalf had to do was find the ghost.

Mack had recently been released from prison; Metcalf knew that much. One witness remembered that when Jones first landed in Woodstock and struggled to buy bulk heroin, a friend had tipped him off to Mack: "When my cousin gets out [of prison], it's game on; he's got the connects."

Mack was by now a pro, with lawyers on retainer and a network of assistants. Earlier, when he learned that Jones threatened to shoot a customer if he didn't pay back his drug debt, Mack rebuked Jones, telling him, "Why would you do that? You're running a business. If you want to harm someone, don't do it yourself. We've got people for that."

But Mack didn't always make the best choices about which details to delegate and which jobs to personally execute. When Shaw paid Mack back for the heroin he'd fronted him, the payments were retrieved in cities across the country—in MoneyGram kiosks from New York to San Diego. Someone was picking up the money for Mack, and Metcalf figured it had to be someone he trusted, a relative or girlfriend, perhaps. (On federal probation, Mack wasn't allowed to leave the state without checking in with his probation officer.)

Late one night, working out of the regional drug task force office in Front Royal, in the upstairs bedroom of an unmarked house, Metcalf reached out to the security department at MoneyGram, read out the transaction numbers from the text messages, and ultimately came away with a woman's name and several seemingly random addresses in Brooklyn, Harlem, and the Bronx.

He cross-referenced the addresses and found one that turned out to be legitimate. He was stunned when, the next morning, he ran that address through the city's probation and parole database and found a single match: a Brooklyn probationer named Matthew Santiago. It had to be Mack.

The thirty-seven-year-old New York native had recently finished a two-year prison stint for his part in a $2 million marijuana-trafficking conspiracy. He'd gotten out of prison just a few weeks before Jones's business in Woodstock picked up.

"What's he look like?" Metcalf asked the probation officer.

"Black male, with a beard."

Metcalf asked for a picture via email, and a few minutes later, there he was on his computer screen: an older version of Matt Doogie.

Metcalf now had everything he needed to arrest Mack: a name, a picture, and an address.

The night before, it had occurred to Bill Metcalf, when he was sorting through MoneyGram receipts, that he was no better than his father. The work had become its own kind of addiction. "We're both chasing the same thing, on different sides of the law," he said. "He enjoyed the streets and friends over family, and the pursuit of this lifestyle. And here I am, chasing those guys, and choosing that over my family."

His wife wanted to try for a boy; it would be their fifth child after four girls. "It's one more jelly sandwich, who cares?" she argued, begging him, again, to ask for a desk job.

After he cut the heart out of the monster, he promised, he'd ask for a transfer. For the first time, he meant it.

He found Mack outside his apartment building in Brooklyn, walking his dog.

"Who are you? Where you from?" Santiago wanted to know.

"I'm an ATF agent from Virginia, and that's where you're going," Metcalf said.

Santiago told him that he'd never been to Virginia, which may have been true.

Santiago had two children. They would be seventeen and fourteen by the time his case rolled through a federal courtroom in Harrisonburg, Virginia, the following year. Judge Michael Urbanski would approve a plea deal negotiated after a series of meetings between Wolthuis and Santiago's lawyer—who, incidentally, had been at the Southern District of New York courthouse in Manhattan waiting for him on the day of his arrest. "The elevators opened, and there was his lawyer; he'd already beaten us there," Metcalf said, believing the quick legal service signified high-level cartel connections.

Wolthuis wasn't so sure, saying that the E-word—evidence—just wasn't there. "If Santiago was truly Mr. Big, why would he be selling to a couple of wahoos in a small Virginia town?"

Santiago had tried to find work when he got out of prison, picking up odd jobs, his attorney wrote in his presentence memorandum. But finding legitimate employment is exceedingly hard for felons, and the odd-job income wasn't enough to provide for his family, so "against his better judgment [he] drifted back into criminal activity," his attorney noted. "He deeply regrets his actions, and is aware of the strict penalty he is about to face. He has let down his children and feels a great sense of guilt and shame for his actions." His father was murdered when he was four months old, and Santiago, a high school dropout, grew up mired in poverty, the report said. In his late twenties, he ran a small party- and event-planning company, called Self-Made, and worked freelance as a music-video stylist.

Compared with Jones, who received a twenty-three-year prison sentence, and Shaw, whose cooperation earned him the lesser sentence of eighteen years, Santiago was merely a "flipper," as Wolthuis described him, not part of the on-the-ground heroin distribution ring. He pleaded guilty to distributing between three and ten kilos of heroin, which equates to an average of sixty-five thousand shots of the drug, and was sentenced to ten years in federal prison.

On the day of his sentencing, Metcalf personally transported him to a federal courthouse in Charlottesville. On the way, Santiago tried to taunt him. He wanted to know if Metcalf had heard about the recent slaying of two New York Police Department officers. They'd been ambushed by a Baltimore man who bragged on Instagram that he was "putting wings on pigs." Metcalf nodded.

"Metcalf, you really think you're doing something, don't you?" Santiago said. "But you ain't changing nothing. This shit ain't going away."

"Man, I'm just doing my job," Metcalf said.

"Helluva thing to take a man away from his family," Santiago said.

"Yes, it is," Metcalf agreed.

Santiago reminded him one more time: There were people out there who were not afraid to put wings on pigs.

Jones and Santiago were right, of course. Shit did not stop. That's not the way addiction works. That's not typically how prison reentry plays out. It didn't stop when Dennis Painter's father moved heaven and earth to get him into treatment again in the wake of Jesse Bolstridge's death—only to have him continually push through the revolving door of rehab, relapse, and jail.

Naming his new baby after Jesse as a reminder didn't stop Dennis's behavior either. Nor did the abstinence-only Nashville treatment center his dad sent him to, his seventh attempt to get clean. "I've never gone through the stages of grief about Jesse," Dennis told me. He said he'd tried to kill himself "like six times, but it just didn't work. I've just been getting high since it happened."

When the Jones/Shaw ring came to a close, Dennis and his friends simply got back on the heroin highway to Baltimore—although in nearby Winchester he could now buy it for $20 a bag, compared with $30 when bought from a runner in Woodstock.

I told Dennis that Jesse's mom, Kristi, really needed to know what happened the morning that Jesse died. "She wants me to vividly describe what I saw when I walked into the bathroom, but she doesn't need that image in her head," Dennis said. He added that he used to go to Jesse's grave but stopped because it was just too hard. "I have a lot of guilt about it. I want to write a letter, get some things off my chest. It feels like if I'd never gone to get the dope that day, he'd still be alive today." Dennis used to spend Thanksgiving at Jesse's house. He, too, had preschool pictures of them at Grasshopper Green.

Dennis described the problem exactly as Metcalf had: If OxyContin had been the economic driver in the Appalachian coalfields, then the heroin highway to Baltimore had become one of the few avenues left for America's small-town working class. Can't get a job in a factory? Drive to Baltimore instead. An investment of $4,000, or 50 grams of heroin, could earn a person $60,000 in a single week.

Don't want to drive all the way to Baltimore? Your returns won't be as high, but you could now drive in just twenty minutes to Little Baltimore: Martinsburg, West Virginia. That's what happens when rural America becomes the new inner city, ranking dead last behind cities, suburbs, and small metro areas in measures of socioeconomic well-being that include college attendance, income, and male labor-force participation.

"They can make all the task forces they want, but they're never gonna stop it because the profits are just too great," Dennis said. "And the heroin is only getting closer and closer and closer."

Dennis's plan, when I talked to him the summer after Santiago went to prison, was to take what some call the geographic cure. He wanted to move to a bigger city with a younger and more ingrained sober-living culture, along with better jobs. "I've already moved from Strasburg to Middletown thinking that would help, but I just found people there. Then I moved to Winchester, but I found people who got high there, too." His girlfriend used to hear him talking to himself in the bedroom, "but I think he's really talking to Jesse," she told me.

His next move, I learned from a sheriff's department Facebook posting, was to get hauled back to jail on a probation violation. In his mug shot, Dennis wore an orange jumpsuit, and his eyes were so squinty you couldn't tell they were blue. He was down to 140 pounds, from his usual 185.

I had just interviewed Dennis's girlfriend, Courtney, the mother of his children. She was attending community college to become a paralegal; her kids went to a federally funded day care facility while Dennis's father paid for their housing. She was working at McDonald's in Strasburg, where Jesse bought his McNuggets on the weekend of his death. One of the low-level dealers in the Jones/Shaw ring—the guy who sold them the heroin that killed Jesse—often showed up at her drive-through window for food.

In 2013, Jesse's was one of 8,257 heroin-related deaths in the nation, by far the majority of them young men, an increase of a staggering 39 percent over the previous year.

Roughly three-quarters of the dead had started down the same painkiller path that led Jesse to his death, the same path as Spencer Mumpower, Scott Roth, and Colton Banks—with a single prescription pill.

A month after Jesse's death, the FDA approved a new high-potency, long-acting version of hydrocodone, Zohydro ER, even after its own expert panel voted 11–2 against it, noting that the drug, which lacked an abuse deterrent, could lead to the same level of addiction and abuse as OxyContin had in its original form. The FDA concluded that "the benefits of this product outweigh the risks."

It would be four more years before the FDA would ask a pharmaceutical company to withdraw an opioid pain medication because of its potential for abuse—Opana ER, and not until 2017—and by then the annual death toll for drug overdose had climbed to 64,000.

Critics pointed out the inherent conflicts of a regulatory agency that both approves drugs and is then supposed to function as a watchdog over those drugs. The Zohydro approval was the OxyContin story all over again, said Dr. Andrew Kolodny, a doctor who lobbies for stronger painkiller restrictions.

"The most damaging thing Purdue did, it wasn't the misbranding of OxyContin they got in trouble for. It was that they made the medical community feel more comfortable with opioids as a class of drugs," Kolodny told me. "But had the FDA been doing its job properly with regards to opioids, we never would have had this epidemic."

Two weeks before Jesse's death, the FDA finally notified Barbara

Van Rooyan via letter that a portion of her petition had been approved—specifically, her call to withdraw its approval of the original OxyContin. The point was by then moot, of course; Purdue had already voluntarily withdrawn it, three years after the reformulation came to market. "I think my petition did ultimately help [push the reformulation], but so many more people died while we were waiting for it," Van Rooyan said. Months later, she said, after reading a *New Yorker* piece on the Sackler brothers, it dawned on her that the reformulation had almost certainly been prompted by the fact that Purdue was losing its patent on the original formulation, "not because they believed the reformulated version was safer, nor because of my petition."

Still, the letter from the FDA disgusted and angered her and made her mourn all over again for Patrick—and the thousands of newly extinguished lives.

In the same letter, the FDA denied her secondary request, which was to have the drug limited to severe, acute, or terminal pain—and not prescribed for chronic use unless all other treatments had first been explored, guidelines most other countries in the world have adopted. Americans, representing 4.4 percent of the world's population, consume roughly 30 percent of its opioids.

Patrick had been dead now for nine years.

It would be three more years before another federal agency would put his mother's suggestions into practice.

PART THREE

"A Broken System"

George's Chicken, Edinburg, Virginia

Note from Tess Henry, Roanoke, Virginia

Chapter Nine
Whac-A-Mole

By 2014, the suburban heroin-dealing scene had become entrenched in Roanoke's McMansion subdivisions and poor neighborhoods alike. But the largest dealers weren't twice-convicted felons like Ronnie Jones with elaborate dope-cutting schemes, multiple cars, and hired mules. They were local users, many of them female, dispatched to buy the heroin from a bulk dealer out of state, in exchange for a cut. And they were as elusive as hell to catch.

Among Roanoke's first long-haul drug runners was a pretty brunet in her midtwenties whose name reflected her Hawaiian heritage: Ashlyn Keikilani Kessler. What distinguished Ashlyn as one of the region's top mules, according to the prosecutor who sent her to prison, wasn't just the volume of drugs she was transporting; it was also her body's astonishing ability to metabolize the drug without overdosing. ("Generally speaking, there are people who overdose all the time, then there are people like me who have *never* overdosed," she told me.) At the peak of her addiction, Ashlyn was using fifty to sixty bags a day. "She had a remarkable liver," her prosecutor said.

She was an unlikely addict, a young mom and paralegal with a criminal justice degree from Jerry Falwell's Liberty University. But her descent into drugs followed a familiar story line: After the birth of her son, in 2008, she was prescribed Lortab for mastitis, an infection not uncommon among breastfeeding mothers. She had lingering lower-back pain, too—the baby's head had been resting on her spine throughout her last trimester. When the Lortab ran out, her obstetrician wrote her another script, for oxycodone. Within six weeks of giving birth, Ashlyn said, she was hooked. When her doctor left town after a few months and his replacement refused her refill requests, she bought black-market OxyContin through a friend of a friend. She occasionally stole Lortab from her disabled octogenarian grandfather.

She switched to Roxicodone in 2010, when OxyContin became abuse-resistant, then to heroin when the black-market Roxys became more expensive and harder to get. "It's unreal how many people followed that same pattern: Oxys-Roxys-heroin," she told me. "If you ask me, OxyContin is the sole reason for all this heroin abuse. If I had the choice between heroin and Oxys, I would choose Oxys.... With pills, you always knew what you were getting."

By the time her son learned to talk, Ashlyn was doing heroin and/or heroin business with most of the Hidden Valley users. She had grown up in the north Roanoke County suburbs, but she had made lots of friends from Hidden Valley and Cave Spring. "Places like Hidden Valley are where you can get some of the best heroin because those are the kids with parents that have money," she said.

From the Kentucky federal women's prison where she was serving a seven-and-a-half-year sentence for distributing between thirteen thousand and twenty-three thousand bags of heroin, Ashlyn charted out, via email, the trajectory of heroin's suburban sprawl, with intersecting spheres of users she knew who were now dead or doing time. She pointed out news articles I'd missed about people she'd once used drugs with, including a young mother named April who'd recently overdosed in the parking lot of a Roanoke Dollar General store, with her infant found crying in the car seat. She knew Spencer Mumpower and Colton Banks. At the height of her addiction, she'd wept through Scott Roth's funeral Mass.

She mapped out her spiral from user to dealer, from patient to criminal. Two years into her addiction, she was fired from her job for too often being late or absent. Her co-workers had no idea she'd been shooting up in a stall of the law-firm restroom where they worked. (She had to have surgery once after a heroin needle became stuck in her arm but told colleagues "some crazy lie that I'd cut it on a fence.")

After her dismissal from the firm, Ashlyn stole from her family to buy drugs: credit cards, checks, even heirloom jewelry from her Hawaiian-born grandmother, who was now, at eighty, raising her elementary-school-age son. A relative visiting from Wahaii had predicted when she was a little girl that "Ashlyn is gonna break your heart," her grandmother Lee Miller told me.

And, sure enough, Ashlyn did. "We enabled her," her grandmother conceded; her grandparents paid for rehabs she typically left after only a few days. They sometimes gave her money to buy Suboxone on the black market, "because she'd get sick and have to turn to heroin if she didn't have it."

It was the car her grandparents bought, a 2013 Nissan Sentra, that led to Ashlyn's undoing and eventually—once she was forced, behind bars, to get clean—her saving grace. A dealer approached Ashlyn about driving him back and forth to New Jersey for three bundles (or thirty bags) of heroin; he had a Newark "connect," a relative with a source willing to sell to them in bulk. When they progressed to bricks, or fifty-bag allotments, they bought them for $100 each, then sold them back in Roanoke for six or seven times that, she said, and made the fourteen-hour round-trip trek three, sometimes four times a week. Her dealer typically sent his girlfriend along on these runs to keep an eye on Ashlyn, who was known to inject the heroin, swiping bags from their mutual stash, at rest stops en route to Roanoke.

"I now know that he enlisted me because I am a well-spoken, young white girl that drives a nice car, therefore it didn't look [to police] like we were there for what we were really there for," she wrote. More important, her craving for the drug was so insatiable—her skinny, desperate look practically screamed *white female addict*—that no Newark dealer would mistake her for an undercover cop.

When Ashlyn first landed in downtown Newark, heroin was so easy to get that the moment she left her car, a man approached her, wanting to know, "Hey, baby girl, what you lookin' for?"

By 2014, when DEA agents and federal prosecutors caught up with her, the government's case laid itself out in the fifteen thousand text messages recovered from her phone—enough evidence to map out a pyramid of addiction, from her New Jersey source to dozens of Cave Spring and Hidden Valley kids. The exchanges were marked by logistics, deals, and despair:

Can you meet me at Sheetz
on Peters Creek Road?

> Whatcha got? Can you do two?

Yeah.

> You got ten more? Can I owe ya?

Ashlyn was almost home when Virginia state police pulled her over on I-81 just north of Roanoke, ten minutes from the end of another Roanoke–Newark round trip. Unbeknownst to her, drug task force officers were following her movements with the help of a GPS tracker they'd hidden on the undercarriage of her car. She'd been on their radar six or seven days, ever since a former classmate overdosed on the heroin

Ashlyn sold him. He lived, selling her out to an undercover cop in exchange for avoiding jail time.

Now, a week later, DEA agents were searching the trunk of her Nissan, beginning with her purple paisley Vera Bradley purse. They found the 722 bags of heroin, not so carefully hidden inside the monogrammed bag. (She and a friend had already blown through half a brick.) Now they were handcuffing the former paralegal and reading her her rights.

Ashlyn realized there was no story to tell herself that didn't begin with the first of the Twelve Steps, she told me: She was powerless to overcome her addiction. She was about to lose her son, who was six at the time, because she had chosen heroin over him.

She watched as officers extracted her belongings from the car, including her Narcotics Anonymous book, left over from two earlier rehab attempts, which had been there all along, next to her purse.

As the interstate traffic roared by, the agents waved the NA book around, laughing about it. Then they tossed it on the ground, next to Ashlyn's other stuff. It was windy and unseasonably brisk that September day, and she remembered shivering by the side of the road in her flower-print skirt, wedge sandals, and shirt, purple to match her purse.

The man in charge of prosecuting Ashlyn Kessler keeps a portrait of the American president James Garfield above his desk. Before he was named brigadier general in command of twenty-five hundred U.S. Army Reservists nationwide, Andrew Bassford was tasked with the job of laying a wreath on the grave of each one of the eight Ohio-born presidents on the anniversary of his birth, then delivering a speech. Bassford viewed it as tedious but important work, the challenge being to say something inspiring while not repeating what he'd expounded on the year before.

Compared with the other Ohio presidents, Garfield is, in Bassford's view, an overlooked gem. He was a beast of a worker, his rags-to-riches story so inspiring that Horatio Alger penned his campaign biography. Among Bassford's favorite Garfield quotes: "Most human organizations that fall short of their goals do so not because of stupidity or faulty doctrines, but because of internal decay and rigidification. They grow stiff in the joints. They get in a rut. They go to seed."

Bassford is also the assistant U.S. attorney in charge of prosecuting many of western Virginia's heroin-distribution and overdose-death cases. That's his primary job, the brigadier general position being a part-time gig that takes him out of town on weekends twice a month. He takes being a prosecutor seriously, this important but sometimes tedious business of sending people like Ashlyn Kessler and Spencer Mumpower to prison—though he's the first to admit the system is inept and flawed.

From his high-and-tight haircut to his dress cowboy boots, Bassford exudes law and order, communicating in staccato sentences and wry one-liners, like a character from the television series *Dragnet*. On the timing of illicit drug sales, for instance: "Heroin is morning, crack is night."

On the federal judge who halved the prison time specified by Ashlyn's plea agreement, saying he was impressed by her perseverance, after her arrest, in a jail-based treatment program: "I think Judge Urbanski is trying to save those that he thinks can be saved." (In 2017, Urbanski knocked Ashlyn's sentence down even more.)

On what he thinks of law enforcement's efforts to quell the opioid epidemic: Not much.

The system is too rigidified, as Garfield would say, not nimble enough to combat heroin's exponential growth. The drug's too addictive, the money too good. "You whack one [dealer], and the others just pop right up, like Whac-A-Mole," Bassford said.

Bassford prosecuted Ashlyn and her dealer in 2015, but only after putting away her first heroin dealer, from southeast Roanoke, the white working-class neighborhood where heroin initially took hold in the city. Thirty-year-old Orlando Cotto had enlisted his girlfriend, his twin brother, an uncle, and a next-door neighbor to help him transport 60 grams of heroin every two weeks for distribution and use. They took turns meeting their supplier in the parking lot of a Burlington Coat Factory in Claymont, Delaware, clearing nearly $60,000 a month.

After Ashlyn went to jail, "I whacked four more," Bassford said of subsequent dealers, all intertwined with Ashlyn's and Cotto's networks.

But the demand for heroin persisted, predicated on the evangelical model of users recruiting new users, and Bassford's whacks could not keep pace. "We'll score a huge drug bust that we've been working on for maybe a year, and all that does is create a vacuum in the market that lasts maybe five to seven days," said Isaac Van Patten, a Radford University criminologist and data analyst for Roanoke city police. "And because the amounts of money involved are so vast, we're not going to stamp it out.

"We don't enjoy the cooperation of the supplier nations," Van Patten explained, referring to drug-cartel production in western Mexico, South America, and Afghanistan, with profits estimated at more than $300 billion a year. "Their attitude is: 'Tell your people who are wanting to consume our product, we're going to supply it.'"

While Roanoke's quietest heroin users were privileged and upper middle-class—Van Patten called them the café crowd—it didn't take long before suburban users like Ashlyn were casting their lot with former OxyContin addicts from the working-class Southeast who were already tapped into illicit networks, he said. "In the suburbs, heroin started out as a trendy drug that people believed they could control. But the rich kids spiraled right down with everybody else and then, suddenly, you couldn't tell between the two."

The rich kids were crashing alongside the poor kids on friends' couches (the lucky ones, anyway), all of them cowering before the morphine molecule and beholden to its spell. Fifteen years earlier, Art Van Zee had predicted that OxyContin would eventually be recalled—but not until rich kids in the suburbs were dying from it. Now they were, and that pained him equally, he told me. "I was absolutely dead wrong."

I thought of Tess Henry, the young mom I met in late 2015. The daughter of a local surgeon and a hospital nurse (they divorced when she was ten), Tess had grown up in multiple homes—one in the nicest section of Roanoke, with mountain-biking trails and the Blue Ridge Parkway abutting her backyard, the other on secluded Bald Head Island, North Carolina, accessible only via ferry.

Tess was a high school track and basketball standout, an honor-roll kid who would go on to study French at Virginia Tech and the University of North Carolina–Asheville, though she didn't complete a degree. Among the things she loved to do before she fell into a raging, $200-a-day heroin habit were writing poetry, painting, reading, and singing to her dog, a black rescue mutt named Koda. (The two were particularly happy when Tess belted out the words to Train's "Hey, Soul Sister" in the car.) Her favorite author in the world was David Sedaris; she'd run into him once in a local coffee shop after a reading, she told me, and he was so, *soooo* unbelievably nice.

Of Patricia Mehrmann's four kids, Tess was the quietest, the one who voluntarily walked the dogs with her on the beach. Patricia emailed me a beach picture of the family Labrador, Charlie, and a ten-year-old Tess, all freckles and a toothy smile, with both arms wrapped around the dog. They liked to head out early at low tide to look for beach treasures. "She was the queen sand-dollar finder," Patricia said.

But Tess struggled with anxiety from a young age, her relatives told me, recalling a panic attack she had as a young teenager on the way home to Roanoke from the beach. ("She thought she was dying," Patricia remembered. "She was throwing up and calling me from the back seat of the car.") At her private Catholic primary school, where students wore blue and khaki uniforms, Tess was stressed that her shoes weren't right.

Tess was twenty-six when we met, a waitress-turned-heroin-addict. With a ruddy complexion and auburn hair, she wore leggings with long sweaters and liked to apply makeup cat-eye style, at the edges of her eyes, which were luminous and shifted color from brown to green depending on the light. She had consorted with most of the Hidden Valley crowd mentioned in this book, working not as a runner or mule but as a lower-level "middleman," as she called herself. She did worse than that, too.

*   *   *

Perhaps she was genetically predisposed to addiction, her mom theorized; there were alcoholic relatives on both sides of the family. Tess's older sister had been in recovery for five-plus years and was a devoted member of Alcoholics Anonymous. Perhaps, during Tess's college experimentation phase, it was the twenty-five Lortab pills a friend gave her, left over from a wisdom-tooth extraction, that set her up for the ultimate fall. Tess knew only that her daily compulsion for opioids began in 2012, the same way four out of five heroin addicts come to the drugs: through prescribed opioids. For Tess, a routine visit to an urgent-care center for bronchitis ended with two thirty-day opioid prescriptions, one for cough syrup with codeine and the other for hydrocodone for sore-throat pain.

"When I ran out, I started looking for them on my own, through dealers," first through the drug-dealing boyfriend of a fellow waitress at the restaurant where they worked, Tess said. Asked how she had known what to do, she told me she Googled it. "Because I was sick. Jittery. Diarrhea. All of it. I looked up my symptoms and what I'd been taking, and I realized, holy crap, I'm probably addicted."

She could get anything she wanted from her dealer. In the beginning, she snorted five pills a day, usually Dilaudid, Roxicodone, Lortab, or Opana. Then, several months into the routine, almost overnight, the pill supply dried up. Tess blamed it on the DEA's reclassification of hydrocodone-based drugs into a more restrictive category. "That made it harder for my dealer to get pills," she said.

In October 2014, hydrocodone-based painkillers such as Vicodin and Lortab were changed from Schedule III drugs to Schedule II, the same category as OxyContin. Regulations now limited doctors to prescription intervals of thirty days or less, with no refills permitted, and patients who needed more had to visit their doctors for a new prescription, as opposed to having it automatically called in to a pharmacy. Before the rule took effect, patients could have their pills refilled automatically as many as five times, covering up to six months—one reason narcotic prescriptions quadrupled from 1999 to 2010, and so did deaths.

The so-called upscheduling had been controversial, with public opinion weighing in pro (52 percent) and con (41). Chronic-pain patients complained loudly about the added cost and inconvenience. "Just because the DEA cannot figure out how to control the illegal use of these drugs should not be a reason to penalize millions of responsible individuals in serious pain," one critic wrote in a published letter to pharmacist Joe Graedon, *The People's Pharmacy* columnist.

On a website set up by the DEA for public feedback, several patients warned that rescheduling the drugs would limit their availability and drive people to street drugs—particularly heroin.

Tess's dealer adapted swiftly to the switch. "He said, here, try this—it's cheaper and a lot easier to get," she told me. Tess took her first snort of the light brown powder, same as she'd done with the crushed-up pills. He was a serious dealer, she said, an African American who sold the stuff but was strict about never using himself. "Not to sound racist or anything, but typically black opiate dealers do not use heroin. Good dealers don't use what they sell because they know they would just use it all," she said.

With the legalization of marijuana in a growing number of states, drug cartels were champing at the bit to meet the demand for heroin, a market they needed to grow. "They were looking at a thirty to forty percent reduction in profits because of legalization," explained Joe Crowder, a Virginia state police special agent and part of the federally funded High Intensity Drug Trafficking Area program that designated Roanoke a heroin hot spot in 2014. "Between the pill epidemic and the less liberal prescribing of pain meds, cartel leaders said, 'Guess what's purer, cheaper, and we can make it all day long?'"

Some dealers encouraged underlings to "hot pack" their product, giving superhigh potencies to new users to hook them quicker. Once the user is hooked, the product gets titrated back, forcing the person to buy more.

*   *   *

Tess said she didn't consider herself a true addict until six months after she started snorting heroin, when she began injecting it. After three shots, though, she knew she'd never return to snorting. She showed me the scars inside her right elbow; right-handed, she learned to use her left hand to mainline the drugs into her right arm because that vein was usually a sure hit.

For a while she was able to keep waitressing at a trendy, upmarket bistro featured in the likes of *Southern Living* and *Garden & Gun*. She wore long sleeves to hide her track marks and was still able, if she concentrated hard, to remember orders without writing them down.

Around this time, a family friend told her mother, "Your daughter's an opiate addict," and Patricia Mehrmann had a reaction not unlike that of many other parents faced with the same accusation: She fumed, incredulous. After all, Tess never missed a day of work. "She did everything she was supposed to do," Patricia said. We were sitting in her comfortable sunroom, surrounded by woods. Patricia was way past denying it now: She'd spent the last six months navigating treatment hurdles, and worse.

"I worked just to use, and I used just so I could work," Tess explained. "There was no in between." But that phase was brief, and neither Tess nor her mom had any idea what was coming next. Or that the molecule had another even higher card to play.

No matter how low Tess got, it seemed there was always a deeper and fresher hell awaiting her.

The addiction would out Tess eventually, as it always does. Even though she was earning $800 a week at the restaurant, even though she'd started middlemanning—recruiting and selling to new users in exchange for her cut of the drugs—she needed more money because she required ever-larger quantities of heroin to keep from feeling shaky and dopesick. She was arrested twice early on—once when officers picked her up for being drunk in public downtown and found an un-prescribed OxyContin in her pocket, and again when police caught her stealing gift cards from a store. The first charge was pleaded down from a felony to a misdemeanor, and Tess was sentenced to a year's probation and a weekend in jail. The second was treated purely as a theft. "I begged her public defender: 'This is not what it looks like; send her to drug court!'" remembered her father, Alan Henry, from whom Tess was sometimes estranged.

On May 15, 2015, an employee manning the security cameras at a Roanoke Lowe's alerted police to Tess. The camera caught her palming a copper plumbing implement and stuffing it into her purse. She'd done it before: stolen an item from one Lowe's, then returned it to another Lowe's, which would issue her a gift card for the value (since she lacked a receipt). But this time they caught her before she left the store.

"I was already in withdrawal at the time" of her arrest, she said.

At the Roanoke city jail that night, with every pore on her body aching and every muscle spasming, a female jailer greeted her with a tiny cup.

"Here, take this," the jailer instructed. The woman handed Tess the medicine, which had been ordered as a result of a routine urine screen.

Inside the cup was a low dose of Tylenol with the opioid codeine. It was designed to keep the fetus growing inside Tess from going into sudden, potentially fatal opioid withdrawal. Twenty-five and five foot seven, Tess was down to 120 pounds. She hadn't had a regular period in two years. She had no idea she was at the end of her second trimester of pregnancy.

At least in jail, for the immediate future, she and the baby were safe.

Six weeks later, the region's new HIDTA task force issued a warning about a spike in opioid-overdose incidents. Between May 1 and June 23, 2015, the local drug task force would investigate eleven overdose calls, four of them fatal. The culprit was fentanyl, once a popularly diverted opioid prescribed in patch form for advanced-cancer patients that was now being illicitly imported from China and mixed with heroin or manufactured into pills. (Some arrived from China via Mexico and, to a lesser extent, Canada.)

A synthetic opioid considered twenty-five to fifty times stronger than heroin, mail-order fentanyl had been arriving direct to residences across the United States, and so were the pill presses that local dealers used to turn the powder into pills. One quarter-ton press arrived in Southern California inside a package labeled HOLE PUNCHER. Cartel lieutenants were setting up clandestine fentanyl labs across America, mixing the powder with heroin to increase the high, in products stamped with names like China Girl, Goodfella, Jackpot, and Cash. "Some of the companies shipping this stuff from China will send you a free replacement package if it gets interdicted on the way to your home," a prevention worker in Baltimore told me.

News that people were dying from fentanyl-laced heroin didn't intimidate heroin addicts, according to several I interviewed. On the contrary, the lure of an even stronger high drew them to it more.

Later that year and again in 2017, China began banning, at the request of the DEA, the manufacture of several fentanyl analogs, which had previously been unregulated. But each time a derivative was banned, a DEA spokesman conceded, new spin-offs emerged from underground Chinese labs, some more potent than the originals. Law enforcement interdiction of the packages is tricky, because it's hard to tell whether the shippers are illicit labs labeling the envelopes "research chemicals," complete with phony return addresses, or legitimate companies providing the powder for pharmaceutical research.

Back in 2015, Roanoke police chief Chris Perkins, forty-six, knew immediately fentanyl was going to be a game changer. It meant more teenagers would be drawn to the ever-potent blends, able to get high simply by snorting the drug and avoiding the stigma new users have about injecting and, later, the telltale track marks. It meant some would buy counterfeit pills that were sold to them as Xanax or oxycodone but were actually fentanyl.

In his earliest days of working undercover drugs, Perkins had gone by the name Woody Call and wore the classic Serpico look, with a goatee and longish dark hair. It was the mid-1990s, when heroin dealers used to "step on," or cut, their product with baby powder. He remembers finding a pair of Radford University coeds at one bust, naked on a couch in a Roanoke drug house, enveloped in a heroin fog. They'd exchanged sex for the drug, injecting it between their toes so their friends and professors wouldn't know. Stunned, Perkins remembers calling their parents in the Washington suburbs and saying, "I can't tell you this over the phone. You just need to come."

But now the cut had switched from baby powder to fentanyl, from mild to often lethal. "The market is so saturated, I can't say it enough: There is so much heroin out there," sold not only by former crack dealers eager to diversify their product but also by subordinates, or subdealers, Perkins said. So much that Roanoke police seized 560 grams of the stuff in 2015 alone—the equivalent of 18,666 doses or shots.

It was Whac-A-Mole on steroids: When police took one source out, there would be a short lag until the next source presented itself. Meantime, the overdoses kept stacking up. And that was before the worst spike in fentanyl hit.

Perkins had long championed community policing in Roanoke, wherein officers engage with teenagers in high-crime areas (often patrolling on bicycle) while always refining where they need to be, using real-time data. Violent crime in the city, much of it previously crack-related, had dropped 64.5 percent and property crime 39.9 percent since 2006. A 2011 program Perkins pioneered called the Drug Market Initiative offered nonviolent offenders the opportunity to bypass jail and receive job training if they agreed to leave the drug trade.

But the cellphone had put an end to open-air drug markets, enabling the coordination of drug buys in gas-station and shopping-mall parking lots. Hotels situated along the perimeter of Roanoke on I-81 and near Interstate 581, which cuts through the city center, were also prime drug-deal spots because higher-level distributors could sell there and quickly get back on the road.

Experienced dealers were hiring addicted middlemen like Tess to conduct street-level business for them, lowering the dealers' risk. And shoplifting fueled by users like Tess had nearly doubled in the past five years. Violent crime was edging upward, too: A thirty-four-year-old woman was murdered at a rent-by-the-week airport motel known to be a hangout for the heroin-addicted. A woman Jamie Waldrop had been coaxing toward treatment for months was found dead of overdose at a Howard Johnson's next to I-81.

"She's next on the list" to be admitted, a rehab intake counselor texted Jamie the next day.

But it was too late. "She died in a motel last night," Jamie wrote back.

It was time to get nimble again.

On the eve of his retirement, Chief Perkins vowed to do something about Roanoke's surging heroin problem. A data geek as well as an incessant worrier—nights and weekends, Perkins had crime reports emailed to his phone every hour, one of the reasons he retired early, after twenty-four years on the force—he was eyeing a program he hoped to implement, if he could just get buy-in from the disparate health care and criminal justice agencies. "This is what I'm going out on!" he told me, almost manically, in late 2015.

He hoped to follow the path of Gloucester, Massachusetts, police chief Joseph Campanello, who'd recently told the growing number of heroin users in his town: Turn in your drugs, and I'll hook you up with treatment instead of handcuffs. By early 2017, the Gloucester model, called Police Assisted Addiction and Recovery Initiative, had been adopted by two hundred police agencies in twenty-eight states.

The Hope Initiative, as the PAARI program in Roanoke would be called, was the impatient police chief's swan song. "We want the carrot to be: We'll treat it like a disease, and if you stay clean, we'll go away," Perkins said.

The idea was to create a public-private partnership where "angels," or trained volunteers, helped funnel addicts into treatment, mentoring them during the cumbersome and usually relapse-ridden march toward sobriety—kind of like an on-call NA sponsor, only with the skills of a social worker able to take advantage of the city's housing, mental health, and job resources. The program would be located at the Bradley Free Clinic, a long-running program for the working poor staffed by physician volunteers and located in Old Southwest, a burgeoning heroin hot spot.

The clinic's executive director, Janine Underwood, wasn't a doctor. In the fall of 2015 she attended the first Hope Initiative meeting not because she ran a nonprofit medical clinic but because her twenty-eight-year-old son, Bobby Baylis, was among the four who died of fentanyl-laced heroin that June, while Tess was in jail.

Janine had spent the previous seven years floundering as she watched Bobby seesaw between rehab and jail after initially becoming addicted to OxyContin prescribed in the wake of ACL surgery following a snowboarding accident. He'd gotten clean—finally, she thought—during a three-year prison sentence, during which he'd participated in drug treatment and become a certified journeyman in heating and air-conditioning. On probation back in Roanoke, Bobby was excelling at his new job, living in her basement, and doing well after his release. "You could see the sparkle again in his eyes, for the first time in years," she said. Three months after leaving prison, a visit with some old Hidden Valley friends led to a single dose of fentanyl-laced heroin. Janine discovered Bobby's body, cold and blue, laid out on the basement floor, the evidence cleaned up and his user-dealer friends long gone from the scene.

Still raw in her grief—Bobby had been dead only six months—Janine could draw a detailed mental map of the flaws in the treatment landscape, from health care privacy hurdles and other treatment barriers to the lack of guidance about what to do the moment you realize your twenty-one-year-old is injecting heroin: Janine had found a box of hypodermic needles hidden in a box in the back of Bobby's closet.

He'd wrapped them up in his baby blanket, sandwiched between soccer trophies and Boy Scout patches.

What Janine did was sob. "It was the worst moment in my life. I didn't understand yet the connection between pills and heroin. I kept thinking, 'He's gonna get better; it's *just* pills.'

"I'm in health care, and there were just so many things I didn't know," she said. "It's almost impossible the way the systems are set up, for a parent to get good treatment for their child."

Janine was the first Hope Initiative angel to tell the chief, "I'm in."

The second was Jamie Waldrop, Christopher's mom—the one who'd personally accompanied her addicted son to the Montana rehab. By now, so many in the Hidden Valley circle of heroin users had become intertwined: Jamie's boys had known Bobby, Janine's son, who'd been in the same court-ordered halfway house as Spencer Mumpower. And Jamie's older son had at one point dated Tess.

"It was like we had a Dementor from *Harry Potter* who was swirling around the households of Hidden Valley, going, 'I want you and you and you and you,'" Jamie told me.

The third volunteer was Terrence Engles, a former pro baseball player who'd progressed from taking injury-prescribed OxyContin to scamming pain-management doctors on Manhattan's Upper East Side to overdosing on a Staten Island ferry in 2011. He'd just landed in Roanoke as a treatment consultant for American Addiction Centers, with three years of sobriety. He spent most of his time in Roanoke trying to persuade addicted twentysomethings to go to treatment, whether it was to one of his company's dozen centers across the United States (for those with insurance) or to the scant few regional or charity options, most of them faith-based and abstinence-only. "I get about twenty calls a week from people in crisis," he said.

In Chief Perkins's ideal world, Carilion Clinic, the region's largest employer with nonprofit hospitals and a new research center already known for its work on addiction research, would provide much-needed inpatient treatment. No comparable treatment was available locally, only short-term detox programs and one privately owned facility that accepted only insurance and cash (a twenty-eight-day stay ran around $20,000), and it didn't allow patients to take maintenance medications.

Unlike Campanello's Massachusetts, Virginia could not rely on anything close to RomneyCare, the 2006 initiative signed into law by then–Bay State governor Mitt Romney, guaranteeing insurance coverage to 99 percent of the state. Virginia's legislature had repeatedly turned down attempts to pass Medicaid expansion in the wake of the Affordable Care Act, sacrificing $6.6 million a day in federal funds and insurance coverage for four hundred thousand low-income Virginians—a frequent source of frustration for opioid-affected families and health care advocates.

In states where Medicaid expansions were passed, the safety-net program had become the most important epidemic-fighting tool, paying for treatment, counseling, and addiction medications, and filling other long-standing gaps in care. It gave coverage to an additional 1.3 million addicted users who were not poor enough for Medicaid but too poor for private insurance.

But in Virginia in June 2014—one year before the first fentanyl spike—statehouse Republicans shut down the Democratic governor's proposal to expand it in a political plot that seemed lifted from *House of Cards:* Democratic coalfields senator Phillip P. Puckett abruptly resigned to give the Republicans an expansion-quashing majority. Alleged motivations for his action included making his lawyer daughter eligible for a judgeship—the senate's policy forbids judicial appointments of relatives—and also allowing him to nab a job with the commission that oversees economic-development investments from Virginia's slice of the tobacco settlement.

The last Democratic legislator west of Roanoke, whose Russell County region in Appalachia remains among the state's hardest hit by the epidemic, Puckett eventually removed himself from consideration for the tobacco post, citing "family matters," while a six-month federal investigation into corruption claims went nowhere.

Perkins hated political maneuvering. In his ideal world, the economics of securing help worked like this: Since addicts would be diverted from jail, the cost savings from their empty jail beds could be put toward treatment. "The problem is, it's easier to give money to the corrections system — to the tune of one billion in the state of Virginia — than it is to take a couple of million dollars and provide inpatient treatment for our problem," he railed, blaming politics and the tendency among jailers and sheriff's departments to cling to bloated incarceration budgets championed during the War on Drugs, even though two hundred of the city jail's eight hundred beds were typically empty.

But Frederick Douglass had it right when he said, "Power concedes nothing without a demand."

Perkins pointed out that most addicted users return to the streets from jail with more drug contacts than they had when they arrived. "I said it all a thousand times, but I couldn't get anybody to listen because the sheriffs are elected officials with powerful lobbyists, and a poor old appointed police chief doesn't stand a chance," he said.

At the first Hope Initiative meeting, stakeholders were so focused on hurdles to treatment that Jamie worried the project would die before it ever got under way. Privately, she reached out to Police Chief Campanello in Massachusetts and asked him to do a conference call with the working group. She even suggested exactly what he should say: that if they waited till they solved all the obstacles, the program would never begin; meanwhile, people were dying every day. By the end of 2015, fifty-one thousand more Americans were dead of drug overdose — a thousand more than died from AIDS in 1995, the peak year. And the epidemic displayed no signs of trending down. In fact, HIV, spurred by the sharing of dirty heroin needles, was on the rise again, with sixty-five new cases reported that year in rural southwestern Virginia alone.

It was exactly what Art Van Zee predicted in one of his first letters to Purdue. "My fear is that these are sentinel areas, just as San Francisco and New York were in the early years of HIV," he had written of Lee County back in November 2000. Van Zee had no idea then that the OxyContin epidemic would become a heroin epidemic, which itself would lead to more deaths from HIV and hepatitis C.

From a distance of almost two decades, it was easier now to see that we had invited into our country our own demise.

Methadone dispensing room, Gray, Tennesse

Chapter Ten
Liminality

I watched the Hope Initiative take hold in early 2016 at the same time I began following Tess Henry and her cheerful five-month-old son. I hoped that one day their stories would converge. But as loved ones and advocates eager to help heroin users navigate treatment have shown me, threading a needle blindfolded over a hot bed of coals might have made for a less complicated odyssey.

Tess was nearly seven months pregnant when she left jail in June 2015. For a month, she lived with her mom and tried to make a go of it with her boyfriend, the baby's father—"disastrous," Patricia and Tess agreed—before they found a private treatment center two hours away that would take Tess during her final month of pregnancy. Private insurance covered most of the $20,000 bill while her dad paid the $6,500 deductible, using the remainder of Tess's college-savings fund. The Life Center of Galax was one of the few Virginia facilities that accepted patients on medication-assisted treatment (methadone or buprenorphine). Tess was now taking Subutex, a form of buprenorphine then recommended for some pregnant mothers. (Suboxone is typically the preferred MAT for opioid users because it also contains naloxone, an opiate blocker; Subutex, which is buprenorphine with no added blocker, was then considered safer for the baby but more likely to be abused by the mom.)

After spending the first half of her pregnancy in the throes of heroin addiction and the second half on Subutex, Tess was nervous about the possibility of delivering a child with neonatal abstinence syndrome, a painful state of withdrawal that sometimes requires lengthy hospital stays. The syndrome is common even among so-called Subutex babies, about half of whom require neonatal intensive care and methadone treatment to facilitate their withdrawal from the medication.

An NAS baby is a portrait of dopesickness in miniature: Their limbs are typically clenched, as if in agony, their cries high-pitched and inconsolable. They have a hard time latching on to either breast or bottle, and many suffer from diarrhea and vomiting. When neonatologist Dr. Lisa Andruscavage showed me the hospital's NAS services, nurses who had just spent the better part of an eight-hour shift coaxing an opioid-dependent baby girl born four weeks early to sleep greeted us, only half joking, with "If you two wake that baby up, we will kill you."

While Tess's son was born two weeks early, he entered the world astonishingly healthy, showing zero signs of distress. He was not among the fifty-five babies born with NAS at Roanoke's public hospital that year, a rate well above the state's average. He was not among the children seen at the region's NAS clinic, where dependent babies released from the NICU come back for weekly check-ins while being very slowly weaned from methadone under their mother's or another family mem-

After the death of her nineteen-year-old son, Jesse Bolstridge, Kristi Fernandez became obsessed with the story of his swift descent into addiction, including finding any missing details that might explain how he went from high school hunk and burly construction worker to heroin-overdose statistic.

From the small sliding-scale clinic where he practices in Virginia's westernmost county, Dr. Art Van Zee was among the first U.S. physicians to warn people about the dangers of OxyContin. The overdose victims showing up in the ER in the late 1990s weren't simply his patients; they were also dear friends, many of them descendants of the coal miners whose pictures line his exam-room walls.

Sister Beth Davies was a plucky activist nun who had already spent decades standing up to coal-mining operators, and she refused to be swayed by Purdue Pharma's marketing or its offers of "blood money." Executives at the company might have been able to intimidate people up north, where their philanthropy held sway, but it didn't work with Sister Beth.

"Mark my words: This is the beginning of a disaster for us," Pennington Gap, Virginia, pharmacist Greg Stewart told Sister Beth Davies in the late 1990s. He had already been the victim of two robbery attempts, including one by the OxyContin-addicted son of a hair-salon owner who crawled in through the ceiling vents connecting the salon to Stewart's store.

The first time Big Stone Gap lieutenant Richard Stallard heard about the new painkiller, a confidential informant told him it was already available on the streets: "This feller up here's got this new stuff he's selling. It's called Oxy, and he says it's great."

"We enabled her," said Ashlyn Kessler's grandmother, Lee Miller, who is raising Ashlyn's young son while Ashlyn finishes a federal prison sentence for heroin distribution. A paralegal with a degree from Jerry Falwell's university, Ashlyn was one of the region's top drug mules, making the trek from Roanoke to New Jersey three, sometimes four, times a week.

Jamie Waldrop, a surgeon's wife and a recovery coach, had two children who became addicted, first to pills, then to heroin. "Until they go off to rehab, you don't realize just how dysfunctional your life has become."

When her twenty-eight-year-old daughter, Tess, checked herself out of a Nevada treatment program, Roanoke nurse Patricia Mehrmann tried desperately to track her movements, including via Facebook Messenger, to prostitution websites featuring her daughter. "There is no love you can throw on them, no hug big enough that will change the power of that drug."

Still raw in her grief—her son Bobby had been dead only six months—Janine Underwood could draw a detailed mental map of the treatment landscape, from health care privacy hurdles to instructions on what to do the moment you realize your twenty-one-year-old is injecting heroin. "I'm in health care, and there were just so many things I didn't know," said Underwood, the administrator of a free clinic for the working poor.

In 2016, psychologist Cheri Hartman teamed up with Jamie Waldrop and Janine Underwood as well as local police officers to try to divert Roanoke users from jail into treatment. Hartman and her husband, psychiatrist Dr. David Hartman, battled bureaucratic logjams, political indifference, and stigma concerning the use of buprenorphine to treat opioid-use disorder.

After her son Spencer's conviction for heroin distribution made front-page news in 2012, prominent Roanoke jewelry store owner Ginger Mumpower became a de facto counselor to worried parents, some of whom drove two hours just to talk to someone about their children's addiction to heroin and pills.

Substance-abuse counselor Vinnie Dabney had been a mostly functioning heroin user for three decades before court-ordered treatment in the late 1990s put him on the path to sobriety. "The moment [heroin] crossed those boundary lines from the inner city into the suburbs, it became an 'epidemic.' But nobody paid any attention to it until their cars were getting robbed, and their kids were stealing their credit cards."

Sergeant Brent Lutz spent nights, holidays, and weekends surveilling a heroin ring that was operating out of a poultry plant on the outskirts of Woodstock, Virginia. "How it transformed from a pill problem to a heroin problem here, it was like cutting off and on a light switch."

ATF agent Bill Metcalf spent the bulk of 2013 relentlessly investigating members of what was then one of Virginia's largest heroin rings, a conspiracy that federal agents informally named "FUBI." "Man, this reminds me of *The Wire*," he told Lutz late one night during a surveillance operation.

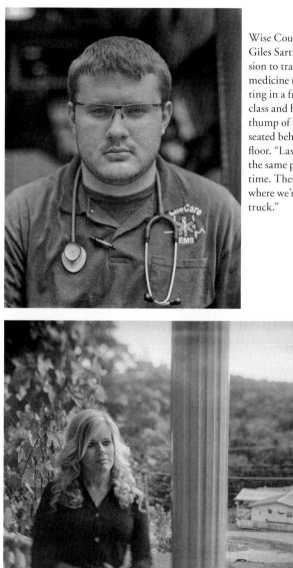

Wise County, Virginia, EMT Giles Sartin made the decision to train for emergency medicine the day he was sitting in a freshman English class and heard the double thump of two classmates seated behind him hitting the floor. "Last week I Narcanned the same person for the fourth time. There's communities where we're like the ice cream truck."

In her mobile Health Wagon, nurse practitioner Teresa Gardner Tyson and her grant-funded staff of twenty are largely left to tend to the health needs of the uninsured in Virginia's coalfields. During repeated attempts to gut the Affordable Care Act in 2017, Tyson grieved for her patients who were dying due to untreated hepatitis C caused by IV injection of opioids and Virginia's repeated failures to expand access to Medicaid.

Of his 1993 Lee County (Va.) High graduate class of two hundred students, A. J. McQueen said more than half were either in prison or battling addiction. "We have to wear rubber gloves now when we make arrests," the drug detective said.

In 2017, public health professor Robert Pack and Dr. Steve Loyd led a coalition to open Overmountain Recovery, a center offering methadone and other treatments in the conservative rural community of Gray, Tennessee, where opposition was fierce. This collaboration among a university, a regional nonprofit hospital, and the state's mental health agency represented one of the strongest models I witnessed for thwarting governmental rigidity and indifference to turning back the crisis.

ber's watch; despite such attention, around 27 percent of the clinic babies end up in foster care.

In fact, Tess's son was a calm baby, happy to sit on your lap looking at a board book or gumming a teething ring or playing peek-a-boo. He had his mother's intense eyes, and his grin was captivating, bell-shaped and wide. Back then, Tess was fiercely protective, to the point of not letting strangers hold him, even for his first picture with Santa. She held him on her own lap instead, saying she was worried Santa might drop the baby or give him germs—a common reaction among drug-addicted new mothers, an NAS nurse told me. "These moms are so over the top after they deliver because they're trying to show everybody how much they care," Kim Ramsey, the hospital's neonatology nurse specialist, explained. Many have been stigmatized by their friends and families, even by members of the hospital staff.

"Our staff used to be really ugly to them," Ramsey admitted. "They'd say, 'This is ridiculous. These moms need to quit having babies and quit doing drugs,' myself included. We had no understanding that these women's brains have been altered, and what they need now more than anything, for the sake of the baby, is our support."

Asked what her goal was in early 2016, Tess told me: "To be a good mom to my son. For right now it's just to get some good sober time, and eventually go back to school and live a normal life. Luckily, I have a nice family, and I'm not dead or serving prison time. I've been given second and third chances, so…"

The buprenorphine made her "feel normal," as Tess thought of it, with insurance covering 80 percent of the medication's costs. Visits to her addiction doctor were cash only, though, requiring $700 up front and $90 to $100 per follow-up visit, as many as four a month, in order to be monitored and receive the buprenorphine, which prevents dopesickness and reduces cravings, theoretically without getting you high. "It's a real racket," Tess's mom, Patricia, said of cash-only MAT practices. "And there are waiting lists just to get into most of these places."

At the time, federal Health and Human Services rules prevented MAT-certified doctors from treating more than 100 patients at a time, a cap adjusted to 275 later that year in response to the opioid crisis. Access to MAT in Virginia would broaden greatly in 2017, thanks largely to the efforts of Dr. Hughes Melton, a Lebanon addiction specialist tapped to help lead the state's Department of Health opioid response. Every week, piloting his own airplane, he would make the round trip between his Suboxone clinic, Highpower, in Lebanon, Virginia, and his office in Richmond. Melton also worked with state Medicaid officials to broaden reimbursements as well as to include payment for mandatory counseling and care coordination, partly as an incentive for cash-only clinics to begin accepting insurance, including Medicaid.

Some eventually did, but the vast human need for treatment was slow to be recognized, and even slower to trickle down to most communities.

As a work-around to the Republicans' refusal to expand Medicaid in Virginia, the Governor's Access Plan, initiated in January 2015, would provide additional addiction treatment and services to fourteen thousand Virginians—but only to a fraction of those in need, and not until 2017, leaving most families to continue navigating wide treatment gaps on their own. "When calling facilities there is rarely a sense of urgency for capturing the addict," Patricia explained, in the middle of a subsequent crisis with Tess. "An application process has to be completed. How many addicts on the streets have insurance, Medicaid, or ability to fax lengthy applications, or access to large amounts of cash?"

For now, Tess and her mom had to pay cash, up front, at every visit.

Among public health officials, buprenorphine is considered the gold standard for opioid-use disorder because it reduces the risk of overdose death by half compared with behavioral therapy alone. It also helps addicts get their lives together before they very slowly taper off—if they do. One researcher recommended that MAT users stay on maintenance drugs at least twice as long as the length of their addiction, while others believe it's too risky for long-term addicts to ever come off the drugs.

But black-market dealing of buprenorphine, especially Subutex, is rampant. And the drug *can* get you high if you inject or snort it, or take it in combination with benzodiazepines, a sometimes fatal blend.

Though I'd visited several Suboxone clinics considered to be best-practice beacons in addiction medicine—including Hughes Melton's in Lebanon and Art Van Zee's in St. Charles—a plethora of shoddy prescribers in rural Virginia and elsewhere in Appalachia had given the good clinics a bad name. Operating at clinics often located in strip malls and bearing generic-sounding names, some practitioners defy treatment protocols by not drug-testing their patients or man-dating counseling, and by co-prescribing Xanax, Klonopin, and other benzodiazepines—the so-called Cadillac high.

"Their treatment is a video playing in the lobby as a hundred patients walk through to get their meds; it's insane!" said Missy Carter, the Russell County drug-court coordinator who has dealt with widespread Subox-one abuse among her probationers as well as in her own family.

Overprescribing among doctors specializing in addiction treatment was rampant, according to several rural MAT patients I talked to who unpacked how Suboxone doctors prescribed them twice as much of the drug as they needed, fully knowing they would sell some on the black market so they could afford to return for the next visit. Others traded their prescribed Suboxone for illicit heroin or pills.

Almost every Virginia law enforcement official I interviewed for this book despised Suboxone, and most Virginia drug-court judges refused to allow its use among participants. (Nationally, roughly half of drug courts permit use of MAT, though the scales seemed to bend toward acceptance as the crisis deepened.) Critics compared the British makers of Suboxone with Purdue Pharma because of their zest for market sat-uration and noted that clinic operators have a financial incentive not to wean someone off the drug. "We have people shooting up Suboxone and abusing it every which way," Mark Mitchell, the Lebanon police chief, told me. "For a town of just thirty-four hundred to have three Suboxone clinics—that's absurd."

"People [outside of Appalachia] don't believe me," said Sarah Melton, a pharmacy professor and statewide patient advocate who helps her husband, Hughes, run Highpower, their Suboxone clinic, which mandates strict urine-screening protocols, with on-site group and individual counseling. Suboxone, with its blocking agent naloxone, "is a wonderful medicine, but we were seeing actual deaths from Subutex here, where people are injecting very high doses of it. And it comes down to these physicians wanting to make so much money, just like they did with the opioid pills!" Subutex is the monoproduct version of buprenorphine; lacking the added naloxone blocker, it is therefore more coveted among some of the addicted, who like the option of being able to take additional opioids such as Percocet at night to get high, multiple users told me.

In Johnson City, Tennessee, just over the Virginia border—where several of the nation's top buprenorphine prescribers have offices—one cash-only prescriber admitted as much in a public forum, saying, "We give 'em enough so they can sell it and stay in treatment," Melton recalled.

Buprenorphine is the third-most-diverted opioid in the country, after oxycodone and hydrocodone.

Hope Initiative angels like Jamie Waldrop and Janine Underwood were opposed to buprenorphine because, based on their sons' experience, it was too easily diverted and abused. Patricia wasn't initially a fan either, because of the expense and the lack of accountability on the part of Tess's doctor, whose drug-testing and counseling protocols seemed lax.

She texted me after taking care of a twenty-five-year-old IV Suboxone user at the hospital where she worked who claimed that 90 percent of all Suboxone was abused. To which I gently replied: "I know Suboxone abuse is awful, but at least no fentanyl is in it, so it's somewhat safer than street heroin."

Tess, too, had clearly figured out how to abuse the drug meant to keep her off heroin—Patricia found spoons and Subutex powder among her things, and Tess told me she doubled her dosage when stressed. Patricia fumed, too, because all but one of the treatment centers she'd called when Tess was pregnant refused to accept her until she'd been detoxed from all drugs, including buprenorphine. Even the hospital where she delivered the baby refused to give her a script for MAT. Instead they arranged for Tess to be seen at a local methadone clinic after Patricia refused for a day to take Tess and the baby home, complaining that it was an "unsafe discharge." They landed at the clinic moments before it closed, with the newborn in tow.

"I'm walking around the methadone clinic parking lot for two hours with a four-day-old baby," Patricia said. "And it was loaded with addicts. It was a place where Tess's circle of addicts would become even bigger than it already was." On days when Patricia had to work, her octogenarian father, who walks with a cane, drove Tess to the clinic.

"It's a broken system," said Ramsey, the nurse clinician. Too few obstetricians chose to become waivered to prescribe Suboxone, and very few drug-tested their pregnant moms, afraid of offending upper-middle-class patients and hiding behind their American Congress of Obstetricians and Gynecologists' recommendation that a verbal screening suffices.

"We need to test all pregnant moms," Ramsey said in a heated NAS-unit policy meeting I sat in on that pitted pediatric against obstetric staff. "We're doing pregnant moms no favors by denying them the proper screening. It's why movie stars and musicians get the crappiest health care—because no one wants to tell Prince he has an opioid problem."

Tess relapsed not long after giving birth, Patricia discovered when she came home from a walk in the woods to find a man lurking around her mailbox. He told Patricia he'd come to return thirty dollars he owed Tess, but Patricia guessed, correctly, that he was a drug dealer. Tess went back to treatment in Galax for another month while the grandmothers kept the baby, then around six weeks old.

By the time I met Tess, she had just returned home and was hoping to transfer to a sober-living or halfway house—but the problem was, many didn't allow MAT, and none of the available facilities would allow her to bring the baby. So she was back at her mom's house and on MAT.

Though she didn't agree with Tess's MAT doctor's protocols and cash-payment restrictions, Patricia was grateful she took Tess on as a patient when all the other area prescribers had long waiting lists.

Tess's problems were growing worse by the minute, and the systems designed to address them were lagging further behind, mired in bureaucratic indifference.

For several months in early 2016, I drove Tess and her baby to Narcotics Anonymous meetings, recording our interviews (with Tess's permission) on my phone as I drove and walking the baby around the back of the meeting room when he cried.

But Tess was edgy and distracted at the meetings, compulsively taking cigarette breaks and checking her phone. She was glad to leave her mother's house but complained about the first meeting we attended, in white working-class southeast Roanoke, pointing out familiar drug dealers lingering outside the church where the group met. In the past, she'd preferred going to meetings in black neighborhoods because participants there were funnier, tended to have more clean time, and were "way more real," she said.

She had been to twelve-step meetings before, both AA and NA, but felt stigmatized for being on buprenorphine, which many participants perceive as not being "clean," or simply as replacing one opioid with another—a cultural gulf that only seemed to widen in the two years I followed Tess. Although NA's official policy was accepting of MAT, longtime NA members who were asked by the meeting leader to sponsor or mentor Tess politely declined—a shunning that must have "felt like daggers" to her, a relative later said.

If you were drawing a Venn diagram comparing Suboxone attitudes among public health experts and criminal justice officials in the Appalachian Bible Belt communities where the painkiller epidemic initially took root, the spheres would just barely touch.

It had been that way since the birth of methadone, a synthetic painkiller developed for battlefield injuries that was discovered in—or rather, recovered from—German labs shortly after World War II. American researchers soon learned that methadone quelled opioid withdrawal, but the Federal Bureau of Narcotics (precursor to the DEA) was rabidly against using drugs to treat drug addiction. The FBN framed methadone as "unsafe"—read: and maybe even pleasurable—after studies revealed that morphine addicts liked it. The FBN also harassed the handful of doctors who used it in the 1960s to treat morphine and heroin addiction. Such controversies continue to this day and illustrate the blurry line between lethal and therapeutic, between the control of pain and suffering and the pleasure of a cozy high.

Over the next decade, into the 1970s, that criticism spurred researchers to improve on methadone and to develop compounds that would both block the euphoric feelings and the dangerous respiratory depression brought on by opioids, including methadone. Such compounds led to the development of next-level maintenance drugs: buprenorphine and naltrexone (now known by the brand name Vivitrol).

Vivitrol, an opiate blocker and anticraving drug given as a shot that lasts around a month, has no abuse potential or street value, and would therefore later become the favored MAT of law enforcement. While naltrexone was approved for treatment of opioid and alcohol addiction in 1984, it was slow to gain social acceptability among doctors or addicted patients despite one researcher's belief that it was the "pharmacologically perfect solution." It wasn't widely used until its maker began aggressively marketing the injection to drug courts and jails, beginning around 2012.

Buprenorphine also blunts cravings, and it's less dangerous than

methadone if taken in excess, which is why regulators allowed physicians to prescribe it in an office-based setting rather than clinics
that have to be visited on a near-daily basis. "I don't think anyone
thought the street value of bupe would be significant," the historian
Nancy D. Campbell told me. "That is generally thought of as quite
a surprise."

But the long shadow of "the heroin mistake," as researchers thought
of Bayer's 1898 development for most of the twentieth century, was
not forgotten by the medical or criminal justice communities. They remained wary of the notion of treating opioid addiction with another
opioid and sought opioid antagonists for that very reason.

Looking back, it was almost quaint how, for most of the last century,
the underdeveloped pharmaceutical industry was dominated by governmental agencies like the National Research Council and the Committee on Drug Addiction. These organizations were composed of
university researchers and regulatory gatekeepers who focused most of
their energies on preventing new addictive compounds from coming
to market in the first place.

As early as 1963, progressive researchers conceded that designing
the perfect cure for addiction wasn't scientifically possible, and that
maintenance drugs would not "solve the addiction problem overnight,"
considering the trenchant complexities of international drug trafficking
and the psychosocial pain that for millennia has prompted many humans to crave the relief of drugs.

When complicated lives need repair, and even the best-intentioned
doctors are rushed, it was as clear then as it is now: Medication can
only do so much.

While methadone remained on the fringes of medical respectability
for decades, the Nixon administration sought it out as a way to control
crime and respond to concerns over the fact that 20 percent of Vietnam veterans (at a rate of fourteen hundred soldiers per month) were
returning home addicted to opium or morphine. Doctors weren't
trusted, though, to both dispense the drugs *and* control for their

illicit diversion in an office setting, so highly regulated, stand-alone methadone clinics became the norm.

Such skepticism toward the medical establishment seems extraordinary now, viewed through the more recent prism of hospital hallways dotted with PAIN AS THE FIFTH VITAL SIGN wall charts and embroidered OxyContin beach hats, hallmarks of an era when doctors were encouraged to prescribe high-powered opioids for months at a time. But as liberally as doctors could prescribe opioid painkillers up through 2016, they remained regulated as hell when it came to treating opioid addiction with methadone and buprenorphine—the latter of which only came to market in 2002, after a thirty-year quest for a new addiction-treatment drug.

The battle lines over MAT persist in today's treatment landscape—from AA rooms where people on Suboxone are perceived as unclean and therefore unable to work its program, to the debate between pro-MAT public health professionals and most of Virginia's drug-court prosecutors and judges, who staunchly prohibit its use. Those unyielding viewpoints remain, I believe, the single largest barrier to turning back overdose deaths. In 2016, not long after a Kentucky appeals court mandated its drug courts to allow MAT, President Obama's Office of National Drug Control Policy announced it would deny funding to drug courts that cut off access to it.

The following spring, President Trump's Health and Human Services Secretary Tom Price would release the first half of the $1 billion appropriated by Congress in the 21st Century Cures Act for treatment and prevention, including expanded access to MAT. But a month later, Price disappointed treatment advocates by publicly dismissing MAT as "substituting one opioid for another." A Tennessee public health official told me Price changed his stance on MAT after NIDA director Nora Volkow showed him the scientific facts: "She worked on him in a hurry." Price resigned a few months later amid a scandal over taxpayer-funded charter flights. In February of 2018, Price's successor, Alex M.

Azar II, signaled the administration would significantly expand access to MAT.

Drug courts remain among the country's models for preventing recidivism and relapse, with intensive daily monitoring of participants—randomly, at all hours of the day and night—and swift consequences, such as being thrown in jail when they fail a drug test or commit another crime. Most of the country's three thousand drug courts drop the charges when offenders complete the twelve- to eighteen-month program. Graduates are roughly a half to a third less likely to return to crime or drugs than regular probationers. Drug courts remain, then, an almost singular place where prosecutors, defense attorneys, judges, and mental health advocates gather around a table to coordinate care and punishment, and discuss the daily challenges of the addicted.

The success rate is so good in opioid-ravaged Russell County that Judge Michael Moore told me strangers approach him at the Food City, begging him to place their addicted children in his drug court, even when they haven't been arrested for anything.

But in a place where illegal diversion of Suboxone dominates the court dockets as well as the landscape—I saw a billboard along I-81 for BRISTOL'S BEST SUBOXONE DOCTOR: MOST PATIENTS ARE IN AND OUT IN 30 MINUTES; CALL TO GET ON THE ROAD TO RECOVERY!—only a handful of Virginia's rural drug-court judges permitted participants to be on MAT. "We've had thirteen babies born to mothers on MAT, and not one of those babies had NAS," Tazewell County judge Jack Hurley told me.

"So tell me: How do you put a price tag on that?"

"The best research says counseling doesn't help: 'Just give 'em the pill. Give 'em the fucking pill,'" said a local addiction counselor, Anne Giles, who was furious about cultural biases against MAT. According to an analysis of international studies published in the *Lancet,* the best treatment for opioid addiction combines MAT with psychosocial support, "although some benefit is seen even with low dose and minimum support."

Giles firmly believes that "courts should not be practicing medicine," and yet, amid growing national consensus about MAT's benefits, criminal justice too often trumps science, she fumed. People buying illicit Suboxone were self-medicating because federal regulators didn't permit enough physicians to prescribe it, in her view, and privately operated clinics accepted only cash because Medicaid reimbursements were delayed and covered only a sliver of the costs.

"We should let doctors be doctors," Giles said. "Because this crisis is a lot like Ebola, where we sent helicopters." Given opioid-related spikes in deaths, HIV, and hepatitis C, she added, "we should be sending helicopters!"

Fury about the fundamental skepticism toward MAT is not restricted to the medical community. Don Flattery, a member of the Virginia Governor's Task Force on Prescription Drug and Heroin Abuse, compared anti-MAT judges and police officers to climate-change deniers. He'd lost his twenty-six-year-old son, Kevin, to an opioid overdose and tortured himself for not insisting that Kevin stick with MAT. His son had been on Suboxone before but abandoned it prematurely, after feeling stigmatized for it, in favor of abstinence-only treatment, Flattery said.

Art Van Zee, too, struggled with law enforcement complaints about buprenorphine, though he conceded that too many Suboxone providers in rural America had lax practices that spawned diversion and abuse. To fix the problem, public policy makers should, in Van Zee's opinion, incentivize more doctors to go into addiction medicine, and MAT should be predominantly expanded in the nonprofit realm of health departments, community service boards, and federally qualified health centers, where salaried doctors are less motivated to overprescribe.

"I think taking an opioid-addicted person and expecting them to do well in drug court [without Suboxone] is almost cruel and unusual punishment," Van Zee said. "In the legal sphere, all the police and judges see is the worst, ugly part—the trafficking, the kids put into foster care because the mother's found injecting Suboxone." A patient had arrived at his St. Charles clinic recently on her sixteenth birthday, only to learn that she'd acquired hepatitis C from injecting black-market Subutex.

It was simple observation bias: MAT opponents failed to see the distinction between people who abused buprenorphine and those who took it responsibly. "They don't see all the patients I have who are going through college, getting their master's degrees, getting jobs and their kids back, some of them drug-free now for ten or twelve years," Van Zee said.

A few of Van Zee's long-term patients had tapered from 16 milligrams of Suboxone to as little as a half-milligram a day, but he hesitated to wean them entirely because, in his experience, it often led to relapse. Though there was scant data about the efficacy of long-term Suboxone treatment, one study showed that 50 percent of users relapsed within a month of being weaned from the drug; the lower the dose at the time of weaning, the better the outcome. Another study, conducted over five years, showed that roughly a third of buprenorphine patients were drug-free after eighteen months, a third were still on MAT, and most of the remainder were back on heroin or illicit opioids.

When a person is weaned too soon, his or her relapse feeds the perception that MAT is ineffective, reinforcing unfair and faulty notions about the treatment, said Nora Volkow, the NIDA official. "All studies—every single one of them—show superior outcomes when patients are treated" with maintenance medications such as buprenorphine or methadone, Volkow told me. She pointed out that most patients buying black-market Suboxone are really trying to avoid dopesickness—"and that is so much safer for them than going back to heroin."

One Roanoke woman was so desperate to avoid relapse that she prepared for an upcoming two-week jail stint by stuffing a vial of Suboxone strips inside her vagina, knowing local jails didn't allow MAT.

"Then, in the middle of the night, she pulled the bottle out, took one, then quickly put it back," said her Roanoke psychiatrist and MAT doctor, Jennifer Wells, who treats indigent pregnant women before and after delivery.

That patient's continued recovery, Wells added, "speaks to the fact that MAT works. And that patients will go to any length not to relapse. They know what they need!"

But the divide between MAT opponents and proponents only deepened as I followed the travails of the Hope Initiative and users like Tess. While treatment providers, police, and family members were arguing about the best way forward, lives hung perilously in the balance.

It was hard being Tess. After four NA meetings, she stopped wanting to go, often texting me just as I was leaving to pick her up. The baby was sleeping, or she was too tired because he'd kept her awake the night before. His father was in jail after an alcohol-related arrest. And though his mother stepped in often to babysit, she was planning to move to North Carolina and hinted that she wanted to take her grandson with her.

Having grown up in an alcoholic household, I knew what it felt like to live on the periphery of addiction—the potential danger of being neglected, taken advantage of, or even raged against. And being with Tess sometimes brought up memories of a much darker time. I worried about her son and felt sorry for him. There were instances when journalistic boundaries blurred, such as the night Tess texted me from an unknown location:

Can yoi please come gwt me.

I was in the middle of organizing taxes, with the help of my spreadsheet-whiz niece, and didn't see the text immediately. An hour later, I weighed what to do, talked to my husband, and ultimately forwarded Tess's plea to both Patricia and Jamie Waldrop, who was Tess's Hope volunteer. The next time I saw Tess, neither of us brought it up.

It was February 2016, and Patricia believed Tess was using again—items from the house started vanishing, including a laptop, and she discovered empty heroin baggies in her bathroom trash—but Tess vehemently denied it.

Family stress was high. Tess's parents had different opinions about the best course of treatment, and Tess believed her siblings looked down on her as the black sheep. Her dad, Dr. Alan Henry, begged her to enroll in a twelve-month residential recovery program at the faith-based Roanoke rescue mission, but the mission banned stimulants of all kinds, from cigarettes to MAT, and Tess was not only still on buprenorphine and a heavy smoker, she was also a proud atheist. "The one thing that becomes clear is, there is misunderstanding with the siblings and with me on the distinction between helping and enabling that remains very murky," Alan Henry told me later, suggesting that whereas he and Tess's siblings preferred a tough-love approach, Patricia and her father were too easily manipulated by Tess, he thought.

Tess's older sister, an AA proponent, begged Tess to adopt the Twelve Steps as she had done, arguing that the program emphasized spirituality over religion. "I told her, 'Use Koda [Tess's dog] as your higher power, for all it matters; just pray to *something*.'" But Tess laughed and said, "That's ridiculous." Soon after, a dopesick Tess asked her for money to buy buprenorphine, and her sister, believing Tess would spend it on heroin, offered her a ride to a meeting instead.

"I'm not trying to go sit in an AA meeting and listen to that bullshit," Tess told her. "And you're not my sister." They stopped speaking.

When Patricia proposed that Tess consider other long-term treatment programs, MAT or not, she refused, turning argumentative and sharp. Her mom had a full-time hospital job with irregular hours; her shifts often ran longer than twelve hours, leaving Tess home alone with her son. Patricia had a security system installed in her home. But two cameras weren't nearly enough.

In March, Patricia arrived home to find Tess stumbling around the house, seemingly high, and clothes from one of the bedrooms vanished—pawned, presumably, for drugs. "I'm meeting with my attorney," Patricia told me, shortly after this incident. "I can't just kick her out because she's been here awhile." A guardian ad litem would be appointed by the court to weigh in on what was best for Tess's son.

"Everything's such a mess, and in the middle of it is this gorgeous, beautiful boy," Patricia said. Now seven months old, he was ahead of developmental schedule and before long he would babble his first word: *Mama*.

Tess maintained she was not using, but evidence to the contrary kept presenting itself. Patricia sometimes arrived home from work to find her security cameras turned to the side. Once, awakened by the baby's cry in the middle of the night, she found him on the couch, "only he could barely sit up, and he's leaning over, and he's crying. He had a piece of a bottle, a plastic tube, and he could have choked."

And where was Tess? "She was in the bathroom putting on makeup! She was superhigh," with her baby about to tip onto the floor. "It is so embarrassing and so painful, trying to make this work," Patricia said. "Your giving starts to give out."

The guardian ad litem saw what was happening, and by late March, Tess lost custody of her son. A judge awarded shared custody to the grandmothers, and Tess was no longer permitted to live at Patricia's, though she could visit her son when Patricia was home.

That spring Tess moved into a cheap motel, a known haven for drug users and dealers, with no car. To regain custody, she had until July 18 to find a job and a place to live, and prove her sobriety. She was mad at her dad for not loaning her money for an apartment down payment and furious about being unfairly painted as an unfit mother in court. "Even if I did take a Xanax when I was with [my son], I've never been fucked up. I've never not changed his diaper," Tess insisted. Asked if it was difficult to stay away from other heroin users, Tess said, "When I'm angry and I have nothing, it's really hard."

She was trying to switch to a Suboxone doctor who accepted Medicaid, which she was now enrolled in, but that physician had long ago reached his federally mandated cap (then a hundred patients). A hundred dollars in debt to her Blacksburg psychiatrist and cash-only MAT provider, Tess had to pay the balance before she could be seen again, and meanwhile she was down to just a week's supply of MAT. She'd tested positive for marijuana on her last doctor's visit: "I was having really bad anxiety, and I thought pot would be better because at least it's herbal," she said.

By May, Tess was couch-surfing in low-rent apartments in southeast Roanoke and using heroin daily. She posted a cry for help on her Facebook page, ending with a quote from a Lil Wayne/Eminem song: "Been to hell and back / I can show you vouchers." She went by the street name Sweet T.

Though the Hope Initiative was still months from opening its doors, Jamie reached out to Tess on Facebook: "Call me if you need help. I might just know of something right up your alley, Girl. Much love."

Tess called immediately. She wanted to hear how Jamie's older son, whom Tess had once dated, had gotten sober. They made plans to meet the next day, but Tess canceled at the last minute.

By early June her son's dad was out of jail. They squabbled, it turned violent, and Tess went deeper underground.

Patricia and Jamie worked their contacts to find her. Jamie's son showed her where they'd once done drugs together while Patricia, worried that Tess was seriously hurt, filed a missing-persons report.

They distributed flyers across the region and on Facebook with a smiling picture of Tess and her description: "Last seen June 11, 2016. Brownish/red hair, green eyes, 5' 7", 130 lbs. Tree of Life tattoo on left shoulder blade." Two days later, police received a report that Tess had stolen a car and a credit card—she'd been sent out for groceries by a woman she was staying with and never returned. Police found and arrested Tess later that day.

Patricia texted Jamie the news: For the first time in months, she told her, she could go to sleep knowing that, at least for that night, her daughter would not die.

The baby was a toddler now, and Tess hadn't witnessed a single one of his steps. He was living with his other grandmother in North Carolina, and Patricia made the twelve-hour round-trip trek to see him monthly, texting me pictures of their visits: her grandson playing on the beach, wearing a silly sock monkey hat.

Summer turned into fall as Tess bounced between the streets, jail, the battered women's shelter, and the psychiatric wards of two local hospitals, the last of which she knew were prevented by federal law from turning suicidal patients away regardless of insurance status or ability to pay. "It's so costly and ineffective," said psychologist Cheri Hartman, another Hope volunteer. "If only [politicians] understood that getting access to Medicaid would actually save money and lives!"

Tess wanted Jamie to find a long-term rehab program for her. "But we all know once her withdrawal gets bad enough she will want to be released and get her fix," Jamie said in July. "Pray that this time we can get her somewhere before that happens."

The moment an addict is willing to leave for treatment is as critical as it is fleeting, Jamie said; she called it the liminal phase. "You only have a very small amount of time; you have to strike while the iron's hot."

But Tess disappeared, again, before they could meet.

The next time Patricia saw her daughter, she was nearly naked, posing for an ad on a prostitution website under the headline SWEET SULTRY SEXY 26. The baby's father had discovered the ad through Tess's cellphone number and told his mother, who alerted Patricia to it.

A half hour for sixty bucks. There were pictures of Tess, crudely posed with her face cropped out, and a cellphone contact. "I looked at it as a way to contact her and let her know I still love her and support her. There's nothing more I can do for her" until she's ready to accept help, Patricia said.

228 • BETH MACY

She was covertly tracking Tess via instant messenger now, a holdover from months earlier, when Tess signed onto Facebook using Patricia's phone but forgot to sign out. She'd read heartbreaking exchanges between Tess, her drug dealers, and her friends, including another young woman from Hidden Valley, Jordan "Joey" Gilbert. Tess and Joey compared notes about dopesickness and black-market Subs (Suboxone or Subutex). They'd arranged to meet once to trade Xanax for crystal meth.

Joey had had earlier success with the monthly naltrexone shot, Vivitrol, which is expensive but also impossible to abuse or to divert. Among the thirty-one states that had then expanded Medicaid under Obamacare, some improved access to naltrexone, even giving Vivitrol shots to people before they left prisons and jails, since they understood that addicted users were most vulnerable to overdose death just following a period of nonuse, when tolerance is low. But Joey lost access to the shot when she turned twenty-six and was no longer on her father's insurance. "Without insurance, it would have cost us fifteen hundred dollars a month," her father, Danny Gilbert, said.

Joey eventually transitioned to buprenorphine, prescribed by Dr. David Hartman, the same Roanoke psychiatrist with the mile-long federally mandated waiting list that had stymied Tess. "Dr. Hartman would not write the prescription unless she passed her weekly drug test," Danny Gilbert said. "And I held all her medication and gave it to her daily so there was control over it," at an average price of around $700 a month.

But there were still so many hurdles Joey faced in her quest for treatment, from the waiting lists that kept her from starting rehab to the byzantine rule that she had to be drug-free upon entry, not to mention her continued drug usage with people like Tess—all of which put her perilously close to relapse and death.

In late October 2016, Jamie Waldrop and I visited Tess in the psych ward of a local hospital; she'd checked herself in, complaining of anxiety and suicidal thoughts. There was an outstanding arrest warrant out for her from a fraudulent seventy-eight-dollar credit-card charge earlier in the year. Her son was now fourteen months old, and Tess hadn't seen him in eight months.

She'd asked me to bring her a copy of my latest book, *Truevine,* which she'd read about in a *People* magazine at the psych ward. She thanked me for it and said it was OK when I asked to take notes. Her writer hero, David Sedaris, was about to publish a new book, and I promised to try to get her an autographed copy when it came out.

Tess told us she was no longer using heroin, that she now favored crack cocaine. "I thought the cocaine would help me get off heroin," she told us. "And it did, actually...but it's very mentally addictive."

Asked if it was a relief to be off the streets, Tess nodded. "When it starts getting cold out, I'm ready to come in for help." She'd been beaten by a drug dealer, she said, but didn't want to go into details. Jamie recommended an Asheville rehab that she had sent other people to, with good results, she said, but it would not accept patients on MAT or the antidepressant Cymbalta, which is sometimes not recommended for people with substance abuse disorder.

"That's the one I'm on," Tess said. But Jamie remained relentlessly upbeat throughout our visit and promised to double-check on the Cymbalta, and Tess seemed brighter and more hopeful than she had in months. The Asheville rehab featured a regimen of horticultural work during the day and intensive group therapy at night.

"It's kinda hippie-ish," Jamie said, knowing that would appeal to Tess.

"Like Warren Wilson?" Tess said, hopefully, referring to the liberal-arts college nearby.

She would not be allowed to talk to anyone back home for six months. It would drive her crazy not to see her son or hear about him, she said, "but my goal is, I want to get him back."

But the liminal window passed, as it usually did, when Tess checked herself out of the hospital before the Asheville rehab bed, or any others, could be secured. "She's back out again," her mother said. "All it takes is one contact, one blinging on the cellphone, and there they go, spiraling again."

The flood of street fentanyl had not slowed. From September to November 2016, Roanoke claimed the highest number of emergency-room overdose visits in the state, most fentanyl-driven. EMS workers reported having to give people as many as five doses of the anti-overdose drug, naloxone, to reverse its effects. One such call ended with a young mother dead in her bedroom, her baby beside her in the bed, cooing.

A week before Christmas, Patricia showed me a card she was mailing to Tess, with pictures of her son tucked inside. She'd found what she believed to be her current address from a series of Facebook exchanges between Tess and her drug dealers, some angry ("Damn man. You stole shit from me") and some matter-of-fact. She was staying in another apartment in southeast Roanoke, catty-cornered from the church where I'd first taken her to NA.

Patricia wanted to tell her about a new Beck song that began:

I met you at JC Penney
I think your nametag said "Jenny"

It was their favorite department store, the place where she bought Tess a new wardrobe every time she left a hospital or rehab stint—only to return home, months later, with just the clothes on her back.

"It scares me now when she comes home," Patricia admitted. She'd locked up her shotguns; a sport shooter, she was afraid they'd end up pawned the way her laptop did. All but two of her spoons were missing from the house, swiped for heroin mixing, she assumed. "It's like there's a demon inside her," Patricia said. "I do get mad at her, and there are times I want to say, 'I quit.' But the truth is, and I want her to know this, I'll never give up on her."

Tess had made her way home briefly at Thanksgiving and insisted on cooking for the entire family, never mind the bandage on her arm, an abscess from a dirty needle that required emergency-room care. But in spite of her efforts, Tess felt her contributions to the meal went unrecognized by her siblings, and she got high the following day on pills and alcohol Patricia had hidden in her shed.

That weekend Patricia bought matching bracelets for the two of them with the inscription "Your heart is my heart." The saying was inspired by an e. e. cummings poem Tess admired and adopted as a kind of mantra about her feelings for her son. Tess had won a national high school poetry competition in 2001; Patricia still kept her winning poem displayed in her kitchen. Over the next several months, whenever she texted me with updates, she referred to Tess as "our poet."

They made an appointment to get Tess's hair highlighted. They were supposed to pick her little boy up from his other grandmother's North Carolina house. It would be his second Christmas, and Tess was eager to see her son. They'd already bought his Christmas presents along with clothes for his Santa picture, complete with a matching sweater and pop-a-collar shirt set, bought used from Once Upon a Child.

"We had all these plans, and then suddenly the switch just goes," Patricia said.

On her way out, the week after Thanksgiving, Tess left a note on her mom's kitchen counter:

Gone to Carilion [psychiatric ward]. Mental Breakdown. I LOVE you so much Mom. You are my everything. I want to get better & I won't stop trying.

*Portrait of Bobby Baylis, held by his mother, Janine
Underwood, Roanoke, Virginia*

Chapter Eleven
Hope on a Spreadsheet

Tess's best chance for recovery, everyone thought, came down to a five-page spreadsheet. The volunteers at Roanoke's new Hope Initiative had spent months crafting it—a list of thirty-six rehab and aftercare providers in the southeastern United States they could contact to arrange treatment, depending on the patient's finances and the centers' availability of beds. A few volunteers also helped arrange outpatient MAT, but the angels were divided on its effectiveness, many believing it was wrong to treat drug addiction with another drug, despite scientific evidence to the contrary. Users could drop in at the Bradley Free Clinic on the second Monday of every month and, if police officers found no outstanding warrants against them, pair them with trained volunteers who would troubleshoot their care. Social service workers would be on hand to help those who qualified apply for Medicaid.

It was now early 2017, and fentanyl-overdose calls were coming in at a rate double that of the same period the previous year. In a region of three hundred thousand people, emergency-room doctors were now seeing drug overdoses daily—sometimes as many as three opioid-involved "gold alerts," or severe trauma cases, at a time. In a single hour that April, three such patients would turn up in the ER of Roanoke Memorial Hospital, including a taxi driver found unconscious along the side of the road and a tree trimmer who'd been dropped off by a friend after injecting himself with two fentanyl-laced shots of heroin; he'd taken a second dose because he didn't think the first one had worked. Emergency-room physician Karen Kuehl begged him not to leave the hospital after he was resuscitated: "I don't want you climbing trees today."

Once revived, the man got up, politely thanked her, and left, saying, "I've got to go to work." An older woman was expecting him to trim her trees that morning, he said, and she'd be disappointed if he didn't show.

In one weekend the following month, a local seventh-grader died of a probable overdose, the region's youngest victim so far. The wife of Janine Underwood's building manager at the clinic was getting her hair done only to be interrupted by the sound of a spectacular crash in the parking lot outside—a middle-aged professional man had passed out while driving, a heroin needle stuck in his arm, and crashed into her car.

Kuehl was studying opioid-related hospital protocols in Ontario, where overdose patients are automatically referred from emergency rooms to outpatient medication-assisted treatment and counseling. "We need to do a smooth handoff here," she said. She was helping local psychologist Cheri Hartman, one of the Hope Initiative coordinators, set up a similar transfer in Roanoke, but they were stymied by bureaucratic, financial, and legal hurdles, including a shortage of MAT providers and not enough opioid-detox and treatment beds.

Both were hopeful about a grant they were applying for to make the handoff smoother. Until then, Kuehl said, hospital social workers were referring revived overdose cases to Hope—among them an increasing number of people who were passing out while driving.

The state was concurrently working, through Carilion and other hospital networks in the state, to free up money to train peer recovery specialists who would facilitate the treatment handoff among overdose patients and others seeking treatment for both opioid-use disorder and mental illness, but the program wouldn't be operational for many months. "Right now everyone is running around in crisis mode, trying anything they can, but there's a lot of mismatched interventions, and no sense to it," one health-system insider told me.

"In the meantime," Kuehl told me, sighing, "I'm definitely getting a bigger car."

Four months later, the women were crushed to learn they did not get the grant.

Though she was still grieving her son's fentanyl-overdose death—Bobby had been dead now for fourteen months—Janine Underwood thrust herself into the Hope project with vigor. She wasn't a believer in harm-reduction strategies or MAT, but she was trying to keep an open mind. When users shot up in the parking lot at the clinic—"getting their last hurrah," she called it—police declined to take action, knowing it would inhibit users from coming.

Like most of the angels, Janine allowed participants to contact her on her personal cellphone. Texts and calls came by the scores, ranging from grieving mothers who wanted the ear of another mom who'd lost a child to a young heroin user named Matthew who'd heard about the program and just wanted to talk. He was suicidal, he said, and they spoke multiple times over the course of several days.

When Janine learned that Matthew had hanged himself the day before he was scheduled to come in, she fell apart. "Before I knew it, I was becoming a crisis center," she told me, a month into the program. "I was in over my head."

The following week, a young woman escorted to the clinic by police staggered indoors, then exhibited signs of overdose in the clinic foyer, necessitating a 911 call and several doses of naloxone to bring her back. And though Janine left follow-up messages with her, she never called or returned.

A conservative Rotarian, Janine realized that barriers to treatment were more formidable than she'd understood, as was the epidemic's scope. It wasn't just the money and limited treatment capacity that waylaid people; it was the morphine-hijacked brain, the scrambled neurotransmitters that kept people from thinking clearly or regulating their pain with nonnarcotic substances, or imagining the possibility of feeling happy again.

Janine wished for a way to force users into treatment, a detention order for the heroin-consumed brain. Bills to involuntarily commit users were increasingly being introduced in state legislatures from Kentucky to Massachusetts, but there were civil liberties concerns, and patients-rights groups and many experts believed coerced treatment backfired more often than not.

Twenty-two people walked into the Hope Initiative in the first month, and the angels felt they were making progress with some, the ones who expressed repeated interest in getting help and continued to text and call. Still, exactly zero of them had entered residential treatment, and only a handful had been able to access outpatient MAT. Janine was so mentally exhausted that her colleagues had to call EMS after she passed out from stress-related vertigo at work one Saturday.

Looking back now, the spreadsheet the angels had so carefully created seemed naive, akin to spraying citronella oil on a termite infestation and expecting your home's crumbling foundation to magically reconstruct itself.

The first Hope Initiative success came months into the program and took weeks of life-and-death negotiations—dozens of phone calls, days of hand-holding, and thousands of dollars, eventually, to arrange

residential treatment placement for a single patient. Janine had personally spent eight straight hours in the emergency room with the family
of "John" (not the person's real name), a ten-year heroin user who
had been a friend and fellow user with her son Bobby. John had tried
detoxing at home, but his parents took him to the hospital when he
became too sick, partly from needle-stick abscesses on his hands and
arms, his temperature soaring to 103.

Janine wiped the young man's dopesick sweaty brow, rubbed his
back when he writhed in pain, and comforted him when nurses
could not find a vein receptive to a medication IV. His parents sat
nearby, paralyzed in their fear and unable to help. "I want to get this
out of me," John told Janine, between screams. "It's like a demon,
and I want to get it out."

Janine had pulled strings to have John directly admitted from the
hospital into detox, a rare handoff with no waiting—only to be
slammed by the emotional wallop of visiting John the next day and
walking the same corridor where she'd once delivered clothes to her
son. "Because of his connection with Bobby, I feel like he's listening to
me, but the truth is, he could walk out any time," Janine said. By day
three of detox, John was already calling his parents and pleading over
the phone, "Dad, come pick me up."

A Hidden Valley couple, his parents were unable to direct his care or
even process what was happening to him. They'd been enabling John's
addiction for ten years, supporting him and allowing him to live in
their home. "They were completely frozen," Janine said.

John's dad, a retired law enforcement officer, told Janine he'd given
many tough-love lectures to parents on the job, but when it came to
his own son he was helpless, even denying that the constellation of
scars on his son's arms were track marks.

"They couldn't even call the detox center from the hospital; they
needed someone to do it for them," Janine said.

And: "They have the disease, too."

When it came time to discharge John from detox, a Hope volunteer working with John's father arranged for him to fly to an out-of-state treatment center, but it was up to Janine to make the transfer work. To do that, she coaxed the detox center to keep John an extra day, then arranged for an intervention between John and his family members off-site. (Detox managers would not allow the meeting to take place there, not even in their parking lot.) "I was starting to panic; I had that sick feeling in my stomach again," Janine said. The liminal window was beginning to close.

John's father hired an "interventionist," a retired cop whose job was escorting, by force if necessary, reluctant patients into treatment. Another local agency offered a conference room, and everyone involved lied to John to get him there, saying it was outpatient counseling he was signing up for on his way home, not residential care.

"I played the Bobby card," Janine admitted the next day on the phone.

And yet it had still taken four hours to persuade John to go, the volunteer angels sighing, finally, when he got on the plane.

As soon as one bureaucratic gap was stitched up—and that could take days—another rip appeared. Government help was on the way in many states, but the national treatment tapestry remained a hodgepodge, divided not only along geographical but also firm ideological lines.

In late 2016, Virginia State Health Commissioner Marissa J. Levine declared the state's opioid crisis a public health emergency, noting that three Virginians were dying every day from drug overdose and that emergency departments across the state were seeing more than two dozen overdose cases a day. Levine also issued a standing order, or blanket prescription, allowing any resident to buy the opioid antagonist naloxone (brand name Narcan), the overdose-reversing drug.

Public health officials in Vancouver were miles ahead of most of America in so-called harm reduction, a social justice movement aimed at reducing the negative consequences of drug use—without necessarily ending the use—and, more broadly, treating users with dignity and respect. The basic theory being: Users can't get sober if they're dead, and it's cheaper and more humane to give them clean syringes, say, than it is to pay for HIV and/or hepatitis C treatment. Vancouver officials launched supervised injection sites where nurses stood by to revive overdosed users, fostered the free exchange of used needles for clean ones, and distributed naloxone. Sites in Toronto and Ottawa were also approved.

Several liberal-leaning American states and cities have used Vancouver as a model, including Seattle, where officials in 2017 approved the nation's first safe-injection program for users of heroin and other illegal drugs, even though it was still illegal under federal law. In Massachusetts, where the opioid death toll now claimed five lives a day, some Bostonians carried naloxone kits, signaling their ability to administer it by placing a purple ALLY patch on their backpacks. Prevention workers were piloting fentanyl test strips so users could gauge the potency of the drugs before they used them, then take smaller doses, avoid using alone, and have naloxone at the ready in case of overdose.

In San Francisco, Seattle, Philadelphia, and even Greensboro, North Carolina, drug-user unions were working to combat the stigma of addiction and advocate for harm reduction, pushing for wider naloxone distribution and needle exchanges, and even negotiating with drug dealers when batches of fentanyl entered the local supply. "Our goal is to end the drug war and to hold treatment providers accountable," said Louise Vincent, who runs a Greensboro needle exchange paid for by state and private funds. "When you pay fifty thousand dollars for treatment and rehab, I believe you should get the gold standard of care," including MAT, she said. She also argued for stricter regulations of "cash-cow Suboxone clinics."

But there is still only one treatment bed available for every five people trying to get into rehab, and at a cost far beyond the financial reach of most heroin users. And for all the treatment money paid by people like Tess's octogenarian grandfather, rehab isn't standardized, nor does it often dovetail with what science says is the gold standard for opioid treatment: medication-assisted therapies. (Only about a third of all U.S. treatment centers allow MAT.)

"It's really going to take doctors standing up for this, and it's going to take going against the very vocal twelve-step recovery community, which is most at odds with the work the harm-reduction movement is trying to do," said Vincent, a recovering heroin user who pays $480 a month, cash, for daily methadone maintenance.

In Baltimore, where the overdose death rate was six times the national average (and where much of Roanoke's heroin supply originates), the health department has long deployed a needle-exchange RV to heroin hot spots six days a week, offering disease testing in addition to clean needles, naloxone training, wound care for injection abscesses, and prenatal care. The initiative is credited with reducing needle-injected HIV instances from 64 to 8 percent. Conservative then–Indiana governor Mike Pence responded, albeit reluctantly, to the 2015 Scott County HIV outbreak that infected 175 people with a limited needle exchange.

In San Francisco, recovering heroin user and certified addiction specialist Tracey Helton Mitchell launched her own renegade harm-reduction movement in 2003 by mailing out free packages of clean needles and naloxone vials. In the opioid-minded Reddit forum where she became known as the Heroine of Heroin, Mitchell still shared counseling and intervention strategies, answering some fifty emails a day.

She continues to receive calls from frantic users in large swatches of the country eager for clean needles, information, and naloxone. "We're in the absolute dark ages in most of this country for syringe exchange," she told me, describing users with worn needles broken off in their arms, or people who reuse needles found in the gutters and then sharpened with matchbooks. "We're years behind catching up, and the drug deaths haven't even peaked yet."

*   *   *

And yet the ideological gulf I witnessed between the criminal justice establishment and families like Tess's seemed to grow wider by the day. Kevin Coffman, a drug task force member who'd worked the Ronnie Jones case, told me he firmly believed we could end the opioid epidemic with a single stroke of Trump's pen: imprison heroin users *for life* the third time they got caught with the drug, and that would have a chilling effect on remaining users, who would logically, he believed, give up their drugs.

We were sitting in the same room where Coffman and Bill Metcalf had mapped out Jones's heroin ring. It was next to the kitchen, where a TRUMP–PENCE sticker was pasted on the refrigerator door. Not only did the detective have zero empathy for the addicted, but he also lacked any scientific understanding of the morphine molecule's pull.

Nor did some of my dear friends, longtime members of AA, who remain staunchly opposed to harm reduction and MAT for those working its twelve-step program. "There's a reason why some people think NA and AA are cults," said Mitchell, who used methadone, needle-exchange programs, and a secular support program called Life-Ring to treat her heroin addiction. "They can't take in any other information because it throws a different light on their own personal recovery."

As Trump-appointed attorney general Jeff Sessions said in March 2017: "We need to say, as Nancy Reagan said, 'Just say no.' Don't do it."

Two months later, the Trump administration proposed gutting the office of the White House drug czar, reducing its budget by $364 million, despite Trump's campaign vow to combat the nation's growing opioid epidemic, and backed health care changes that would have put the most vulnerable users at risk. After a backlash, Trump rolled back his proposal to relatively modest trims. But more than a year after his inauguration, the office still lacked a permanent director, Trump remained more focused on law enforcement than public health strategies, and a comprehensive list of recommendations written by his own presidential commission remained a work in progress or unaddressed.

*   *   *

Harm reduction remained slow to catch on in most of the Bible Belt, including Roanoke. When I told Janine about an idea hatched at an opioid brainstorming session in Boston—to segregate users on a boat in international waters, where they could legally inject under medical supervision, ideally then transitioning to counseling and MAT—she was repulsed. "That's crazy! We've created this problem, and now we decide we're just going to continue to let it happen, and that's the answer?"

And yet she was miles ahead of most leaders in her conservative community. She'd told her son's story recently to the local school board and county officials, hoping to raise money for the county's risk prevention council, which was currently running on fumes and a few small federal grants. She'd explained how she'd pulled strings to get her kids into the Hidden Valley school zone because she considered it a superior place to raise children. But the affluence she believed would protect her family had instead allowed the festering of shame and inaction. Almost daily the Hope Initiative took a call about a heroin user from Hidden Valley or nearby Cave Spring, and police data showed that the problem was worse by far in those two communities than in other, less affluent areas of the county.

"I was just a mom trying to make them aware of what's happening here, that they should be aware. But there was dead silence in the room," Janine said. "Nobody asked me a question. I just spoke, and I sat down."

The school board declined to support the program, and the county gave its usual $2,000.

Of the fifty-seven people who came seeking treatment in the Hope Initiative's initial months, the volunteers had persuaded only two people to begin residential treatment. About fifteen were referred to MAT outpatient programs—seven of whom were still in recovery a year later. Neither Tess nor her friend Joey was among the successes, though both were regularly in touch with Hope volunteers.

Tess seemed to be nowhere close to accepting help, Patricia told me, in early 2017. We sat next to each other at a drug-prevention forum put on at Tess's alma mater, Cave Spring High, as judge after cop after grieving parent talked about rising overdose calls (thirty in the first six weeks of the year), more than a doubling of Narcan administrations, and increasingly potent seizures of fentanyl-spiked heroin.

Janine told Bobby's story publicly for maybe the twelfth time. She finished by describing a recent visit to an urgent-care center with her teenage daughter, who'd sprained her thumb playing softball. After an X-ray and an exam to rule out a break, the doctor wrote her fifteen-year-old a prescription for a twenty-five-day supply of oxycodone.

"I tore it up," Janine said. She also called clinic official Dr. John Burton, who said of the incident: "This was a provider who was still doing things the way we used to do them five years ago, and he didn't get the memo." A come-to-Jesus ensued, with Burton reminding the doctor of the hospital system's ER policy of no more than three days' worth of oxycodone or hydrocodone per prescription, sans refills.

During the Q&A at the end, Patricia stood in the audience and described Tess's descent from Cave Spring honor-roll student and athlete to heroin addict and prostitute, preyed on by a growing network of drug dealers and pimps.

"I never saw it coming," she told the crowd. "And I don't know what the answer is, but I know it's important we take heroin out from under a dirty rug. We should be talking about it the same way we talk about cancer."

At the moment, Tess was back in the psych ward of a local hospital, Patricia said later. Hope volunteers Jamie and Terrence Engles were trying to coax her into a long-term rehab center in Nevada, but they were concerned, again, about the problem of the fleeting liminal phase—having a bed available the moment Tess was released from the hospital, not to mention coming up with the $12,000 she still needed for treatment, less the last bit of her college fund. She considered asking her eighty-five-year-old father for an early release of the inheritance he planned to leave for Tess, knowing the money would be no good to her dead.

Patricia had visited Tess at the hospital the night before, taking her grandson with her, and Tess beamed at the sight of her boy. It was the first time she had seen him in ten months.

But she had a methamphetamine rash on her face, and track marks extended from her biceps to her wrists. She was newly diagnosed, too, with hepatitis C, her weight down to ninety pounds. When Tess got on the hospital floor to crawl around with her son, Patricia saw abscesses on the back of her head. "She's the sickest I've ever seen her, but she has no idea how sick she is!" Patricia told me.

After the forum, Tess's onetime track coach walked up as we were talking and told Patricia he was stunned by her remarks. "She was such a good kid, I mean . . . Tess was just an awesome kid."

The latest research on substance use disorder from Harvard Medical School shows it takes the typical opioid-addicted user eight years—and four to five treatment attempts—to achieve remission for just a single year. And yet only about 10 percent of the addicted population manages to get access to care and treatment for a disease that has roughly the same incidence rate as diabetes.

But Patricia wasn't giving up on her father's generosity, and she wasn't giving up on Tess. Neither was Jamie. "We all knew that if we didn't actually have a car waiting to take her to the airport from the hospital, she'd never go," Jamie said.

Tess had lost her ID, and Patricia persuaded a kindly hospital employee who happened to be a notary public to create a new, makeshift one for her so she could get on the plane. Hope volunteer Terrence Engles, in recovery for five years, coordinated the transfer between the hospital and the cab that ferried Tess to the airport on February 26, 2017. The Nevada treatment center did not accept patients on MAT. Tess had quit Suboxone months earlier—she'd lost her Medicaid coverage when her son was removed from her care—and was mostly now using crack and heroin.

Tess would end up being the Hope Initiative's fifth person to be funneled into residential treatment, though only time would tell if the Nevada attempt would be her last. "I feel like a spectator watching a movie and just hoping and praying it ends well," Jamie said.

Patricia compared the precariousness of the situation to a balloon with a pin poised a millimeter from the edge. "It's like, dear God, please *please* do not pop this balloon," she said. "Because there is no love you can throw on them, no hug big enough that will change the power of that drug; it is just beyond imagination how controlling and destructive it is."

After an initial hiccup—Tess transferred in her second week to a smaller women's facility nearby called the We Care House, saying the first place wasn't a good fit—Patricia said she was "doing great" a month in, and would soon transition to aftercare. Her granddad had stepped in with her early inheritance, putting $12,000 toward her treatment.

Jamie Waldrop and I both sent cards of encouragement, and I included a copy of Mitchell's *Big Fix: Hope After Heroin* because it offered the clearest framework for getting sober that I had read. The author, in recovery for nearly two decades, was not opposed to MAT (even though replacement medication had not been her ultimate path), and her book was full of hopeful data like this:

If Tess could remain sober for a year, she had a 50 percent chance of relapsing. If she stayed sober five years, her chance of relapse was less than 15 percent.

At the Hope Initiative, triaging Tess now shifted to triaging her friend Joey Gilbert. The two had couch-surfed together in southeast Roanoke, trading intermittent texts about dopesickness, Xanax, and crystal meth. Joey had arrived at Hope with her mom in early 2017. She tried going cold turkey during a brief stint at the abstinence-only rescue mission program—and didn't last twenty-four hours before fleeing, telling Jamie she was too sick and couldn't handle it. "She told me, 'As long as I can use the Suboxone, I can wean myself down,'" Jamie said. Her goal was to become someone who helps other people get off drugs.

"I know I can do it," she'd tell Jamie.

"I know you can, too," Jamie said.

A beautiful young woman, with long blond hair and blue eyes like crystal orbs, Joey had graduated from Hidden Valley High in 2007, the same year as Tess. She excelled in art and music, and once had a three-year string of near-daily Goodwill shopping fueled by a personal style rule that every accessory or piece of clothing had to match the color she'd chosen that day—if her outfit was green, then her earrings, shoes, and tights had to all match, down to her rings. Joey liked to share her opinions on everything from Freddie Mercury to eye makeup to the best dance moves when making a Facebook workout video to the Prince song "When Doves Cry."

"She's the funniest person I've ever known; she's literally a ball of fire," said her best friend, Emma Hurley. A boyfriend had introduced Joey to pills in high school, then heroin shortly after that. They were part of the Hidden Valley group of early opioid users that included the late Scott Roth and Janine's son Bobby. Over the next decade, Emma would lose three close friends and ten acquaintances to opioid overdose. A friend of many of the Hidden Valley users told me he no longer asks what happened when people phone him to say that another friend has passed. "I already know," he tells them.

"Hidden Valley was where it all started with my friends," Emma said. "I just happened to say no to the harder stuff. You'd be at a party, and it was, 'Hey, try this, have a beer, pills, cocaine, anything you could use to get a little bit higher.'" She separated herself from the group when IV heroin became part of the mix, she said.

"It was just overwhelming, the ups and downs of clean Joey and relapsed Joey," Emma said, recalling that supposedly sober Joey had talked her into sharing an apartment in 2013, and swore that she no longer used heroin. "I wouldn't have let her move in with me if I had known," Emma said. "Eventually, she'd do it [heroin] right in front of me; it was tough." They parted ways over a missing six dollars, and for six months they didn't speak.

"This too shall pass," Joey had written around that time on her Facebook page. "It might pass like a kidney stone, but it will pass."

Joey was not only still using, but she had also allowed an abusive drug dealer and the dealer's girlfriend to move in with her in exchange for drugs, unbeknownst to her dad. "She was ashamed of how low she'd gotten herself in her own eyes," Jamie said. She and Cheri Hartman, a Hope volunteer, worked to find Joey a residential-treatment bed, according to the new Hope policy of volunteers working only in pairs, which allowed them to share the heartache as well as the tasks.

Several interventions later, including a visit with her at the emergency room, the women persuaded Joey, battered and with bruises around her neck, to move away from the dealer. As Jamie helped her pack up, they found some of Tess's clothes.

Cheri Hartman talked her psychiatrist husband into taking Joey on again as a Suboxone patient. (He'd once prescribed her Vivitrol, during an earlier period of sobriety, before she turned twenty-six.) Joey's divorced parents shared the cost of the prescription, visits, and lab work, and uninsured Joey applied to the hospital-run clinic for charity care.

But Joey bumped into treatment barriers in March 2017, just as Tess had with waiting lists and funding hurdles: The only inpatient facility willing to accept her at the moment was a free, faith-based program in Charlotte that did not permit the use of Suboxone or any other drugs.

To get into the rehab, Joey decided to wean herself off MAT, even though she knew the dangers. And while Jamie tried to be encouraging, privately both she and Cheri worried. "She was so motivated and wanted to do it, and we all felt like it would really be a good fit," Cheri said, even though the MAT tapering presented a catch-22.

"Her addiction was so severe, I don't think she was fighting withdrawal symptoms as much as she was fighting her mental illness demons," including bipolar depression and probably PTSD, Cheri said. In her experience, those who have serious psychiatric problems on top of their addictions and who also use multiple drugs (not just opioids) are the very hardest cases to treat, even with MAT. In an ideal world, Joey would have gone from Vivitrol, which lasts about a month, directly to rehab, with the shot providing a bridge to fight her cravings, Cheri said.

Jamie worried, too, telling Joey's dad, "I don't know what makes her think she can do it now when she couldn't do it before. We're just doing the same old thing here." Her dad pointed out that Joey had never had much tolerance for pain. "She felt she couldn't get off anything unless she was on something else, but that's what a lot of drug addicts do; it's the addictive personality," Danny Gilbert said. "I think it's asinine to tell a drug addict you've got to be clean before you can come to my facility." (In the treatment center's defense, it couldn't afford to have medical staff on hand to supervise detox and/or medications, Jamie said.)

Joey had two halves of a Suboxone pill left. She was trying to stretch them out, self-weaning in preparation for rehab. The next day, Danny Gilbert was traveling in northern Virginia with his wife when he took a frantic call from Joey. She and her boyfriend had had another fight, and she felt her resolve slipping.

"Daddy, I don't want to die!" she told him. They argued on the phone.

A few hours later, she texted her father:

I just left goodwill, can you please transfer $4 so I can get a pack of cigarettes please?

Eight minutes later he texted Joey back:

Say what you want but everyone loves you . . . we want you back!!!!
Get Cigarettes but get your life back, not more BS.

The next morning, Cheri phoned Jamie but had a hard time choking out the news: Joey had lain inside a Roanoke County house for *almost eight hours* before 911 was called. Police were investigating, but the so-called friends she was using with had cleaned up the scene, fearing prosecution, after Joey passed out. She died of an overdose of illicit methadone on March 26, 2017, the nineteenth lethal overdose in the Roanoke County suburbs so far that year. She was twenty-seven years old.

"She fought hard against the demon of addiction and God has delivered her to a place of unconditional love, laughter and no more pain," her mother wrote in her obituary. "Watch over us, Jo, and smile down on us until we can hold you in our arms again."

Two days later, the moms of the Hidden Valley fraternity of users—only a few of their sons and daughters now among the living—took their seats among the memorial service pews. Patricia wept, marveling at how much the Gilbert family loved their troubled daughter. Even with all the sorrow she'd caused them, they had tried so hard to keep her safe.

"I was thinking to myself, 'If this was Tess, how would you feel right now, family?'" She firmly believed that Tess still had the potential to recover, to become a loving mother to her son. Patricia was still showing her grandson family pictures, coaching him to say "Mama" when she pointed to Tess. But new custody issues were emerging that Patricia kept secret from Tess—and she knew that Tess could die before they were resolved. She had already chosen the spot where she would sprinkle her daughter's ashes if it came to that: at a confluence of the Cape Fear River and the ocean where they had loved walking the dogs and searching for sand dollars, not far from the family's old beach house.

*　　*　　*

Six weeks later, Patricia intercepted a Facebook message between a Las Vegas drug dealer and Tess, now communicating through her rehab roommate's phone.

She was still at the facility the next day, when Patricia fired off a letter expressing her disappointment to her daughter. "If she fails, she is on her own," she told me.

It was Mother's Day 2017. Tess wished Patricia a happy one, via text. "I love you," Tess wrote. "But this [is] bullshit all of it," especially being away from her son.

"I'm going to [find] a way home," she said.

She signed the text to her mother ominously, using her street name: Sweet T.

United States Penitentiary, Hazelton, Bruceton Mills,
West Virginia

Chapter Twelve
"Brother, Wrong or Right"

In *The Odyssey*, Homer described a drug that would "lull all pain and anger and bring forgetfulness of every sorrow." A Victorian poet said taking opium felt as if his soul was "being rubbed down with silk."

In Virginia's coalfields, a long-addicted OxyContin user spoke in hyperbolic terms about the first time she crossed paths with the molecule, back in 1998. "I thought, that's all I need from here on out. I will *live life* like this," Rosemary Hopkins, in recovery and on MAT under the care of Van Zee since 2009, told me in a counseling room at Sister Beth Davies's office.

Rosemary had a theory about the way corporations had been allowed to unleash a flood of painkillers, a notion I heard more than once as I traversed Appalachia's former factory and mining towns:

"For that strong of a drug, for it to be everywhere you looked, it was like the government was controlling it, trying to get rid of the lowlifes."

She laughed when she said it, but I could see what she was getting at. Although her hypothesis was somewhat different, it was a version of what federal prosecutor Andrew Bassford meant when, quoting President Garfield, he proposed that governments fail their citizens "not because of stupidity or faulty doctrines, but because of internal decay and rigidification."

"I used to do eighty cases in a good year, but in recent years it's been twenty-six, forty, whatever," Bassford said in April 2017. "So the amount of cases being done does not match the problem, and we have found ways to make it more difficult to do cases—more boxes that have to be checked, more things to do in the service of perfection."

When I offered that I was leaving his office after our third interview depressed—again—he said, "Well, you should be. Rehab is a lie. It's a multibillion-dollar lie."

An annual $35 billion lie—according to a *New York Times* exposé of a recovery industry it found to be unevenly regulated, rapacious, and largely abstinence-focused when multiple studies show outpatient MAT is the best way to prevent overdose deaths. "I'm afraid we don't have good data on outcomes from residential programs," said John Kelly, the Harvard researcher. While research supports users remaining in their home environments on outpatient MAT, desperate families continue to grasp for "cures" offered by companies marketing abstinence-only rehabs. "Part of it is, when you spend that much money, you think it's going to work," Cheri Hartman said. "But it is killing people for that myth to be out there—that the only true cure is abstinence."

I hoped the stories of Ronnie Jones and his victims would illuminate the ruts in both a criminal justice system that pursues a punishment-fits-all plan when the truth is much more complicated and a strained medical system that overtreats people with painkillers until the moment addiction sets in—and health care scarcity becomes the rule.

I hoped, too, that my interview with Jones would help answer Kristi Fernandez's questions about what led to her son Jesse's premature death. Was Ronnie Jones really the monster that law enforcement officials made him out to be? Had the statewide corrections behemoth that returns two thousand ex-offenders a year to Virginia's cities, counties, and towns played a role in his revolving door of failures?

I had come to interview Ronnie Jones expecting I would have two hours, no recording devices allowed. On the day of our meeting, though, the visit stretched from morning into late afternoon, with the prison handler monitoring our visit from the other side of a glass wall and inexplicably allowing us to talk for more than six hours.

I had the better part of a day to try to discern how a sleepy agricultural county nestled in the Blue Ridge Mountains, with covered bridges and lovingly preserved two-hundred-year-old log homes, had gone from having a handful of heroin users to hundreds in a few short months, and how much Ronnie Jones was to blame for it.

Understandably guarded at first, Ronnie, thirty-nine, was gentlemanly and polite throughout the visit. During the two years he'd spent there, he said, he spent his time working out, studying Arabic and Swahili, and reading the works of Guy Johnson, Eric Jerome Dickey, and Maya Angelou. On my way to the prison, I'd been listening to the audiobook of Michelle Alexander's *New Jim Crow*, I told him, the seminal book on mass incarceration that likens the War on Drugs to a system of racial control comparable to slavery and Jim Crow.

"I've read *The New Jim Crow* twice," Ronnie said. He'd also read lawyer Bryan Stevenson's majestic *Just Mercy*, a memoir about his work against the racial bias and economic inequities inherent in the criminal justice system, which included efforts on behalf of falsely accused death row inmates. "It had me crying when I read it," he said. These books we had both read challenged the tough-on-crime government narrative of the past forty years, one that fostered the shift in public spending from health and welfare programs to a massive system of incarceration, with a fivefold increase in imprisonment and corrections spending that soared from $6.9 billion in 1980 to $80 billion today.

Whereas Bill Metcalf, the ATF agent largely responsible for Jones's twenty-three-year prison sentence, took inspiration for his life's work from the image of the brain frying like an egg and Nancy Reagan's "Just Say No" slogan, Alexander and Stevenson saw fearmongering and institutional racism in mandatory minimum sentences, three-strikes sentencing laws, the abolishment of parole, and "stop and frisk" policing.

This was Ronnie's third time in prison. He already knew that one in three black men was destined to end up incarcerated, only to find himself branded as a felon and second-class citizen the moment he got out, blocked from the mainstream economy and propelled into a dystopian loop of jail, joblessness, and back to jail. He knew that drug-involved offenders, who represent half the incarcerated population, had a recidivism rate of 75 percent. His own story was a case in point.

"We can't arrest our way out of this problem," I'd heard again and again, from everyone from police chiefs to public health providers. But that sentiment seemed to apply only to the mostly white group of opioid users who were dealing or committing property crimes to stave off dopesickness—not to people like Ronnie, in prison for armed heroin distribution, or to the majority of other black and brown people arrested for selling the drugs, even though they were statistically less likely to use or to deal. (Three-quarters of federal drug offenders are black or Hispanic while 57 percent of state-imprisoned drug offenders are people of color.)

Why had blacks failed to become ensnared in opioid addiction? That question was addressed in 2014 data issued by the Centers for Disease Control and Prevention: Doctors didn't trust people of color not to abuse opioids, so they prescribed them painkillers at far lower rates than they did whites. "It's a case where racial stereotyping actually seems to be having a protective effect," marveled researcher Dr. Andrew Kolodny of Brandeis University. Put another way: By 2014, while young whites were dying of overdose at a rate three times higher than they did in 2002, the death rate for people of color was relatively unchanged.

If, as Shannon Monnat had proposed, the hollowing out of the predominantly white working class was the kindling in the heroin epidemic, and the mounds of opioid pills in America's communal medicine chest was the spark, I was beginning to wonder whether the fragile transition of ten thousand prisoners a week from state and federal prisons into U.S. communities fanned the flames of the fire.

At the same time that Ronnie and I were speaking, the city of Winchester was launching the region's first drug court just a half hour north of the heart of Ronnie's Woodstock heroin ring. It was designed not only to connect offenders to treatment, including MAT, but also to help them access free housing and taxi vouchers to get to work (a serious barrier in rural areas), the latter paid for by grants from the local Rotary Club.

While the government's response to the opioid crisis had been molasses-slow, mired in bureaucracy, funding woes, and slow-to-close treatment gaps, here was an example of volunteers stepping in to patch up the holes. Winchester was becoming a magnet for people in recovery across the state, including ex-offenders who came for treatment and ended up staying because of its multitude of halfway houses—fourteen in a city of just twenty-seven thousand people—and of newly announced jobs.

Amazon was soon to open a warehouse and distribution center in the county, and Procter and Gamble was building a Bounce fabric-softener factory twenty minutes north. The fastest-growing church in town was led by an ex-offender and opioid addict, a charismatic pastor who held Sunday services at the downtown mall—in a bar.

What if Winchester's Rotarians and drug-court champions had been around to assist Ronnie Jones when he got out of prison, instead of one probation officer responsible for keeping up with 104 ex-offenders on her rolls?

"Right away they run into issues of having a paycheck that doesn't cover rent, utilities, and food, not to mention their court fines and child-support arrears—and that's when the issues really start," said Ronnie's probation officer, who asked not to be named because she wasn't authorized to speak. "That's usually when they commit new crimes." In 2016, the Woodstock office had two probation officers tasked with doing monthly check-ins, field visits, and drug screening for 204 people, though an additional officer was scheduled to join the team.

Many ex-offenders have no driver's license and no way to get one until they pay back the thousands they owe in court fines and child-support arrears. In some states, people with drug charges are permanently barred from getting food stamps, a holdover from a 1996 federal ban. (Virginia is one of twenty-six states that have eased some restrictions on the ban.)

"Think about it: You can do without a roof, but you can't do without food," said Mark Schroeder, a repeat drug-dealing offender and recovering crack addict who successfully opened his own garage-door-hanging business in the Shenandoah Valley in 2016 after a ten-year federal prison stint. He and hundreds like him were given reduced sentences following the 2015 decision *Johnson v. United States,* a U.S. Supreme Court ruling that redefined the status of "armed career criminals."

"To feed yourself, you're either going to rob somebody, or you're going to go back to dealing or prostitution," Schroeder said. "I've been there and done it myself.

"The whole thing is designed for you to come back."

What if Ronnie's reentry had been managed not by an overburdened and apathetic system but instead by workers from Bryan Stevenson's

Equal Justice Initiative, which sends clients to felon-friendlier cities like Seattle? There, jobs and harm-reduction measures are more plentiful, and police divert low-level drug and prostitution offenders who are addicted from prosecution before they're booked, assisting with housing, case management, and employment services. Such a two-pronged approach not only addresses the need of former drug dealers to find legitimate work but also works to dry up the demand for drug dealing.

"It makes a huge difference," Stevenson told me. "If we reduced our prison population by twenty-five percent, that's twenty billion dollars we could save. And if we invested half of that in treatment, we could really increase people's likelihood of success."

In the 1970s, America decided to deal with drug addiction and dependence as a crime problem rather than a health problem, "because it was popular to find a new community of people to criminalize," Stevenson explained. "And everybody was preaching the politics of fear and anger."

As that narrative of addicts as criminals further embedded itself into the national psyche, the public became indifferent to an alternative response that could have eased treatment barriers, he said. As an example he cited Portugal, which decriminalized all drugs, including cocaine and heroin, in 2001, adding housing, food, and job assistance—and now has the lowest drug-use rate in the European Union, along with significantly lowered rates of drug-related HIV and overdose deaths. In Portugal, the resources that were once devoted to prosecuting and imprisoning drug addicts were funneled into treatment instead.

Ronnie Jones's story was tough to fit into a neat arc of redemption, but it seemed to turn on poor decision making fueled by family instability and quick-fix desires. His rap sheet began with a felony grand larceny charge the summer before his senior year of high school. He'd borrowed a car from a girlfriend, then used that car to meet up with another girl, resulting in a catfight and, ultimately, his arrest and conviction for theft. While he was on probation for that offense, he nabbed another felony for driving another car, sans license, that contained stolen goods.

Growing up, he told me, he wanted Nikes instead of Reeboks, steak instead of hot dogs and fish sticks. He wished for a closer relationship with his single mother, a hospital nursing assistant and, later, nurse. But she got along better with his easier-going little brother, Thomas, who was into music and sports and was promoted to his school's gifted program. "I'd get jealous of my brother, of his attention from my mom. I'd get mad at her and threaten all the time, 'I'll go live with my dad.'"

Ronnie was obstinate to a fault, recalled Thomas Jones III, and would talk back to teachers and to their mom. "The weird thing is, he wasn't a very bad kid; it was more of his total disregard, at times, for authority. I learned that it was best just to try to stay out of his warpath."

Now a music promoter based in Charlotte, Thomas Jones said his brother had a brilliant business mind and had helped him, when he was younger, with his advanced math homework even as he refused to do his own.

Their family was not without connections. His uncle Petey Jones was a linebacker on the 1971 state-champion team memorialized in the movie *Remember the Titans,* which was set against a backdrop of racial tensions brought on by the integration of Alexandria's high schools. In 1990, his maternal grandfather, Thomas "Pete" Jones Sr., was such a fierce fighter for equal housing that then–president George H. W. Bush met with him and other residents to discuss ways to rid Alexandria's public housing units of drugs.

Ronnie and his brother grew up in Section 8 housing in northern Virginia, moving every few years as their mom worked her way up to better jobs. A no-holds-barred fight between the brothers when Ronnie was fifteen taxed his mother's nerves to the breaking point. She sent him to live in Alexandria with his father, dropping his belongings on the curb in trash bags and telling his dad, as Ronnie recalled it: "He your responsibility now. I'm done."

Ronnie's father and uncle were regular drug users. He remembered them going down into the basement regularly to freebase powder cocaine. Six months after moving in with his dad, Ronnie moved in with his maternal grandmother, Rosie, his favorite relative. Her husband was an Air Force mechanic who took Ronnie to air shows at Andrews Air Force Base, in Maryland, and let him sit in the pilot's seat. He was fascinated with airplanes and wanted to be an Air Force pilot. It was a short but happy time in a tumultuous upbringing: His grandmother helped him get a dishwashing job at a nearby retirement home, and he sold cookie dough for a door-to-door nonprofit organization on the side, developing an acumen for sales.

His grandmother gave him anything he wanted—as long as he stayed in school. But he had already switched schools ten times before his sixteenth birthday, often butting heads with his teachers. One memorable clash with authority came during a class discussion that spiraled into a debate about who had been persecuted most: African Americans, native Americans, or Jews. The exchange grew so heated that Ronnie was asked to leave the classroom, which he did, forcefully pushing the door on his way out in a way the teacher perceived as threatening. The incident culminated in a fine and his first juvenile probation stint.

"I play those incidents over and over in my head," he said of his first few legal charges. "If I had never drove that girl's car and then [the car with the stolen goods], I could've been probably in the military now and having a regular life."

Jobs were hard to get. Because of Ronnie's felony record, his applications were turned down by Burger King, McDonald's, Walmart, and Lowe's. For a time, he worked at Food Lion in Maryland, driving an hour each way to get there. A cousin introduced him to cocaine dealing, he said, whereupon Ronnie realized that he could stock shelves for two weeks and not come close to making what he could dealing drugs in a single day. The math was irresistible.

Ronnie said he hated hard drugs and didn't want to end up like his dad. So he drank only on his birthday and New Year's Eve, and eschewed marijuana entirely. But dealing drugs gave him the two things he craved most: money and respect. He says he was profiled in early 2000 when he and a black friend were pulled over on Interstate 66 near Herndon, Virginia, and naïvely consented to being searched, ostensibly for not having a county sticker on their car. (They were driving a car with Maryland plates, he said.) Police found 3 grams of crack cocaine tucked into his sock. "I was guilty. I did have the drugs."

Bonded out of jail by his grandmother, he was arrested a short time later for selling drugs to an undercover cop, and the two state charges plus a probation violation combined for a state-prison sentence of eight and a half years. His court-appointed attorney was overworked and "just wanted to get me over with," Jones said; he didn't answer the letters Jones wrote about his case from jail. He was encouraged to accept the prosecutor's first plea deal, and to remain mum in court. This was 2001, a time when prosecutors across the country were doubling the number of felonies they filed in state courts despite declining crime rates. In his 2017 book, *Locked In*, Fordham Law School professor John F. Pfaff argues that it's politically safer and economically cheaper to charge a person with a felony, which sends them to prison—on the state's dime—than it is to incarcerate someone locally or put them on probation, paid for by local budgets.

"No matter where you turn in this epidemic," East Tennessee State University public health professor Robert Pack told me, "there are systems in place to address the problems, but none of them are working together." The biggest barrier to collaboration is the fact that everyone involved views the problem too rigidly—through the lens of how they get paid, according to Pack.

Ronnie finished high school in jail, then took computer-repair classes in the state prison system, earning a GPA of 3.6. He tutored other inmates working toward their GEDs and earned a certificate in computer-repair tech. His goal was to get a job as a certified network administrator, maybe land a government job.

His brother's career was on a high when Ronnie got out of prison in 2008. Thomas, also known by the stage name "Big Pooh," had been traveling in Asia on a contract with Atlantic Records, recording with the rap band Little Brother.

"I gave him five thousand dollars for a laptop and helped him get on his feet," Thomas told me. Ronnie was working for T-Mobile, selling cellphones for a time, but grew frustrated that he wasn't advancing in the company, a failure that he attributed to his record. He was too impatient, too clever by half. "I kept telling him, 'Man, the system is set up for you to fail. Just be happy you found some employment because most people who are felons can't,'" Thomas recalled. "Ronnie has a knack for quickly reading people and knowing how to talk to 'em and reel 'em in. I said, 'You just got to work that opportunity till you get another one.' But it wasn't fast enough for him."

Thomas was on the road in 2010 when he took another collect call from Ronnie. His brother had been locked up again, this time for credit-card fraud.

"I was like, 'Come on, we just did all this stuff trying to help you get on your feet?'" Thomas remembered, exasperated.

Thomas rapped about devotion and disappointment in a song called "Real Love," from an acclaimed solo album released in 2011:

> Brother, wrong or right
> The fact that you were incarcerated
> After being free let me know you never made it
> To that point where the old you is not outdated...
> No matter how this picture looks
> I'm still putting money on your books.
> I told you... we family.

It was the credit-card fraud charge that landed Ronnie in the diversion program at George's Chicken, and for a time following his release from it, his family believed he had turned a corner. He told his brother and mom he'd launched a computer-repair startup, which was certainly within his abilities, given the skills he'd picked up in prison programs. Thomas's own business was in a lull at the moment, so Ronnie floated the idea of starting a joint venture. He wanted Thomas's help opening a Caribbean jerk-chicken restaurant in Winchester. He didn't turn to his brother because he needed the money; Ronnie needed Thomas's help securing a liquor license, which wasn't possible for a felon.

"I didn't understand the urgency for him wanting to buy something legitimate," Thomas said. "I just kept saying, 'I don't live in Virginia, and I'm not going to have my name on nobody's liquor license and I can't be there. And anyway, who's going to come to a restaurant in this dead little small town?'"

Thomas began doubting his brother during their final visit, when Ronnie and a girlfriend drove to Charlotte to see him and his wife. "I'm like, I don't know if the computer business is this good? He had a Mercedes-Benz truck. And he had a motorcycle that he couldn't really ride, and another car back at home."

Thomas said he wondered if the girlfriend, who worked at a federal agency, owned some of the vehicles but admits that he didn't really want to know. Thomas now believes his brother was trying to phase out of drug dealing so that if and when he got arrested, there would be a legitimate revenue stream already established to help support his daughters.

Ronnie Jones has frustrated his younger brother his entire life—and that pattern of behavior included his initial refusal to cooperate with Bill Metcalf and Don Wolthuis, the ATF agent and prosecutor responsible for his conviction. Ronnie thought he deserved a ten-year sentence, so he fired his first court-appointed attorney, Sherwin Jacobs, who'd negotiated a plea deal of fifteen years with Wolthuis—a decision Ronnie regretted the moment it backfired.

Thomas was on a month-long European touring stint when a relative texted him the stomach-sinking news that Ronnie's federal sentence was in: twenty-three years. "I told him, the last to talk is always the last to walk," Thomas said.

Though he's never been in legal trouble, Thomas said he is regularly profiled, pulled over ostensibly for speeding—presumably because he's a thirtysomething black man with tattoos driving a Lexus through his middle-class Charlotte neighborhood. Though the experience is frightening, he always looks forward to the moment in the exchange when the officer runs his license, and it comes back crystal clean, with the vehicle registered to his wife, a third-generation operator of a successful bail-bonding company. "I don't have the leverage to get smart or act crazy when I get pulled over," he said. "My goal every day is to make it back to my wife in one piece so I can live to fight another day, so I'm just 'yes, sir, no, sir,' and all that."

He feels for Ronnie and other ex-offenders getting out of prison. "They don't rehabilitate you in prison, and they don't make it easy for you to get a job. I truly believe they don't make it easy because they want you back, and they want you back because that's the new factory work in so many places now—the prison.

"You have to be very strong mentally when you get out to not make those same mistakes."

Ronnie Jones said he initially felt welcomed in Woodstock. When he first landed there to work, in 2012, he found it charming that drivers waved to one another on the country roads, and his minimum-wage paycheck from George's Chicken went further than it had in the city. "It was almost a culture shocker for me. I could count on one hand the number of black people. I loved it. I actually thought I couldn't get into anything there," he told me.

He didn't even mind the early shift, he said, even though "you're standing in chicken shit, and you be dealing with 'em while they're live, and they be scared." He kept working at George's after his twenty-one-week diversion sentence was complete but lost the job several months later when he got sick and had to be hospitalized for a week.

At the time, he hoped to open a small diner with ten chairs—he'd learned to cook from his mother, and his first job at the diversion center, where he worked before going to George's, had been as a cook—but no one would rent to him. He said the same thing happened when he contacted a landlord about renting space for a computer-repair shop and was told the space was already leased. ("I got a white girl to call, and he was willing to rent to her, and I was like, 'This is bullshit.'")

At the time, he owed $5,000 in medical bills and $20,000 in court fines and restitution. Jurisdictions across the country increasingly inhibit ex-offenders' ability to reenter society by assessing hefty court fines and fees, requiring them to pay thousands or face more jail time.

Jones was hired at another chicken plant but netted only $300 to $400 a week. "I was at the second chicken plant for less than thirty days before I decided, 'I'm making too much money; let me concentrate on this,'" he said, deciding to deal drugs full-time—temporarily, he told himself—until he could pay off his fines and go legit.

In a convoluted feat of logic twisting, Ronnie justified his heroin enterprise by declaring himself the ring's wholesaler, far removed from the moment the needle touched the vein. He clings to the narrative that he was providing an actual service—offering the drug cheaper and in a much safer environment than Baltimore. Like Purdue Pharma announcing it had created the perfect time-release painkiller that was addictive in "less than 1 percent" of cases and then reproaching the hordes of addicted people who misused its drug, Ronnie had an easy time shifting the blame, with responsibility often lost in the cloudy penumbra of bureaucratic disconnects and cops-and-dealers Whac-A-Mole.

If you were a user-dealer, you would, employing Ronnie's model, buy your heroin from his subdealers for $100 a gram, which was substantially cheaper than driving to Baltimore and paying $150, plus it saved you the driving time and the risk of dealing with armed inner-city dealers (though Ronnie and some of his lieutenants were also armed).

"Herr-on was already there," he insisted, a truth confirmed in interviews with survivors of people who died of heroin overdose before Ronnie arrived in Woodstock. "I never introduced herr-on to the area. The only thing I did: I gave it to 'em at a cheaper price."

Ronnie believes he was made out to be a monster in the federal government's case against him, vehemently denying that he had sex with underage females and dopesick users—an accusation that Wolthuis said fueled him and the task force in their quest to put him behind bars for many years and possibly even for life. "I would pay for sex before I'd have sex with someone doing drugs," Ronnie said.

Jacobs, the fired first attorney, believes Ronnie on this point, even as he called him a "con man" and "a pain in the ass." Jacobs saw Ronnie as someone who dealt drugs because it "was easier than working, and you can be a big guy in your own eyes, and people follow you, and it's like you're the head of a business, which you are—until it all comes crashing down."

Female user-dealers are incentivized to lie in their quest for what the government calls substantial assistance, and they exaggerate their addictions so they'll be given less time, according to Jones and Jacobs. Keith Marshall, the dealer whose expletive "Fuck. You. Bring it." gave the case its informal name, said the women not only cooperated for less time but also played up their addictions to their advantage. When Kareem Shaw's girlfriend was arrested, "she batted her eyes and talked about how she was just an addict forced into this and used up by everybody when the reality was quite the opposite. She was selling and setting up new people to move [drugs] just like myself," Marshall told me in an email, mad that she'd gotten a lighter sentence than him and was due to be released from prison in late 2018.

Ronnie turns the case over in his mind, including his own complicity. "I promised myself I'd never grow up to be like my father, and while I may not have an addiction to an actual drug, I do feel my addiction," he said. "I'm addicted to that lifestyle. It wasn't my intention. I didn't want to do it. But no one would give me a job in the field I'd trained for, and no one would let me create my own."

He was disappointed in himself and felt bad about hurting his relatives, especially his daughters. He no longer has relationships with their mothers, one of whom told me, "Ronnie was just not mentally mature enough to be a father. His biggest thing was, he felt entitled."

Ronnie ended the interview with a version of the same old saw I'd heard at so many of my stops along the heroin highway: He predicted that "ten more dealers would pop up to take my place," which was accurate. It was hard to envision a future where shit in fact stopped.

It was a long drive back to Roanoke. I was too tired to stop in Woodstock, where I'd arranged to meet with Kristi. She was eager to learn what light Ronnie had shed on Jesse's death, but I dreaded telling her just how little he seemed to think or care about the victims of his crimes. Since our last meeting, she had arranged to view the pictures police took of Jesse lying dead on the floor. He looked surprisingly peaceful. "What I'd been imagining was actually much worse," she said. When Sergeant Lutz called them up for her on his computer screen, the task force had noted a lull in overdose deaths in the wake of the prosecution of Ronnie Jones and others in the FUBI ring. But that was also before fentanyl and other synthetic analogs came roaring onto the scene.

Kristi still went by her son's grave overlooking the football field several times a month, less often since her family moved to the other side of the county. But she still decorated it for every holiday. "I feel bad every day that I don't go," she said.

She had recently met Dennis Painter's son, the curly-haired toddler named for Jesse. His mother, Courtney, had awakened him in his car seat after she and Kristi ran into each other at the Dollar Store. "He woke up reaching for me," Kristi said, as if it were Jesse reaching out from beyond the grave. "I got in my car and cried for ten minutes."

It was almost three years since Jesse's death. His grave was now decorated with red-white-and-blue pinwheels, an American flag, and a brand-new 55 metal sculpture painted in school colors. Over the next year, Kristi would hatch plans for a memorial five-kilometer race for opioid awareness that she envisioned meandering past Jesse's old football field and the Shenandoah River. Photos of overdose victims, including another friend of Jesse's who had recently died, would be placed along the runners' path; the money raised would benefit the area's substance abuse coalition.

In one week in October 2016, nineteen people in the northern Shenandoah Valley region would overdose, seventeen of them brought back with Narcan. Baltimore dealers continued to hot-pack their heroin with fentanyl, an area naloxone trainer told me, because when someone dies, customers flock to his or her dealer, chasing a better high. "It's like, 'I might lose three of my customers, but in the long run I'll gain ten of yours,'" theorized the trainer, a mom who'd lost a son to fentanyl-laced heroin. The fentanyl-packing strategy is also sometimes employed with known snitches or suspected confidential informants, the goal being to kill them.

After a day passed, I tried to break the news gently to Kristi over the phone that Ronnie hadn't even recognized Jesse's name.

In that respect, Ronnie Jones was no different than the drug reps in their tailored suits and SUVs: He had failed to see the harm his drugs had caused.

And why should he be any different?

A few months before I sat down with Ronnie, Purdue Pharma executive J. David Haddox gave a speech urging members of the Richmond Academy of Medicine not to be swayed by the narrative taking shape around the opioid epidemic. His company was working to create new and "safer" painkillers, he said. The assembled doctors were unimpressed. What can we do, they wanted to know, when our patients need pain relief but we don't want them to become addicts? Haddox could only suggest using local pain specialists—including the friend of his who'd invited him down to deliver the speech. But there weren't enough pain specialists, and the doctors were increasingly aware of studies showing that long-term opioids in fact created more pain in many patients, a condition known as opioid-induced hyperalgesia.

Eight years after the 2007 sentencing of the company and three top executives for criminal misbranding, more lawsuits were being filed against Purdue and/or other opioid makers and distributors by the month, and they would grow to include such plaintiffs as the city of Everett, Washington; the state of Ohio; Cabell County, West Virginia; and Virginia's tiny Dickenson County, not far from Lee. Purdue had followed Big Tobacco's playbook when it downplayed the risks of its drug, and now some of America's best legal minds were trying to make it and other pharmaceutical companies pay for the "public nuisance" burdening their communities. The states of West Virginia and Kentucky had already garnered modest settlement payments from Purdue, to the tune of $10 million and $24 million, respectively, victories that brought to mind the civil litigation brought by forty-six states and six other jurisdictions against the tobacco industry in 1998. Cigarette companies then agreed to pay billions to the states, in perpetuity, for the funding of prevention and public health programs.

But painkillers aren't tobacco, and the cases differ partly because opioids have legitimate medical benefits when prescribed and used correctly, and the companies who make them use as fall guys the out-of-work coal miners and furniture makers and underchallenged youth who have illegally abused and diverted their drugs. "The cigarette companies finally caved, but only because the litigation costs were eating them alive," said legal scholar Richard Ausness at the University of Kentucky. He foresaw the possibility of such a settlement being forged with opioid makers, but to a much smaller degree. "It's a tough call because you want to punish them, but you may not want to put them out of business, because then you're largely forgoing the right to any future claims," he said. Tightening new opioid prescriptions through physician monitoring programs, then shifting the government's focus to treatment and prevention, were more effective strategies than litigation, Ausness believed.

Haddox punctuated his talk with slides touting the work Purdue was undertaking to create new, "safer" painkillers. When his thirty-minute speech was over, the general practitioners in the audience grumbled a bit. Despite Haddox's great slides and optimistic plans for new and improved opioids, the doctors were still slogging it out in the trenches. They knew they'd be the ones left holding the prescription pads when it came time to juggle their patients' pleas for pain relief and addiction treatment with their patient satisfaction ratings, still used by many insurers to gauge reimbursements.

But Haddox remained firmly on point. "What's getting lost here is the prevalence of chronic pain in this country," he said. The optics of the opioid epidemic had clearly been bad for business. While Ronnie turned gray in prison and Kristi prepared the next seasonal decorations for Jesse's grave, the Sacklers' rank among "America's Richest Families" slid from sixteenth to nineteenth on the *Forbes* list.

Powell Valley Overlook, Wise County, Virginia

Chapter Thirteen
Outcasts and Inroads

"If you want to treat an illness that has no easy cure, first of all treat it with hope."

—Psychiatrist George Vaillant, Harvard Medical School

I n 1925, the psychiatrist Lawrence Kolb Sr. published a set of groundbreaking articles arguing that addiction afflicted only people who were born with personality defects. He distinguished between "normal" users, who had been prescribed opiates by their doctors, and users who were "vicious" (a word deriving from "vice"), who had become addicted via illicit channels. The latter were much worse than the former, he initially believed, and this notion led him to categorize the addicted person as a criminal rather than a patient deserving of treatment and care.

In the mid to late 1930s, Kolb oversaw the opening of two U.S. Narcotics Farms, in Lexington, Kentucky, and Fort Worth, Texas, part of the federal government's so-called New Deal for the Drug Addict. In bucolic rural settings, the government provided treatment both to the addicted who had arrived by court mandate and those who had volunteered, along with job training and medical care. Meanwhile, the government scientists were allowed to conduct research on the farms' captive populations.

Kolb changed his beliefs about addiction after his colleagues proved to him that "normal" people, including the 10 to 15 percent of patients who were health care professionals, could become addicted, too, if they were opioid-exposed.

The work at the Narcotics Farm labs led to the field of addiction medicine. Both farms closed in the mid-1970s—due to an ethics scandal over experimentation on the addicted who were improperly exploited as research subjects. But their legacy includes the establishment of the National Institute on Drug Abuse and the scientific notion that addiction is a chronic, relapse-ridden disease.

Today, courts largely continue to send the addicted to prisons when reliable treatment is difficult to secure, and many drug courts controlled by elected prosecutors still refuse to allow MAT, even though every significant scientific study supports its use.

Not every patient wants or needs maintenance drugs, because every human experiences addiction differently, and what works for one might not work for another. Still, it is crucial to preserve treatments for people with addiction and help them obtain the means needed to get off drugs, rather than simply treat them as criminals who have no right to health care.

If my own child were turning tricks on the streets, enslaved not only by the drug but also criminal dealers and pimps, I would want her to have the benefit of maintenance drugs, even if she sometimes misused them or otherwise figured out how to glean a subtle high from the experience. If my child's fear of dopesickness was so outsized that she refused even MAT, I would want her to have access to clean needles that prevented her from getting HIV and/or hepatitis C and potentially spreading them to others.

As the science historian Nancy D. Campbell, who documented Kolb's work, has written: "Perhaps the day will come when more sensible views prevail—that relapse is the norm; that drug addiction should be treated as a chronic, relapsing problem that affects the public health; and that meeting people's basic needs will dampen their enthusiasm for drugs."

But there is so much more work to be done.

Why, in less than two decades, had the epidemic been allowed to fester and to gain such force? Why would it take until 2016 for the CDC to announce voluntary prescribing guidelines, strongly suggesting that doctors severely limit the use of opioids for chronic pain—recommendations that echoed, almost to the word, what Barbara Van Rooyan begged the FDA to enact a decade before? Why did the American Medical Association wait two decades before endorsing the removal of "pain as the fifth vital sign" from its standards of care? If three-fourths of all opioid prescriptions still go unused, becoming targets for medicine-chest thievery, why do surgeons still prescribe so many of the things?

While it is true that doctor junkets funded by Big Pharma are no longer the norm, and physicians no longer ask reps to sponsor their kids' birthday parties, more than half of all patients taking OxyContin are still on dosages higher than the CDC suggests—and many patients in legitimate pain stabilized by the drugs believe the pendulum has swung too far the other way.

A journalist and former colleague of mine was so worried about the epidemic's chilling effect on painkillers that she emailed me an X-ray of her back, showing a sixty-four-degree curve in her lumbar spine—from the front, it resembled a question mark—and slipped disks that caused severe arthritis pain. Painkillers had allowed her to work and actively pursue gardening, cooking, and beekeeping, and they precluded risky and potentially debilitating surgery.

And yet her scoliosis specialist had recently discontinued her pain management "without any notice and with no discussion during appointments to come up with a pain management strategy" because the new CDC guideline "frightened him into abandoning his patients," she said. (For her arthritis, she takes the synthetic opioid Tramadol; for neuropathy, she takes the seizure medication gabapentin, which is increasingly sought on the black market for its sedative effects.) "My life is not less important than that of an addict," my friend wrote, in bold letters, explaining that her new practitioner requires her to submit to pill counts, lower-dose prescriptions, and more frequent visits for refills, which increase her out-of-pocket expense.

"The system taking shape treats me like an addict, like a morally dubious person who must be treated with the utmost suspicion," she said.

The CDC guideline had become so controversial among pain patients that the two employees charged with drafting it received death threats.

To follow the physician's imperative of "Do no harm" in a landscape dominated by Big Pharma and its marketing priorities, the medical community only recently organized behind renewed efforts to limit opioid prescribing, teach new doctors about the nuances of managing pain, and treat the addicted left in the epidemic's wake. The number of residency programs in the field of addiction medicine has grown in recent years from a dozen to eighteen.

"We live in an era where for a century now the pharmaceutical industry has invested enormous capital investments in new drugs, and there's no turning back that clock," said Caroline Jean Acker, an addiction historian. "So, as a society, we're going to have to learn to live with possibly dangerous or at least risky new drugs—because Big Pharma's going to keep churning them out."

*   *   *

The birthplace of the modern opioid epidemic—central Appalachia—deserves the final word in this story. It is, after all, the place where I witnessed the holiest jumble of unmet needs, where I shadowed yet more angels, in the form of worn-out EMTs and preachers, probation officers and nurse-practitioners. Whether they were attending fiery public hearings to advocate for more public spending, serving suppers to the addicted in church basements, or driving creaky RVs-turned-mobile-clinics around hairpin curves, they were acting in accordance with the scripture that nurse-practitioner Teresa Gardner Tyson had embroidered on the back of her white coat:

Verily I say unto you, inasmuch as ye have done it unto one of the least of these my brethren, ye have done it unto me. (Matthew 25:40)

One three-day weekend every summer in far southwest Virginia, Tyson plays host to the nation's largest free medical outreach event. Held at the Wise County Fairgrounds, Remote Area Medical serves the uninsured, from children with undiagnosed diabetes to adults on walkers with infected teeth, some caused by lack of dental coverage and others by years of meth use. It's where I crossed paths with people like Craig Adams, a construction worker and recovering opioid addict, who brought his wife, Crystal, to RAM so they could both get their teeth fixed: They'd used so many tubes of temporary dental repair glue, he told me, they'd lost count. Craig had spent eight years in the state prison system for breaking into Randy's Gateway Pharmacy in nearby Richlands, trying to steal OxyContin. But he was taking Suboxone now—"responsibly," he told me, "because my wife wouldn't have it any other way." Having lost scores of people to opioid overdose, including his mom and grandmother, he hadn't used illicit drugs in more than three years. "I had put off going to RAM for years because I figured they'd make you feel like shit about yourself, like ninety percent of the social service people do," he said. "But everyone was just...so...kind."

If there's an argument to be made for a single-payer health care system with mental health and substance abuse coverage, this is the lumpy ground on which to make it, a gravel lot in which upward of three thousand Appalachians camp out for days in 100-degree heat to be treated in exam rooms cobbled together from bedsheets and clothespins. Behind a banner for the VIRGINIA-KENTUCKY DISTRICT FAIR & HORSE SHOW, patients wait in bleachers while volunteers pass out bottles of water as they triage them to pop-up clinics for medical, dental, and eye care.

I interviewed Tyson several times in the spring and summer of 2017, before and after the July RAM event that her organization helps plan and host. In the weeks leading up to it, she liaised with media from as far away as Holland and made frantic phone calls, once when her assistant struck out trying to secure enough bottled water for the RAM crowds. A nonprofit they usually counted on said this year's pallets were already reserved for natural-disaster relief. "If this isn't a disaster, I don't know what is!" Tyson said, managing to sound both desperate and upbeat.

In rural America, where overdose rates are still 50 percent higher than in urban areas, the Third World disaster imagery is apt, although the state of health of RAM patients was actually far worse. "In Central America, they're eating beans and rice and walking everywhere," a volunteer doctor told the *New York Times* reporter sent to cover the event. "They're not drinking Mountain Dew and eating candy. They're not having an epidemic of obesity and diabetes and lung cancer."

I had made a similar comparison two years before, when Art Van Zee drove me through the coal camps on my first visit to Lee County, just west of Wise. Though I'd covered immigration in rural Mexico and the cholera epidemic in northern Haiti, I told him, never before had I witnessed desolation at this scale, less than four hours from my house. Most of America would be shocked by the caved-in structures, with their cracked windows and Confederate flags, and burned-out houses that nobody bothered to board up or tear down. It felt completely out of scale with the rest of the nation I knew. But these conditions were hardly limited to St. Charles or Wise County, Van Zee pointed out. "On the other side of the cities [many Americans] live in, there's poverty and poor health probably just as bad," he said.

In Appalachia, he conceded, poverty and poor health were not only harder to camouflage; they were increasingly harder to recover from. For decades, black poverty had been concentrated in urban zones, a by-product of earlier inner-city deindustrialization, racial segregation, and urban renewal projects of the 1950s and 1960s that decimated black neighborhoods and made them natural markets for heroin and cocaine.

Whites had historically been more likely to live in spread-out settings that were less marred by social problems, but in much of rural America that was clearly no longer the case. These were the same counties where Donald Trump performed best in the 2016 election—the places with the most economic distress and the highest rates of drug, alcohol, and suicide mortality.

The national media's collective jaw-dropping at the enormity of needs displayed at the RAM event underscored the fact that the outside world had zero clue. As the Appalachian writer and health care administrator Wendy Welch noted: "We're not victims here, except for when it comes to Purdue Pharma. But when one of us makes a mistake, it tends to be a fatal one."

I found hope in the stories of Tyson's staff and patients as I set out, in multiple visits, to discern what happened after the volunteer doctors departed for their urban enclaves, and the politicians and pundits went home. I felt hope as I witnessed Tyson, a bubbly, every-curl-in-place blonde, manage her workaday free clinic as she seamlessly steered her rattling 2001 Winnebago through southwest Virginia's serpentine roads, juggling phone calls from nurses, patients, and the media alike—in high-heeled, rhinestone-studded sandals. With her sorghum-thick accent, Tyson was camera-ready and thoroughly put together each time we met, except once, when mascara smudged her doctor's coat.

I would find out soon enough why she'd been crying for days, and it wasn't because the battery on her Winnebago had just conked out. (The nonprofit's marketing manager was dispatched with the battery booster to give us a jump, while Tyson's husband offered real-time jump-starting counsel via FaceTime.)

It was a fitting state of affairs for what happens after the out-of-state RAM do-gooders depart and Tyson's grant-funded Health Wagon staff of twenty is left to tend to the health needs of the region's uninsured. The program is called the Health Wagon because it was founded in 1980 by a Catholic nun and medical missionary named Sister Bernie Kenny, now retired, who first provided care out of the back of her red Volkswagen Beetle.

At our first stop, Tyson treated the swollen wrist of a substitute teacher whose pay had just been reduced from $70 to $56 a day. She was a casualty of school district depopulation and austerity, measures that included closing two schools in the town of Appalachia, one of which was now a food bank. In St. Paul, where our RV was presently stalled, the middle-school roof had become so tattered that buzzards had descended on it a few months earlier to eat the rotting tiles. With no money for repairs, school administrators resorted to temporary measures to divert the vultures, erecting giant inflatable tube men, the silly beacons you see waving from car dealerships.

The fifty-four-year-old teacher hadn't had insurance in decades, not since she was pregnant and qualified for Medicaid; her husband, a former Walmart worker disabled by a series of strokes, was on Medicare. Because Virginia hadn't approved the Affordable Care Act Medicaid expansion, she patched together free coverage at RAM events and occasional visits to Tyson's mobile unit when it came to town. She had to be practically dying before she went to see her family doctor, who accepted cash at a discount rate of $63 per visit.

* * *

In a state with an increasingly flimsy safety net, people like Tyson had been left to clean up the politicians' mess. As the health care debate over repeated attempts to repeal the ACA raged in Washington and opioid activists waited for President Trump to declare the epidemic an official national emergency—to free up immediate federal disaster relief funds for cities and states—between patients Tyson followed the machinations on her phone, fuming as she scrolled.

A devoutly religious wife and mother from nearby Coeburn, she was finding it hard to remain optimistic. In our first interview, she'd been distraught over the recent death of a forty-two-year-old patient caused by untreated hepatitis C. Though he hadn't used or injected drugs for eight years, he could not afford to see a specialist. And by the time treatment could be arranged, "the damage was already done, and he couldn't overcome it," said his father, who owns a twenty-seven-acre cemetery.

The man buried his son near his office so he could visit him daily, he said. He invited me to tour the Wise County graveyard, where he offered to point out the scores of people he'd personally buried thanks to "OxyCoffin," as the pills are now known here.

Months later, Tyson found herself crushed by a repeat in the continuing tragedy: In spite of 24/7 news cycles and a dense web of interconnectedness, here was one more death that gained no media traction and inspired zero public action. She could give all the interviews she wanted during the month of RAM, but the truth was that the extent of the suffering here garnered very little attention outside the spectacle of the annual health care event.

Unremarked on were the slow-simmering and increasingly common stories of people for whom no treatment could be secured. This time Tyson was crying about Reggie Stanley, forty-five, who died in a Charlottesville hospital while awaiting a liver transplant, after twelve years of untreated hepatitis C. "This patient was such a good person. He did make the wrong decisions initially," Tyson said of Stanley's IV drug use, but he'd been sober for several years. She'd tried desperately to get him into treatment, but like 90 percent of her patients, he was uninsured, and Tyson could not persuade a gastroenterologist to take him on as charity care. (She has since had success dispensing free medication provided by the company that makes Harvoni, the expensive hepatitis-curing drug.) By the time Stanley made it to a liver-transplant list, his disease was too advanced.

"You can fix it upstream, when it's affordable, or you can wait till they present back in the ER with stage-four cancer or cirrhosis, and they still need extended hospital stays," Tyson said. "It's a drain on the system no matter what, so why can't we fix it upstream?"

Tyson kept looking at Stanley's obituary on her phone, which included a photo of him beaming in his Clintwood High graduation gown. "He was a great guitar player, great singer, and a good soul who was loved by many," one of the guest-book mourners wrote.

The region's health-department director, Dr. Sue Cantrell—the same one who'd warned state supervisors about the epidemic two decades before, only to have her pleas dismissed as "a regional problem"—was slowly making inroads. With the Scott County, Indiana, HIV epidemic still in mind, Cantrell had been holding town-hall meetings in the coalfield counties throughout the summer of 2017 to sound the alarm. Though Virginia had recently passed legislation paving the way for syringe exchange programs, every legislator in the coalfields had voted against the bill, citing widespread local law enforcement concerns, even though crime historically has not risen in communities with access to clean needles. Across the border in West Virginia, a 2015 syringe exchange had resulted in lowered overdose deaths and five-times-greater access to treatment and disease prevention services. Cantrell was hoping to arrange a visit from a West Virginia police chief to talk to local authorities, and her staff was already teaching users to clean their syringes between injections, giving out Clorox packets and plastic cups. She sometimes offered free food to entice patients both to be tested and to return for their results.

The RAM clinic offered free hepatitis C testing for the first time—a pharmacy professor estimated that 75 percent of IV drug users in the region have contracted it "and have no idea"—and handed out take-home naloxone kits with training to almost four hundred people. "In a rural area like this, just trying to get people to their appointments is huge," Cantrell told me. Two patients in the MAT clinic she runs in nearby Lee County, Virginia, either hitchhike or walk to their appointments, some from a distance of more than five miles.

She'd floated the idea of turning some of the area's subsidized housing units into "clean living facilities," with wraparound services and support group offerings, not unlike substance-free college dorms. "We need to support this as a chronic disease the same as we support cancer and other diseases," Cantrell said. "Not just evidence-based treatment and drug prevention programs but broadening it to meaningful education that leads to jobs with a living wage so there are options to stay in the area—or to leave."

At the Narcotics Farm in Lexington, Kentucky, researchers had once referred to the latter as "the geographic cure."

The idea of moving away from the site of addiction's onset appealed to younger people who grew up among addicted family members as well as to the recovering addicts themselves, and it had worked for some, like many of the returning Vietnam soldiers. But opioids are much more available today than they were then—summonable by text or via online cryptomarkets, aka the dark web—and vastly more potent.

"The biggest lesson of the science behind drug addiction is that alternate reinforcers are essential," Nancy D. Campbell, the Narcotics Farm historian, told me. "If you want to keep people away from drugs and drug-related crime, you have to have rewarding activities. It's work. It's play. It's an emphasis on the kinds of activities and relationships that people build their lives around. If we don't do something to rebuild these communities, I don't see this current drug configuration ebbing in the way that drug waves of the past historically have."

The question echoed louder by the day in rural America: How do you inspire hope in a middle-school boy whose goal in life is to become a "draw-er," like his parents before him and their parents before them? Did a president who bragged about winning a swing state—telling the president of Mexico, "I won New Hampshire because New Hampshire is a drug-infested den"—win because voters genuinely thought he could fix it, or because too many people were too numbed out to vote?

Voters should judge politicians at all levels on the literal health of their communities, lawyer Bryan Stevenson explained. And while most Americans support federal financing of health care and even a slim majority approves of single-payer, those reforms will likely remain political nonstarters until more voters begin defining themselves in contrast to the billionaire class holding sway in Washington. Also needed are more efforts to court nonwhite voters, including Hispanics (of whom 74 percent are currently registered to vote), African Americans (69 percent), and Asian Americans (57 percent).

"You've got too many leaders just not responding to problems," Stevenson said. "Think about with HIV, with smoking, with Zika, you had this energetic leadership from people who were saying, 'We're going to win this.' The mind-set of 'This is unacceptable' has to be brought into the way we think about addiction and the opioid epidemic. But part of the problem now is, we're so hopeless...that we don't try very hard."

America's approach to its opioid problem is to rely on Battle of Dunkirk strategies—leaving the fight to well-meaning citizens, in their fishing vessels and private boats—when what's really needed to win the war is a full-on Normandy Invasion.

Rather than puritanical platitudes, we need a *new* New Deal for the Drug Addicted. But the recent response has been led not by visionaries but by campaigners spewing rally-style bunk about border walls and "Just Say No," and the appointment of an attorney general who believes the failed War on Drugs should be amped up, not scaled back. Asked in August 2017 why he hadn't taken his own commission's recommendation to label the epidemic a national emergency, President Trump dodged the question. He said he believed the best way to keep people from getting addicted or overdosing was by "talking to youth and telling them: No good, really bad for you in every way." A few days later, he seemed to change his mind, saying he *would* make the emergency official, even as he remained tethered to a law-and-order approach.

But months later, he still had not followed through. When the so-called emergency was retrumpeted in an October 2017 press conference, Trump sounded bold and even hopeful, but his ballyhoo fell short of an official declaration, and included no additional treatment funding. At the time, seven Americans were dying of overdose every hour.

To be fair, the crisis had been cruelly ignored by both sides of the political aisle. The Obama administration had also been slow to address the crisis and tepid when it did. Caroline Jean Acker, the historian who is also a harm-reduction activist, told me she was scolded during a 2014 NIDA meeting for championing needle exchange and naloxone distribution after a speaker attempted to separate "good" addicts, or people who became medically addicted, from the illicit, or "bad," users—as if there were no fluidity between the two. "The worst thing for politicians, I was told, was for them to appear they were being soft on drugs. Even under Obama, federal [Substance Abuse and Mental Health Services Administration] employees were told not to use the term 'harm reduction,'" she said, sighing.

No matter where I turned in central Appalachia, the biggest barriers to treatment remained cultural. Stigma pervaded the hills and hollows, repeating itself like an old-time ballad, each chorus featuring a slightly different riff.

At the RAM event in Wise, a kerfuffle erupted when a local judge volunteering at the event accused a pharmacist of giving Narcan training to a local Boy Scout troop without their parents' permission; she claimed the kids would party harder knowing they had Narcan to revive them. "Just ridiculous," one trainer told me.

But across the region, where it seemed every family had at least one soul crusher of a story, it would take more than one fairground debate to convince people that harm reduction was necessary to save lives, even as the region had the worst hepatitis C rate in the state. One-third of children in central Appalachia now lived with a nonparent adult, and 96 percent of the adopted kids weren't orphaned—they'd been removed from their drug-addicted parents by social service workers.

At another Health Wagon event, a man overdosed on meth in the parking lot while his friends took off, running up the mountain, according to the responding EMT, who recognized a familiar unconscious face. "Repeats," as Giles Sartin refers to many of his overdose calls, saying: "It's rare you'll get somebody who's just now getting hold of it." Sartin, twenty-one, has been an EMT since the tenth grade. He made the decision to train the day he was sitting in a freshman English class and heard the double thump of two classmates seated behind him hitting the floor.

They'd overdosed on OxyContin during a lesson on grammar and punctuation.

"Last week I Narcanned the same person for the fourth time," Sartin said. When the man woke up, he punched Sartin's EMT partner and broke his nose. He'd been speedballing painkillers with meth, which makes users paranoid and gives them "ridiculous strength." It was such a problem that Sartin's rescue squad had to adopt a new protocol: Even though people could die, they waited now for police to arrive before they went inside the patients' homes.

"There's communities where we're like an ice cream truck," Sartin said of the ambulance. "They'll try to steal our needles, our gloves, everything," especially in the Lee County hamlets of Keokee and St. Charles.

When I explained that my book began with OxyContin abuse in Lee County in the late nineties, Sartin cut me off with a warning: "Ma'am, there are spots in St. Charles where I would advise you not to be there at night. If they catch ya and don't know ya, well...I don't know."

Tyson had revised the Health Wagon's safety procedures, too. Whereas in Lebanon she tends to set her RV up outside a Food City grocery, or near the town square in St. Paul, she has learned to avoid residential neighborhoods in smaller communities. In the former coal camp of Clinchco, a close call had persuaded her to switch locales from a neighborhood to the police station parking lot.

Some neighbors had rushed to her RV, screaming and banging on the door for help. "We get to their trailer, and in the living room we get ready to work on the first person we see on the floor, but that wasn't even who they were talking about," Tyson recalled. The real patient was in the rear room, they were told, but her body was already growing cold. Meanwhile, others in the trailer were screaming at Health Wagon staffers "to get the f—outta here!"

"I still stand by what we did, trying to revive her, but the dynamics here are changing, and you can no longer just go blindly in," said Tyson, who was genuinely afraid during the exchange.

Even law enforcement tightened up procedures. In June 2017, the DEA recommended that first responders wear safety goggles, masks, and even hazmat suits to avoid skin contact with fentanyl and other powerful synthetics after reports of officers having to be Narcanned when they inadvertently brushed up against them on calls.

But these guidelines came way too late for caregivers in the coal-fields: Tyson's life-and-death scare in Clinchco took place more than a decade earlier—in 2006.

As a Lebanon prevention leader put it in a recent town-hall meeting called Taking Our Communities Back: "We are pioneers when it comes to this drug epidemic. We can tell people what will happen in their other communities in twenty years because it's already happened here to us. We are the canaries in the coalfields."

If it sounds like alarmist antidrug hyperbole—a version of Nixon's speech identifying drug abuse as "public enemy number one"—it's not. University of Pittsburgh public health dean Don Burke recently published a study forecasting the epidemic's spread. Charting drug-overdose deaths going back to 1979, he added a new wrinkle to the work of Anne Case and Angus Deaton, the economists who pointed out the soaring "deaths of despair" among midlife white Americans.

Drug-overdose deaths had doubled every eight years over that time: Three hundred thousand Americans had died of overdose in the past fifteen years, and lacking dramatic interventions, the same number would die *in just the next five*.

"The numbers by themselves are disturbing, but more disturbing is the pattern—a continuous, exponential, upward-sloping graph," Burke told me in 2017. A year before, more than a hundred Americans a day were dying from opioid overdose. Some epidemiologists were predicting the toll would spike to 250 a day as synthetic opioids became more pervasive.

Opioids are now on pace to kill as many Americans in a decade as HIV/AIDS has since it began, with leveling-off projections tenuously predicted in a nebulous, far-off future: sometime after 2020. In past epidemics, as the public perception of risk increased, experimentation declined, and awareness worked its way into the psyche of young people, who came to understand: "Don't mess with this shit, not even a little bit," as another public health professor put it. But that message has not yet infiltrated the public conscience.

What about the more than 2.6 million Americans who are already addicted? Will the nation simply write them off as expendable "lowlifes," as Van Zee's patient still believed?

"My hope is that there is an end in sight," Burke told me. "Some natural limit, or some policy where we deflect the curve downward." But even in states where downturns have intermittently appeared—

such as in Florida, following the crackdown on pill mills—"eventually those places snapped back to that curve, and we don't know why," he said.

In the carefully couched words of an academic, Burke suggested that the War on Drugs should be overhauled, with input gathered from other countries, including Portugal, that have decriminalized drugs and diverted public monies from incarceration to treatment and job creation.

He wondered whether drug cartels were the economy's new invisible hand—a modern-day Adam Smith creeping around America's suburbs, cities, and small towns, proffering stamped bags of dope. The economist had assumed the free-market economy would operate efficiently as long as everyone was able to work for his or her own self-interest, but he had not foreseen the elevation of rent-seeking behavior: the outsized greed of pharmaceutical companies and factory-closing CEOs, and the creation of a class of people who were unable to work.

In 2017, two decades after OxyContin erupted in Lee County, Virginia's Board of Medicine ordered that, to prevent doctor-shopping, all doctors were to check the drug-monitoring system every time they issued a prescription. This mandate arrived at the same time new CDC figures showed that residents of two rural Virginia towns had been prescribed more opioids per person than any other place in the country. (The top locality was Martinsville, and the fourth was Galax, the small cities where my book *Factory Man* was largely set.)

As far behind as Virginia had been in its initial response, state health-department officials were now working hard to expand MAT as well as to crack down on its abuse. The expansion was mostly modeled after a Suboxone clinic in rural Lebanon, called Highpower, where a younger version of Art Van Zee, Dr. Hughes Melton, set up practice in 2000 because he wanted to treat the underserved. Melton was helping direct the state's response to the opioid crisis; among his initiatives was a new statewide push for syringe exchange and some tighter controls on MAT prescribing. His wife, Sarah Melton, a pharmacy professor and naloxone trainer, hadn't just given training sessions to more than four thousand doctors about the perils of opioids; she'd turned in a fair number for overprescribing them, too.

The Meltons were so busy that often the only times I could interview them were at night or when they were in their cars. It was in their Highpower clinic that several patients had first explained the diversion and abuse of buprenorphine to me—a practice harm-reduction proponents elsewhere in the country dismissed every time I brought it up.

Finding a balance between treating and perpetuating addiction had been pursued in the United States since the 1800s, when doctors used morphine to wean patients from laudanum, then later used heroin to get patients off morphine. Soldier's disease had sparked a period of stern prohibition in the Harrison Act and, eventually, the War on Drugs. "Our wacky culture can't seem to do anything in a nuanced way," explained Dr. Marc Fishman, a Johns Hopkins researcher and MAT provider.

While Fishman believed buprenorphine, methadone, and naltrexone were all imperfect solutions, they remain, scientifically speaking, the best death-prevention tools in the box. "I apologize for my white-coated, nerdy scientist colleagues who have not invented better yet, I get it!" he said. The naysayers would be more open to MAT if its proponents would more openly acknowledge the drawbacks of maintenance drugs—significant relapse rates when patients stop treatment, for instance—instead of portraying them as a kind of perfect chemical fix, Fishman argued.

The explosive costs of addiction-related illness will eventually force health systems to integrate addiction treatment into general health care, he predicted, including a smoother transition of overdose patients from hospital ERs to outpatient MAT. "Too often, we're still giving them Narcan, then sending them along with a tired old Xerox of AA meeting phone numbers, and telling them, 'Have a nice life.'"

In a treatment landscape long dominated by twelve-step philosophy, only a slim minority of opioid addicts achieve long-term sobriety without the help of MAT, Fishman reminded me. "AA is not a scalable solution in an epidemic like this, and most opioid addicts just can't do it" without MAT, he said.

In the Appalachian Bible Belt, a blend of MAT and twelve-step programs seemed to work best, which is why Art Van Zee and Sister Beth Davies still communicate daily about their patients, the nun letting the doctor know, for instance, when a shared patient suffers a personal setback, like a death in the family or a job loss. It had happened in the spring of 2017 with one of their longtime patients, Susan (not her real name), whose brother died of overdose. Then, a few months later, Sister Beth emailed me that it had happened again: Another of Susan's brothers died of overdose, the youngest, whom she'd "practically raised. The loss is tremendous."

Among Susan's ten siblings, only three had managed not to become opioid-addicted, although one of the three was a pill dealer who didn't himself use, Susan had told me. She'd been in Van Zee's Suboxone program for six years and was now transitioning off disability via a program called Ticket to Work. She was putting in twelve-hour shifts as a nursing-home licensed practical nurse and going to the local community college to earn her registered-nurse degree.

"Some of my family's like, 'Why don't you just keep your [disability] check and stay home?'

"And I'm like, 'I've always wanted to go to school to be a nurse, and I can't make it on seven hundred and forty dollars a month, and besides, you just feel so much better about yourself when you work.'"

Asked how the epidemic had changed her community, Susan sighed and told me it was now just an ingrained part of the culture. Her fifteen-year-old son believes the only way to avoid its perils is to move away. "I can't live here, Mom," he told her. "There's nothing here but drugs and nursing homes."

The first time Susan saw Van Zee, he spent two hours with her, learning her medical history, including the details of her addiction and childhood abuse. She'd recently had surgery for lung cancer, and he did not make her feel like crap for continuing to smoke (though he suggested she stop).

The members of her twelve-step support group—the one led by Sister Beth—like to joke: "When you go to Van Zee's office, you might as well take a pillow and a blanket and a book, because you're going to wait there a long time." They worry, though, about what they will do if something happens to the seventy-year-old doctor and the eighty-three-year-old nun. "There's so many of us who would just be—lost," Susan said.

Van Zee was still working sixteen-hour days, much to Sue Ella's chagrin. He was still conferring daily with Sister Beth over their growing roster of opioid-use-disorder patients (now the preferred term)—not counting the 150 people on his waiting list—either on the phone or via email multiple times a day.

Van Zee told me his greatest fear now was of being hit by an intoxicated driver while he jogged the winding roads—not because he feared his own death but because where, then, would his patients go?

Nationwide, attitudes about the drug-addicted were shifting, faster in urban settings than rural. At the edge of Boston's South End, in a neighborhood some derisively called Methadone Mile, I stood in the low light of a homeless shelter clinic where users converged on a former conference room to be medically monitored as they rode out their heroin highs, often staggering in, propped between friends. In the facility's public restrooms, a clever maintenance worker had rigged reverse-motion detectors that sounded visual and audible alarms to summon help if a person hadn't moved for four minutes. The initiatives were the brainchild of the shelter's medical director, who had sometimes tripped over bodies on her way to work, some of them having been fatally struck by cars. Dr. Jessie Gaeta's goal in opening

Supportive Place for Observation and Treatment inside the shelter was to keep users alive until they were ready to be funneled into treatment, as well as to separate them from those in the homeless community already in recovery (almost a third of the shelter's clients have opioid-use disorder).

But the brownstone-filled neighborhood was rapidly gentrifying, and the cultural obstacles, even in liberal Boston, were significant. Neighbors were worried that SPOT would just attract more heroin users, dirty needles, and crime. Many accused Gaeta and her staff of enabling continued drug use.

The project got the neighbors' reluctant blessing, but only after Gaeta invited community leaders and officials to the shelter and showed them what would happen in the small, ten-recliner room.

Over the course of more than fifty neighborhood meetings, "I got my ass kicked, basically," she said.

But many skeptics were won over when they realized she was treating the problems that were already happening outside *indoors*. In a program that didn't even keep patients' names on file (a strategy called low threshold, to build trust), staffers monitored those who stumbled in on heroin combined with an increasing multiplicity of other drugs.

The SPOT room was the first place where skittish rape victims would let Gaeta administer proactive treatments for sexually transmitted illness as they tentatively told her their stories in an adjoining kitchenette. Only then would they allow her to stanch the bleeding brought on by forced sodomy with a gun or by duct tape ripped from their mouths.

"Even in a mission-based organization, there's still so much stigma around how we should treat addiction," Gaeta said. "You have to constantly fight this notion that we shouldn't wrap our arms around people who don't want treatment."

Everywhere in America, it was painstaking to walk skeptics through the social, criminal, and medical benefits of helping the least of their brethren, but worth it—even if you had to get your ass kicked.

*   *   *

In Appalachia, harm reduction was very slowly making inroads. In Lebanon, Virginia, where anti-MAT drug-court workers had once been castigated by harm-reduction proponents, Judge Michael Moore's hair had turned from salt-and-pepper to white in the year since I'd first interviewed him.

But the top Russell County prosecutor had recently signed off on allowing the drug court's first Vivitrol participant, a thirty-year pill addict who admitted she could not stop abusing buprenorphine. Moore praised the prosecutor's decision and viewed it as a harbinger of greater sensitivity in the criminal justice system to the realities of addiction. Half the probationers from his regular circuit-court docket were now on Suboxone, and "we do see good things with it," he said. If his own kids were addicted, he told me, he, too, would want the option of MAT.

"Last fall the governor declared opioids an epidemic and I was like, 'Are you kidding me? We've had the epidemic since 2002!'" Moore said. One of his present drug-court participants, in fact, was born dependent on the drugs.

"It's really discouraging and scary because what kid, sixteen or seventeen, doesn't know that opiates are addictive? They can see it in their family, so how can they not know, and yet they take them anyway. And there are parents out here just like me, or better, who have drug-addicted kids."

The local schools had recently adopted new prevention models, after studies showed kids were more likely to use drugs after DARE. (One advocate told me she remembered her classmates sharpening the DON'T off their DARE pencils so they actually read DO DRUGS.) A new school policy diverted first-time juvenile offenders into treatment instead of expulsion or jail.

On Thursday nights, Judge Moore helps serve dinners to participants in a twelve-step program at a local church. He also persuades his friends in the community—from fast-food managers to local contractors—to hire his drug-court participants.

At a recent jury orientation, Moore's bailiff was approached by two boys, ages four and five. Neil Smith thought they were the grand-children of a potential juror, but it turned out they were only tem-porarily with him as foster children, and they were looking for a permanent parent—a fact that became clear when the boys took one look at his bailiff's uniform and asked him, "Will you be our daddy?"

Smith is on the far end of middle-aged, a kindly-looking sort. Both his parents worked in the mines, and they grew a twelve-acre plot of tobacco on the side near the hamlet of Cleveland. His first memory of the judge was from when they were both kids: He remembered an adolescent Michael Moore getting on the same Russell County school bus that he rode, his face obscured by an armload of books, his bright future laid out before him.

One of the truest things I heard in my reporting came from David Avruch, a Baltimore therapist who works with a largely homeless, heroin-addicted clientele. In his experience, the base problem wasn't a dearth of harm reduction but an economic structure that created more foster kids and fewer Michael Moores.

"The more we talk about the epidemic as an individual disease phe-nomenon or a moral failing, the easier it is to obfuscate and ignore the social and economic conditions that predispose certain individuals to addiction," Avruch said. The fix isn't more Suboxone or lectures on morality but rather a reinvigorated democracy that provides a pathway for meaningful work, with a living wage, for everybody.

Judge Moore asked me, three times in one sitting, what I had learned from my reporting that he could feel hopeful about. He chuckled as he said, "I can't wait to read your book, because then maybe we'll know what to do"—but he seemed closer to tears than laughter.

I told him what Sue Ella Kobak had said, more times than I could count: "The answer is always community." I told him about Teresa

Tyson's Health Wagon and Sue Cantrell's commitment to stopping the spread of hepatitis C. The elusive gap between law enforcement and health care seemed as if it were finally beginning to close, I explained, even in a few remote Appalachian towns.

I described a faith-based treatment center in nearby Bristol that had just turned a donated former nursing home into a rehab with 240 beds. Geared to housing addicted people, veterans, aging-out foster kids, and ex-offenders getting out of jail, it had been brought to fruition by Bristol Recovery Center director Bob Garrett, who had spent three years forging collaborations with local courts, police, churches, and social service agencies. Participants would eventually pay to live in the center, nestled in a peaceful wooded compound, after they found jobs with the center's help.

At first, Garrett told me, he wasn't going to allow participants to be on MAT, but he changed his mind after serving on a community coalition spearheaded by East Tennessee State University public health professor Robert Pack. Since then, he's preached the benefits of "evidence-based treatment" to churches across the state at dinners and presentations on addiction. "We want to show [the addicted] that they're loved and cared about," he told me. "And we're trying to teach the lay folk, 'They're not really bad people,' and 'That's a sin' doesn't really work."

I told Judge Moore, finally, that Pack's coalition—an alliance of mental health and substance abuse administrators who call themselves the working group—had just scored another coup. Of all the upstart recovery programs I had surveyed in my reporting, this collaboration represented the strongest model for thwarting governmental rigidity and bureaucratic indifference to the crisis, and it had the potential to be replicated elsewhere.

In a rural town between Johnson City and Kingsport, Tennessee, the alliance was about to open a treatment clinic called Overmountain Recovery. It was deliberately named: Overmountain, for the disparate group of local farmers and frontiersmen, called the Overmountain

Men, who beat back the British in the Battle of Kings Mountain, turning the tide in the Revolutionary War; and Recovery, because the treatment is meant to go beyond MAT to include group and individual counseling, yoga, and other alternative therapies, plus job-training support. Though the outpatient clinic would eventually offer Suboxone, it would predominantly be a methadone clinic, because methadone is cheaper and harder to divert (participants drink the liquid daily in front of a nurse), and the nearest methadone facility in the region was over a mountain some sixty miles away.

"We would not have pulled this off without the working group," said Pack, who began his addiction research after losing a dear friend to opioid-related suicide in 2006. With the backing of his university, the region's nonprofit hospital corporation, and the state's mental health agency, Overmountain was the latest project of Pack's working group, which had secured $2.5 million in grants, eight funded projects, twenty-five research proposals, and the opening of a Center for Prescription Drug Abuse geared toward research. And, maybe even more important, it was co-led by Dr. Steve Loyd, a charismatic physician with local roots who had been opioid-addicted himself.

Located in Gray, Tennessee, a solidly middle-class community of farmers and suburbanites, with Daniel Boone High School just a mile and a half away, Overmountain fought a mighty resistance on its march to opening its doors, in September 2017. Headed by a respected area farmer, Citizens to Maintain Gray worried that patients taking methadone would be too high to drive safely. And, while the members of the group weren't exactly against the idea of the center, they didn't want it anywhere near them, even as some admitted privately to Loyd and Pack, "My son is dealing with this." But the working group showed up and heard them out. They brought in outside police chiefs and methadone providers, giving decision makers examples and studies from other communities that overrode their safety concerns. To win near-unanimous approval from the city zoning board and the state, they willingly endured more than a year of public ass kicking. In a

In a community of just 1,222 residents, more than 300 people had spoken out publicly against the project, some referring to Pack and Loyd as drug lords.

In recovery for more than a decade, Loyd knew exactly how to explain himself to people in his hometown, to make them see the struggle anew: Before seeking treatment, he had doctor-shopped his own colleagues, stolen from relatives' medicine cabinets, and even faked an ankle injury so he could have orthopedic surgery and get discharged with painkillers. His father called him out on his addiction in 2004 and forced him to get help, funneling him into ninety days of inpatient rehab, followed by five years of random drug screens, support services, and intensive monitoring.

A key component of Loyd's success was the threat of punishment; his medical license could be yanked if he relapsed and/or made a critical medical error while treating a patient. He still checks in daily for the possibility of a random drug screen, via an app on his cellphone, even though he's now Tennessee's assistant commissioner for Substance Abuse Services. The daily routines of his life as a recovering addict and physician keep him committed to recovery, just as the scar on his left ankle reminds him how desperately low the drug-addicted can go.

Though Loyd's treatment was too expensive to be replicated to scale—he paid $40,000 cash up front (limited coverage is now available to those with insurance, but it would cost almost twice that today)—he believes the five-year treatment model, common for addicted doctors and airline pilots, is ideal. It's why they tend to have opioid-recovery rates as high as 70 to 90 percent.

"There's nothing scientific at all about twenty-eight days of [residential] treatment," Loyd said of the kind heralded in movies and on reality TV. "It takes the frontal lobe, the insight and judgment part that's been shut down by continued drug use, at least ninety days just to start to come back online and sometimes two years to be fully functioning."

But most users don't have access to ninety days of treatment, much less two years. Only one in ten addicted Americans gets any treatment at all for his or her substance use disorder—which is why there's such a push for outpatient MAT and, increasingly, programs that divert the addicted from jail to treatment.

While drug courts rightly provide not only intensive monitoring but also the threat of a swift jail sentence, Loyd believes that all people in recovery, especially those who relapse, should be allowed MAT, even if they have to sue to get it. "The judges who don't allow it are in violation of the Americans with Disabilities Act. They just are!" he said. Denying opioid-addicted participants medicine they have legitimately been prescribed is akin to denying diabetics their insulin on the grounds that they're fat.

If 90 percent of people with diabetes were unable to access medical treatment, there would be rioting in the streets.

Loyd made his MAT argument repeatedly as he tried to sell the idea of Overmountain to the doubters in Gray, ten minutes down the road from his Boones Creek hometown. The crowd was tougher than he anticipated.

To intimidate him, they filmed him as he spoke. They yelled, "Put it in *your* neighborhood!" and placed condemning signs in the hands of their ten-year-old children as they marched.

At one meeting, Loyd tried to explain the science behind addiction—that it was a chronic brain disease, and relapses were to be expected—when a woman in the audience interrupted to ask, "Just how many chances are we supposed to give somebody?"

He tried to appeal to the group's humanity, as Gaeta had done in Boston, pointing out that addiction *already was* in their neighborhood. Simply turning their heads away out of fear or sanctimonious denial was equivalent to enabling the spread of overdose deaths—quite possibly, even, in their own families.

From the community center where he stood, in the heart of the Bible Belt, Steve Loyd could make out four church steeples. He had played ball and gone to Sunday school with many of the people in the room.

There were leaders here and elsewhere who agreed with the woman, he knew, including an Ohio sheriff who'd recently proposed taking naloxone away from his deputies, claiming that repeated overdose reversals were "sucking the taxpayers dry."

Loyd thought immediately of the answer Jesus gave when his disciple asked him to enumerate the concept of forgiveness. Should it be granted seven times, Peter wanted to know, or should a sinner be forgiven as many as seventy times?

In the shadow of the church steeples, Loyd let Jesus answer the woman's question: "Seventy times seven," he said.

If the federal government wouldn't step in to save Appalachia, if it steadfastly refused to elevate methods of treatment, research, and harm reduction over punishment and jail, Appalachia would have to save itself.

Epilogue
Soldier's Disease

Back in my adopted hometown of Roanoke, where I'd been following families for going on six years, the addicted people I came to know were in widely ranging states of wellness, some far more fragile than others. Their relatives were worn out. Many seemed to age before my eyes, like a video on fast-forward.

The day his mother arrived to pick him up from the Petersburg, Virginia, penitentiary in February 2017, Spencer Mumpower was exuberant when he spotted her walking toward him. "I want to run to you, but I still have these prison clothes on, and I'm afraid they'll shoot me!" he shouted, only half joking.

"That's OK," Ginger hollered back. "I'll run to you." There was almost no weekend since Spencer began his prison sentence, in 2012, when she hadn't visited him in federal prison and/or put money on his commissary account, almost no month in which she had not tried to coax prosecutors, lawyers, politicians, probation officers, and even judges to grant her only son an early release.

That August, exactly a year after my prison interview with Ronnie Jones, Ginger left her Roanoke jewelry store, located on the fringes of Hidden Valley, and drove to a North Carolina halfway house to pick up Spencer, who had been living there for six months since his prison release. He was free to finally leave his confinement, all exquisitely toned 165 pounds of him, with a body that could deadlift five hundred pounds, in sets of five reps.

Sober for seven years, Spencer had replaced his heroin and methamphetamine addiction with martial arts even before he'd left for federal prison. The jujitsu practice had sustained him throughout his incarceration—even when his girlfriend dumped him and when his former martial-arts teacher and onetime father figure was arrested and jailed for taking indecent liberties with a teenage female student.

Spencer stuck to his recovery and to his prison workouts, ignoring the copious drugs that had been smuggled inside, and he read voraciously about mixed martial arts. Using the Bureau of Prisons' limited email system, he had Ginger copy articles about various MMA fighters—laboriously pasting in one block of text at a time—so he could memorize pro tips and workout strategies and, eventually, through her, reach out directly to fighters and studio owners for advice.

If all goes well, Spencer will be taking the geographic cure when he moves to another Virginia city, which he doesn't care to name, to work for one such studio—once his probation officer signs off. While he was enjoying his new freedom, the reality of life after prison was also settling in. Prison had given him post-traumatic stress disorder, he told me, and his transition to the outside world was proving to be far harder than he'd imagined. Sleeping in a room without the lights on or anyone else nearby made him nervous, as did driving a car. Ginger drove him to the gym most days, or he took an Uber, which didn't exist in

Roanoke when he left for prison in 2012. To help with his PTSD, he planned to get a service dog.

Scott Roth's mom, Robin, still texted me regularly with pictures of sunflowers, along with images of Vanilla Rice pretending to cook with a sword, and another jokey one of him donning her fur coat the Christmas before he died. She texted a picture of an eighth-grade Scott, blond and bespectacled and wearing a classy black tux to his Catholic-school dance. He'd insisted she buy him a dozen roses for the dance, not just for his date but also for the girls who didn't have one, she wrote; a trail of sunflower emojis decorated her note.

Still engulfed in her grief, Robin Roth had been mourning her son's death now for eight years, and she was occasionally asked by his old friends for help getting into treatment, which she happily extended. She wanted me to convey both the depth of her grief and the ways in which she believed she had failed her son: "I wish I would have built him a stronger support system. I thought I could do it all as a single mom. I made a mistake. Find at least four adults your young adult can trust and turn to. Know their names and let them know that you are counting on them to help you assist your child to make good choices.

"Whatever rules you make, you better stick to them. Your son or daughter depends on it. They will call your bluff on everything. Don't you budge. Changing the rules only confuses a young, developing mind."

Two years earlier, Robin had moved into an apartment, downsizing from the suburban split-level where she'd raised her only child. It had been hard to leave the Hidden Valley home: the place where she'd removed all the bathroom doors, thinking that might keep Scott from shooting up; the yard where she'd grown the massive sunflower field after his death.

Occasionally, stray sunflowers still sprout up in the yard of her former home—eight feet tall, some of them, with a dozen or more blooms. They are not just memorials to Scott Roth but also to the epidemic's intractability. The young woman who bought Robin's house had not only been addicted to heroin herself (she's been sober now for more than four years), but her sister, twenty-seven-year-old Joey Gilbert, is the one who relapsed and died in March 2017, despite the Hope Initiative angels' herculean efforts to help her. Had Joey had access to Medicaid health insurance and a clear path forward for continuing her MAT, her family firmly believes, she'd be alive today.

In the early fall of 2017, I sat down again with the Hope Initiative director, Janine Underwood, Bobby's mom, who grew more despairing by the day. All the overdoses and all the deaths—none of it seemed to inspire more awareness of the tragedy or its toll on families, many of whom were still cowering in shame.

Bobby's old friends continued showing up to Hope every week. Some had been using for almost a decade, and "they are so, so very tired of the way they're living," Janine said, and yet they were so equally afraid to give it up.

One friend, a thirty-year-old man, had broken down when he realized Janine was Bobby's mom. Though his mother had driven him to the Hope clinic from the suburban ranch-house-turned-meth-lab where he now lived, she was so ashamed that she waited outside in her car.

Betsy (not her real name), a young woman who had once babysat for Bobby's sister, showed up recently at Hope, too, determined to get sober. But by the time Janine and Hope volunteer Nancy Hans went to her home to help arrange a transfer to detox, Betsy was nodding out. During a brief coherent moment, she pulled out her Hidden Valley High yearbook, pointing to a homecoming-dance picture of herself and her friends: Three of the five were now active heroin users, she said, her voice slurring as she spoke.

Then, abruptly, she pointed to the window. "Look, it's raining," she said. "That's Bobby looking down on us."

Nancy and Janine made dozens of phone calls to get Betsy into the community services board-run detox. Janine even drove her to the facility, but it wasn't yet providing buprenorphine for detox, and Betsy left after just twelve hours, saying she couldn't take the pain of being dopesick.

By the time the women lined up a facility that would allow her to be on MAT, Betsy had fled to New York, partly to avoid an upcoming court date for drug charges. A few days later, she overdosed on fentanyl-laced heroin in Central Park, where EMS workers revived her and let her go. The last Janine heard from Betsy, she had taken off for New Jersey, where she was now presumably trading sex for drugs.

Unlike the Tennessee Tri-Cities collaboration that had birthed Overmountain, Roanoke had not created a working group to transcend bureaucratic logjams, but perhaps in time it would. Nonfatal overdoses in 2017 had more than doubled the previous year's count, and fatal overdoses had nearly tripled (and those figures were likely an undercount).

At a sparsely attended public forum at Tess's alma mater, police recounted the August 2017 seizure of 4.4 pounds of fentanyl along I-81—enough for 1 million fatal overdoses. They'd also recently arrested a Cave Spring High graduate attempting to sell 700 "Xanax bars" at the local community college that contained fentanyl he'd mail-ordered via the dark web from Hong Kong.

Ronnie Jones was right again: Shit had not stopped at all, but with continued regional-media cutbacks—the *Roanoke Times* was down to just a single Roanoke Valley police reporter, and there were now sprawling heroin-ring prosecutions that received zero media attention—the public was left to believe that it had.

Warren Bickel, the world-class addiction researcher, had just nabbed a $1 million grant for his Virginia Tech Carilion Research Institute to pilot new MAT protocols for the streamlining of ER-to-outpatient transfers: Patients who overdosed would be directly connected to outpatient buprenorphine via a newly FDA-approved once-monthly injection called Sublocade. Bickel had recently lost a family friend to overdose. The young man had been taking Suboxone, but when he tested positive for additional opioids during a follow-up visit, his doctor cut his Suboxone dosage back as punishment. "What he needed was an increased dose, not less," Bickel said. When I told Bickel that Tess was still living homeless on the streets of Las Vegas, paying for illicit drugs with sex work, he called up a study he'd coauthored in 1988, showing that buprenorphine definitively protects the addicted from overdose death and leads to reduced crime and better health. "Holy mackerel, this is such an old study, but people still aren't aware," he said.

The community services board in Roanoke had recently added MAT treatment for twenty-one patients, but only if they first engaged in counseling. Carilion still had a three-week wait for its outpatient MAT. When I floated the idea at a Carilion-sponsored forum that every doctor who'd accepted a Purdue Pharma freebie should feel morally compelled to become waivered to prescribe Suboxone as a way to beef up treatment capacity, the response among the doctors in the room was...crickets.

As Philadelphia edged closer to launching the nation's first supervised safe-injection facility, efforts to start a syringe-exchange program in Roanoke remained sluggish and mired in politics—even as the rural health department director Dr. Sue Cantrell finally won permission to open one in Wise, in the most conservative part of the state. The Virginia General Assembly seemed on the verge of passing a Medicaid expansion, finally, but with a provision that the "able-bodied" be required to work.

The changes weren't trickling down fast enough for Tess. When I told her mom about the limited MAT expansions in the fall of 2017, paid for via state and federal grants, she called the community services board office and was told that only pregnant women were being accepted at the time. Soon after, Tess messaged me at 4 a.m. from someone else's phone, saying she planned to enter another Nevada rehab and asking if I'd send her more books when she got there.

I texted back that I already had the new David Sedaris book ready to send.

"Oh, awesome!" she said, thanking me for my "positivity" and support. She didn't have an address where she could receive the book, but she would let me know when she checked herself into a rehab. Her elderly grandfather had agreed to fund another round of treatment, even though Tess had recently talked him into wiring her $500, allegedly to pay a friend to drive her back to Roanoke. "He knew he was being played, but he loves her so much, and he was probably thinking, 'What if she's hungry?'" said Patricia, who learned about her dad's cash transfer after the fact. Though the ploy was likely another con for drug money, Patricia was buoyed by Tess's having reached out to her family and me, and updating her Facebook page with pictures of her son. Unknown to us at the time, Tess had applied for Medicaid in Nevada, which expanded access in 2014 under the ACA—another indication that she was actively seeking treatment and MAT.

"The problem is, we don't even know where she is" or, worse, what pimp and/or drug dealer she was now beholden to. In a November 2017 phone call, Tess was hopped up on crystal meth, Patricia believed, and paranoid that "gang stalkers" were trying to kill her. As she walked down the streets of Las Vegas, she thought people in passing cars were flashing their lights at her. She thought strangers were shouting her son's name.

"All Tess has to do is tell us where she is, and the treatment people will come and pick her up."

Of the 132 addicted users who had come to the Hope Initiative in its first year, fewer than ten had gone to residential treatment and stayed sober.

But Patricia still slept with her cellphone every night, waiting and praying that Tess would one day be among them.

*   *   *

In early December, Tess seemed better, judging from sporadic text messages and calls to her mom. She'd decided to make her way home to Roanoke, though her plans for the journey were vague. Patricia lined up a bed at an abstinence-only treatment center fifteen minutes from her home, Tess's grandfather agreed to cover the flight and rehab, and Patricia spent a week navigating the Department of Motor Vehicles bureaucracy to get Tess a temporary ID that would allow her to board an airplane.

But where to send the ID? Tess was still homeless, and another week passed before she called Patricia with an address via a borrowed phone, possibly belonging to a current or former pimp. "Are you in danger?" her mom asked, and Tess claimed she was not, repeating a line she often said: "I'm a soldier, Mom. I'll be fine."

"Yes, love," Patricia responded. "But sometimes even soldiers fall."

On December 9, Tess may have used that same borrowed phone to respond to one of my Facebook posts, about an early reading I'd given in a Richmond bookstore from the prologue of this book. "Yay," she wrote. "I helped make it!"

I told her, via instant messenger, that her mother and I were eager to see her. She asked if she could read an advance copy of this book, I said she could, and later she texted that she really wanted to "work on it." It was unclear whether she was referring generally to her recovery or to the trip back to Roanoke for her fourth rehab attempt.

Tess was walking the Las Vegas streets at night, I would later learn, often picking up johns, sometimes sleeping in corners of a casino. Her last known residence was an abandoned minivan in a parking lot. During one winter freeze, she turned up at a friend's house wrapped in a blanket. "Some nights I've talked to her, and she'd just be up walking all night," said Mark Sharp, who befriended Tess in rehab in the spring. "She missed her son a lot. She wanted her mom. She said she was all right, but I was like, 'No, you're not.'"

A construction laborer and former heroin user now working in Portsmouth, Virginia, Sharp said he offered to fly out and drive her back in a rental car, but Tess told him not to worry; her mother was making arrangements to fly her home.

"For a drug addict trying to be clean, Vegas is really no place to be," Sharp said. Tess was aware of Las Vegas gangs, but she wasn't mixed up in them, to Sharp's knowledge. "She wasn't afraid to go into the wrong part of town, though," he added. "She really weren't scared of nothing."

Tess gave Sharp the same line she gave her mother: She was a soldier, not to worry, she would make it home.

In the days leading up to Christmas, Tess sent her mother scattered texts with mixed messages, telling her she loved her, thanking her for looking after her son and her beloved dog, Koda. She'd be home soon, she insisted, though she had yet to pick up her ID.

"Our poet has been begging for money, saying she is sick but no trip to ER," Patricia texted me on December 22.

The next day, Tess wrote to say she'd just gotten on Suboxone, to prevent her from becoming dopesick during her trip. But she still hadn't picked up her ID.

"I am thankful for my dad and have peace of mind knowing that when she is ready I can make something happen quickly," Patricia said, the day before Christmas Eve. "It is for the angels to watch over her."

The morning after Christmas, Patricia got the call. Las Vegas police had traced Tess's identity through her fingerprints and her tattoos—the Tree of Life on her shoulder and another on her side that said "God forgive me my sins."

On Christmas Eve, in the Dumpster of a central Las Vegas apartment complex, a homeless man foraging for cans discovered Tess. She was naked, inside a plastic bag, and there were partial burns on her body and the bag, as if whoever murdered her had tried to erase the evidence of her death. The cause of death was blunt head trauma.

The story made national news, and Patricia, determined that people should understand both the disease of addiction and her daughter's incredible strength, spoke to every reporter who contacted her. The attention made some family members uncomfortable.

I saw a family riven by Tess's death as it had been throughout the last five years of her life, some members second-guessing each other's actions and still debating enabling versus helping and the meaning of tough love. "As my son is fond of saying, 'Whenever Tessy was presented with choices, she was expert at making the very worst choice,'" said her father, Alan, enumerating the many times that he and Tess's siblings had tried to help, paying for rent, rehab, or food. But those efforts were primarily in the earlier years of Tess's addiction.

By the time Tess left for Nevada, as she wrote in her journal around that time, "I was stealing, robbing, selling my body, and anything else I could do to make money for drugs. I was beaten, raped, robbed, and malnourished. I ended up in the hospital with my mom's help where I detoxed and got on medication and where I am writing this now. I am going to die if I keep living the way I am."

She was dead now, her grieving family a perfect microcosm of the nation's response to the opioid epidemic: well-meaning but as divided as it was helpless, and utterly worn out.

Police were investigating, but Alan Henry theorized that Tess "had gotten crosswise with somebody she owed something to," possibly a drug dealer or a pimp—an argument Patricia rejected outright as blaming and unjust "when we have no idea of what happened to her."

A former counselor of Tess's who works with addicted and sex-trafficked women in Las Vegas said it was entirely possible that Tess had in fact been a victim of gang stalking. Addicted women who do sex work are sometimes threatened with rape or murder if they refuse to join a gang trying to "turn them out," or coerce them into prostituting themselves on the gang's behalf.

Another rehab worker who knew Tess and had herself been a heroin-addicted sex worker from 2003 to 2010 told me that four of her prostitute friends had been murdered by gangs and left in Dumpsters and, in one case, the air-conditioning ducts of a motel. "These gangs will stalk you and hurt you and block you from making money," said Kathleen Quirk, who does street-level counseling with addicted prostitutes in Las Vegas, offering cookies she bakes in her home as a way to forge an initial bond. "They make your life miserable until you do what they say—or you end up dead."

The scenarios were almost beyond comprehension for those at home closest to Tess.

Her grandfather, a retired auditor for IBM, was struggling to grasp the violent nature of Tess's death. As Patricia relayed the details in the booth of a steakhouse chain, where they stopped after making arrangements for Tess's cremation, his eyes welled with tears and he said, "Oh . . . That means somebody hit her."

Tess finally made her flight home the night of December 30. It was unseasonably cold in Virginia, the winds howling and furious. The snow flurries reminded Patricia of all the cold nights she'd spent worrying about Tess. She was still sleeping with her cellphone, awaiting Tess's transport to Roanoke. Just after midnight, she texted me:

Her body has arrived.

It took funeral-home technicians two days to make Tess presentable enough for Patricia to view her body. Her head had been shaved in Las Vegas, for the collection of evidence, and Tess's older sister had picked out an outfit from one of Tess's favorite shops, including an embroidered vest, leggings, and a bright silk-cashmere headscarf with a boisterous, smiling Frida Kahlo.

In a windowless nook of a downtown Roanoke funeral parlor, not far from where Tess once roamed the streets, Patricia caressed the back of the scarf, as if cupping a baby's head, and told her poet goodbye.

It was January 2, Tess's birthday. She would have been twenty-nine.

Patricia tucked the treasures of her daughter's life inside the vest—a picture of her boy and one of his cotton onesies that was Tess's favorite, some strands of Koda's hair, and a sand dollar.

Acknowledgments

This book stands on the shoulders of several important works about the opioid crisis that came before it: Barry Meier's *Pain Killer,* Sam Quinones's *Dreamland,* Anna Lembke's *Drug Dealer, MD,* and Tracey Helton Mitchell's *Big Fix.* My take on the epidemic as I witnessed it landing in the western half of Virginia began with reporting I did in 2012 for the *Roanoke Times,* and I remain grateful to my former newspaper for giving me the time and guidance to see the epidemic unfolding before me, particularly editors Carole Tarrant and Brian Kelley. Longtime reporter Laurence Hammack not only unearthed the devastation caused by rampant overprescribing in Virginia's coalfields as early as 2000, he was also the first in the nation to write about the heroics of Dr. Art Van Zee, Sue Ella Kobak, and Sister Beth Davies, whose insights were invaluable to me throughout my reporting.

My agent, Peter McGuigan, helped frame my initial reporting into the idea for this book, and Vanessa Mobley, my editor at Little, Brown, shaped my further reporting with razor-sharp analysis and offered masterful guidance on structure and theme while never letting me forget that, above all, it was America's grieving families who were being left to figure a way out of this mess. John Parsley gave critical early advice to cast my reporting net wide and to be patient.

If I ran my own journalism action-figure factory (#LifeGoals), I would fashion caped likenesses of my most intrepid and generous journalist pals: Martha Bebinger, Andrea Pitzer, Carole Tarrant, and Brian

Alexander, along with my photojournalist collaborator of many years, Josh Meltzer, who shot the portraits for this book.

I'm thankful, too, for the generous legal, medical, journalistic, and historical insights offered in multiple conversations with Dr. Anna Lembke, Dr. Molly O'Dell, Dr. Steve Huff, Dr. Art Van Zee, Sister Beth Davies, Robert Pack, Dr. Steve Loyd, Sarah Melton, Dr. Sue Cantrell, Dr. Hughes Melton, Dr. Jody Hershey, Dr. Karl VanDevender, Teresa Gardner Tyson, Tammy Bise, Don Wolthuis, Andrew Bassford, Nancy D. Campbell, Elizabeth Jamison, John Kelly, Caroline Jean Acker, Sergeant Chad Seeberg, Agent Bill Metcalf, Sergeant Brent Lutz, Lieutenant Richard Stallard, Christine Madeleine Lee, Heath Lee, Dean King, Andy Anguiano, Barbara Van Rooyan, Cheri Hartman, Nancy Hans, Janine Underwood, Jamie Waldrop, Wendy Welch, Bryan Stevenson, Danny Gilbert, Thomas Jones III, Drenna Banks, Dr. Karen Kuehl, Dr. Lisa Andruscavage, Kim Ramsey, Dr. Jennifer Wells, Ed Bisch, Lee Nuss, Barry Meier, Laura Hadden, Lisa Wilkins, Marianne Skolek Perez, Isaac Van Patten, Chris Perkins, Jeremiah Lindemann, Richard Ausness, Vinnie Dabney, Laura Kirk, Warren Bickel, Aaron Glantz, Rob Freis, Judge Michael Moore, Missy Carter, Emmitt Yeary, Shannon Monnat, Nikki King, Sue Ella Kobak, Dr. Martha Wunsch, Destiny Baker, Kristi Fernandez, Ginger Mumpower, Robin Roth, David Avruch, and with the patients (named and unnamed) of Dr. Art Van Zee, Dr. Hughes Melton, Sister Beth Davies, and Ron Salzbach. For the insights they shared from behind prison walls, I offer heartfelt thanks to Ronnie Jones, Ashlyn Kessler, and Keith Marshall.

Portions of this book were written and rewritten at the Virginia Center for the Creative Arts and Rivendell Writers Colony; their fishponds and wooded lands were a balm of beauty, quiet, and support. As usual, my librarian pro team of Piper Cumbo, Edwina Parks, and Belinda Harris cheerfully augmented my research. I'm also grateful for the creative support of Sheila Pleasants, Mason Adams, Amy Friedman, Kim Cross, Kirk Schroder, Richie Kern, Mim Young, Doug

Jackson, Chloe Landon, Chris Landon, Mary Bishop, Anna Quindlen, Mary-Chris Hirsch, Kate Khalilian, Mindy Shively, Max Landon, and Will ("You Got This, Ma") Landon. Special thanks to my friend Elizabeth Perkins, who introduced me to Patricia Mehrmann and Tess Henry in November 2015, after rescuing a dog of theirs that had gotten loose, and who "had a feeling" I needed to know their story.

At Little, Brown, I'm lucky to have the spirited backing of publishers Reagan Arthur and Terry Adams, copyeditor Deborah P. Jacobs, production editor Pamela Marshall, jacket designer Lauren Harms, editorial assistant Joseph Lee, and the fabulous publicity/marketing team of Sabrina Callahan, Alyssa Persons, Lena Little, and Pamela Brown.

As always, I thank my secret ingredient, Tom Landon, who supports everything I do, from first-line editing and technical assistance to hashing out story lines with tough questions and cheerful reminders to be patient with my interviewees and myself.

In my thirty-two years of journalism, I have never known a source to be as open and unvarnished about hard truths as Patricia Mehrmann, who let me into her life over the course of hundreds of text messages and scores of emails, phone calls, and visits, and whose courage to confront the stigma of addiction is astonishing. May our poet rest in peace.

Notes

PROLOGUE

Interviews: Ronnie Jones, Don Burke, Kristi Fernandez

I walked along the manicured entranceway: Author interview, Ronnie Jones, Hazelton Federal Correctional Institution, Bruceton Mills, WV, Aug. 11, 2016.

the prison had taken over: Hazelton is the largest employer in Preston County, according to the Preston County Economic Development Authority website and Hazelton management, via email to author, July 13, 2017.

"Exactly who have you spoken to": Email to author via CorrLinks federal prison monitored email: July 18, 2016.

a single batch of heroin was about to land: "26 Overdoses in Just Hours: Inside a Community on the Front Lines of the Opioid Epidemic," Andrew Joseph, *STAT,* Aug. 22, 2016.

West Virginia's indigent burial-assistance program: Christopher Ingraham, "Drugs Are Killing So Many People in West Virginia That the State Can't Keep Up with the Funerals," *Washington Post,* March 7, 2017.

Drug overdose had already taken: Jeanine M. Buchanich, Lauren C. Balmert, and Donald C. Burke, "Exponential Growth of the USA Overdose Epidemic," https://doi.org/10.1101/134403 (extrapolates 300,000 more opioid deaths in the next five years, based on graphs studied from 1979 to 2015); other forecasts using similar data are outlined in Max Blau, "STAT Forecast: Opioids Could Kill Nearly 500,000 Americans in the Next Decade," *STAT,* June 27, 2017.

It is now the leading cause: Josh Katz, "Fentanyl Overtakes Heroin as Leading Cause of U.S. Drug Deaths," Global NAIJA News, Sept. 3, 2017.

Kristi Fernandez and I stood: Author interview, Kristi Fernandez, May 23, 2016.

When a new drug sweeps the country: Author interview, historian David Courtwright; the advent of the opioid epidemic was masterfully chronicled for the first time in Paul Tough, "The Alchemy of OxyContin," *New York Times Magazine,* July 29, 2001.

the German elixir peddlers at Bayer: Martin Booth, *Opium: A History* (New York: St. Martin's, 1996), 69; David Courtwright, *Dark Paradise: A History of Opiate Addiction in America* (Cambridge, MA: Harvard University Press, 2001), 47; Courtwright, "Preventing and Treating Narcotic Addiction—A Century of Federal Drug Control," *New England Journal of Medicine*, Nov. 26, 2015. Per capita consumption of opiates tripled in the 1870s and 1880s.

CHAPTER ONE. THE UNITED STATES OF AMNESIA

Interviews: Lt. Richard Stallard, Nancy D. Campbell, Dr. John Burton,
Dr. David Davis

young parents can die of heroin overdose one day: Kristine Phillips, "A Young Couple Died of Overdose, Police Say. Their Baby Died of Starvation Days Later," *Washington Post*, Dec. 25, 2016. The deaths occurred in the Kernville neighborhood of Johnstown, Pennsylvania, sixty miles east of Pittsburgh.

"Half a million people are dead": Lenny Bernstein and Joel Achenbach, "A Group of Middle-Aged Whites in the U.S. Is Dying at a Startling Rate," *Washington Post*, Nov. 2, 2015.

"diseases of despair": That wording became a shorthand for Case and Deaton's work in the wake of a subsequent study by the pair, published in March 2017, according to Joel Achenbach and Dan Keating, "New Research Identifies a 'Sea of Despair' Among White, Working-Class Americans," *Washington Post*, March 23, 2017. The language is also used in a follow-up story, Jeff Guo, "The Disease Killing White Americans Goes Way Deeper Than Opioids," *Washington Post*, March 24, 2017.

Kaiser Family Foundation poll: Bianca DiJulio, Jamie Firth, Liz Hamel, and Mollyann Brodie, "Kaiser Health Tracking Poll: November 2015," http://kff.org/health-reform/poll-finding/kaiser-health-tracking-poll-november-2015/.

Nationwide, the difference in life expectancy: Steven Rattner, "2016 in Charts. (And Can Trump Deliver in 2017?)," *New York Times*, Jan. 3, 2017.

in Appalachia, those disparities are even starker: A 65 percent higher overdose mortality rate in Appalachia: Michael Meit et al., "Appalachian Diseases of Despair," prepared for the Appalachian Regional Commission, Walsh Center for Rural Health Analysis, August 2017.

people hadn't yet begun locking: The early history of the modern-day epidemic shows that some of the largest concentrations of overdose deaths were in Appalachia, the Southwest, and New England, according to Lauren M. Rossen et al., "Drug Poisoning Mortality: United States, 2002–2014," National Center for Health Statistics, Centers for Disease Control and Prevention, Aug. 25, 2016.

Stallard was sitting in his patrol car: Author interview, Big Stone Gap police lieutenant Richard Stallard (now retired), April 29, 2016.

snorters overcame their aversion to needles: Paul Tough, "The Alchemy of OxyContin," *New York Times Magazine,* July 29, 2001.

"Delayed absorption, as provided by OxyContin": Attachment B to Plea Agreement, United States v. The Purdue Frederick Company, Inc., and Michael Friedman, Howard R. Udell, and Paul D. Goldenheim, filed in the U.S. District Court for the Western District of Virginia, Abingdon Division, from lawsuit's "Agreed Statement of Facts" outlining the company's original claims, 6; last modified May 8, 2007.

The company was virtually unheard of: Michael Moore, "Lodi Plant Owners Known for Wealth, Philanthrophy," *Hackensack Record* (NJ), April 27, 1995.

As its patent was set to expire: Stacy Wong, "Thrust Under Microscope, Stamford Drug Company's Low Profile Shattered by Controversy Over Abuse of Painkiller OxyContin," *Hartford Courant,* Sept. 2, 2001.

launched in the nation's best-known corporate tax haven: Leslie Wayne, "How Delaware Thrives as a Corporate Tax Haven," *New York Times,* June 30, 2012. Because corporations can lower their taxes by shifting royalties and other revenues to holding companies in Delaware, where they are not taxed, the state is particularly appealing to shell companies.

"If you take the medicine": Barry Meier, *Pain Killer: A "Wonder" Drug's Trail of Addiction and Death* (New York: Rodale Press, 2003), 43.

"exquisitely rare": Ibid., 190.

at the end of Alexander Hamilton's ill-fated duel: John C. Miller, *Alexander Hamilton and the Growth of the New Nation* (New Brunswick, NJ: Transaction Publishers, 2004; originally published in 1959), 574. Hamilton recovered from a 1793 bout of yellow fever after taking laudanum, 380.

one of Boston's leading merchants: Opium money made by Thomas S. Perkins helped spawn the Industrial Revolution, according to Martha Bebinger, "How Profits from Opium Shaped Nineteenth-Century Boston," WBUR, July 31, 2017.

the opioid-addicted in China had long referred to as "yen": Thomas Nordegren, *The A–Z Encyclopedia of Alcohol and Drug Abuse* (Parkland, FL: Brown Walker, 2002), 691. "Yen" refers both to restless sleep during withdrawal and to the craving for drugs.

(What modern-day addicted users): William S. Burroughs, *Junkie* (New York: Ace Books, 1953), 155.

"I consider it my duty": Martin Booth, *Opium: A History* (New York: St. Martin's, 1996), 69.

it became standard practice: Soldier's disease as defined in Gerald Starkey, "The Use and

Abuse of Opiates and Amphetamines," in Patrick Healy and James Manak, eds., *Drug Dependence and Abuse Resource Book* (Chicago: National District Attorneys Association, 1971), 482–84. While Starkey puts the number of addicted veterans at 400,000, some modern-day historians believe the figure is lower and are more likely to cite Horace Day's 1868 *Opium Habit,* which estimated that 80,000 to 100,000 Americans were addicted, as also described in Dillon J. Carroll, "Civil War Veterans and Opiate Addiction in the Gilded Age," *Journal of the Civil War Era,* Nov. 22, 2016. David F. Musto puts the 1900 figure at 250,000 in *The American Disease: Origins of Narcotic Control* (New York: Oxford University Press, 1973), 5.

The addiction was particularly severe: Carroll, "Civil War Veterans."

"Since the close of the war": "Opium and Its Consumers," *New York Tribune,* July 10, 1877.

"I know persons": Letter by Dr. W. G. Rogers, *Daily Dispatch* (Richmond, VA), Jan. 25, 1884.

It was a safe family drug: David F. Musto, ed., *One Hundred Years of Heroin* (Westport, CT: Auburn House, 2002), 4.

it also seemed to strengthen respiration: Ibid.

Free samples were mailed: David Courtwright, *Dark Paradise: A History of Opiate Addiction in America* (Cambridge, MA: Harvard University Press, 2001), 91, 231.

"almost criminal": "Women Victims of Morphine; Physicians Discuss the Danger in the Use of the Drug," *New York Times,* Oct. 25, 1895.

By 1900, more than 250,000 Americans: Musto, *The American Disease,* 5.

for eight years you could buy heroin: Some states had regional versions of the Harrison Act before 1914, but that didn't prevent a person from going the mail-order route, according to historian Nancy D. Campbell; author interview, Oct. 25, 2017.

then called "vicious": Author interview, Campbell, Sept. 3, 2017.

"the American Disease": Musto, *One Hundred Years of Heroin,* xvi.

now reliant on criminal drug networks: The drug had been interdicted on Chinese ships, where it was hidden inside the rinds of oranges and bars of soap and, once, in 1924, in the bodies of dead kittens found in a passenger's basket, according to "China Again in Grip of Opium and Morphia," *New York Times,* Aug. 24, 1924.

Think of the "Des Moines woman": *Daily State* (Richmond, VA), May 3, 1873 (wire report).

"'contain nothing injurious to the youngest babe'": "Secretary Warns Mothers of Doped Medicines," *Evening News* (Roanoke, VA), March 1, 1914 (wire reports).

David Haddox touted OxyContin: "If you take the medicine like it is prescribed, the risk of addiction when taking an opioid is one-half of 1 percent," said Purdue's medical director Dr. J. David Haddox, as outlined in Meier, *Pain Killer,* 45.

The 1996 introduction of OxyContin coincided: Laurie Tarkan, "New Efforts Against an Old Foe: Pain," *New York Times,* Dec. 26, 2000.

Purdue's bean counters gushed: All budget plans cited in this book came from internal documents I obtained that were originally subpoenaed for the federal investigation.

"We have an opportunity…": Purdue Pharma's 2000 Budget Plan, 51–52.

A 2000 *New York Times* article: Tarkan, "New Efforts Against an Old Foe."

No one questioned whether: John Walsh, "The Enduring Mystery of Pain Measurement," *Atlantic,* Jan. 10, 2017.

not only did reliance on pain scales not correlate: Effectiveness of pain scales dissected in Anna Lembke's *Drug Dealer, MD: How Doctors Were Duped, Patients Got Hooked, and Why It's So Hard to Stop* (Baltimore: Johns Hopkins University Press, 2016), 66–67.

"Every single physician I knew…": Author interview, Dr. John Burton, March 20, 2017.

The Press Ganey survey upped the pressure: Author interview, Dr. David Davis, March 16, 2017.

financial toll of $1 trillion: As reported in Altarum, "Economic Toll of Opioid Crisis in U.S. Exceeded $1 Trillion Since 2001," Feb. 13, 2018. "An additional $500 billion is estimated through 2020 if current conditions persist," the health care firm estimated. The White House Council of Economic Advisers calculated the costs at $504 billion in 2015 alone, according to "Council of Economic Advisers Report: The Underestimated Cost of the Opioid Crisis," Nov. 20, 2017, https://www.whitehouse.gov/briefings-statements/cea-report-underestimated-cost-opioid-crisis/.

only a few voices of dissent: Seddon R. Savage, "Long-Term Opioid Therapy: Assessment of Consequences and Risks," *Journal of Pain and Symptom Management,* May 1996: 274. Dennis Turk wrote in that same paper: "Arguments both pro and con are based on small segments of the pain populations with unique psychosocial and behavioral, as well as disease characteristics."

CHAPTER TWO. SWAG 'N' DASH

Interviews: Dr. Steve Huff, Rosemary Hopkins, Ray Kohl, Dr. Sue Cantrell, Dr. Art Van Zee, Sue Ella Kobak, Dr. Vince Stravino, Jan Mosley, Greg Stewart, Dr. Molly O'Dell, Debbie Honaker, Jennifer Ball, Crystal Street, Sister Beth Davies, John Kelly, Doug Clark, Dennis Lee, Emmitt Yeary, Sheriff Gary Parsons, Rev. Clyde Hester, Tony Lawson

detailed television ads touting specific medical claims: Dylan Scott, "The Untold Story of TV's First Prescription Drug Ad," *STAT,* Dec. 11, 2015, https://www.statnews.com/2015/12/11/untold-story-tvs-first-prescription-drug-ad/.

companies spent more plying: Chris Adams, "Doctors 'Dine 'n' Dash' in Style, as Drug Firms Pick Up the Tab," *Wall Street Journal,* May 14, 2001.

there were scant industry or federal guidelines: U.S. General Accountability Office report, "OxyContin Abuse and Diversion and Efforts to Address the Problem," December 2003, 15–17, https://www.gao.gov/new.items/d04110.pdf. Voluntary guidelines regarding drug company marketing and promotion were issued by July 2002 by the Pharmaceutical Research and Manufacturers of America. In April 2003, voluntary guidelines were issued by the Office of Inspector General, U.S. Department of Health and Human Services.

Purdue handpicked the physicians: Barry Meier, *Pain Killer: A "Wonder" Drug's Trail of Addiction and Death* (New York: Rodale Press, 2003), 99–101.

If a doctor was already prescribing lots of Percocet: Ibid., 103. High-prescriber target was also outlined in Purdue Pharma's 1996 Budget Plan for OxyContin, 56.

a term reps use as a predictor: Deciles are based on volume, past prescribing history, managed care mix, and adopter status, and are used as a way of getting reps to prioritize time and resources; author interview, longtime pharmaceutical sales rep, Dec. 18, 2017.

the more visits that doctor received: Purdue Pharma's 1999 Budget Plan, 65. Meier, 99–103. GAO report, "OxyContin Abuse and Diversion," 15–20: "Purdue directed its sales representatives to focus on the physicians in their sales territories who were high opioid prescribers."

who often brought along "reminders": Purdue Pharma's 1999 Budget Plan, 65.

the higher the milligrams a doctor prescribed: Author interview, former Purdue Pharma OxyContin sales rep, Jan. 26, 2017.

family doctors now the largest single group: Paul Tough, "The Alchemy of OxyContin," *New York Times Magazine,* July 29, 2001.

Reps began coming by before holidays: Author interview, pharmaceutical sales rep, July 28, 2016.

Purdue reps were heavily incentivized: David Armstrong, "Secret Trove Reveals Bold 'Crusade' to Make OxyContin a Blockbuster," *STAT,* Sept. 22, 2016.

"We were impressionable young doctors": Author interview, Dr. Steve Huff, Aug. 7, 2016.

When he set about trying to coax: Ibid., Sept. 26, 2017.

"Cadillac high": Author interview, Rosemary Hopkins, Sept. 23, 2016.

in nearby Galax, a factory town: Author interview, Ray Kohl, director of tourism for Galax, Aug. 8, 2016.

Cantrell remembered setting up: Author interview, Dr. Sue Cantrell, March 23, 2016.

Jobs in coal mining: Brad Plumer, "Here's Why Central Appalachia's Coal Industry Is

Dying," *Washington Post,* Nov. 4, 2013; Nathan Bomey, "Coal's Demise Threatens Appalachian Miners, Firms as Production Moves West," *USA Today,* April 19, 2016.

That's where he met his wife: Author interview, Dr. Art Van Zee, Sept. 3, 2017.

"'The best doctor in America'": Author interview, Dr. Vince Stravino, March 13, 2017.

Locals often compared Van Zee...to Abraham Lincoln: Author interview, Jan Mosley, June 30, 2016.

"When his patients are admitted to the ER": Ibid.

accompany a patient in cardiac arrest: Author interview, Greg Stewart, Sept. 23, 2016.

The time when he cracked three ribs: Author interviews, Van Zee and Sue Ella Kobak, March 3 and 4, 2017.

a physician colleague treated a septuagenarian: Author interview, Stravino.

"Nobody would listen to her": Author interview, Dr. Molly O'Dell, March 22, 2016.

In 1997, the Roanoke-based medical examiner: Rex Bowman, "28 Deaths Linked to Drug—OxyContin Plagues Southwest Virginia," *Richmond Times-Dispatch,* Feb. 9, 2001.

"a little bit unique": Bowman, "Drug Sparks Crime Surge—Southwest Virginia Hit Hard by Opiate Abuse," *Richmond Times-Dispatch,* Oct. 21, 2000. The overdose deaths weren't reported until Bowman's report the following February.

So it happened that in the early 2000s: Author interview, Debbie Honaker, March 16, 2016; follow-up interview, Aug. 8, 2016.

The Board of Medicine suspended Dr. Dwight Bailey's: Lindsey Price, "Doctor's License Suspended Amid Prescription Drug Allegations," WCYB, Aug. 6, 2014, and confirmed in the Board of Medicine's License Lookup: https://dhp.virginiainteractive.org/Lookup/Detail/0101031921. "Had he not given her that junk, my sister would still be here," said Jennifer Ball, who said her sister sought help from Bailey after injuring her back while lifting her handicapped son. She died at forty-one from a heart attack brought on by a combination of blood-pressure medicine, Xanax, and opioids; author interview, Ball, Aug. 5, 2016.

"It's our culture now": Author interview, Crystal Street, March 16, 2016.

24 percent of Lee High School juniors: Author interview, Van Zee, Sept. 23, 2016.

Machias, Maine, was a remote town: The population of Washington County in Maine has been in decline for the last three census periods; the median household income is $38,083, according to U.S. Census data from 2010 and 2016. Nearly one in three children in the county lives in poverty, according to Tom Walsh, *Bangor Daily News,* Feb. 7, 2012.

The plainspoken sheriff: Donna Gold, "A Prescription for Crime," *Boston Globe,* May 21, 2000.

"That's us!": Author interview, Sister Beth Davies, Sept. 23, 2016.

"The extent and prevalence": Letter from Van Zee to Dr. J. David Haddox, Aug. 20,

2000. Van Zee's medical partner, Dr. Vince Stravino, had already filed official complaints about children in the area "crushing, snorting and injecting Oxycontin" and "come to the hospital with overdoses and abscesses because of injections," according to a Purdue response written by Mayra Ballina, the company's associate medical director, on May 8, 2000.

"My fear is that these are sentinel areas": Letter from Van Zee to Dr. Daniel Spyker, Purdue's senior medical director, Nov. 23, 2000.

Forty to 60 percent of addicted opioid users: George E. Woody, "Advances in the Treatment of Opioid Use Disorders," National Institutes of Health, Jan. 27, 2017: https://www.ncbi.nlm.nih.gov/pmc/articles/PMC5288680/#ref-1; M. J. Fleury et al., "Remission from Substance Use Disorders: A Systematic Review and Meta-Analysis," *Drug and Alcohol Dependence,* Nov. 1, 2016; studies interpreted by Harvard Medical School's John Kelly, author interview, Aug. 31, 2017.

"Among the remedies which it has pleased": Meier, *Pain Killer,* 42.

makers of the painkiller Talwin: C. Baum, J. P. Hsu, and R. C. Nelson, "The Impact of the Addition of Naloxone on the Use and Abuse of Pentazocine," *Public Health,* July-August 1987: 426–29.

Unemployed Tazewell miners: Author interview, Doug Clark, Aug. 9, 2016.

and he seemed intimidating: Author interview, then–Tazewell County prosecutor Dennis Lee, now in private practice, May 2, 2016.

"There's just no comparison": Tom Angleberger, "Panel Discusses OxyContin Problem," *Roanoke Times,* Sept. 25, 2000.

Sales-rep bonuses were growing exponentially: In 2001, the average salary for a Purdue sales rep was $55,000, and the average bonus was $71,500, according to U.S. General Accountability Office report, "OxyContin Abuse and Diversion and Efforts to Address the Problem," December 2003, https://www.gao.gov/new.items/d04110.pdf.

"starter coupons": Ibid., 23. "In 1998 and 1999, each sales representative had 25 coupons that were redeemable for a free 30-day supply....Approximately 34,000 coupons had been redeemed nationally when the program was terminated in July 2001."

The trips were free: Ibid., 22.

"The doctors started prostituting themselves": Author interview, Emmitt Yeary, Jan. 24, 2017.

Purdue had passed out fifteen thousand copies: GAO report, "OxyContin Abuse and Diversion," 27.

"pseudo addiction": Explained in the Purdue Pharma "I Got My Life Back: Patients in Pain Tell Their Story" video, narrated by Dr. Alan Spanos, 1997.

"go to sleep" before they stopped breathing: Thomas Catan and Evan Perez, "A Pain-Drug Champion Has Second Thoughts," *Wall Street Journal,* Dec. 17, 2012.

The region had now buried forty-three: Laurence Hammack, "Deaths from OxyContin Overdoses on the Rise," *Roanoke Times,* Feb. 10, 2001, and author interviews, Van Zee.

At the Lee County jail: Hammack, "Lee County Is the Epicenter of Abuse," *Roanoke Times,* June 10, 2001.

"stacking 'em on the floor": Author interview, Lee County sheriff Gary Parsons, March 3, 2017.

one of the prisoners had bought four OxyContin tablets: Rex Bowman, "Prescription for Crime," *Time,* March 21, 2005.

While attempting to make a night deposit: Harless Rose was sentenced to life in prison for murdering the thirty-five-year-old store manager, Timothy Hughes; author interview, Richard Stallard, March 3, 2017; and "Life Term Imposed in Wise Slaying," *Richmond Times-Dispatch,* March 31, 2003 (wire reports).

a man made the bold move: Billy Gene Lawson fired a shot at two young men trying to get his wife's pills, shooting twenty-six-year-old Shannon Fleenor in the back of the head. Lawson was charged with second-degree murder, but a jury of twelve county residents voted to acquit; author interview, Stallard.

" 'spot and steal' ": Author interview, Rev. Clyde Hester, March 3, 2017.

petition drive asking the FDA: Originally at recalloxycontinnow.org, but the website is no longer live.

"In a place where people barely have money": Author interview, Stravino.

"the crack of Southwest Virginia": Hammack, "Deaths from OxyContin Overdoses on the Rise."

marked the first time in the agency's history: GAO report, "OxyContin Abuse and Diversion," 36. Laurence Hammack, "OxyContin," *Roanoke Times,* June 10, 2001.

ten-point plan to curb abuse: Ibid.

pills taped to their back: Author interview, Stallard.

black-box warning on the drug: Reuters Health, "Purdue Pharma's OxyContin to Get Black Box Warning," July 25, 2001.

It was now possible for a rep: Author interviews, former Purdue sales reps, Jan. 26 and Nov. 1, 2017.

"The issue is drug abuse, not the drug": Laurence Hammack, "Seeing OxyContin Abuse Firsthand Pushes St. Charles Doctor's Petition," *Roanoke Times,* Nov. 25, 2001.

"We are an average family": Meier, *Pain Killer,* 138; author interview with banker, name withheld by request, Jan. 12, 2017.

" 'tremendous insult' ": Author interview, Kobak, March 3, 2017.

the newspaper ad never ran: Meier, *Pain Killer,* 140.

The next day Friedman gathered with: Author interview, Stewart, Sept. 23, 2016;

banker interview (name withheld by request), Jan. 12, 2017; and Meier, *Pain Killer,* 140–42 .

"except broken bodies": Author interview, Kobak.

executives might be able to intimidate the people: Author interview, Sister Beth Davies, Aug. 10, 2016. "Beth, my hands are tied," she remembered her former student telling her, apologetically.

Sister Beth had stood up to a crowd: Greg Edwards, "Plant Moves to Clean Up Spill," *Roanoke Times,* Oct. 31, 1996.

That event pitted company miners: Author interview via email, Sister Beth Davies, Feb. 3, 2017.

"She was absolutely the most fearless": Author interview, Tony Lawson, Jan. 30, 2017.

"Greed makes people violent": "A Connecticut Yankee Meets Ol' King Coal," excerpted from John G. Deedy, *The New Nuns: Serving Where the Spirit Leads* (Chicago: Fides/ Claretian, 1982), in *Salt,* September 1982.

all the mining-company executives who'd flown in: Author interview, Davies, Sept. 22, 2016.

she was wearing the same gray sweatpants: Hammack, "Lee County Is the Epicenter of Abuse."

CHAPTER THREE. MESSAGE BOARD MEMORIAL

Interviews: Dr. Steve Huff, Ed Bisch, David Courtwright, Eric Wish, Nancy D. Campbell, Lee Nuss, Barbara Van Rooyan, Dr. Art Van Zee, Dr. Steve Gelfand, Richard Ausness, Laurence Hammack, Barry Meier, Lisa Nina McCauley Green, Lt. Richard Stallard, Randy Ramseyer, John Brownlee

New York Times reporter Barry Meier and a colleague: Francis X. Clines with Barry Meier, "Cancer Painkillers Pose New Abuse Threat," *New York Times,* Feb. 9, 2001.

The news was disseminating, finally: Paul Tough, "The Alchemy of OxyContin," *New York Times Magazine,* July 29, 2001. The extent of the spread of the drug was also chronicled early on by Seamus McGraw, "The Most Dangerous Drug to Hit Small-Town America Since Crack Cocaine?," *Spin,* July 2001.

"pharming": Author interview, Dr. Steve Huff, Sept. 27, 2017.

his son was dead from it: Author interview, Ed Bisch, Jan. 26, 2017.

"After the old-time addicts died out": Author interview, David Courtwright, July 21, 2016.

hipster counterculture: Courtwright, *Dark Paradise: A History of Opiate Addiction in America* (Cambridge, MA: Harvard University Press, 2001), 148–52.

Progressive doctors championed the carefully restricted use: Courtwright, "Preventing and Treating Narcotic Addiction—A Century of Federal Drug Control," *New England Journal of Medicine,* Nov. 26, 2015.

"sour, puritanical shits": Burroughs to Allen Ginsberg, April 25, 1955: Oliver Harris, ed., *The Letters of William S. Burroughs, 1945–1959* (New York: Penguin, 1994), 273.

they returned to spread-out social networks: Lee N. Robins et al., "Vietnam Veterans Three Years After Vietnam: How Our Study Changed Our View of Heroin," *American Journal on Addictions,* May 2010: 203–211; author interview, Eric Wish, April 22, 2016.

the veterans who continued to struggle with addiction: Author interview, historian Nancy D. Campbell, Aug. 9, 2017.

"In the early 1990s, probably ninety percent": Author interview, Courtwright.

bluntest moniker he could think of: After some heated exchanges with Purdue that ended with the company giving him a $10,000 "grant" for equipment to facilitate drug-awareness presentations, Bisch was persuaded to change the name to OxyAbuseKills.com, a decision he later regretted. "I was duped," Bisch told me.

the drug's sales in 2001 hit $1 billion: Barry Meier and Melody Petersen, "Sales of Painkiller Grew Rapidly, But Success Brought a High Cost," *New York Times,* March 5, 2001.

Nuss, too, had lost an eighteen-year-old son: Author interviews, Lee Nuss, Jan. 23 and March 3, 2017.

only to have an unidentified woman: Author interview, Nuss, Jan. 23, 2017, and Doris Bloodsworth, "Crowd Protests Drug Maker," *Orlando Sentinel,* Nov. 20, 2003.

Purdue's marketing of OxyContin had been "appropriate": Bloodsworth, "Group to Target OxyContin Maker in Orlando Rally," *Orlando Sentinel,* Nov. 17, 2003.

"At the time, I knew very little about the drug": Author interview, Barbara Van Rooyan, Jan. 16, 2017. The right-wing radio host made national headlines in 2003 after checking himself into rehab for an addiction to OxyContin, publicly admitting that he had tried to kick his painkiller habit twice before: Jerry Adler, "In the Grip of a Deeper Pain," *Newsweek,* Oct. 20, 2003.

Sue Ella admired the way her mild-mannered husband was stifling: Author interview, Sue Ella Kobak, March 4, 2017.

Wright had signed off on a 1995-filed NDA review and **"Care should be taken":** "Medical Officer Review," NDA #20-553, 14, written by Curtis Wright, Team Medical Review Officer. The 68 percent figure, also included in the NDA, comes from the Center for Drug Evaluation and Research Pilot Drug Evaluation Staff, "Pharmacology Review," submitted Dec. 28, 1994, NDA #20-553, 6.

"the biggest form of drug abuse today": Chris Mullikin testimony, outlined in transcript of FDA's "Anesthetic and Life Support Drugs" Advisory Committee hearing,

Jan. 30, 2002, Gaithersburg, MD. Online at http://www.fda.gov/ohrms/dockets/ac/02/transcripts/3820t1.htm.

a decade later Portenoy conceded: Thomas Catan and Evan Perez, "A Pain-Drug Champion Has Second Thoughts," *Wall Street Journal,* Dec. 12, 2012. "Did I teach about pain management, specifically about opioid therapy, in a way that reflects misinformation? Well, against the standards of 2012, I guess I did," Portenoy told the reporters.

Van Zee pressed on, raising similar concerns: Barry Meier, *Pain Killer: A "Wonder" Drug's Trail of Addiction and Death* (New York: Rodale Press, 2003), 185–91; author interviews, Dr. Art Van Zee, Sept. 23, 2016, and Feb. 11, 2017.

an ethical quandary a *Milwaukee Journal Sentinel* reporter: John Fauber, "E-mails Point to 'Troubling' Relationship Between Drug Firms, Regulators," *Milwaukee Journal Sentinel,* Oct. 6, 2013.

The same *Journal Sentinel* reporter, John Fauber: Fauber and Ellen Gabler, "Doctors with Links to Drug Companies Influence Treatment Guidelines," *Milwaukee Journal Sentinel,* Dec. 18, 2012.

results of that investigation would end up: Paul D. Thacker, "Senators Hatch and Wyden: Do Your Jobs and Release the Sealed Opioids Report," *STAT,* June 27, 2016.

"nothing's come of it": Author interview, Dr. Steve Gelfand, Feb. 9, 2017.

(That initial application would be rejected): John O'Brien, "Blumenthal Calls Out FDA Over OxyContin Petition," Legal NewsLine, July 31, 2007. Rejection of it: Harriet Ryan, "Purdue Pharma Issues Statement on OxyContin Report; L.A. Times Responds," *Los Angeles Times,* May 6, 2016.

"I'm a stubborn Dutchwoman": Author interview, Van Rooyan.

Among RAPP's first courtroom targets: Karen White v. Purdue Pharma, Circuit Court for the Tenth Judicial Circuit Court, Polk County, FL, Civil Division, 2003.

White claimed in her legal filing: Ibid.

the company bragged in a press release: Laurence Hammack, "OxyContin Settlement a Reversal of Fortune," *Roanoke Times,* May 12, 2007.

"Personal injury lawyers" and the firm's legal bills: Meier, *Pain Killer,* 232–33.

Purdue still had 285 lawsuits pending: "Former Drug Firm Worker Says He Was Fired for Being a Whistle-Blower," *Record-Journal* (Meriden, CT), Aug. 25, 2003, quoting spokesman Timothy Bannon; Julie Fishman-Lapin, "Fired Former Employee Withdraws Lawsuit Against OxyContin Manufacturer," *Stamford Advocate,* March 9, 2004.

His bosses banned him from undertaking: Described in Marek Zakrzewski v. Purdue Pharma, Superior Court of Danbury, CT, 2003. Case dismissed: Fishman-Lapin, "Fired Former Employee Withdraws Lawsuit."

calling the allegations "baseless": Fishman-Lapin, "Fired Former Employee Withdraws Lawsuit."

to convince "public officials they could trust Purdue": Barry Meier and Eric Lipton, "Under Attack, Drug Marker Turned to Giuliani for Help," *New York Times,* Dec. 28, 2007.

2001 arrest of two Purdue employees: Ashanti Alvarez, "Arrests Heighten Battle Over Painkiller," *Bergen Record* (NJ), July 6, 2001.

Giuliani brokered a behind-the-scenes negotiation: John Solomon and Matthew Mosk, "The Importance of Being Rudy—Close Up," *Washington Post,* May 15, 2007. Giuliani role in DEA settlement: Meier and Lipton, "Under Attack, Drug Marker Turned to Giuliani."

Purdue Pharma heaped praise on its American hero: Meier and Lipton, "Under Attack, Drug Marker Turned to Giuliani."

Time **magazine's Person of the Year 2001:** http://content.time.com/time/specials/packages/article/0,28804,2020227_2020306,00.html.

Purdue spent $500,000 defending the case: Elaine Silvestrini, "OxyContin's Maker Cleared in Suit Over Sales Tactics," *Tampa Tribune,* Feb. 9, 2005.

She'd been a champion of the drug's painkilling properties: Ibid.; Silvestrini, "Firing Was Retaliation for Ethics Fight, Suit Says," *Tampa Tribune,* Feb. 1, 2005.

one opioid-addicted Orange County veterinarian: Doris Bloodsworth, "Legal Drugs May Be Tracked—Jeb Bush Is Pushing for a Databank to Fight Abuse of Prescriptions," *Orlando Sentinel,* March 25, 2003.

her lawyer had not proved the illegality: Order, White v. Purdue Pharma, Inc., U.S. District Court, Middle District of Florida, Tampa Division, Jan. 26, 2005. From Richard Ausness, "The Role of Litigation in the Fight Against Prescription Drug Abuse," *West Virginia Law Review,* Spring 2014: 1165: "Suits against Purdue by individual consumers have almost always failed because the company has successfully argued lack of causation, misuse, wrongful conduct, and expiration of the statute of limitations."

"'Don't tell us what you believe'": Author interview, Richard Ausness, Jan. 27, 2017.

he had a boyish appearance that belied: Jen McCaffery, "Brownlee Voted into Attorney Post for Virginia," *Roanoke Times,* Oct. 13, 2001. The showboating earned Brownlee a reputation: Mike Gangloff, "Brownlee Resigns—May Run for Office," *Roanoke Times,* April 17, 2008. Brownlee retried Knox after the 2006 acquittal and hung jury, a trial that ultimately saw the doctor convicted of racketeering, health care fraud, and distribution of marijuana, and losing his medical license in 2006.

Brownlee needed a big legal win: Brownlee prosecuted National D-Day Memorial Foundation president Richard Burrow twice for fraud, after which Burrow filed a prosecutorial misconduct complaint with the Justice Department, but Brownlee was exonerated from wrongdoing, according to Gangloff, "Brownlee Resigns." Both of Burrow's cases ended in hung juries.

With plans to seek elected office: Author interview, Laurence Hammack, April 14, 2016; Brownlee himself announced he was running for Virginia attorney general in 2008, a year after the Purdue case was closed. He yielded the nomination to Ken Cuccinelli in 2009.

Udell wanted Meier taken off the beat: Daniel Okrent, "The Public Editor: You Can Stand on Principle and Still Stub a Toe," *New York Times,* Dec. 21, 2003. Okrent said that Meier's 2003 reporting on Rush Limbaugh's addiction was "probably a mistake," quoting Meier's editor at the *Times.* "Certainly, the paper's reputation could have been served by removing even the slightest hint of conflict," Okrent wrote.

"Their agenda was to shut me down": Author interview, Barry Meier, Jan. 24, 2017.

(Meier would not write about Purdue Pharma): Meier covered only two stories on the company between the publication of his book and the 2007 settlement, both of limited, technical scope: "Court Says OxyContin Patent Is Invalid," *New York Times,* June 8, 2005; and, with Andrew Ross Sorkin, "Drug Maker May Buy Rival for $7.5 Billion," *New York Times,* July 25, 2005.

"Never assume I already know!": Van Zee loaned me a copy of the Wood Reports, compiled by Gregg Wood, from March 2004, which he'd saved on CD and which took up 361 pages of a Word document.

"elephant to a blind man": Author interview, Emmitt Yeary, Jan. 24, 2017.

"he worked": Author interview, Lisa Nina McCauley Green, Feb. 2, 2017.

"For a miner who avoids being crippled": John C. Tucker, *May God Have Mercy: A True Story of Crime and Punishment* (New York: Delta, 1998).

the country doctor was the perfect conduit: Yeary initially asked for $5.2 billion in damages in what he predicted would become a class-action lawsuit, but his quest for class-action certification was later dropped and folded into a civil case brought on behalf of McCauley and two similarly injured laborers from the region.

a patient Van Zee was by then treating: From an affidavit of Art Van Zee, filed in McCauley v. Purdue Pharma, Van Zee testified: "It was clear to me that he had developed profound opioid addiction during the course of his treatment with OxyContin. By opioid 'addiction,' I specifically mean...McCauley demonstrated tolerance to increased amounts of OxyContin; increased his dosage on his own; a characteristic withdrawal syndrome when he was attempting to come off OxyContin;...and continued use of OxyContin despite harm (physical, social, personal, and family harm) from his continued use of OxyContin." McCauley v. Purdue Pharma, U.S. District Court for the Western District of Virginia, Big Stone Gap Division, filed

Oct. 31, 2004. McCauley initially went to Van Zee for help in weaning himself off methadone.

It didn't matter that the septuagenarian: Author interview with Green; McCauley deposition, Jan. 22, 2003, Abingdon, VA; filed in *McCauley.*

Norton was sentenced to five years: Associated Press, "Four Sentenced in Lee County Scam—Corruption Plot Led to Hospital's Bankruptcy," Nov. 17, 2000. Norton's treatment of McCauley in 1999 was outlined in McCauley's medical records, subpoenaed from Van Zee for the case.

federal prosecutors were also investigating Norton: Sales-rep notes written by Kimberly Keith explain that Norton "has been convicted of money laundering etc and last week was sentenced to 5 years in fed prison, pulled me into a room to tell me that the US attorney's office was going to get him with over prescribing of narcotics but got him with this one first, said we, as a company, should know that they are after us and making us enemy #1 with oxycontin"; written about a Nov. 20, 2000, visit to Norton's office.

"the Shadow Company": Author interview, Richard Stallard, March 3, 2017.

His family had sent him to rehab seven times: Author interview, Green.

Brownlee's belief that Purdue had knowingly concealed: Author interview, Van Zee, Sept. 24, 2016.

***New York Post* reporter broke the news in 2005:** Brad Hamilton, "Jury Eyes RX Bigs in OxyContin 'Coverup'; Allegedly Hid Painkiller Peril," *New York Post,* June 12, 2005.

"Sometimes people get intimidated by big companies": Author interview, Randy Ramseyer, March 17, 2016.

only to leave his post in 2001: Gregory D. Kesich, "Former Prosecutor Backs Drug Company—Maine's One-Time U.S. Attorney Tells Senators the Maker of Oxycontin Has Worked to Curb Abuse," *Portland Press Herald,* Aug. 2, 2007. "The drug diversion problem was not caused by OxyContin, and it will not be solved by going after OxyContin as a whipping boy," McCloskey said.

doling out prescriptions from the back seat: Author interview, Ramseyer; Dr. Denny Lambert, who was also addicted to opioids, was sentenced to fifty-two months in prison for illegally distributing OxyContin, Ritalin, and Dilaudid: Laurence Hammack, "Doctors or Dealers?," *Roanoke Times,* June 11, 2001.

"Look, my view of the case was": Author interview, John Brownlee, Sept. 30, 2016.

"his star power alone": Author interview, U.S. assistant attorney, March 2, 2017.

a memo written by the federal prosecutors to Brownlee: From a memo draft written Sept. 28, 2006, from the assistant prosecutors to Brownlee.

"Brownlee, you are fine": "Evaluating the Propriety and Adequacy of the OxyContin Criminal Settlement," hearing before the Committee on the Judiciary, U.S. Senate,

July 31, 2007, online at https://www.gpo.gov/fdsys/pkg/CHRG-110shrg40884/html/CHRG-110shrg40884.htm.

senior Justice Department officer phoned Brownlee: Ibid.

eleventh-largest fine paid by a pharmaceutical firm: David Armstrong, "Purdue Says Kentucky Suit Over OxyContin Could Be Painful," *Bloomberg News,* Oct. 20, 2014.

two thousand cardboard containers they'd filled: Hammack, "OxyContin Settlement a Reversal of Fortune."

falsified charts created by Purdue: "Agreed Statement of Facts," United States of America v. The Purdue Frederick Company, Inc., and Michael Friedman, Howard R. Udell, and Paul D. Goldenheim, filed in the U.S. District Court for the Western District of Virginia, Abingdon Division, May 7, 2007, 7–8.

("I would not write it up at this point"): Point No. 36 of Attachment B to Plea Agreement, *The Purdue Frederick Company, Inc.,* et al., 13.

68 percent of the drug: Point No. 20(a.), *The Purdue Frederick Company, Inc.,* et al., 6.

oxycodone was harder to extract: Ibid.

OxyContin caused less euphoria: Point No. 43, 14, *The Purdue Frederick Company, Inc.,* et al.

CHAPTER FOUR. "THE CORPORATION FEELS NO PAIN"

Interviews: Sister Beth Davies, Dr. Art Van Zee, Andrew Bassford, Randy Ramseyer, Dr. Sue Cantrell, Barry Meier, Judge James Jones, Andrew Bassford, Jeff Udell, Lee Nuss, Laurence Hammack

the Barter stage featured a homegrown comedy: *The Quiltmaker,* a comedy by Catherine Bush, Barter's playwright in residence, premiered at the Barter in the spring of 2007.

even written a poem: "OxyContin," by Dr. Art Van Zee, *Annals of Internal Medicine,* April 6, 2004: 527.

"Everything I'd written was now justified": Author interview, Barry Meier, Jan. 24, 2017.

voices broke periodically as they choked out: From a host of names submitted in memorial to Ed Bisch's memorial website (no longer active, but Bisch provided me with a document he had archived that contained hundreds of names).

two moms in matching rain scarves held each other: Barry Meier, "3 Executives Spared Prison in OxyContin Case," *New York Times,* July 21, 2007. Don Petersen took the photograph.

"What if it was your son or daughter": Testimony of Victor Del Regno, about his son, Andrew, from the transcript of United States of America v. The Purdue Frederick

Company, Inc., and Michael Friedman, Howard R. Udell, and Paul D. Goldenheim, sentencing hearing, U.S. District Court for the Western District of Virginia, Abingdon Division, July 20, 2007: 10–12.

"Brian is here in the courtroom with me today" and **"I think jail is too good for you guys":** From the transcript of *The Purdue Frederick Company, Inc., et al.,* sentencing hearing, 28–30.

"I think you should go spend some time in a rehab facility": Ibid., 20–21.

"a personal tragedy for Mr. Udell": Ibid., White testimony, 92–102.

"a criminal, and that is horrendously harsh punishment": Ibid., Good testimony, 103–109. Goldenheim left the company in 2004.

to jail him would be virtually unprecedented: Ibid., Mark D. Pomerantz testimony, 83–91.

"the enormous benefits of OxyContin far outweigh": Ibid., Purdue Frederick attorney, Howard Shapiro testimony, 73–83.

"unprecedented" to hold pharmaceutical corporate officers: Ibid., Randy Ramseyer testimony, 67–72.

"they didn't seem as unhappy as those three guys": Author interview, Ramseyer, March 17, 2016.

every American adult around the clock: 2010 data released by the Centers for Disease Control and Prevention.

Super Bowl ads now targeted relievers: The 2015 ad was meant to promote Movantik, a first-of-its-kind constipation drug for painkiller users, though the ad didn't directly mention the drug. The U.S. market for treating opioid constipation is projected to reach $500 million by 2019, according to Matt Pearce, "What the Super Bowl Constipation Ad Did Not Say," *Los Angeles Times,* Feb. 10, 2016.

Purdue had earned over $2.8 billion: Caitlin Sullivan, "Punishing OxyContin's Maker," *Time,* July 20, 2007.

earn its way onto *Forbes*'s: Alex Morrell, "The OxyContin Clan: The $14 Billion Newcomer to Forbes 2015 List of Richest U.S. Families," *Forbes,* July 1, 2015. The family dropped to number nineteen on the list in 2016, its estimated worth down to $13 billion, even though it had reaped some $700 million the preceding year, the magazine estimated, according to Chase Peterson-Withorn, "Fortune of Family Behind OxyContin Drops Amid Declining Prescriptions," *Forbes,* June 29, 2016.

Mortimer Sackler even had a pink climbing rose: Bruce Weber, "Mortimer D. Sackler, Arts Patron, Dies at 93," *New York Times,* March 31, 2010.

Arthur pioneered the idea: Jesse Kornbluth, "The Temple of Sackler," *Vanity Fair,* September 1987.

put the figure as high as 56 percent: From a systematic review of Bridget A. Martell et al., "Opioid Treatment for Chronic Back Pain: Prevalence, Efficacy, and Association with Addiction," *Annals of Internal Medicine,* January 2007: 116–27.

"Arthur built his own temple": Kornbluth, "The Temple of Sackler."

Public Citizen, a consumer advocacy group: Laurence Hammack, "OxyContin Settlement a Reversal of Fortune," *Roanoke Times,* May 12, 2007.

"The corporation feels no pain": Author interview, Andrew Bassford, Jan. 16, 2016. He admitted his point of view was in the minority "and maybe even heresy" to his colleagues in the office.

The $634.5 million fine: According to Brownlee's news release, May 10, 2007, the fine included the following directives: $276.1 million forfeited to the United States; $160 million to federal and state agencies to resolve liability for false claims made to Medicaid and other government health care programs, $130 million to resolve private civil claims; $5.3 million to the Virginia Attorney General's Medicaid Fraud Control Unit to fund future fraud investigations; $20 million to Virginia's prescription monitoring program. "In addition, Purdue will pay the maximum statutory criminal fine of $500,000." The executive fines were assessed at $19 million for Friedman, $8 million for Udell, and $7.5 million for Goldenheim, and each executive was also fined an additional $5,000.

"independent, associated companies": Corporate Crime Reporter, "Corporate Drug Pushers," *Counterpunch,* May 16, 2007, http://www.counterpunch.org/2007/05/16/corporate-drug-pushers/.

a decision they repeatedly appealed: Barry Meier, "Restrictions Are Upheld for Executives in OxyContin Case," *New York Times,* Jan. 23, 2009.

"Plaintiffs appear to misunderstand": Federal judge Segal Huvelle wrote in rejecting the executives' arguments that their disbarment from doing business with taxpayer-financed health care programs should be overturned; the executives did get their initial disbarment reduced from twenty to twelve years, Meier, "Ruling Is Upheld Against Executives Tied to OxyContin," *New York Times,* Dec. 15, 2010. Ramseyer said they were ultimately excluded for eight years.

But the Abingdon federal judge's hands were tied: U.S. District Judge James Jones testimony, from the transcript of *The Purdue Frederick Company, Inc., et al.,* 110–21.

"Opioid addiction continues to be": Author interview, Judge James Jones, Feb. 3, 2017.

Udell went on to found the Connecticut Veterans Legal Center: Anne M. Hamilton, "Helping Veterans with Legal Problems," *Hartford Courant,* Sept. 1, 2013.

the government presented zero proof: Author interview, Jeffrey Udell, April 5, 2017.

she brandished the tiny brass urn: Lee Nuss testimony, from the transcript of *The Purdue Frederick Company, Inc., et al.,* 21–22, and author interview, Nuss, Jan. 31, 2017. Laurence Hammack is the reporter who told me he thought Nuss was going to throw the urn.

CHAPTER FIVE. SUBURBAN SPRAWL

Interviews: Chief Chris Perkins, Dr. Steve Huff, Sgt. Chad Seeberg, Dr. Jennifer Wells, Don Wolthuis, Warren Bickel, Robin Roth, Kristi Fernandez, Lt. Chuck Mason, Spencer Mumpower, Ginger Mumpower, Tony Anderson, Vinnie Dabney

the *Cincinnati Enquirer* became the first newspaper: Kristen Hare, "The Cincinnati Enquirer Now Has a Heroin Beat," Poynter Institute, Feb. 15, 2016.

Viewers loved watching them: Lindsey Nair and Marques G. Harper, "Another WSLS Weatherman Admits Struggle with Heroin," *Roanoke Times,* Feb. 18, 2006. Gilbert Dennis Hadden, a twenty-one-year-old dealer from Detroit, was sentenced to two years in prison later that year.

"The weathermen were skin popping": Author interview, Chief Chris Perkins, Dec. 29, 2015 (since retired). Some users skin pop when their veins are too scarred to inject, according to Dr. Steve Huff, author interview, Oct. 2, 2017.

an unconscious man on the floor: Author interview, Sgt. Chad Seeberg of Marysville, Ohio, Aug. 8, 2016.

"Train City to Brain City": Colin Woodard, "Trains Built Roanoke. Science Saved It," *Politico Magazine,* Sept. 15, 2016. The quote was from Chris Morrill, Roanoke's city manager from 2010 to 2017.

"Roanoke is just big enough where all the stories meet": Author interview, Dr. Jennifer Wells, May 1, 2017.

"maybe a few dozen people were doing heroin here": Author interview, Don Wolthuis, Jan. 7, 2016.

an addicted user's idea of the future: Author interview, Warren Bickel, July 25, 2016.

The first bags sold in Roanoke: Mike Gangloff and Mike Allen, "Rise in Heroin Use Among Youth Alarms Officials," *Roanoke Times,* Feb. 24, 2009.

"They're skipping over pot and going straight to heroin": Julia Dudley, U.S. attorney for the Western District of Virginia, quoted in Gangloff and Allen, "Rise in Heroin Use."

"You think of heroin as seedy street slums": Author interviews, Robin Roth, 2012–2017. Interviews in 2012 and 2013 were research for my *Roanoke Times* series "The Damage Done," Aug. 20–22, 2012, and follow-up articles.

Kristi defended her son: Author interview, Kristi Fernandez, May 23, 2016.

Brandon Perullo had become so desperate: Preston Knight, "Robber to Serve 3½ Years in Heist," *Northern Virginia Daily,* Feb. 9, 2011.

Brandon's mother, Laura Hadden, begged: Author interview, Laura Hadden, May 18, 2017.

At Spencer Mumpower's 2012 federal court sentencing: Transcript of sentencing hearing, United States v. Spencer Cruise Mumpower, U.S. District Court for the Western District of Virginia, Roanoke, March 1, 2012.

But Robin declined, saying she wasn't ready: Beth Macy, "The Damage Done."

oversimplification that police only partially confirmed: Author interview, Chuck Mason (then Roanoke County police lieutenant), May 5, 2012: "Catch-and-release implies we're not going to charge them, but we are. They're to be out on the road so they can work for us, but they are going to be charged at some point so they can face what they've done.... If we take the guy dealing fifty bags and put him in jail, then we don't have a shot at the guy dealing five hundred bags."

His lawyer, Tony Anderson, recalled: Ibid.

Vinnie Dabney remembered it: Ibid.

Spencer was alternately immature and wise: Ibid.

stamped with names like Blue Magic or Gucci: Author interviews, Roanoke County native Ashlyn Kessler, conducted via CorrLinks, federal prison monitored email, multiple times beginning May 26, 2016.

CHAPTER SIX. "LIKE SHOOTING JESUS"

Interviews: Sgt. Joe Crowder, Dr. Anna Lembke, Cheri Hartman, Tony Lawson, Judge Bob Bushnell, Andrew Nester, Shannon Monnat, Nikki King, Spencer Mumpower, Dr. William Massello, Dr. Martha Wunsch, Vinnie Dabney, Nancy Hans, Dr. Hughes Melton, Andrew Bassford, Dr. John Burton, Ron Salzbach, Jamie Waldrop, Drenna Banks, Christopher Waldrop

ill-designed training for displaced Americans: Trade Adjustment Assistance is outdated, with poor participation and efficacy, according to Beth Macy, "The Reality of Retraining," *Roanoke Times*, April 22, 2012.

"not a social experiment": Bassett Furniture CEO Rob Spilman, as relayed in Macy, *Factory Man* (New York: Little, Brown, 2014), 300.

soaring crime, food insecurity, and disability claims: America's overall work rate for Americans age twenty and older dropped 5 percentage points between early 2000 and late 2016, as analyzed in Nicholas N. Eberstadt, "Our Miserable 21st Century," *Commentary*, Feb. 15, 2017.

unemployment rates rose to above 20 percent: Food stamp increase courtesy of Supplemental Nutrition Assistance Program data from Martinsville and Henry County social services; disability hike factored from statistics, compiled here: http://www.ssa.gov /policy/docs/statcomps/oasdi_sc/2008/va.html.

mental health and substance use disorders: Anna Lembke, *Drug Dealer, MD: How Doctors Were Duped, Patients Got Hooked, and Why It's So Hard to Stop* (Baltimore, MD: Johns Hopkins University Press, 2016), 92, based on the work of economists David Autor and Mark Duggan, "The Growth in the Social Security Disability Rolls: A Fiscal Crisis Unfolding," National Bureau of Economic Research, Working Paper No. 12436, August 2006. Mental illness is the reason cited in 25 percent of disability awards, and chronic pain is cited in 26 percent.

"Ritalin is a pipeline to disability here": Author interview, Tony Lawson, Jan. 30, 2017.

"a *draw-er*": Author interview, Nikki King, July 20, 2017.

Well over half of Lee County's working-age men: U.S. Census data collated by Syracuse University sociologist Shannon Monnat.

for every unemployed American man: Eberstadt, "Our Miserable 21st Century."

Disability claims nearly doubled: From a *Washington Post* analysis of Social Security Administration statistics, as reported in Terrence McCoy, "Disabled or Just Desperate? Rural Americans Turn to Disability as Jobs Dry Up," March 30, 2017.

"one of the unemployed masses": Author interviews, Henry County judge and former prosecutor Bob Bushnell and commonwealth attorney Andrew Nester, June 23, 2015.

"Crystal meth controls all the dockets now": Author interview, Virginia state police special agent Joe Crowder, March 24, 2017. Methamphetamine was the most common drug involved in federal drug-trafficking offenses in 2015 (31.5 percent of all cases), followed by powder cocaine (20.5 percent), marijuana (17.1 percent), and heroin (13.3 percent), according to the U.S. Sentencing Commission, "Drug Trafficking Offenses: Quick Facts," 2005–2015 Datafiles.

Drug epidemics unfold "like a vector": Lembke, *Drug Dealer, MD,* 16, and author interviews, Lembke, via email, April 15 and Oct. 26, 2017.

"One time I got pulled over, I had ten bags": Author interview, Spencer Mumpower, April 19, 2012.

"one overdose where the son would die": Author interview, Dr. William Massello, March 21, 2017. By the time he left the position in 2007, accidental drug overdose deaths in western Virginia had quadrupled, rising from about 65 a year in the early 1990s to 250.

"The issue is Interstate 81": Author interview, Dr. Martha Wunsch, now an addiction medicine doctor in Northern California, Jan. 27, 2017.

Opioids infiltrated the toniest suburbs: OxyContin was the first drug to receive an "abuse-deterrent" designation from the FDA, according to Christopher Ingraham, "How an 'Abuse-Deterrent' Drug Created the Heroin Epidemic," *Washington Post,* Jan. 10, 2017.

One of the most segregated cities in the South: Matt Chittum and Sara Gregory, "Decades of Inequality and Lack of Opportunity Have Generational Cost in Roanoke," *Roanoke Times,* May 6, 2017.

beginning to migrate to the more affluent: Author interview, Crowder, March 24, 2017.

"nobody paid any attention to it until their cars": Author interviews, Vinnie Dabney, Dec. 29, 2015, and Dec. 31, 2016. Dabney also told his story in a talk to at-risk kids at the Roanoke Higher Education Center, May 11, 2017.

"The early suburban wave mostly stayed hidden": Author interview, Dr. Hughes Melton, April 2, 2017.

"We didn't understand the connection": Author interview, Nancy Hans, April 4, 2017.

***Vice* magazine swooped into Roanoke:** Rob Fischer, "Bath Salts in the Wound," Vice.com, Dec. 30, 2012. Bath-salt ban: Matthew Perrone, "Many Drugs Remain Legal After 'Bath Salts' Ban," Associated Press, July 25, 2012.

"How dare you tell the newspaper these things?": Author interview, Andrew Bassford, Jan. 6, 2016.

"If you tried to crunch 'em": Author interview, Victoria (real name withheld, by request, to protect her job), Jan. 19, 2017.

the number of prescribed stimulants increased tenfold: Lembke, *Drug Dealer, MD,* 45–46.

2014 data review that illustrates the discrepancies: Frances Rudnick Levin and John J. Mariani, "Co-occurring Addictive Disorder and Attention Deficit Hyperactivity Disorder," published by the American Society of Addiction Medicine, 2014, available at https://basicmedicalkey.com/co-occurring-addictive-disorder-and-attention-deficit-hyperactivity-disorder.

"A lot of us think that doctors": Author interview, Cheri Hartman, Jan. 14, 2018.

the abuse of prescription drugs increased: Lembke, *Drug Dealer, MD,* 48.

Dr. John Burton watched the cultural shift: Author interview, Dr. John Burton, March 20, 2017.

two-thirds of college seniors reported: Lembke, *Drug Dealer, MD,* 48, and author interviews, Lembke; also http://drugfree.org/newsroom/news-item/full-report-and-key-findings-the 2012-partnershipattitude-tracking-study-sponsored-by-metlife-foundation/.

"I'd take just a couple": Author interviews, Brian, May 1, 2012, and in several follow-up interviews and email exchanges.

"like shooting Jesus up in your arm": Author interview, counselor and Suboxone support group facilitator Ron Salzbach, Jan. 4, 2106; confirmed by author interviews, Brian, May 1, 2012, Dec. 28, 2015, and April 9, 2017.

"It's been seven days": Author interview, Brian, May 1, 2012.

"cellphone is the glue": Author interview, Brian, Sept. 3, 2012.

their chance meeting have lasting implications: Author interviews, Jamie Waldrop, Dec. 5, 2015, and multiple interviews through 2017.

"I just knew [Jamie] was this cool blond-haired chick": Author interviews, Drenna Banks, Dec. 15, 2015, and March 23, 2017.

"I was a pretty bad robber": Author interview, Christopher Waldrop, April 11, 2017.

a painkiller-selling scheme that placed Colton: From the Roanoke police search warrant, filed Nov. 4, 2012, by Detective P. B. Caldwell: "Based on my training and expertise, the currency [$1,350 found on site in cash] and the extreme shortage of oxycodone would indicate the distribution of these pills."

supposed to be his last hurrah: Author interview, Banks, Dec. 15, 2015, and March 23, 2017.

chucking her prepared remarks in favor of: Remarks by Drenna Banks, Nov. 9, 2012, transcribed from a CD of Colton's memorial service.

"I wanted to drink again": Author interview, Christopher Waldrop, April 17, 2017.

Fewer than one-quarter of heroin addicts: Lembke, *Drug Dealer, MD,* 133; John Strang et al., "Drug Policy and the Public Good: Evidence for Effective Interventions," *Lancet,* Jan. 7, 2012: 71–83; author interview, Dr. Hughes Melton, March 31, 2017.

for every one opioid-overdose death, there were 130: 2011 data sets compiled by Substance Abuse and Mental Health Services Administration, Drug Abuse Warning Network, Treatment Episode Data Set, and Coalition Against Insurance Fraud, "Prescription for Peril: How Insurance Fraud Finances Theft and Abuse of Addictive Prescription Drugs," December 2007, courtesy of epidemiology mapmaker Jeremiah Lindemann, April 7, 2017.

CHAPTER SEVEN. FUBI

Interviews: Sgt. Brent Lutz, James Kendrick, Sheriff Tim Carter, Don Wolthuis, Shannon Monnat, Sgt. Kevin Coffman, Mark O'Brien, Dennis Painter, Courtney Fletcher, Kristi Fernandez, Agent Bill Metcalf, Lauren Cummings, Dana Cormier, Keith Marshall

Lutz was tracking the movements: Author interviews, Sgt. Brent Lutz, Jan. 19, 2016, and subsequent interviews about the FUBI ring, including May 24, 2016, and Oct. 27, 2016.

drug users are arrested four times more often: Human Rights Watch and American Civil Liberties Union, "25 Seconds: The Human Toll of Criminalizing Drug Use in the United States," 2016: https://www.aclu.org/sites/default/files/field_document/us-drug1016_web.pdf.

$7.6 billion spent nationwide: C. S. Florence et al., "The Economic Burden of Prescription Opioid Overdose, Abuse, and Dependence in the United States, 2013," National Institutes of Health, *Medical Care,* October 2016, 901–906, https://www.ncbi.nlm.nih.gov/pubmed/27623005.

"that one that starts with a D": "Makers of Dilaudid to Officially Change Name to 'That One That Starts with a D,'" http://gomerblog.com/2017/03/makers-of-dilaudid/.

"You go crazy if you can't laugh": Author interview, Health Wagon nurse-practitioner James Kendrick, May 24, 2017.

"but they don't put the resources to monitor them": Author interview, Shenandoah County sheriff Tim Carter, July 10, 2017.

three people died of overdose: Virginia Department of Health statistics, 2012. (Five died that year of prescription opioid overdose.) Two NAS babies were reported for Shenandoah County in 2012.

"it was like cutting off and on a light switch": Author interviews, Lutz.

demanding sex from female addicts: Ibid.; author interview, Don Wolthuis, Jan. 7, 2016 (and many subsequent interviews with Lutz, Wolthuis, and others).

diseases of despair: Anne Case and Angus Deaton, "Rising Morbidity and Mortality in Midlife Among White Non-Hispanic Americans in the 21st Century," National Academy of Sciences of the United States of America, at http://www.pnas.org/content/112/49/15078.full.

"The places with the lowest overdose mortality rates": Author interview, Shannon Monnat, June 6, 2017. Lewis County, NY, schools' payment in lieu of taxes from Maple Ridge Wind Farm: Joanna Richards, "Wind Farm a Windfall to Lewis County Communities," North Country Public Radio, May 15, 2013.

opioid-prescribing rate in the Woodstock region: Opioid-prescribing rates comparing Lee County's (10.23 percent) to Shenandoah County's (2.96), Virginia's (5.49), and the nation's (5.03); data comes from Medicare Part D enrollees, 2013, compiled by Monnat. The statewide figure was 5.49 percent.

journalist Sam Quinones: Sam Quinones, *Dreamland: The True Tale of America's Opiate Epidemic* (New York: Bloomsbury, 2015), 327–28.

Declining workforce participation wasn't just: Author interview, Monnat. Princeton economist Alan B. Krueger's 2017 study also backs Monnat's thesis: "The opioid crisis and depressed labor force participation are now intertwined in many parts of the U.S.," he said, in the Brookings Institution paper "Where Have All the Workers Gone? An Inquiring into the Decline of the U.S. Labor Force Participation Rate," Sept. 7, 2017, found here: https://www.brookings.edu/bpea-articles/where-have-all-the-workers-gone-an-inquiry-into-the-decline-of-the-u-s-labor-force-participation-rate/. Related: Fred Dews, "How the Opioid Epidemic Has Affected the U.S. Labor Force, County-by-County," Brookings Institution, Sept. 7, 2017.

Packaged in Harlem, the heroin was shaped: Details of the FUBI ring were gleaned from interviews with numerous law enforcement officers who worked the case, 2016–2017, including Lutz, Stafford County drug task force officer Kevin Coffman, ATF agent Bill Metcalf, and Wolthuis, along with numerous users and their relatives, and with Ronnie Jones.

D.C. was so afraid of the drug: Author interview with one of his subdealers, "Marie," name withheld to protect her job, May 23, 2016, confirmed by several drug task force officers.

wouldn't even know where to put the needle: Author interview, Jones, Hazelton Federal Correctional Institute, Aug. 11, 2016.

"you don't have people shooting at you": Author interview, Coffman, May 31, 2016. Coffman also described the regular weight of the Harlem heroin haul.

important subset of the drug trade in Baltimore: Jean Marbella and Catherine Rentz, "Heroin Creates Crowded Illicit Economy in Baltimore," *Baltimore Sun*, Dec. 19, 2015, quoting a RAND Corporation study and Baltimore's heroin task force.

With the highest per capita rate of heroin use: Baltimore has the worst heroin problem in the country, according to incoming Maryland governor Larry Hogan: Jenna Johnson, "Hogan Says He Will Declare Heroin 'Emergency' Once Sworn in as Md. Governor," *Washington Post*, Dec. 6, 2014. A 2000 DEA report said Baltimore had the highest per capita rate for heroin: Julia Beatty, "Baltimore: The Heroin Capital of the U.S.," *The Fix*, March 30, 2015.

Baltimore residents were six times: "We have oh-point-two percent of the country's population and one-point-two percent of the drug overdoses," and locals are six times more likely to die of an opioid overdose, according to Mark O'Brien, Baltimore City Health Department's opioid overdose prevention and treatment director: Author interview, Sept. 4, 2016.

Little Baltimore: Jennifer Donelan and Dwayne Myers, "Heroin Highway: Part 5—Hagerstown, Md. 'Round the Clock Emergency,'" WJLA, Washington, D.C., Feb. 19, 2016.

A 2017 *New Yorker* profile of Martinsburg: Margaret Talbot, "The Addicts Next Door," *The New Yorker*, June 5 and 12, 2017.

Intended to aid police surveillance: Luke Broadwater and Justin George, "City Expands Surveillance System to Include Private Cameras of Residents, Businesses," *Baltimore Sun*, Oct. 30, 2014.

"Sometimes the dealers will flash their lights": Author interview, Dennis Painter, June 17, 2016.

His girlfriend had to pick him up late that night: Author interview, Courtney Fletcher, Dennis's then-girlfriend, May 17, 2017.

The first time Jesse shot up heroin: Author interview, Kristi Fernandez, May 23, 2016.

Gray was driving on a suspended license: Outlined in "Statement of Facts," United States v. Devon Renard Gray, U.S. District Court for the Western District of Virginia, Harrisonburg Division, Feb. 5, 2015.

"we've almost come to blows": Author interview, Coffman, May 31, 2016.

a squealing chase through Middletown: Author interviews, Wolthuis, June 2, 2016, and Metcalf, May 23, 2016; and Joe Beck, "Officer: Strasburg Chase Speeds Reached 60 to 90 MPH," *Northern Virginia Daily,* April 9, 2013.

Responding to a nearly sixfold increase: The per capita rate of imprisonment increased from 93 per 100,000 to 536 per 100,000, according to David Cole, "The Truth About Our Prison Crisis," *New York Review of Books,* June 22, 2017.

"Too many Americans go to too many prisons": Charlie Savage, "Justice Dept. Seeks to Curtail Stiff Drug Sentences," *New York Times,* Aug. 12, 2013.

"My story was, I was recently out of jail": Author interviews, Metcalf, May 16, 2016, and multiple subsequent interviews.

Rose had forgotten it was a territory: Author interview, Marie (name withheld), May 23, 2016.

"two hundred people I know of would get sick": From the courtroom testimony of Marie (name withheld): Joe Beck, "Sentencing Depicts Dealer's Role in Heroin Ring," *Northern Virginia Daily,* June 3, 2015.

a woman's chipper recorded voice intoned: Author interview, Marie.

"Never get high on your own supply": Ibid.; Notorious B.I.G. lyrics from "Ten Crack Commandments." Other details of Jones's spending came from Jones, Lutz, Metcalf, Coffman, and Wolthius.

"reminds me of *The Wire*": Author interview, Lutz, Jan. 19, 2016.

"We were disgusted": Ibid.

overdose deaths in the region would surge: Author interview, Lauren Cummings, executive director of the drug abuse and prevention coalition Road to Recovery, July 3, 2017.

addicted user-dealer from Stafford County: Author interview, Metcalf, May 23, 2016, and sentencing memorandum, United States v. Kimberle Ann Hodsden, U.S. District Court for the Western District of Virginia, Harrisonburg Division, April 15, 2015.

It was heady stuff: Sentencing memorandum prepared by Hodsden's lawyer, Rhonda Quagliana, for *Hodsden,* April 15, 2015. Hodsden was sentenced to five years in federal prison for her role in the Jones/Shaw ring.

Marshall was a functioning heroin addict: Keith Marshall letter to author, received

June 27, 2017. In separate emails from prison, Marshall also confirmed Metcalf's account.

His lawyer told me he'd overdosed five times: Author interview, Dana Cormier, May 25, 2016.

"Mr. Metcalf unfortunately is": Keith Marshall letter to author, received June 27, 2017.

FUBI: Author interview, Wolthuis, Jan. 7, 2016, and with agents and task force officers who worked the case.

CHAPTER EIGHT. "SHIT DON'T STOP"

Interviews: Agent Bill Metcalf, Don Wolthuis, Lauren Cummings, Thomas Jones III, Ronnie Jones, Kristi Fernandez, Dennis Painter, Courtney Fletcher, Dr. Nora Volkow, Tracey Helton Mitchell, Dr. John Kelly, Dr. Andrew Kolodny, Barbara Van Rooyan

former Marine who'd been kicked out: Author interview, Bill Metcalf, June 9, 2017, and Joshua Pettyjohn's presentencing report.

trying to distance himself from his buyers: Author interview, Don Wolthuis, June 2, 2016.

not only had overdose deaths surged: Increases from 2012 to 2013 in substance abuse determinants in the northern Shenandoah Valley, data tracked by Lauren Cummings.

the family had no idea Ronnie was a big-time: Author interviews, Ronnie Jones (in person and via prison email), and his brother, Thomas Jones III, Aug. 16, 2016.

delivering cupcakes to his daughter's school: Jones's account of his arrest and the weeks leading up to it came from my interview with him and from multiple exchanges via prison-monitored email.

The quest had become deeply personal: Author interviews, Metcalf, May 16, 2016, and June 13, 2017.

***Charleston Gazette-Mail* reporter Eric Eyre:** https://www.wvgazettemail.com/news/cops _and_courts/drug-firms-poured-m-painkillers-into-wv-amid-rise-of/article_99026dad-8ed5 -5075-90fa-adb906a36214.html.

"These country bumpkins'": Author interview, Metcalf, July 10, 2017.

heroin stuffed into the false bottom: Wolthuis's sentencing memo, United States v. Kareem Shaw, U.S. District Court for the Western Division of Virginia, Harrisonburg Division, April 21, 2015.

Wolthuis tallied the offense: Sentencing memo, United States of America v. Ryan Kenneth McQuinn, U.S. District Court for the Western District of Virginia, Harrisonburg Division, Feb. 27, 2015. McQuinn's release date was scheduled for May 13, 2018, including a sentence reduction for prison drug addiction and/or mental health treatment.

One of his first death cases: Author interview, Wolthuis, June 28, 2017.

And as far as she knew, Jesse's problem: Author interviews, Kristi Fernandez, May 23 and Aug. 17, 2016; Dennis Painter, June 17, 2016; and Courtney Fletcher, June 10, 2016, and May 17, 2017.

"So glad to be sober on this date": Postings by Jesse Bolstridge, from April 2013, at https://www.facebook.com/jesse.bolstridge.

"To be clear, the evidence supports long-term maintenance": Author interview, Dr. Nora Volkow, April 27, 2016. Volkow's testimony, presented to the Senate Judiciary Committee, Jan. 27, 2016: https://www.drugabuse.gov/about-nida/legislative-activities/testimony-to-congress/2016/what-science-tells-us-about-opioid-abuse-addiction.

even Hazelden, the Betty Ford–affiliated: Maia Szalavitz, "Hazelden Introduces Anti-addiction Medications into Recovery for First Time," *Time,* Nov. 5, 2012.

Jesse still owed $25,000 for that earlier rehab stint: Author interview, Fernandez, Sept. 10, 2017.

"The whole system needs revamped": Author interview, Tracey Helton Mitchell, May 8, 2017.

"in any given episode, they only see": Author interview, Dr. John Kelly, May 25, 2017.

He was forty-eight hours away from a do-over: Author interview, Fernandez, June 20, 2016.

"I'm not trying to do dope": Details from the last weekend of Jesse's life came from interviews with Fernandez, Painter, Fletcher, and Sgt. Brent Lutz.

"Arthur, I have been hearing a lot of foul shit lately": Ronnie Jones's letter to Arthur (no last name given), written by Jones on Jan. 13, 2015, and submitted by Wolthuis as evidence of continued harassment and drug dealing, even after Jones's arrest, in the government's case.

"Most agents would have written it off": Author interview, Wolthuis, June 2, 2016.

The thirty-seven-year-old New York native had recently: Details of how Metcalf tracked Santiago came from multiple author interviews with Metcalf as well as from pre-sentencing memoranda prepared in the case by his lawyer, Alberto Ebanks, and federal prosecutor Wolthuis, filed July 15, 2015.

"He deeply regrets his actions": Ebanks's presentencing memorandum, United States v. Matthew Santiago, U.S. District Court for the Western District of Virginia, Harrisonburg Division, filed July 7, 2015.

"wings on pigs": "Gunman 'Assassinates' 2 NYPD Officers in Brooklyn, Kills Self," NBCNewYork.com, Dec. 21, 2014.

in nearby Winchester he could now buy it: Compared with thirty dollars for a bag, or point, of heroin in Woodstock: Author interview, Lutz, Oct. 26, 2017.

when rural America becomes the new inner city: Janet Adamy and Paul Overberg, "Rural America Is the New 'Inner City,'" *Wall Street Journal,* May 27 and 28, 2017. Economic activity is more concentrated now in cities, and even many companies (for example, Amazon fulfillment centers) that were initially drawn to rural areas for lower taxes have picked up and moved to metro areas. The rural/urban divide has widened further following the 2007–2009 recession, with wages one-third higher in cities than rural areas, an inequality gap that is 50 percent wider than it was in the 1970s.

to get hauled back to jail: Painter's mug shot was posted on the Shenandoah County Sheriff's Office Facebook page, June 28, 2016, and noted that he was arrested for possession of a Schedule I/II drug, possession of drug paraphernalia, and possession of marijuana (second offense).

Jesse's was one of 8,257 heroin-related deaths: "Drug-Poisoning Deaths Involving Heroin: United States, 2000–2013," Centers for Disease Control and Prevention, March 2015: https://www.cdc.gov/nchs/data/databriefs/db190.htm. Overall, there were 43,982 drug-overdose deaths in 2013.

even after its own expert panel voted 11–2: Barry Meier, "Addiction Specialists Wary of New Painkiller," *New York Times,* Nov. 15, 2013.

"the benefits of this product outweigh the risks": Cathryn Jakobson Ramin, "Why Did the F.D.A. Approve a New Pain Drug?," *The New Yorker,* Dec. 2, 2013.

withdraw an opioid pain medication because of: Melanie Eversley and Sara Wise, "Risk of Abuse: FDA Wants Opioid Painkiller Pulled from Market," *USA Today,* June 8, 2017.

annual death toll for drug overdose: Sixty-four thousand deaths reported in 2017 for 2016: https://www.drugabuse.gov/related-topics/trends-statistics/overdose-death-rates.

"The most damaging thing Purdue did": Author interview, Dr. Andrew Kolodny, Jan. 6, 2016.

The point was by then moot: Author interviews, Barbara Van Rooyan, Jan. 16, 2017, and several follow-up correspondences, including letter from Department of Health and Human Services to Barbara and Kirk Van Rooyan, Sept. 10, 2013: "The Agency is requiring certain other modifications to the labeling, including the indication, for ER/LA [extended release, long-acting] opioid analgesics to help improve the safe use of these products. We decline to make the specific labeling changes you request, however." The *New Yorker* article Van Rooyan refers to is Patrick Radden Keefe, "Empire of Pain," Oct. 30, 2017.

approval of the original OxyContin: "FDA Actions on OxyContin Products, 4/16/2013," U.S. Food and Drug Administration, which noted that it was withdrawn from the market "for safety reasons": https://www.fda.gov/Drugs/DrugSafety/Informationby DrugClass/ucm347857.htm.

Americans, representing 4.4 percent of the world's population: Gary Garrison, "Claire McCaskill Cites Disproven Figure on Opioid Use," PolitiFact.com, May 10, 2017, citing International Narcotics Board data.

CHAPTER NINE. WHAC-A-MOLE

Interviews: Ashlyn Kessler, Lee Miller, Andrew Bassford, Dr. Isaac Van Patten, Tess Henry, Patricia Mehrmann, Dr. Alan Henry, Terrence Engles, Special Agent Joe Crowder, Mark O'Brien, Chief Chris Perkins, Jamie Waldrop

("Generally speaking, there are people who overdose"): Author interviews, Ashlyn Kessler, via prison-monitored email, video exchanges, and letters, June 2016 to September 2017.

a young mother named April who'd recently: Tiffany Stevens, "Baby Turned Over to CPS After Police Find Adults Passed Out in Vehicle," *Roanoke Times,* Feb. 28, 2017. April Lynne Maxwell was revived by EMTs with naloxone and taken to jail and charged with felony child neglect. Two other adults in the car with her also overdosed and were charged with being intoxicated in public.

"Ashlyn is gonna break your heart": Author interview, Lee Miller, June 13, 2016.

fifteen thousand text messages: Author interview, Andrew Bassford, Jan. 6, 2016, and follow-up interviews in person and via email.

"Can you meet me at Sheetz on Peters Creek Road?": Ibid.

after putting away her first heroin dealer: Ibid. and Jeff Sturgeon, "Roanoke Heroin Ring Shut Down," *Roanoke Times,* Nov. 14, 2014.

"We don't enjoy the cooperation": Author interviews, Dr. Isaac Van Patten, May 1, 2016, and April 19, 2017; United Nations' International Narcotics Control Board data on where heroin is produced: Christopher Woody and Reuters, "Here's Where America's Heroin Comes From," March 3, 2016.

I thought of Tess Henry: Dozens of author interviews with Tess Henry and her mother, Patricia Mehrmann, took place beginning Dec. 2, 2015, and continued in person, over the phone, and via text and Facebook Messenger, up until this book went to press.

the same way four out of five heroin addicts: "79.5% of new heroin initiates in the National Survey on Drug Use and Health reported that their initial drug was a prescription opioid," according to Richard C. Dart et al., "Trends in Opioid Analgesic Abuse and Mortality in the United States," *New England Journal of Medicine,* Jan. 15, 2015.

Regulations now limited doctors: Laurence Hammack, "DEA Rule Targets Popular Painkillers," *Roanoke Times,* Oct. 5, 2014. Quadrupling of prescription opioids: "Understanding the Epidemic," Centers for Disease Control and Prevention, Aug. 30, 2017, https://www.cdc.gov/drugoverdose/epidemic/index.html.

upscheduling had been controversial: John J. Coleman, "Rescheduling Hydrocodone Combination Products: Addressing the Abuse of America's Favorite Opioid," *American Society of Addiction Medicine,* April 10, 2015.

one critic wrote in a published letter: Joe Graedon, "Patients in Pain Are Outraged About New Hydrocodone Rules," *People's Pharmacy,* Oct. 20, 2014.

"hot pack" their product: Author interview, Joe Crowder, May 1, 2016.

"I begged her public defender": Author interview, Dr. Alan Henry, Dec. 20, 2017.

the fetus growing inside Tess: "Abrupt discontinuation of opioid use during pregnancy can result in premature labor, fetal distress, and miscarriage," according to "A Collaborative Approach to the Treatment of Pregnant Women with Opioid Use Disorders," Substance Abuse and Mental Health Services Administration, Aug. 2, 2016, available at https://ncsacw.samhsa.gov/files/Collaborative_Approach_508.pdf.

now being illicitly imported from China: David Armstrong, " 'Truly Terrifying': Chinese Suppliers Flood US and Canada with Deadly Fentanyl," *STAT,* April 5, 2016.

(Some arrived from China via Mexico): "Fentanyl: China's Deadly Export to the United States," staff report, U.S.–China Economic and Security Review Commission, Feb. 1, 2017, https://www.uscc.gov/Research/fentanyl-china's-deadly-export-united-states.

"Some of the companies shipping this stuff": Author interview, Mark O'Brien, then-director of opioid overdose prevention and treatment, Baltimore City Health Department, Sept. 4, 2016.

But each time a derivative was banned: As cited by DEA spokesman Russ Baer in Sara Ganim, "China's Fentanyl Ban a 'Game Changer' for Opioid Epidemic, DEA Officials Say," CNN, Feb. 16, 2017; Kathleen McLaughlin, "Underground Labs in China Are Devising Potent New Opiates Faster Than Authorities Can Respond," *Science,* March 29, 2017.

Roanoke police seized 560 grams: "Roanoke Valley Needs Assessment Partnerships for Success," Roanoke Area Youth Substance Abuse Coalition (RAYSAC), Sept. 30, 2016, 22. The majority of those arrested were white males in their mid to late twenties.

Perkins had long championed community policing: Amy Friedenberger, "One Last Walk on the Old Beat," *Roanoke Times,* March 1, 2016.

Hotels situated along the perimeter of Roanoke: Highways that pass by or cut through the city include I-81, I- 581, and U.S. 220; nearby hotels become prime heroin-dealing hot spots, according to RAYSAC survey, "Executive Summary," 1.

shoplifting fueled by users like Tess: Author interviews, Chief Chris Perkins, Dec. 29, 2015, and April 24, 2017, and Tiffany Stevens, "Drug Initiative Faces New Street Realities," *Roanoke Times,* Feb. 21, 2016.

A thirty-four-year-old woman was murdered: Violent crime up: Author interview, Van Patten; hotel murder: Neil Harvey, "Suspect in Roanoke Woman's Death Is Denied Bond," *Roanoke Times,* April 18, 2017.

Police Assisted Addiction and Recovery Initiative: Brian MacQuarrie, "'Angel' Opioid Initiative Thrives Despite Exit of Gloucester Police Chief," *Boston Globe,* Feb. 21, 2017.

Janine had spent the previous seven years: Bobby's story and the beginnings of the Hope Initiative outlined in multiple author interviews, Janine Underwood, beginning Aug. 3, 2016.

"It was like we had a Dementor from *Harry Potter*": Author interview, Jamie Waldrop, Nov. 6, 2017.

a former pro baseball player who'd progressed: Author interviews, Terrence Engles, Jan. 4, 2016, and subsequent interviews.

"RomneyCare": Kenneth Rapoza, "If ObamaCare Is So Bad, How Does RomneyCare Survive?," *Forbes,* Jan. 20, 2012.

sacrificing $6.6 million a day in federal funds: "McAuliffe Pushes Virginia Medicaid expansion After GOP's Failure to Repeal Obamacare," CNN Wire, March 27, 2017. Republican House of Delegates speaker William Howell claimed an expansion would take state resources from education, transportation, and public safety, even though 90 percent of the bill would be footed by the federal government.

In states where Medicaid expansions were passed: Noam N. Levey, "Tens of Thousands Died Due to an Opioid Addiction Last Year. With an Obamacare Repeal, Some Fear the Number Will Rise," *Los Angeles Times,* June 21, 2017.

It gave coverage to an additional 1.3 million: Sally Satel, "Taking On the Scourge of Opioids," *National Affairs,* Summer 2017: 21.

political plot that seemed lifted from: Laura Vozzella, "Virginia Democratic Senator Puckett to Resign, Possibly Dooming Push to Expand Medicaid," *Washington Post,* June 8, 2014. Political wrangling for favors: Jeff Schapiro, "McAuliffe, Others Pressed Puckett to Stay," *Richmond Times-Dispatch,* June 10, 2014.

removed himself from consideration for the tobacco post: Puckett denied the quid pro quo, saying his talks with the Republican-controlled tobacco commission began only after he'd decided to leave. "At this point in my life, I feel that I cannot allow my political career to hamper my daughter's future," he said in a statement, according to Trip Gabriel, "State Senator's Resignation Deepens Political Turmoil in Virginia," *New York Times,* June 9, 2014.

while a six-month federal investigation: Andrew Cain, "U.S. Attorney's Office Closes Puckett Probe, Will Not Seek Charges," *Richmond Times-Dispatch,* Dec. 12, 2014.

a thousand more than died from AIDS in 1995: Centers for Disease Control and

Prevention, as outlined in charts in German Lopez and Sarah Frostenson, "How the Opioid Epidemic Became America's Worst Drug Crisis Ever, in 15 Maps and Charts," *Vox*, March 29, 2017.

sixty-five new cases reported that year: NAS cases in Virginia had climbed from 88 in 1999 to 493 in 2013; in the Southwestern health district, there were 65 new HIV cases in 2015 and 46 in 2016, according to the Virginia Department of Health: http://www.vdh.virginia.gov/data/opioid-overdose/.

"My fear is that these are sentinel areas": Dr. Art Van Zee's letter to Purdue senior medical director Dr. Dan Spyker, Nov. 23, 2000.

CHAPTER TEN. LIMINALITY

Interviews: Tess Henry, Patricia Mehrmann, Dr. Hughes Melton, Dr. Lisa Andruscavage, Kim Ramsey, Dr. Cheri Hartman, Kate Neuhausen, Missy Carter, Chief Mark Mitchell, Sarah Melton, Nancy D. Campbell, Dr. Steve Loyd, Judge Jack Hurley, Anne Giles, Don Flattery, Dr. Art Van Zee, Dr. Nora Volkow, Dr. Jennifer Wells, Jamie Waldrop

Suboxone is typically the preferred MAT: Standards shifted in 2017; Virginia Board of Medicine guidelines now recommended pregnant mothers use Subutex for no more than seven days before transitioning to Suboxone. Author interviews, Dr. Hughes Melton, March 31, July 1, Oct. 3, and Oct. 28, 2017.

Subutex babies, about half of whom require: Half of babies born in Roanoke to mothers on MAT require NICU care, usually involving methadone given twice a day, for an average in-hospital period of 7.7 days, according to author interviews with neonatologist Dr. Lisa Andruscavage, May 10 and 11, 2017, and clinical nurse specialist Kim Ramsey, May 11, 2017.

"If you two wake that baby up": Author interview and NAS unit visit with Andruscavage, May 10, 2017.

the fifty-five babies born with NAS: Carilion NAS data from Ramsey and Andruscavage; statewide NAS data compiled from Virginia Department of Health: http://www.vdh.virginia.gov/data/opioid-overdose/.

dependent babies released from the NICU: Among the 55 NAS babies born between 2015 and 2016, 37 went home with a parent, 5 with another caregiver, and 13 went directly into foster care (though 2 of the 37 eventually landed in foster care); Andruscavage and Ramsey data. Babies typically wean off their low doses of methadone within three months.

Many have been stigmatized: Author interview, Ramsey.

Access to MAT in Virginia: Author interviews, Melton and Department of Medical Assistance Services director Kate Neuhausen, July 27, 2017.

As a work-around to the Republicans' refusal: Author interview, Neuhausen.

"When calling facilities there is rarely": Text to author from Patricia Mehrmann, Oct. 5, 2017.

most families to continue navigating: Author interview, psychologist and Hope Initiative volunteer Cheri Hartman, Aug. 8, 2017.

"Their treatment is a video playing": Author interview, Missy Carter, June 20, 2017.

(Nationally, roughly half of drug courts): According to the National Drug Court Institute, 56 percent of drug courts allowed MAT, 2016: https://www.ndci.org/resources/training/medication-assisted-treatment/.

"abusing it every which way": Author interview, Lebanon police chief Mark Mitchell, May 4, 2016.

"a wonderful medicine, but we were seeing": Author interview, pharmacist and professor Sarah Melton, July 24, 2017.

several of the nation's top buprenorphine prescribers: Using data from a *ProPublica* study of Medicaid reimbursements in 2013, John Ramsey, "Clinic Operators See Benefits of Careful Suboxone Use," *Richmond Times Dispatch,* Aug. 6, 2016.

Buprenorphine is the third-most-diverted opioid: Sally Satel, "Taking On the Scourge of Opioids," *National Affairs,* Summer 2017: 13.

She texted me: Author interview, Patricia Mehrmann, Sept. 3, 2017.

"no one wants to tell Prince": Monthly meeting of NAS policy board, Roanoke Memorial Hospital, Kim Ramsey, May 11, 2017.

The FBN framed methadone: Multiple interviews about the history of addiction maintenance drugs with historian Nancy D. Campbell, August and September 2017. Campbell and Anne M. Lovell, "The History of the Development of Buprenorphine as an Addiction Therapeutic," *Annals of the New York Academy of Sciences,* February 2012: 124–39.

"pharmacologically perfect solution": Campbell and Lovell, "The History of the Development of Buprenorphine," citing the researcher P. F. Renault from 1978. First use of Vivitrol in jails in Barnstable County, MA, according to Tina Rosenberg, "Medicines to Keep Addiction Away," *New York Times,* Feb. 16, 2016. Aggressive marketing of Vivitrol, with sales going from $30 million in 2011 to $209 million in 2016: Jake Harper, "To Grow Market Share, a Drugmaker Pitches Its Product to Judges," NPR, Aug. 3, 2017.

While methadone remained on the fringes: Campbell and Lovell, "The History of the Development of Buprenorphine."

20 percent of returning Vietnam veterans: Lee N. Robins, "The Sixth Thomas James Okey Memorial Lecture: Vietnam Veterans' Rapid Recovery from Heroin Addiction: A Fluke or Normal Expectation?," *Addiction,* August 1993.

The battle lines over MAT: My op-ed on the MAT controversy, "Addicted to a Treatment for Addiction," *New York Times,* May 28, 2016.

In 2016, not long after a Kentucky appeals court: The shift of Kentucky drug courts to allow MAT was prompted by a *Huffington Post* investigation by journalist Jason Cherkis, "Kentucky Reforms Drug Court Rules to Let Heroin Addicts Take Prescribed Meds," April 17, 2015.

Price disappointed treatment advocates: Harper, "Price's Remarks on Opioid Treatment Were Unscientific and Damaging, Experts Say," NPR, May 16, 2017.

"She worked on him in a hurry": Author interview, Dr. Steve Loyd, Tennessee's assistant commissioner for Substance Abuse Services, Aug. 25, 2017.

resigned a few months later: Juliet Eilperin, Amy Goldstein, and John Wagner, "HHS Secretary Tom Price Resigns Amid Criticism for Taking Charter Flights at Taxpayer Expense," *Washington Post,* Sept. 29, 2017.

signaled the administration would significantly expand: Sheila Kaplan, "F.D.A. to Expand Medication-Assisted Therapy for Opioid Addicts," *New York Times,* Feb. 25, 2018.

Graduates are roughly a half to a third less likely: National Association of Drug Court Professionals, as cited in Satel, "Taking On the Scourge,"17.

"We've had thirteen babies born": Author interview, Tazewell County drug court judge Jack Hurley, April 20, 2016.

"The best research says counseling doesn't help": Author interview, counselor Anne Giles, Sept. 8, 2016. Giles was referring to a British study on 150,000 patients showing that people in abstinence-only care had double the death rate of those who received ongoing MAT, though that study doesn't compare MAT-only with MAT with counseling: Matthias Pierce et al., "Impact of Treatment for Opioid Dependence on Fatal Drug-Related Poisoning: A National Cohort Study in England," *Addiction,* February 2016.

"although some benefit is seen even with low dose and minimum support": Research on opioid-substitution protocols: John Strang et al., "Drug Policy and the Public Good: Evidence for Effective Interventions," *Lancet,* Jan. 7, 2012.

only cash because Medicaid reimbursements were: Author interview, Giles, Sept. 8, 2016. Reimbursements improved in Virginia in April 2017, under new regulations meant to nudge cash-only clinics toward adopting best practices; author interview, Dr. Hughes Melton.

He'd lost his twenty-six-year-old son: Author interview, Don Flattery, Dec. 30, 2015.

Art Van Zee, too, struggled with: Author interview, Dr. Art Van Zee, June 25, 2016.

he hesitated to wean them entirely because: "If tapered off buprenorphine-naloxone, even after twelve weeks of treatment, the likelihood of an unsuccessful outcome is high, even in patients receiving counseling in addition to standard medical management," according to Roger D. Weiss et al., "Adjunctive Counseling During Brief and Extended Buprenorphine-Naloxone Treatment for Prescription Opioid Dependence," *Archives of General Psychiatry,* December 2011.

one study showed that 50 percent of users: Brandon S. Bentzley et al., "Discontinuation of Buprenorphine Maintenance Therapy: Perspectives and Outcomes," *Journal of Substance Abuse Treatment,* May 2015: 48–57.

roughly a third of buprenorphine patients: Roger D. Weiss et al., "Long-Term Outcomes from the National Drug Abuse Treatment Clinical Trials Network Prescription Opioid Addiction Treatment Study," *Drug and Alcohol Dependence,* May 2015: 112–19.

his or her relapse feeds the perception: Author interview, Dr. Nora Volkow, April 22, 2016.

One Roanoke woman was so desperate to avoid: Author interview, Dr. Jennifer Wells, May 1, 2017.

"Can yoi please come gwt me": Text to author from Tess Henry, Feb. 11, 2016.

"misunderstanding with the siblings and with me": Author interview, Dr. Alan Henry, Dec. 30, 2017.

They stopped speaking: Author interview, April Henry, Jan. 3, 2018.

She was furious with the baby's other grandmother: Author interview, Tess Henry, at her mom's house during a visit to see her son, April 20, 2016.

"I've never been fucked up": Author interview, Tess Henry and Mehrmann, April 20, 2016.

Jamie reached out to Tess: Tess Henry's Facebook page, May 22, 2016.

"Last seen June 11, 2016": Tess Henry's missing poster, disseminated by Help Save the Next Girl.

"If only [politicians] understood that getting access": The Emergency Medical Treatment and Labor Act (EMTALA) requires anyone coming to an emergency department to be stabilized and treated, regardless of his or her insurance status or ability to pay: author interview, Cheri Hartman, Oct. 13, 2017.

"Pray that this time": Text to author from Jamie Waldrop, July 28, 2017.

Vivitrol shots to people before they left prisons: Sam Quinones, "Addicts Need Help. Jails Could Have the Answer," *New York Times,* June 16, 2017. Maine became the thirty-second state to expand Medicaid and the first to do it via a ballot initiative: Michelle Hackman and Jennifer Levitz, "Maine Votes to Expand Medicaid Under the Health Law," *Wall Street Journal,* Nov. 7, 2017.

Joey eventually transitioned to buprenorphine: Author interview with Joey's father, Danny Gilbert, April 14, 2017.

Jamie Waldrop and I visited Tess in the psych ward: Author interview, Tess Henry, LewisGale Pavilion, Oct. 31, 2016.

Roanoke claimed the highest number of emergency-room: RAYSAC needs assessment summary, compiled using Virginia Department of Health data.

young mother dead in her bedroom: Author interview, Vinton EMS volunteer Jordan Fifer, May 1, 2017.

e. e. cummings poem: Tess had memorized the poem, "[I carry your heart with me (I carry it in)]," available here: https://www.poetryfoundation.org/poetrymagazine/poems/49493/i-carry-your-heart-with-mei-carry-it-in.

"Gone to Carilion": Mehrmann texted me a photo of the note, Jan. 13, 2017.

CHAPTER ELEVEN. HOPE ON A SPREADSHEET

Interviews: Janine Underwood, Dr. Karen Kuehl, Erin Casey, Cheri Hartman, Louise Vincent, Mark O'Brien, Tracey Helton Mitchell, Sgt. Kevin Coffman, Nancy Hans, Dr. John Burton, Dr. John Kelly, Jamie Waldrop, Emma Hurley, Danny Gilbert, Charles Cullen, Patricia Mehrmann, Wendy Gilbert, Britney Gilbert, Skyler Gilbert

Fentanyl-overdose calls were coming in: From the first six months of 2016, combined Roanoke city and county counted 85, compared with 38 during the same window the prior year: EMS data and author interview, Janine Underwood, Aug. 3, 2016.

Karen Kuehl begged him not to leave: Author interview, Carilion Clinic emergency-room doctor Karen Kuehl, May 9, 2017.

In one weekend: Author interview, Underwood, May 8, 2017.

the program wouldn't be operational until 2018: Author interview, Erin Casey, Dec. 14, 2017. Casey led Carilion's peer recovery specialist efforts.

the women were crushed to learn: Author interview, Cheri Hartman, Oct. 9, 2017.

a way to force users into treatment: Massachusetts and thirty-nine other states allow involuntary commitment for drug treatment: Karen Brown, "Some See Uptick in 'Voluntary' Addiction Treatment Commitments as Problematic," WBUR, Oct. 25, 2016.

many experts believed coerced treatment: William L. White and William R. Miller, "The Use of Confrontation in Addiction Treatment: History, Science, and Time for Change," *Counselor,* January 2007: 12–30. Maia Szalavitz outlines a host of reasons in "Attract Patients to Addiction Treatment, Don't Force Them Into It," *New York Times,* May 4, 2016.

"They have the disease, too": Author interview, Underwood, Jan. 6, 2017.

Levine also issued a standing order: Gregory S. Schneider, "Virginia Declares Opioid Emergency, Makes Antidote Available to All," *Washington Post*, Nov. 21, 2016.

Vancouver officials launched supervised: Gordon Omand, "B.C. Naloxone Kits Flood Province to Reverse Overdoses Amid Fentanyl Crisis," *Canadian Press*, Sept. 21, 2016.

Several liberal-leaning American states and cities: Katie Zezima, "Awash in Overdoses, Seattle Creates Safe Sites for Addicts to Inject Legal Drugs," *Washington Post*, Jan. 27, 2017.

a purple ALLY patch: Martha Bebinger, "Hacking a Solution to Boston's Opioid Crisis," WBUR, Sept. 12, 2016.

piloting fentanyl test strips: Bebinger, "As Fentanyl Deaths Rise, an Off-Label Tool Becomes a Test for the Killer Opioid," WBUR, May 11, 2017.

drug-user unions: Author interview, Louise Vincent, May 4, 2017, and http://ncurbansurvivorunion.org.

About a third of all U.S. treatment centers: National Survey of Substance Abuse Treatment Services (N-SSATS), Department of Health and Human Services, July 2017.

In Baltimore, where the overdose death rate was: Author interview, Mark O'Brien, Sept. 4, 2016.

reducing needle-injected HIV instances: Address by Dr. Leana Wen, Baltimore City Health Department director, Poynter Institute's "Covering the Opioid Crisis," Washington, D.C., Sept. 26, 2016.

Conservative then–Indiana governor Mike Pence responded: Alan Schwarz and Mitch Smith, "Needle Exchange Is Allowed After H.I.V. Outbreak in an Indiana County," *New York Times*, March 26, 2015. A year later, HIV in the county had plateaued at around 210 cases.

Mitchell launched her own renegade: Andrew McMillon, "The Heroin Heroine of Reddit," BackChannel.com (also published on Medium.com), July 21, 2015. Tracey Helton Mitchell would go on to author *The Big Fix: Hope After Heroin* (Berkeley: Seal Press, 2016).

"We're in the absolute dark ages": Author interview, Mitchell, May 8, 2017.

imprison heroin users *for life*: Author interview, Sgt. Kevin Coffman, July 10, 2017.

"Don't do it": Cameron Joseph, "AG Jeff Sessions Calls for Return to 'Just Say No,'" *New York Daily News*, March 15, 2017.

backed health care changes that would have put: Andrew Taylor and Jonathan Lemire, "Trump Moving to Slash Budget for White House Drug Czar," ABC News, May 5, 2017.

After a backlash, Trump rolled back: Andrew Joseph, "After Outcry, Trump Budget Largely Preserves 'Drug Czar' Funding," *STAT*, May, 23, 2017.

the office still lacked a permanent director: *Politico* staff, "Trump to Nominate Jim Carroll for 'Drug Czar,'" *Politico*, Feb. 9, 2018.

remained a work in progress or unaddressed: Tamara Keith, "Trump Says Administration Working on 'Very Very Strong' Policies to Combat Opioids," NPR, March 1, 2018. The White House was criticized as viewing the drug czar position (and the opioid epidemic) as an afterthought, with Carroll nominated for it only after disappointing Trump as deputy chief of staff: Matthew Yglesias, "A Telling Anecdote About Trump and the Opioid Abuse Crisis," *Vox,* March 1, 2018. White House counselor Kellyanne Conway was now Trump's opioid point person, "quietly freezing out drug policy professionals and relying instead on political staff to address a crisis claiming about 175 lives a day," according to *Politico* staff, "Trump to Nominate Jim Carroll for 'Drug Czar,'" *Politico,* Feb. 9, 2018.

showed definitively that the problem was: According to Roanoke County police data: "Interoffice Memorandum," compiled by Brittni Money at author's request, May 3, 2017, with 513 heroin arrests between 2010 and March 2017, most in Southwest County (Cave Spring/Hidden Valley area), and 81 heroin overdoses between 2014 and early 2017, 19 of them fatal.

The school board declined to support the program: Author interview, Nancy Hans, April 25, 2017.

drug-prevention forum put on at: Prevention council forum at Cave Spring High School, Feb. 21, 2017.

A come-to-Jesus ensued: Author interviews, Dr. John Burton, March 20, 2017, and Kuehl.

"She was such a good kid": Track coach Tommy Maguire, exchange with Patricia Mehrmann, prevention council forum at Cave Spring High School, Feb. 21, 2017.

The latest research on substance use disorder: John Kelly, "Reasons for Optimism: Recovery Science," Association of Health Journalists Conference, Orlando, FL, April 2017, slide 14.

10 percent of the addicted population manages: Address by then–drug czar Michael Botticelli, Poynter Institute's "Covering the Opioid Crisis," Washington, D.C., Sept. 26, 2016. There are about 23 million Americans diagnosed with diabetes, according to 2017 Centers for Disease Control and Prevention figures—roughly the same as those with some form of substance use disorder (22 million); author interview, Dr. John Kelly, Nov. 6, 2017.

"It's like, dear God": Author interview, Patricia Mehrmann, May 17, 2017. Tess's admission to the Nevada center also recounted in interviews with Terrence Engles and Jamie Waldrop.

If Tess could remain sober for a year: Michael L. Dennis, Mark A. Foss, Christy K. Scott, "An Eight-Year Perspective on the Relationship Between the Duration of Abstinence and Other Aspects of Recovery," *Evaluation Review,* December 2007.

when making a Facebook workout video: Joey's Facebook workout video, with Emma Hurley, April 25, 2013: https://www.facebook.com/permalink.php?story_fbid=10106610813798632&id=68137950&comment_id=10106705958198492&notif_t=comment_mention&notif_id=1494943625490149.

"ball of fire": Author interview, Emma Hurley, May 15, 2007.

"I already know": Author interview, Charles Cullen, May 11, 2017.

uninsured Joey applied to the hospital-run clinic: Danny Gilbert said he used the website goodrx.com with each prescription to figure out which pharmacy in town had the best prices that week; author interview, Oct. 27, 2017. After Joey's death, Carilion Clinic wrote off more than $10,000 of her bills as charity care.

those who have serious psychiatric problems: Author interview, Hartman, Aug. 8, 2017.

Jamie worried, too: Author interviews with Jamie Waldrop, Hartman, Hurley, Cullen, and Danny and Wendy Gilbert, April and May 2017.

"asinine to tell a drug addict you've got to be clean": Author interview: Danny Gilbert, April 11, 2017. Account of Joey's death and cause of death: Author interview, Danny, Wendy, Britney, and Skyler Gilbert, Sept. 22, 2017.

"She fought hard against the demon of addiction": Obituary for Jordan Racquel (Joey) Gilbert, *Roanoke Times*, March 29, 2017.

"If she fails, she is on her own": Author interview, Mehrmann, May 15, 2017.

Sweet T: Mother's Day text exchange between Tess and Mehrmann, May 14, 2017.

CHAPTER TWELVE. "BROTHER, WRONG OR RIGHT"

Interviews: Rosemary Hopkins, Andrew Bassford, Cheri Hartman, Ronnie Jones, Anthony West, Dr. Andrew Kolodny, Lauren Cummings, Pastor Brad Hill, Mark Schroeder, Christine Madeleine Lee, Bryan Stevenson, Thomas Jones III, Robert Pack, Don Wolthuis, Sherwin Jacobs, Kristi Fernandez, Beth Schmidt, Richard Ausness, Chip Jones

"lull all pain and anger and bring forgetfulness": *The Odyssey of Homer,* translated by S. H. Butcher and Andrew Lang (New York: Macmillan, 1906), 47.

soul was "being rubbed down with silk": From Druin Burch's *Taking the Medicine: A Short History of Medicine's Beautiful Idea, and Our Difficulty Swallowing It* (London: Random House UK, 2010), 16. A worthwhile examination of the morphine molecule's pull in literature, art, and film offers several other examples: Lecture by Susan L. Mizruchi, "Opioids: The Literary, Experiential Point of View," Boston Athenaeum, June 13, 2017, available at https://vimeo.com/221754272.

"trying to get rid of the lowlifes": Author interview, Rosemary Hopkins, Sept. 23, 2016.

"more boxes that have to be checked": Author interview, Andrew Bassford, April 10, 2017.

An annual $35 billion lie: Michael Corkery, Jessica Silver-Greenberg, and David Segal, "Addiction, Inc.: Marketing Wizards and Urine-Testing Millionaires: Inside the Lucrative Business of America's Opioid Crisis," *New York Times,* Dec. 27, 2017.

"we don't have good data": Author interview, Dr. John Kelly, Jan. 2, 2018.

"killing people for that myth to be out there": Author interview, Cheri Hartman, Jan. 16, 2018.

statewide corrections behemoth that returns: Author interview, Anthony West, chief operations officer, Virginia CARES, July 14, 2017.

likens the war on drugs to a system: Michelle Alexander, *The New Jim Crow: Mass Incarceration in the Age of Colorblindness* (New York: New Press, 2010). Alexander's thesis was further delineated by a 2017 book by scholar John F. Pfaff, in which he argues that the incarceration spike was fueled more by elected local prosecutors, the vast majority of them white men who operate behind a veil of secrecy and aggressively forge plea deals in 95 percent of cases: *Locked In: The True Causes of Mass Incarceration—and How to Achieve Mass Reform* (New York: Basic Books, 2017).

shift in public spending from health and welfare programs: "Fact Sheet: Trends in U.S. Corrections, U.S. State and Federal Prison Population, 1925–2015," Sentencing Project: http://sentencingproject.org/wp-content/uploads/2016/01/Trends-in-US-Corrections.pdf; Bryan Stevenson, *Just Mercy: A Story of Justice and Redemption* (New York: Spiegel & Grau), 2014, introduction.

one in three black men was destined to end up: Marc Mauer, Sentencing Project, "Addressing Racial Disparities in Incarceration," *Prison Journal,* 2011. The *Washington Post* elucidated those statistics (and found them to be somewhat outdated by 2015) in Glenn Kessler, "The Stale Statistic That One in Three Black Males Will End Up in Jail," June 16, 2015. In the Washington, D.C., area where Jones hailed from, the statistic was three out of four, according to Alexander, *The New Jim Crow,* 6–7, citing 2000 corrections data.

recidivism rate of 75 percent: Matthew R. Durose, Alexia D. Cooper, and Howard N. Snyder, "Recidivism of Prisoners Released in 30 States in 2005: Patterns from 2005 to 2010," U.S. Department of Justice, Bureau of Justice Statistics, April 2014. Among prisoners released in 2005 and tracked for five years: 32 percent had drug-related offenses, and of those, 77 percent reoffended within that five-year period, compared with 57 percent of all offenders released who reoffended, and 75 percent of drug traffickers reoffended: https://www.bjs.gov/content/pub/pdf/rprts05p0510.pdf.

statistically less likely to use or to deal: Blacks are far more likely to be arrested for selling or possessing drugs than whites, even though whites use drugs at the same rate, and whites are also more likely to sell drugs: Analysis of National Survey on Drug Use and Health data by Jonathan Rothwell, Brookings Institution, outlined in Christopher Ingraham, "White People Are More Likely to Deal Drugs But Black People Are More Likely to Get Arrested For It," *Washington Post,* Sept. 30, 2014.

(Three-quarters of federal drug offenders are black): https://www.bjs.gov/content/pub/pdf/dofp12.pdf. State rates: http://www.drugpolicy.org/issues/drug-war-statistics.

"racial stereotyping actually seems to be having": Author interview, Dr. Andrew Kolodny, Jan. 6, 2016.

young whites were dying of overdose: Centers for Disease Control and Prevention data, "Drug Poisoning Mortality, United States, 1999–2015," Jan. 19, 2016, and Allan Smith, "There's a Disturbing Theory About Why America's Overdose Epidemic Is Primarily Affecting White People," *Business Insider,* Jan. 25, 2016.

Winchester was launching the region's first drug court: Author interviews, Lauren Cummings, July 3 and July 17, 2017.

Winchester was becoming a magnet: Ibid.; Matthew Umstead, "P&G Still Looking for Workers for New W.Va. Plant," *Herald-Mail Media,* Dec. 8, 2016; and staff report, "Governor Announces Amazon's E-Commerce Facility and 1,000 New Jobs in Frederick," *Winchester Star,* March 28, 2017.

Sunday services at the downtown mall: Author interview, Pastor Brad Hill, July 14, 2017.

"That's usually when they commit new crimes": Author interview with Ronnie Jones's probation officer, name withheld because she said she wasn't authorized to speak, June 30, 2016. Of the 5.2 million people across the United States who owed child support in 2010, 662,000 were incarcerated, according to federal data from the Office of Child Support Enforcement.

holdover from a 1996 federal ban: States that still have full bans preventing felons from getting food stamps are Arizona, Florida, Indiana, Mississippi, Nebraska, South Carolina, and West Virginia, according to Teresa Wiltz, "States Ease Access to Welfare and Food Stamps for Convicted Drug Felons," *PBS NewsHour,* Aug. 9, 2016; Yale study: Helen Dodson, "Ban on Food Stamps Leads to Hunger, HIV Risk Among Former Drug Felons," *YaleNews,* March 25, 2013.

(Virginia is one of twenty-six states): Eli Hager, "Six States Where Felons Can't Get Food Stamps," Marshall Project, Feb. 4, 2016. Six states still have full bans—Alaska, Georgia, Mississippi, South Carolina, West Virginia, and Wyoming. Virginia's partial-ban restrictions are listed here: https://vacode.org/2016/63.2/II/5/63.2-505.2/.

were given reduced sentences: Author interview, Christine Madeleine Lee, Mark Schroeder's federal public defender, July 5, 2016. Ann E. Marimow, "One of Scalia's Final Opinions Will Shorten Some Federal Prison Sentences," *Washington Post,* June 24, 2016, referring to Johnson v. United States, Supreme Court of the United States, Washington, D.C., June 2015. A 2013 Yale School of Medicine study found that 91 percent of people recently released from prison didn't have reliable access to food: https://news.yale.edu/2013/03/25/ban-food-stamps-leads-hunger-hiv-risk-among-former-drug-felons.

"designed for you to come back": Author interview, Mark Schroeder, July 17, 2017.

felon-friendlier cities like Seattle?: People in Seattle's Law Enforcement Assisted Diversion program are 60 percent less likely to commit further crimes, according to an independent review conducted by the University of Washington, http://leadkingcounty.org/lead-evaluation/who, and Sarah Jarvis, "Innovative LEAD Program for Drug Criminals Expands to Seattle's East Precinct," *Seattle Times,* Aug. 4, 2016.

"If we reduced our prison population": Author interview, Bryan Stevenson, July 14, 2017.

Portugal, which decriminalized all drugs: Drug-related pathologies including sexually transmitted diseases and deaths due to drug usage have also decreased dramatically, attributable to increased treatments made possible by decriminalization and money diverted from criminal justice to treatment, according to Glenn Greenwald, "Drug Decriminalisation in Portugal: Lessons for Creating Fair and Successful Drug Policies," Cato Institute (white paper), April 2, 2009.

drug addicts were funneled into treatment instead: Portugal's shift toward a health-centered approach to drugs was even more responsible than decriminalization for drug-rate reductions, Christopher Ingraham, "Why Hardly Anyone Dies from a Drug Overdose in Portugal," *Washington Post,* using data from George Murkin's "Drug Decriminalisation in Portugal: Setting the Record Straight," published in "Transform: Getting Drugs Under Control," June 11, 2014, available here: http://www.tdpf.org.uk/blog/drug-decriminalisation-portugal-setting-record-straight.

Ronnie was obstinate to a fault: Author interview, Thomas Jones III, Aug. 6, 2016.

Their family was not without connections: Alex Prewitt, "Petey Jones, Immortalized in 'Remember the Titans,' Still Works at T.C. Williams High School," *Washington Post,* Oct. 13, 2014; and author interviews, Ronnie and Thomas Jones III.

his maternal grandfather, Thomas "Pete" Jones Sr.: Author interviews, Ronnie and Thomas Jones III, and http://www.alexandriaafricanamericanhalloffame.org/?p=41.

2001, a time when prosecutors: Pfaff, *Locked In,* 22.

politically safer and economically cheaper: Pfaff, *Locked In,* and Pfaff, "The Never-Ending 'Willie Horton Effect' Is Keeping Prisons Too Full for America's Good," *Los Angeles Times,* May 14, 2017.

everyone involved views the problem too rigidly: Author interview, Robert Pack, May 23, 2017.

recording with the rap band Little Brother: Brandon Soderberg, "Little Brother's Retirement Party," *Village Voice*, April 27, 2010. Thomas Jones III goes by the rapper name Big Pooh and went on to have a solo career under that name. He now writes music and manages rap artists.

"Real Love": From the 2011 Big Pooh album, *Dirty Pretty Things*, reprinted with permission of Thomas Jones III.

Jurisdictions across the country increasingly inhibit: Alexes Harris, *A Pound of Flesh: Monetary Sanctions as Punishment for the Poor* (New York: Russell Sage Foundation, 2016).

quest to put him behind bars for many years and possibly even for life: Had Jones gone to trial, his maximum sentence could have been 360 months, or thirty years, to life imprisonment: Author interview, Don Wolthuis, Nov. 2, 2017.

Jacobs, the fired first attorney: Author interview, Harrisonburg defense attorney Sherwin Jacobs, July 18, 2017.

the women not only cooperated for less time: Keith Marshall letter to author via CorrLinks, federal prison monitored email, July 8, 2017.

"His biggest thing was, he felt entitled": Author interview, Alicia Catney, Nov. 26, 2016.

"What I'd been imagining was actually much worse": Author interview, Kristi Fernandez, Aug. 17, 2016.

In one week in October 2016: Regional overdoses and naloxone attributed to a fentanyl-laced batch in Joe Beck, "Heroin Deaths, Overdoses Increase," *Northern Virginia Daily*, Nov. 3, 2016.

"'I might lose three of my customers, but in the long run'": Dealers purposely hot-pack fentanyl-laced heroin, according to naloxone trainer Beth Schmidt, who lost her twenty-three-year-old son, Sean, to a fentanyl overdose in 2013 near Baltimore; author interview, Schmidt, May 19, 2017.

studies showing that long-term opioids: Marion Lee et al., "A Comprehensive Review of Opioid-Induced Hyperalgesia," *Pain Physician*, March-April 2011, available at https://www.ncbi.nlm.nih.gov/pubmed/21412369.

more lawsuits were being filed against Purdue: Everett mayor Ray Stephanson sued Purdue Pharma for gross negligence, claiming the company turned a blind eye to pills being funneled into its streets: Stephanie Gosk and David Douglas, "OxyContin Maker Purdue Pharma Hit With Unprecedented Lawsuit by Washington City," NBC News, March 9, 2017. Ohio attorney general Mike DeWine sued for the state of Ohio to make Purdue and other companies pay for the consequences of the crisis: Alana Semuels, "Are Pharmaceutical Companies to Blame for the Opioid Epidemic?," *Atlantic,* June 2, 2017. Cabell County, West Virginia, sued ten wholesale drug distributors, not Purdue, for flooding the state with painkillers, including forty million doses sold from 2007 to 2012: Keegan Hamilton, "Opioid Overload," *VICE News,* March 10, 2017. The U.S. Attorney's Office in Connecticut began a new criminal probe into Purdue's marketing of OxyContin, according to Nate Raymond, "Opioid Drugmaker Purdue Pharma Faces U.S. Investigation," Reuters, Oct. 25, 2017.

"The cigarette companies finally caved": Author interviews, Richard Ausness, Jan. 27 and July 22, 2017.

Haddox punctuated his talk with slides: Author interview, Chip Jones, Richmond Academy of Medicine marketing director, July 25, 2017.

"What's getting lost here is the prevalence of chronic pain": Coverage of Haddox's November 2015 lecture as reported in Lisa Crutchfield, "Opioid Abuse: No Quick Fix," *Ramifications* (Richmond Academy of Medicine), Winter 2016.

CHAPTER THIRTEEN. OUTCASTS AND INROADS

Interviews: Nancy D. Campbell, Tonia Moxley, Caroline Jean Acker, Teresa Gardner Tyson, Craig Adams, Dr. Art Van Zee, Wendy Welch, Dr. Sue Cantrell, Sarah Melton, Tammy Bise, Dr. Marc Fishman, Bryan Stevenson, Lori Gates-Addison, Giles Sartin, Don Burke, Robert Pack, Tim Allen, Dr. Jessie Gaeta, Neil Smith, David Avruch, Judge Michael Moore, Bob Garett, Robert Pack, Sue Ella Kobak, Dr. Steve Loyd, Ginger Mumpower, Robin Roth, Janine Underwood, Nancy Hans, Danny Gilbert, Wendy Gilbert, Skyler Gilbert, Britney Chitwood Gilbert, Patricia Mehrmann

"treat it with hope": Nancy D. Campbell, J. P. Olsen, and Luke Walden, *The Narcotic Farm: The Rise and Fall of America's First Prison for Drug Addicts* (New York: Abrams, 2008), 190.

Lawrence Kolb Sr. published a set of: Campbell, *Discovering Addiction: The Science and Politics of Substance Abuse Research* (Ann Arbor: University of Michigan Press, 2007), and author interview, Campbell, Aug. 9, 2017.

due to an ethics scandal over: In 1975, Senator Ted Kennedy led Senate hearings on human experimentation that included harmful LSD and morphine research done on patients, some of it funded by the CIA: Campbell, Olsen, and Walden, *The Narcotic Farm,* 166–80.

"Perhaps the day": Ibid., 28.

the CDC to announce voluntary prescribing guidelines: https://www.cdc.gov/mmwr/volumes/65/rr/rr6501e1.htm.

Why did the American Medical Association: Joyce Frieden, "Remove Pain as 5th Vital Sign, AMA Urged," *MedPage Today,* June 13, 2016.

why do surgeons still prescribe so many: Sally Satel, "Taking On the Scourge of Opioids," *National Affairs,* Summer 2017: 9; Mark C. Bicket et al., "Prescription Opioid Analgesics Commonly Unused After Surgery: A Systematic Review," *JAMA Surgery,* Nov. 1, 2017: https://jamanetwork.com/journals/jamasurgery/article-abstract/2644905.

legitimate pain stabilized by the drugs: Bob Tedeschi, "A 'Civil War' over Painkillers Rips Apart the Medical Community—and Leaves Patients in Fear," *STAT,* Jan. 17, 2017.

A journalist and former colleague of mine: Tonia Moxley email, with X-ray, to author, July 24, 2017.

gabapentin, which is increasingly sought: Carmen Heredia Rodriguez, "New on the Streets: Gabapentin, a Drug for Nerve Pain, and a New Target of Abuse," Kaiser Health News, July 6, 2017.

two employees charged with drafting it: Told to me privately by a Centers for Disease Control and Prevention program analyst at the Poynter Institute's "Covering the Opioid Crisis," Washington, D.C., Sept. 26, 2016.

residency programs in the field of addiction medicine: Author interview, Campbell, and David E. Smith, "The Evolution of Addiction Medicine as a Medical Specialty," *AMA Journal of Ethics,* December 2011. As of 2014, the list of residency programs: http://www.abam.net/wpcontent/uploads/2013/04/ABAMFAccredited-ProgramSummaries-2013-14-1.pdf.

"because Big Pharma's going to keep": Author interview, Caroline Jean Acker, June 15, 2017.

largest free medical outreach event: Author interviews, Teresa Gardner Tyson, Feb. 23, July 6–7 (on Health Wagon), and May 24, 2017 (Health Wagon event that was precursor to Remote Area Medical event), and follow-up interviews by phone and text over the summer of 2017.

hadn't used illicit drugs in more than: Author interview, Craig Adams, July 25, 2017.

state of health of RAM patients: Higher overdose death rates in rural America as outlined in these CDC statistics: https://www.cdc.gov/mmwr/volumes/66/ss/ss6602a1.htm?s_cid=ss6602a1_e.

"In Central America, they're eating beans": Quote by RAM volunteer Dr. Joseph F. Smiddy, in Trip Gabriel, "When Health Law Isn't Enough, the Desperate Line Up at Tents," *New York Times,* July 23, 2017.

"On the other side of the cities": Author interview, Dr. Art Van Zee, Sept. 24, 2016.

For decades, black poverty had been concentrated: Caroline Jean Acker, *Creating the*

American Junkie: Addiction Research in the Classic Era of Narcotic Control (Baltimore: Johns Hopkins University Press, 2002), 225.

same counties where Donald Trump performed: Shannon Monnat, "Deaths of Despair and Support for Trump in the 2016 Presidential Election," Pennsylvania State University, Department of Agricultural Economics, Sociology, and Education Research Brief, Dec. 4, 2016. (Monnat now works at Syracuse University.)

"when one of us makes a mistake": Author interview, Wendy Welch, May 22, 2017. Welch is the director of the Graduate Medical Education Consortium and author of *Fall or Fly: The Strangely Hopeful Story of Adoption and Foster Care in Appalachia* (Athens: Ohio University Press, 2018).

founded in 1980 by a Catholic nun: The Health Wagon was started by a Massachusetts native who'd served as a midwife in Africa before volunteering in Appalachia. Sister Bernie Kenny regularly got carsick on the twisty roads: "Every scratch on the old RV, Sister Bernie put it there," Tyson said, grinning.

school district depopulation and austerity: Sara Gregory, "Final Bell Tolls at Coalfields School—Wise County, the Beacon of the Coalfields School Divisions, Closes Another School," *Roanoke Times,* May 28, 2017.

The fifty-four-year-old teacher hadn't had insurance: Author interviews, Brenda Bolling, St. Paul Health Wagon stop, July 6 and 24 (telephone follow-up), 2017.

recent death of a forty-two-year-old patient: Author interviews, Tyson and patient's father, Tony Roberts, March 28, 2017.

Reggie Stanley, forty-five, who died: Author interview, Tyson.

"He was a great guitar player": Written on his Mullins Funeral Home guest book, July 5, 2017.

Cantrell had been holding town-hall: Author interview, Dr. Sue Cantrell, Aug. 8, 2017.

every legislator in the coalfields had voted: Author interview, Sarah Melton, July 24, 2017. No substantive crime increase in needle-exchange areas: Melissa A. Marx et al., "Trends in Crime and the Introduction of a Needle Exchange Program," *American Journal of Public Health,* December 2000: 1933–1936, available at: https://www.researchgate.net /publication/12217407_Trends_in_crime_and_the_introduction_of_a_needle_exchange _program.

Across the border in West Virginia: Early results from Huntington needle exchange were positive, according to Christine Vestal, "Early Results of W.Va. Towns' Needle Exchange Program Show Progress," *PBS NewsHour,* June 6, 2016. Even bare-bones exchanges operating on as little as $10,000 annually were found to be cost-effective, considering that the cost to treat a single hepatitis C infection ranged from $65,000 to $500,000. In other localities, needle-stick injuries to police officers were reported 66 percent less often; Tessie Castillo, "Law Enforcement Lead West Virginia Efforts to Implement Syringe Exchange Programs," *Huffington Post,* Dec. 15, 2015.

IV drug users in the region: Author interview, Melton.

like many of the returning Vietnam soldiers: Among the 20 percent of American servicemen in Vietnam who became hooked on heroin, only 20 percent went on to abuse the drug once they returned to their hometowns. Some attributed this low rate to the fact that the people and places associated with prior heroin use were powerful triggers to reuse: Lee N. Robins et al., "Vietnam Veterans Three Years After Vietnam: How Our Study Changed Our View of Heroin," *American Journal on Addictions,* April 2, 2010.

"I won New Hampshire because": Donald Trump explaining why he won the Republican primary in New Hampshire (though he did not win the state's general election), from Liam Stack, "Trump Called New Hampshire a 'Drug-Infested Den,' Drawing the Ire of Its Politicians," *New York Times,* Aug. 3, 2017.

most Americans support federal financing: "Public Ranks Children's Health Insurance, Marketplace Stabilization Higher Priorities Than ACA Repeal," Kaiser Family Foundation poll, Sept. 22, 2017. The poll found that Medicaid and Medicare buy-in ideas are more popular than single-payer, which was affirmed by 54 percent of those polled. Data analysis from Eric Levitz, "America Is Not a 'Center-Right Nation,'" *New York Times,* Nov. 1, 2017.

to court nonwhite voters, including Hispanics: U.S. Census Bureau, "Voting and Registration in the Election of November 2016," released in May 2017.

"You've got too many leaders just not responding": Author interview, Bryan Stevenson, July 12, 2017.

"really bad for you": Aubrey Whelan and Don Sapatkin, "Advisers: Trump Won't Declare Opioid Crisis a National Emergency," *Philadelphia Inquirer,* Aug. 9, 2017.

A few days later, he seemed to change his mind: Brianna Ehley, "Trump Says He Will Declare Opioid Crisis a 'National Emergency,'" *Politico,* Aug. 10, 2017.

the so-called emergency was retrumpeted: In ninety-day increments, federal agencies could more freely use existing money to mitigate the crisis, and Trump's aides pledged that eventually Trump would release more money for treatment: Julie Hirschfeld Davis, "Trump Declares Opioid Crisis a 'Health Emergency' But Requests No Funds," *New York Times,* Oct. 26, 2017.

seven Americans were dying of overdose: Zachary Siegel, "Where Are the Opioid Recovery Activists?," *Slate,* Oct. 29, 2017.

The Obama administration had also been slow: Author interview, Acker.

One-third of children in central Appalachia: Lori Gates-Addison, area prevention council director, quoting Kids Count data, presentation for Taking Our Communities

Back, Big Stone Gap, VA, May 23, 2017; and author interview, Gates-Addison, May 23, 2017.

96 percent of the adopted kids: Author interview, Welch.

"Repeats": Author interview, Giles Sartin, May 24, 2017.

DEA recommended that first responders wear: http://iaclea.org/visitors/PDFs/Fentanyl_BriefingGuide_June2017.pdf.

"already happened here to us": Gates-Addison, presentation for Taking Our Communities Back.

study forecasting the epidemic's spread: Jeanine M. Buchanich, Lauren C. Balmert, and Donald C. Burke, "Exponential Growth of the USA Overdose Epidemic," https://doi.org/10.1101/134403. The study is critically lauded though not yet peer-reviewed, as outlined in Jeremy Berg, "Modeling the Growth of Opioid Overdose Deaths," *Science,* June 5, 2017.

"more disturbing is the pattern": Author interview, Don Burke, May 30, 2017.

predicting the toll would spike to 250 a day: Max Blau, "STAT Forecast: Opioids Could Kill Nearly 500,000 Americans in the Next Decade," *STAT,* June 27, 2017.

"Don't mess with this shit": Author interview, Robert Pack, Aug. 25, 2017.

2.6 million Americans who are already addicted: Of the 20.5 million Americans with a substance use disorder in 2015, 2 million had prescription opioid-use disorder, and 591,000 were addicted to heroin: Results from 2015 National Survey on Drug Use and Health at https://www.samhsa.gov/data/.

residents of two rural Virginia towns: CDC statistics ranked Martinsville, VA, first for opioid prescribing and Norton, VA, second, using 2015 statistics. Andrew Joseph, "More Opioids Were Prescribed Here Per Person Than Anywhere Else in the U.S.," *STAT,* July 7, 2017, using data from this CDC report: https://www.cdc.gov/mmwr/volumes/66/wr/mm6626a4.htm?s_cid=mm6626a4_w.

It was in their Highpower clinic: Among the patients who explained the practice to me were Crystal Street and Debbie Honaker; author interviews, March 16, 2016, and in follow-up phone calls.

"Our wacky culture can't seem to do": Author interview, Dr. Marc Fishman, May 9, 2017.

a slim minority of opioid addicts: Ibid. Half of buprenorphine patients drop out within six months of beginning MAT, and poor outcomes often follow dropout, according to Kathleen M. Carroll and Roger D. Weiss, "The Role of Behavioral Interventions in Buprenorphine Maintenance Treatment: A Review," *American Journal of Psychiatry,* Dec. 16, 2016.

only three had managed not to become: Author interview, Susan (real name withheld to protect job prospects), May 22, 2017.

"The loss is tremendous": Email to author from Sister Beth Davies, Oct. 13, 2017.

Van Zee told me his greatest fear: Author interview, Van Zee, June 25, 2016.

I stood in the low light: Author interviews, maintenance director Tim Allen and Dr. Jessie Gaeta, Boston Health Care for the Homeless Program medical director, who designed SPOT over the objections of several community groups; June 23, 2017.

Judge Michael Moore's hair had turned: Author interviews, drug court judge Michael Moore, March 16 and April 1, 2016, and June 20, 2017.

studies showed kids were more likely to use: Multiple studies showed that DARE was ineffective, including a GAO report: Christopher Ingraham, "A Brief History of DARE, the Anti-Drug Program Jeff Sessions Wants to Revive," *Washington Post,* July 12, 2017.

Neil Smith thought they were the grandchildren: Author interview, Russell County bailiff Neil Smith, June 20, 2017.

"The more we talk about the epidemic": Author interview, David Avruch, Nov. 1, 2017.

"The answer is always community": Author interview, Sue Ella Kobak, March 13, 2017.

former nursing home into a rehab: Author interview, Bob Garrett, July 5, 2017.

treatment clinic called Overmountain Recovery: Author interviews, Pack, Dec. 16, 2016, and July 5, 2017, and follow-ups via email and phone.

a mighty resistance on its march: Dr. Stephen Loyd, as featured in the documentary *The Gray Area,* by David Floyd, available at https://www.youtube.com/watch?v=qGQy0NcnK2Q&feature=youtu.be.

Loyd knew exactly how to explain himself: Author interview, Loyd, Aug. 25, 2017.

via an app on his cellphone: The app prompts Loyd to check in daily for the possibility of a random drug screen. He is drug-tested at least four times a year.

repeated overdose reversals were: Corky Siemaszko, "Ohio Sheriff Says His Officers Won't Carry Narcan," NBC News, July 7, 2017.

EPILOGUE. SOLDIER'S DISEASE

Interviews: Ginger Mumpower, Robin Roth, Danny Gilbert, Wendy Gilbert, Britney Gilbert, Skyler Gilbert, Janine Underwood, Nancy Hans, Joe Crowder, Warren Bickel, Steve Ratliff, Dr. Sue Cantrell, Tess Henry, Patricia Mehrmann, Mark Sharp, Lindsey Turner, Kathleen Quirk, Louis Mehrmann, Dr. Alan Henry, April Henry, Sergeant Brian Kowalski

"That's OK," Ginger hollered: Author interviews, Ginger Mumpower, Sept. 18 and Oct. 22, 2017.

onetime father figure was arrested: "Karate Instructor Pleads No Contest to Sex

Crimes," WDBJ-7, April 18, 2016; Rikk Perez, owner of Perez Kenpo Karate, pleaded no contest to taking indecent liberties with a minor and carnal knowledge of a minor.

Scott Roth's mom, Robin: Text exchanges between author and Robin Roth, 2012–2017.

her family firmly believes, she'd be alive today: Author interview, Danny, Wendy, Britney, and Skyler Gilbert, Sept. 22, 2017.

Bobby's old friends continued showing up: Author interviews, Janine Underwood and Nancy Hans, Sept. 22, 2017.

Nonfatal overdoses had more than doubled in 2017: Community forum, Virginia State Police special agent Joe Crowder, Cave Spring High School, Jan. 22, 2018. Of the 334 overdose calls police in the region responded to in 2017, 36 people died and 298 were nonfatal.

4.4 pounds of fentanyl…arrested a Cave Spring High graduate: Ibid.

nabbed a $1 million grant: Author interview, Dr. Warren Bickel, Dec. 12, 2017.

only if they first engaged in counseling: Author interview, Steve Ratliff, division director of adult and family services, Blue Ridge Behavioral Healthcare, Jan. 26, 2018.

Dr. Sue Cantrell finally won permission: Author interview, Dr. Sue Cantrell, Jan. 26, 2018.

only with a provision that the "able-bodied": Laura Vozella, "Virginia House Passes Medicaid Work Requirements at Session Midpoint," *Washington Post,* Feb. 13, 2018.

"Oh, awesome!": Text exchange between author and Tess Henry, Sept. 12, 2017.

Patricia still slept with her cellphone: Author interviews, Patricia Mehrmann, Aug. 11, Sept. 14, and Nov. 28, 2017, with numerous text exchanges in between.

A construction laborer and former heroin user: Author interview, Mark Sharp, Dec. 29, 2017.

"Our poet": Text to author from Patricia Mehrmann, Dec. 22, 2017.

"I am going to die": Journal entry by Tess Henry, sometime between November 2016 and February 2017.

possible that Tess had in fact been: Author interviews, Lindsey Turner, Dec. 29 and 30, 2017. Turner, assistant director of the We Care House in Las Vegas, where Tess lived in the spring of 2017, had been one of Tess's counselors.

"They make your life miserable": Author interview, Kathleen Quirk, Jan. 8, 2017. Quirk operates a street-level ministry doing well-being checks on Las Vegas sex workers under the name Cookies and Hope. "If you take cookies from me, I get to talk to you. I walk around where I used to work in brothels, strip clubs, and on the streets," she told me. Quirk was profiled in Kimberly De La Cruz, "Former Prostitute Fights Sex Trade with Cookies," *Las Vegas Review-Journal,* April 13, 2015.

was struggling to grasp the violent nature: Author interview, Patricia and Louis Mehrmann, Dec. 27, 2017.

"Her body has arrived": Text to author from Patricia Mehrmann, Dec. 31, 2017.

Index

DOPESICK

DEALERS, DOCTORS, AND THE DRUG

COMPANY THAT ADDICTED AMERICA

by

Beth Macy

A Conversation with Beth Macy

It's been a year since *Dopesick* was published. How has the opioid crisis changed since you finished writing the book in early 2018?

The crisis has continued to worsen in most states. Americans are now more likely to die of an accidental opioid overdose (1 in 96) than they are from a car crash (1 in 103). And while I pointed out in chapter 12 that African Americans were initially less likely to become ensnared in the opioid crisis that erupted in the early 2000s—probably because of racist attitudes among physicians who were less likely to trust them to take painkillers responsibly—opioid overdose rates have risen among blacks, according to data released in 2018. That increase was highest among forty-five-to-sixty-five-year-old users in urban areas, largely due to fentanyl, though the total death toll remained higher for whites.

This disease spares no one.

As I sat in the church pews at the funeral of Tess Henry—a young woman who was abandoned, over and over, by a medical system that had helped get her addicted—I was feeling pretty hopeless. But we are starting to see positive shifts, including small decreases in overdose deaths in hard-hit New England states like Massachusetts, Rhode Island, and Vermont.

Why there? These states were early adopters of expanded Medicaid, the number one tool for helping the addicted access medication-assisted treatment. (As I write this in February 2019, fourteen states still have not adopted the expansion.) Vermont, for instance, created a hub-and-spoke system for treatment that opened up access points, embedding addiction treatment within its wider health-care system. Rhode Island began offering, among other initiatives, buprenorphine and methadone in its prisons and jails; and Massachusetts made naloxone, the overdose antidote, widely accessible along with on-demand buprenorphine treatment in some emergency departments.

We can see in the shifting data what works. We just aren't doing enough of it. If you're addicted, where you live in the United States can determine whether you live or die. Alas, in the southern mountains of Appalachia, where the crisis first erupted, treatment and harm-reduction initiatives remain the exception rather than the rule.

What has the response been to *Dopesick,* and how has it differed among readers in various regions of the country?

When I speak in cities, the audience usually consists of concerned citizens and people who want to help, including many who are still struggling to process how bad the epidemic really is. But in rural communities and towns, readers in the signing line tell me the equivalent of "It's worse than you know." A public defender in Harlan County, Kentucky, said her office was thinking of building a memorial wall, they've lost so many people. A writer in Tennessee who is raising her grandchild told me that fewer than half of the kids at her granddaughter's rural school are being raised by their parents, having been orphaned by the epidemic—their parents dead, in jail, or still in active addiction.

No matter where I go, parents ask me to inscribe their books in memory of their lost child. A mother in Floyd, Virginia, with tears in her eyes, asked me to write directly to her addicted adult son in a message she'd copied out for me on a bookstore Post-it note in shaky all caps. It said: THIS WILL BE THE YEAR.

What I most love about traveling for the book is learning about grassroots innovations. At an event at Shenandoah University, a public-health nurse director from hard-hit Martinsburg, West Virginia, explained how she'd coaxed a reluctant police department to sign off on the opening of a syringe exchange, where she offers testing and treatment referrals in addition to clean needles and wound-care services, and, in the winter months, much-coveted socks.

What has been the most revealing response to the book?

My favorite response to the book was a text I received from Dr. Steve Loyd, the Tennessee doctor I write about in chapter 13. He still works day and night, trying to coax his physician colleagues, rehab administrators, drug court judges, and other community leaders to understand that patients on medication-assisted treatment (MAT) can have a greater than 60 percent success rate, unlike those not on the maintenance medications.

Loyd wrote: "I think you found the answer [to the opioid crisis], but it's not one anyone will like a whole lot. It's community. Arguments will rage on between abstinence and MAT...and politicians and lawyers have their two cents' worth. But the truth is that it's about Tess and her family and how we as a community of human beings can provide the environment for each other to thrive as well as recover from sometimes unspeakable hurt." He signed his note the same way he answered a woman who was angry about his support for a proposed methadone clinic in Gray, Tennessee. How many times should a person with opioid-use disorder be given another chance? The same as any sinner, according to Loyd, who quoted Jesus telling his disciple: seventy times seven. As many times as it takes.

In Roanoke, Virginia, where you've been a journalist for three decades and where much of *Dopesick* is set, are you starting to see change?

Thank God, yes! The innovation I'm most excited about is a new buprenorphine initiation protocol in the emergency department at Carilion Roanoke Memorial Hospital, part of our nonprofit hospital system, with same-day referrals to outpatient MAT. Up until recently, emergency doctors there simply Narcanned people who had overdosed and then released them, which is still standard practice in most of America. Dr. John Burton, the head of the emergency department, told me in a 2017 interview that he didn't think addiction treatment fell under his department's purview and that prescribing buprenorphine was simply "replacing a drug with another drug."

But not long ago he had a revelation. "I realized that I've been erring throughout this entire time, thinking it was something I couldn't do. I went back to the medical literature and the science, and I thought, 'How could I not be'" offering evidence-based treatment?

Six weeks into the new protocol, his department had referred eighteen people for treatment, accompanied by counseling and peer-recovery coaching. And 90 percent of them had returned for outpatient care. When I asked him how it felt, Burton said, "I am pretty much doing mental handsprings."

I thought of Tess Henry, who had described becoming addicted at an urgent-care center the first time I interviewed her and offered, "What we really need is urgent care for the addicted." Between 2012 and 2017, Tess had been released many times from Carilion, in active withdrawal with no follow-up care. I know she would have been thrilled to learn about this lifesaving shift.

What can we as readers do to help turn the crisis back?

Whenever I interview experts, I call this my "magic-wand question." The opioid epidemic is festering and growing because it takes advantage of long-standing fissures in American society: the fundamental philosophical difference between providing treatment for the addicted and punishing them via a War on Drugs that costs American taxpayers $47 billion a year.

I've written about the critical need to expand harm-reduction measures, Medicaid, and easy-access MAT. I've spoken at length about the need for expanded drug court programs, especially in distressed rural areas, where overdose death rates remain highest and conservative mentalities often favor incarceration over treatment or even doing nothing at all—a mind-set known as "thinning the herd," as one police officer told me. But I've recently met rural innovators, too, ranging from a Tennessee judge who set up a treatment center in the woods, where he houses his drug court, to an Indiana hospital administrator who talked local judges into letting her open a de facto treatment operation inside the courthouse. In Ohio, I met a pharmacy-board investigator operating a pilot program to identify people who are doctor-shopping for opioids and funnel them into treatment before they are charged (and for many, before they're even fully cognizant of their addiction).

"If I could wave a magic wand, I'd want everybody to get educated about addiction," said Angie Gray, the Martinsburg public-health nurse—a sentiment that consistently rose to the top among the experts I talk to. "In Appalachia, it used to be we'd mow each other's grass, take food to people who were needy. But because of this opioid crisis, we've started to turn on each other, and we're trying to find someone to blame, when the blame is much higher above us."

Every person can play a role, Travis N. Rieder told me. His recently published book, *In Pain: A Bioethicist's Personal Struggle with Opioids,* deftly exposes a health-care system conflicted about opioids and woefully inept at managing them. "The paucity of harm-reduction and addiction-treatment services is tied to beliefs and attitudes that individual people have and can reject, like disgust and stigma, and the accompanying belief that those suffering from opioid-use disorder aren't worth spending resources on—that they aren't worth saving," he said. "What each of us can do is expand our circle of compassion and empathy, and urge others—including our elected officials—to do the same."

Martin Luther King Jr. wrote that "the moral arc of the universe is long, but it bends toward justice." History will eventually prove these addiction-treatment innovators correct. But how many people struggling with opioid-use disorder will die before bureaucratic gatekeepers in our courts, health departments, governments, and police departments figure out that it's actually their job to foster change and that they, too, could be turning handsprings?

Beth Macy's Recommended Reading

In Pain: A Bioethicist's Personal Struggle with Opioids by Travis N. Rieder

Drug Dealer, MD: How Doctors Were Duped, Patients Got Hooked, and Why It's So Hard to Stop by Anna Lembke, MD

The Big Fix: Hope After Heroin by Tracey Helton Mitchell

The Recovering: Intoxication and Its Aftermath by Leslie Jamison

If You Love Me: A Mother's Journey Through Her Daughter's Opioid Addiction by Maureen Cavanagh

American Overdose: The Opioid Tragedy in Three Acts by Chris McGreal

Glass House: The 1% Economy and the Shattering of the All-American Town by Brian Alexander

Factory Man: How One Furniture Maker Battled Offshoring, Stayed Local—and Helped Save an American Town by Beth Macy

What You Are Getting Wrong About Appalachia by Elizabeth Catte

Trampoline and *Weedeater,* illustrated novels by Robert Gipe

Ohio, a novel by Stephen Markley

Cherry, a novel by Nico Walker

I Know Your Kind, poems by William Brewer

Dopesick: Finding Tess
An Audible Original available in Fall 2019

The more Patricia and I learned in the wake of Tess's murder, the more we wanted to see Tess's world in Las Vegas for ourselves. A month after the funeral, Patricia gave me a gold locket inscribed with an e. e. cummings poem that Tess loved — the one that begins "i carry your heart with me(i carry it in my heart)."

On one side of the locket, I put my favorite picture of Tess, with her arms wrapped around Koda, her rescue dog. And on the other side, I put a picture of James Baldwin, who said, "Not everything that is faced can be changed, but nothing can be changed until it is faced." That quotation would become a kind of mantra for me in the aftermath of publishing Dopesick. *I would recite it at every book lecture and in almost every interview I was called upon to give.*

Over beer and pizza, I asked Patricia if she wanted to go to Las Vegas with me. We clinked our IPAs together and toasted "our poet," deciding then and there that we would face what happened to Tess as Baldwin instructed, and if we were lucky, we would maybe even inspire some change.

The Audible Original *Dopesick: Finding Tess* is a coda to this book. It is a psychosocial autopsy of sorts, not just a retracing of Tess's final steps on the streets of Las Vegas but also a dissection of what went wrong during the six-year span of her opioid addiction. This exclusive audio documentary features interviews with Tess, her family, and many of those who tried to help her along the way, as well as the systems and the people who failed her.